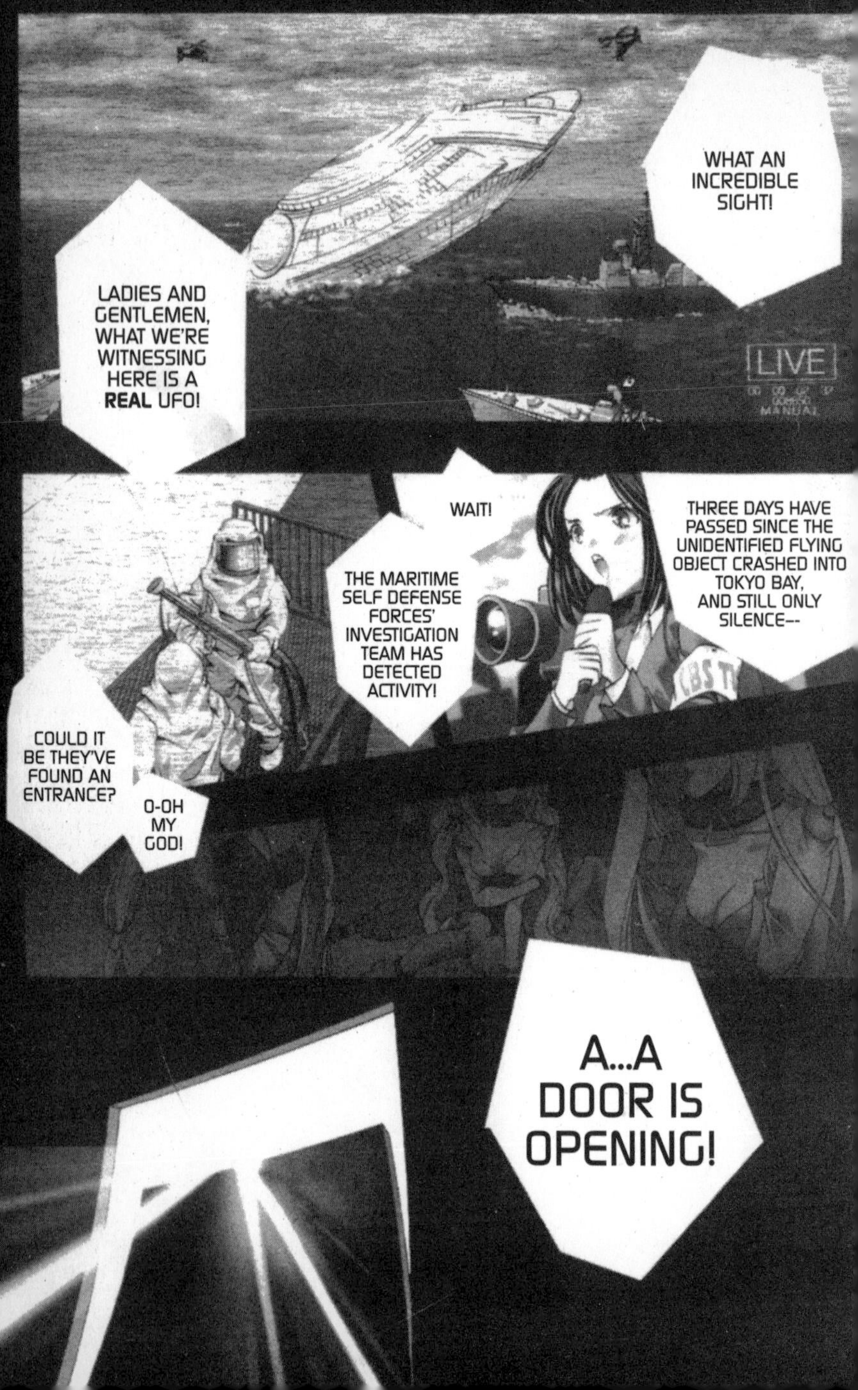
WHAT AN INCREDIBLE SIGHT!
LIVE
MANUAL
LADIES AND GENTLEMEN, WHAT WE'RE WITNESSING HERE IS A **REAL** UFO!
THREE DAYS HAVE PASSED SINCE THE UNIDENTIFIED FLYING OBJECT CRASHED INTO TOKYO BAY, AND STILL ONLY SILENCE--
WAIT!
THE MARITIME SELF DEFENSE FORCES' INVESTIGATION TEAM HAS DETECTED ACTIVITY!
COULD IT BE THEY'VE FOUND AN ENTRANCE?
O-OH MY GOD!
A...A DOOR IS OPENING!

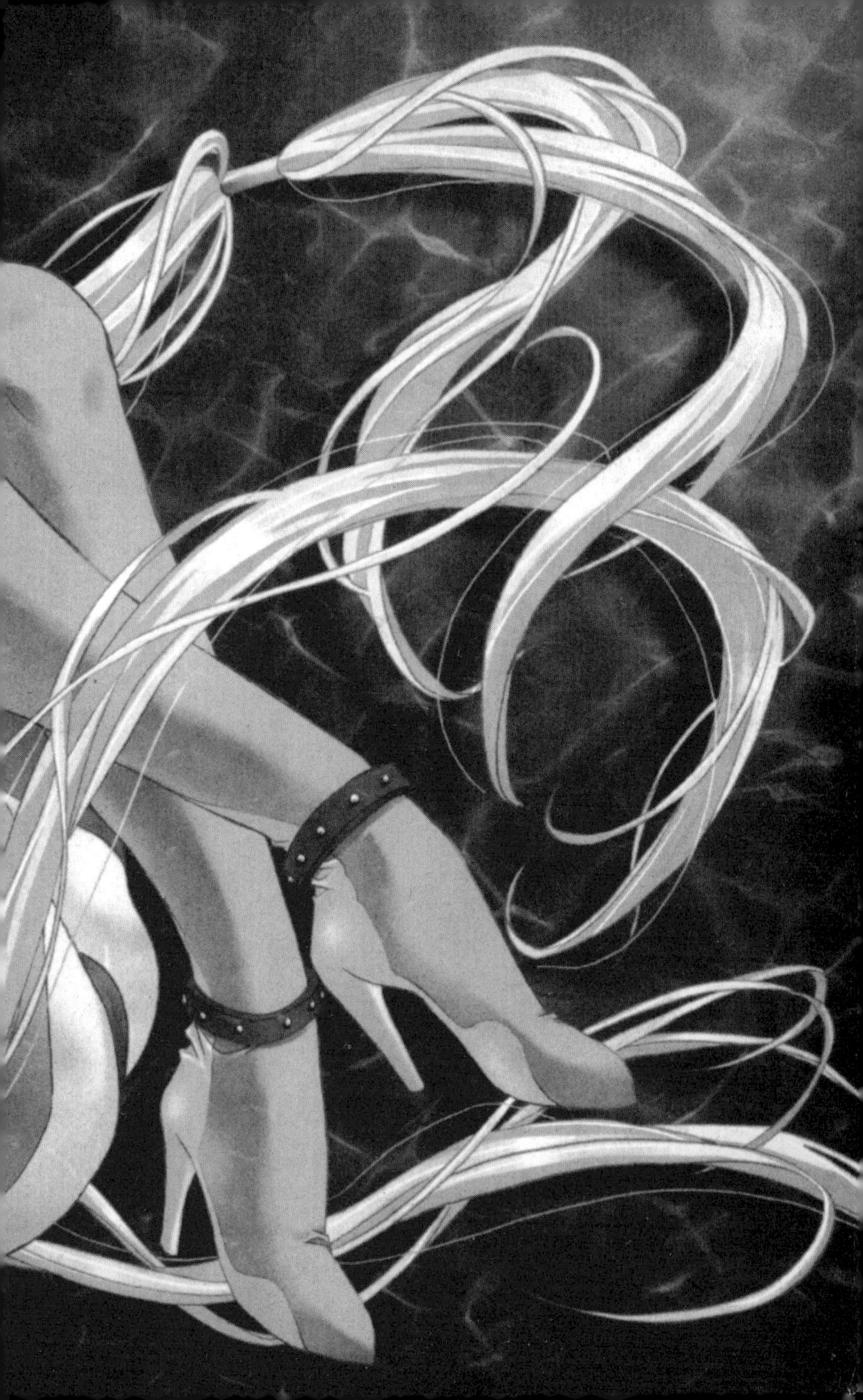

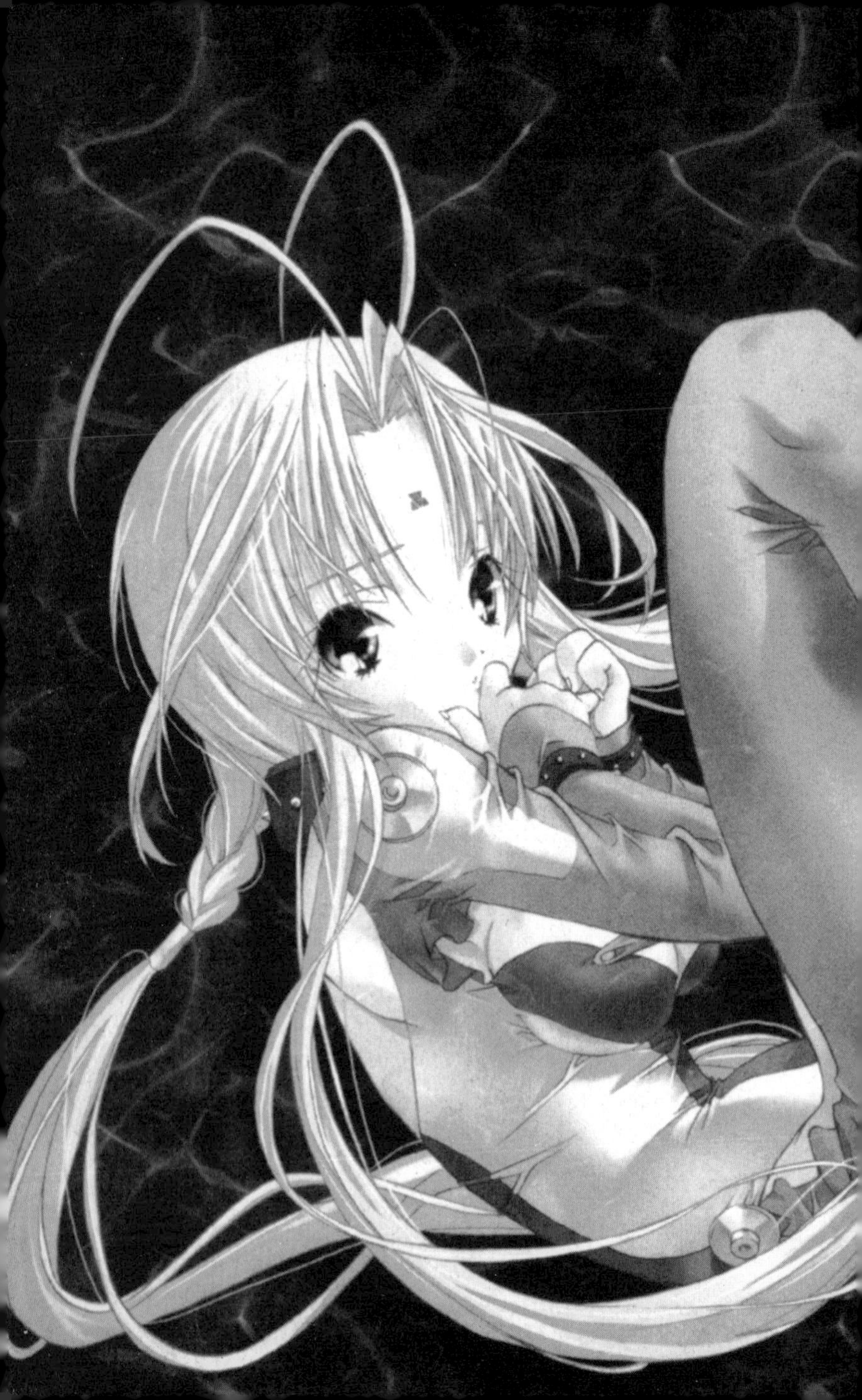

DearS Vol. 1
Created by Peach-Pit

Translation - Christine Schilling
English Adaptation - Hope Donovan and Katherine Schilling
Associate Editor - Brandon Montclare
Retouch and Lettering - Christine Schilling
Production Artist - Yoohae Yang
Cover Design - Gary Shum

Editor - Luis Reyes
Digital Imaging Manager - Chris Buford
Pre-Press Manager - Antonio DePietro
Production Managers - Jennifer Miller and Mutsumi Miyazaki
Art Director - Matt Alford
Managing Editor - Jill Freshney
VP of Production - Ron Klamert
Editor-in-Chief - Mike Kiley
President and C.O.O. - John Parker
Publisher and C.E.O. - Stuart Levy

A  Manga

TOKYOPOP Inc.
5900 Wilshire Blvd. Suite 2000
Los Angeles, CA 90036

E-mail: info@TOKYOPOP.com
Come visit us online at www.TOKYOPOP.com

ISBN: 1-59532-242-6
First TOKYOPOP printing: January 2005
10 9 8 7 6 5 4 3 2 1
Printed in the USA

DearS

VOL. 1

by
PEACH-PIT

HAMBURG // LONDON // LOS ANGELES // TOKYO

DearS

01

PEACH-PIT
presents

CONTENTS

1st Contact

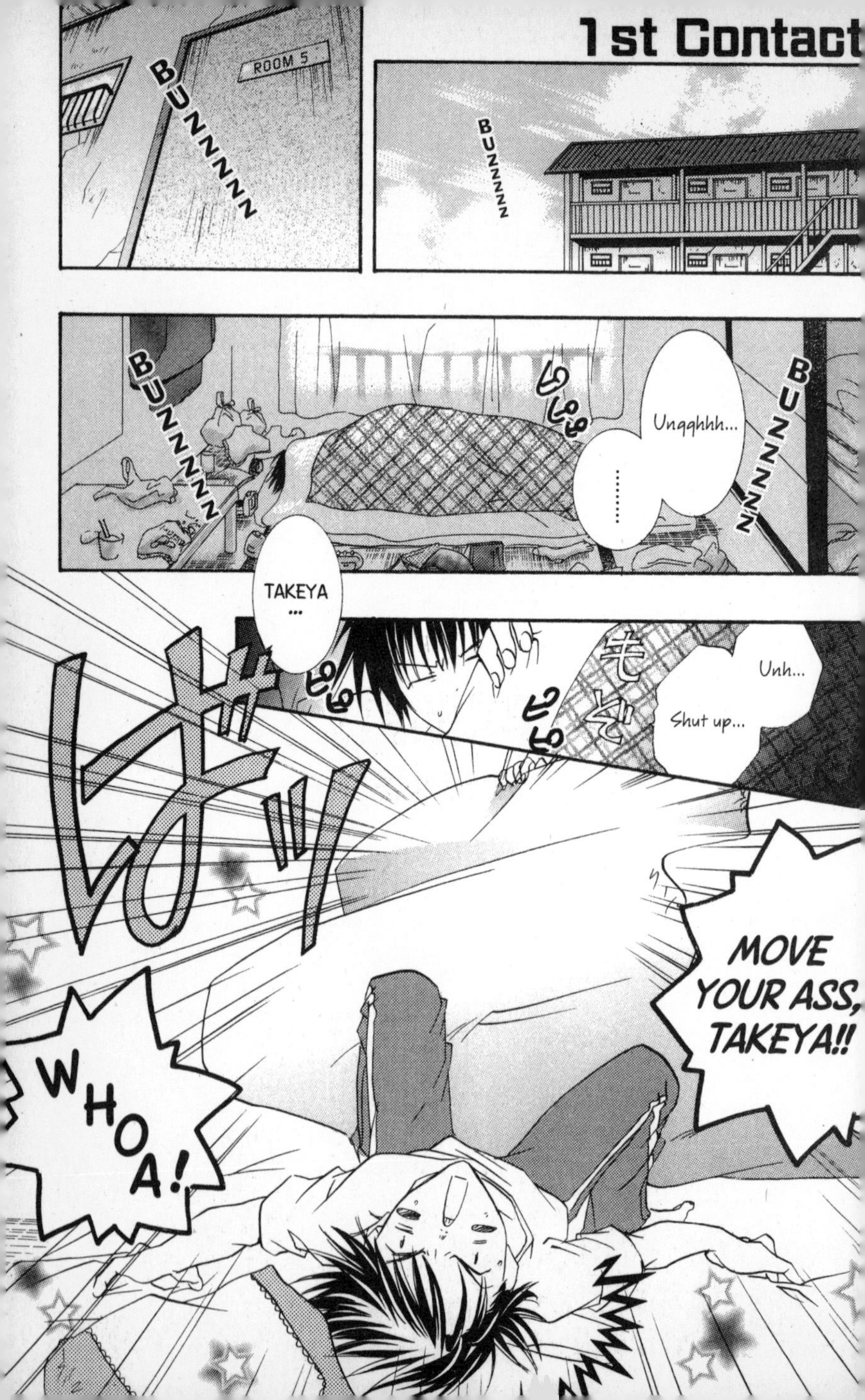
BUZZZZZ
ROOM 5
BUZZZZZZ
BUZZZZZZ
Unqghhh...
....
BUZZZZZZ
TAKEYA ...
Unh...
Shut up...
もぞ
MOVE YOUR ASS, TAKEYA!!
WHOA!

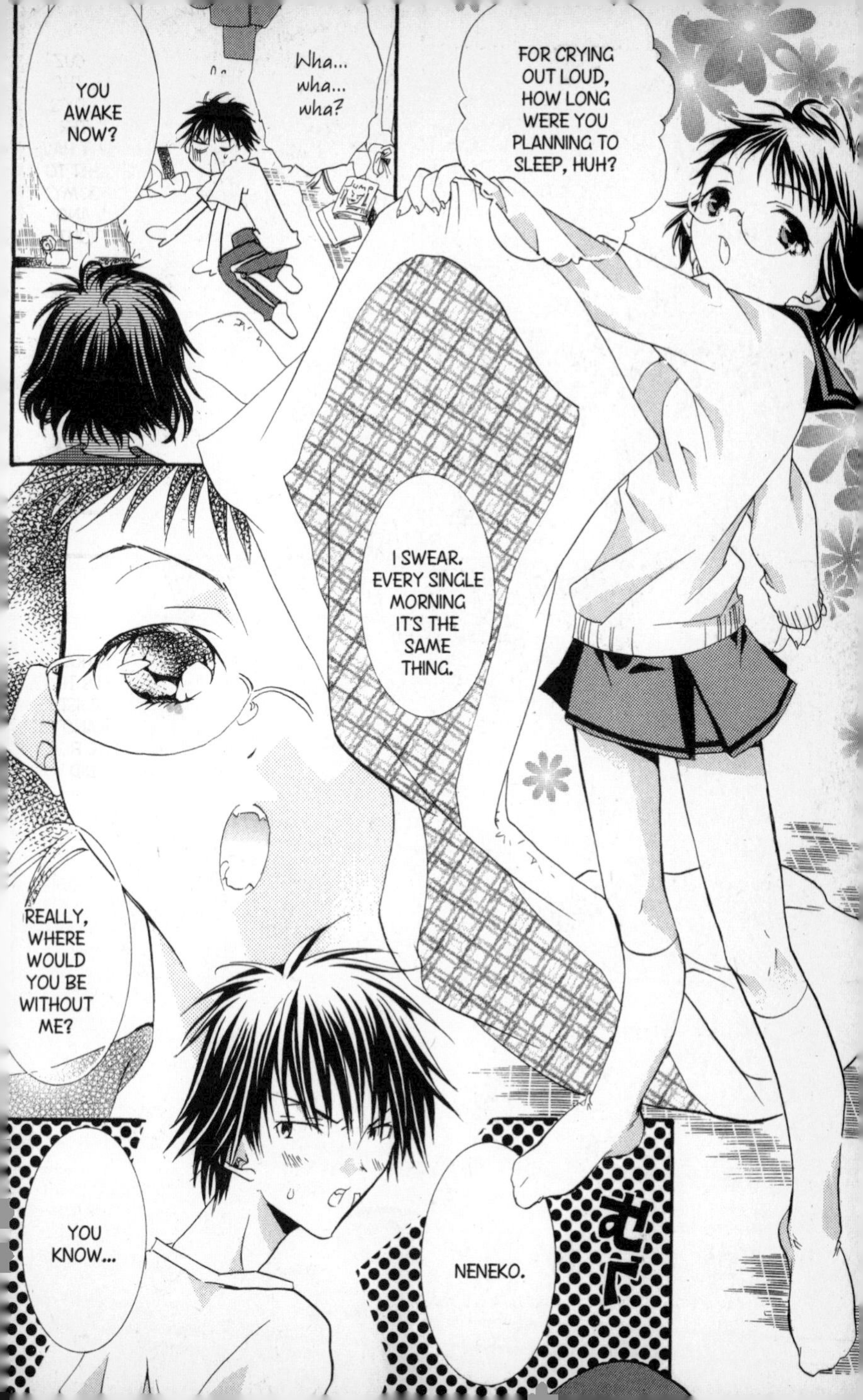

FOR CRYING OUT LOUD, HOW LONG WERE YOU PLANNING TO SLEEP, HUH?
Wha... wha... wha?
YOU AWAKE NOW?
I SWEAR. EVERY SINGLE MORNING IT'S THE SAME THING.
REALLY, WHERE WOULD YOU BE WITHOUT ME?
NENEKO.
YOU KNOW...

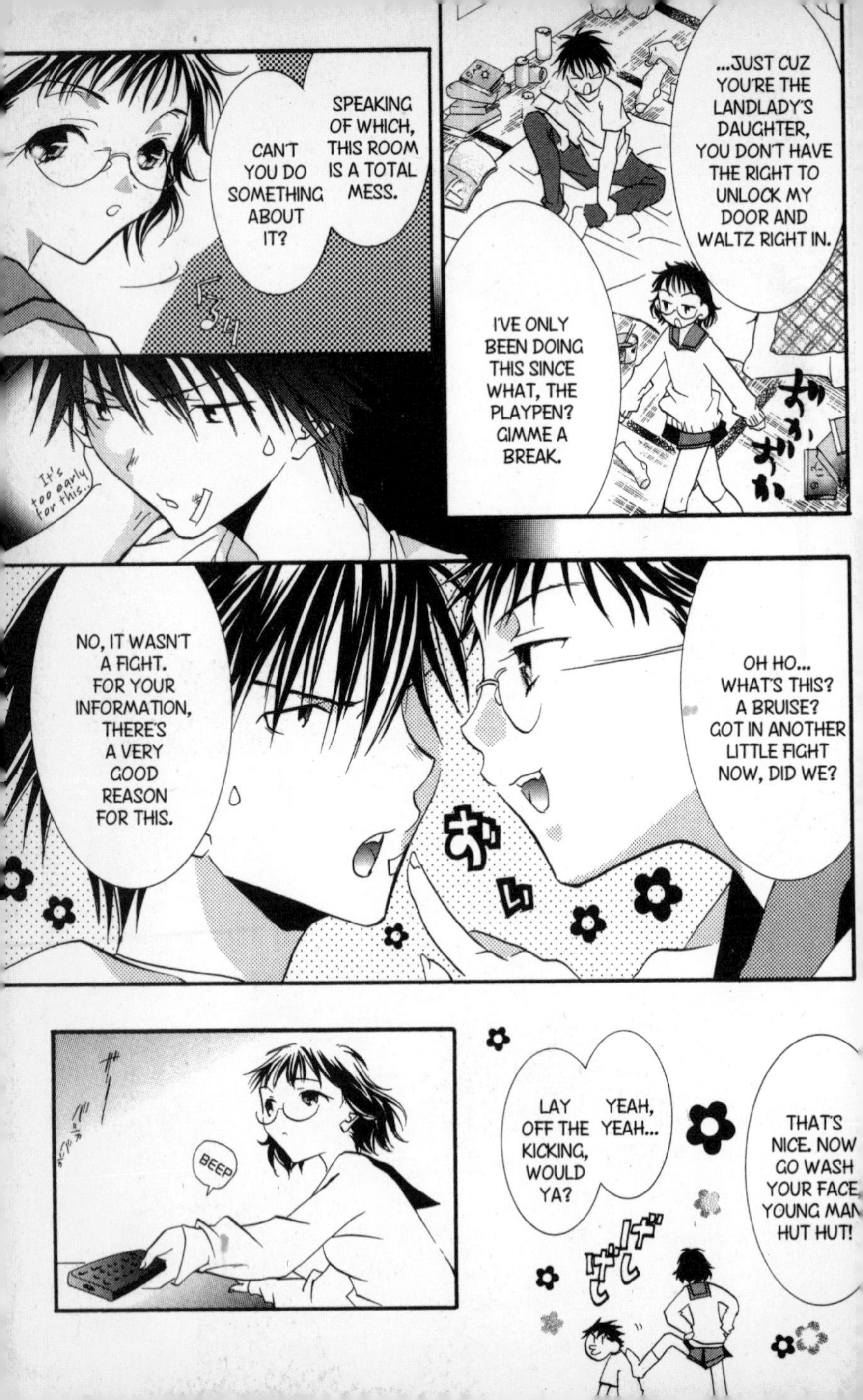
...JUST CUZ YOU'RE THE LANDLADY'S DAUGHTER, YOU DON'T HAVE THE RIGHT TO UNLOCK MY DOOR AND WALTZ RIGHT IN.
I'VE ONLY BEEN DOING THIS SINCE WHAT, THE PLAYPEN? GIMME A BREAK.
SPEAKING OF WHICH, THIS ROOM IS A TOTAL MESS.
CAN'T YOU DO SOMETHING ABOUT IT?
It's too early for this...
OH HO... WHAT'S THIS? A BRUISE? GOT IN ANOTHER LITTLE FIGHT NOW, DID WE?
NO, IT WASN'T A FIGHT. FOR YOUR INFORMATION, THERE'S A VERY GOOD REASON FOR THIS.
THAT'S NICE. NOW GO WASH YOUR FACE, YOUNG MAN HUT HUT!
YEAH, YEAH...
LAY OFF THE KICKING, WOULD YA?
BEEP

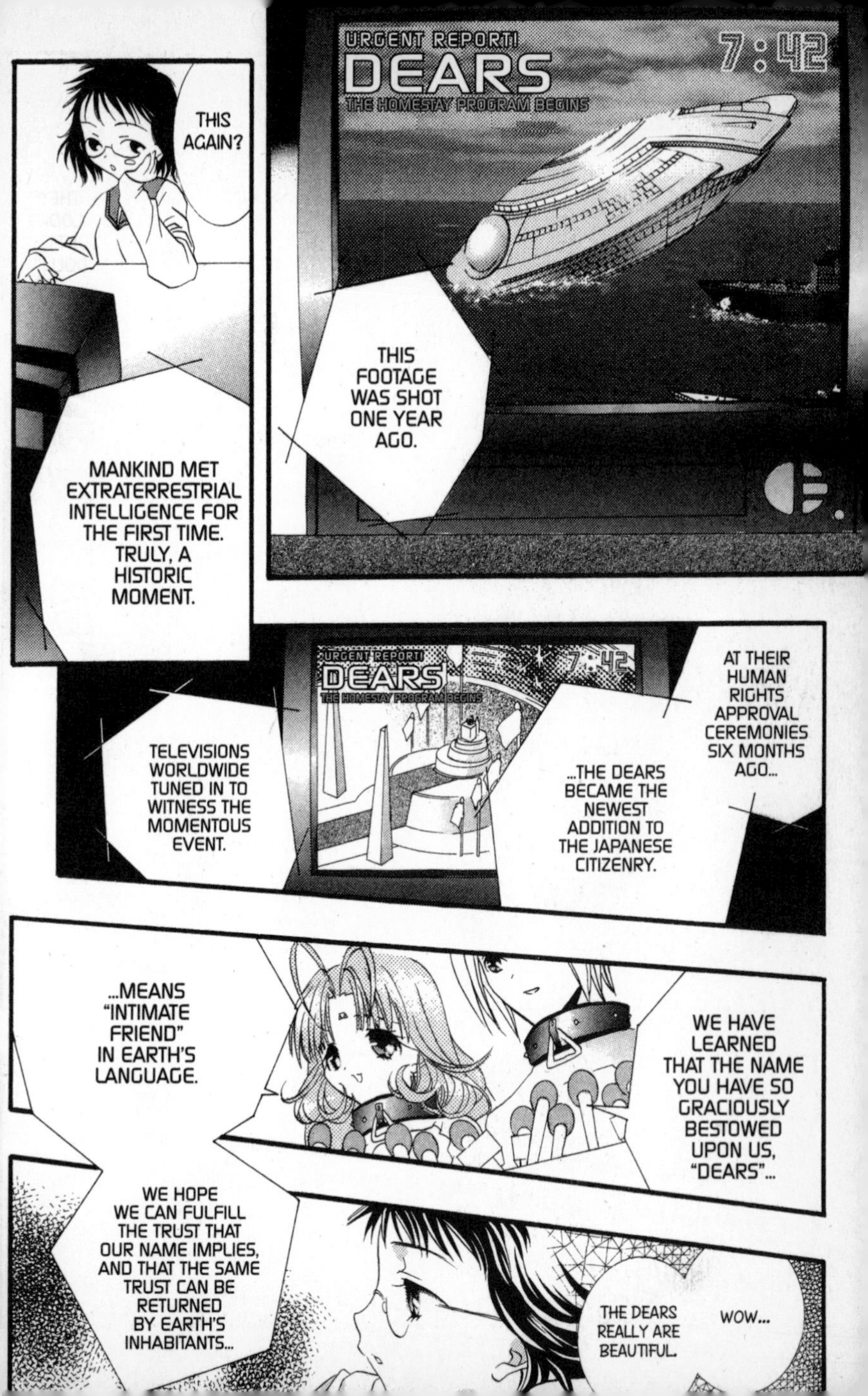
URGENT REPORT!
DEARS
THE HOMESTAY PROGRAM BEGINS
7:42
THIS FOOTAGE WAS SHOT ONE YEAR AGO.
THIS AGAIN?
MANKIND MET EXTRATERRESTRIAL INTELLIGENCE FOR THE FIRST TIME. TRULY, A HISTORIC MOMENT.
AT THEIR HUMAN RIGHTS APPROVAL CEREMONIES SIX MONTHS AGO...
...THE DEARS BECAME THE NEWEST ADDITION TO THE JAPANESE CITIZENRY.
URGENT REPORT!
DEARS
THE HOMESTAY PROGRAM BEGINS
7:42
TELEVISIONS WORLDWIDE TUNED IN TO WITNESS THE MOMENTOUS EVENT.
WE HAVE LEARNED THAT THE NAME YOU HAVE SO GRACIOUSLY BESTOWED UPON US, "DEARS"...
...MEANS "INTIMATE FRIEND" IN EARTH'S LANGUAGE.
WE HOPE WE CAN FULFILL THE TRUST THAT OUR NAME IMPLIES, AND THAT THE SAME TRUST CAN BE RETURNED BY EARTH'S INHABITANTS...
WOW...
THE DEARS REALLY ARE BEAUTIFUL.

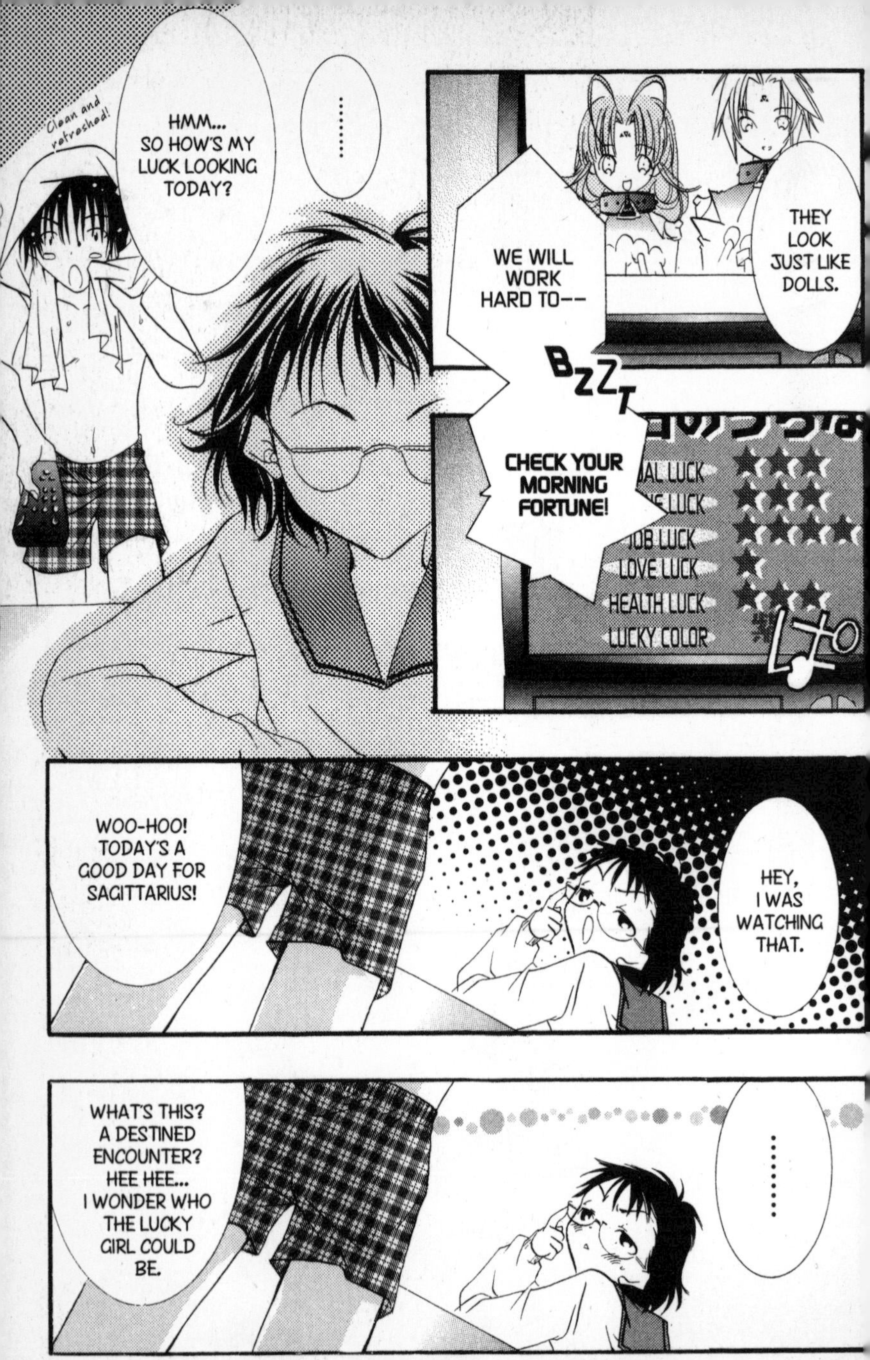
THEY LOOK JUST LIKE DOLLS.
WE WILL WORK HARD TO--
BZZT
CHECK YOUR MORNING FORTUNE!
JOB LUCK
LOVE LUCK
HEALTH LUCK
LUCKY COLOR
......
HMM... SO HOW'S MY LUCK LOOKING TODAY?
Clean and refreshed!
HEY, I WAS WATCHING THAT.
WOO-HOO! TODAY'S A GOOD DAY FOR SAGITTARIUS!
......
WHAT'S THIS? A DESTINED ENCOUNTER? HEE HEE... I WONDER WHO THE LUCKY GIRL COULD BE.

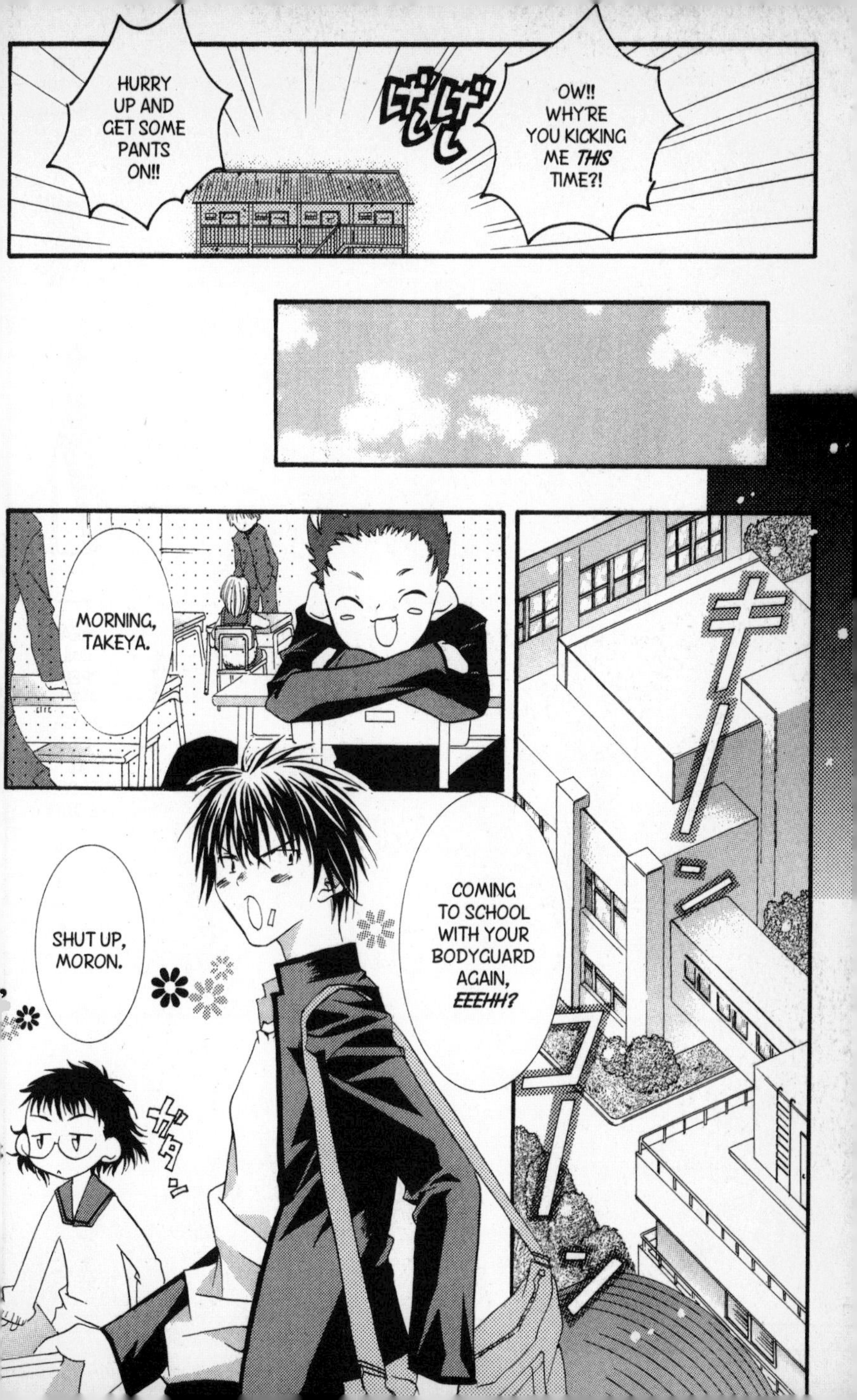
OW!! WHY'RE YOU KICKING ME *THIS* TIME?!
HURRY UP AND GET SOME PANTS ON!!
MORNING, TAKEYA.
COMING TO SCHOOL WITH YOUR BODYGUARD AGAIN, *EEEHH?*
SHUT UP, MORON.

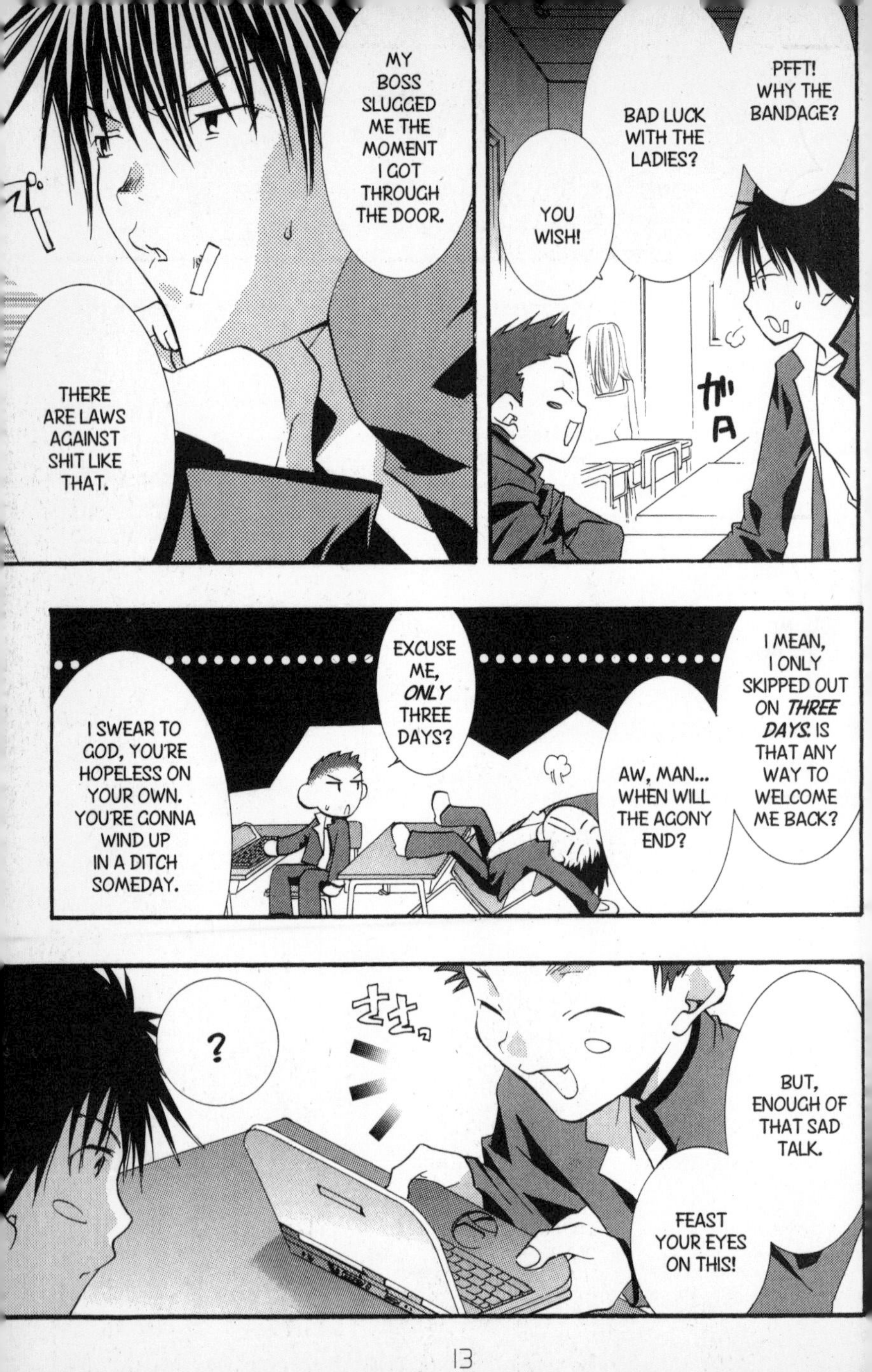
PFFT! WHY THE BANDAGE?
BAD LUCK WITH THE LADIES?
YOU WISH!
MY BOSS SLUGGED ME THE MOMENT I GOT THROUGH THE DOOR.
THERE ARE LAWS AGAINST SHIT LIKE THAT.
I MEAN, I ONLY SKIPPED OUT ON *THREE DAYS.* IS THAT ANY WAY TO WELCOME ME BACK?
AW, MAN... WHEN WILL THE AGONY END?
EXCUSE ME, *ONLY* THREE DAYS?
I SWEAR TO GOD, YOU'RE HOPELESS ON YOUR OWN. YOU'RE GONNA WIND UP IN A DITCH SOMEDAY.
BUT, ENOUGH OF THAT SAD TALK.
FEAST YOUR EYES ON THIS!
ささっ
?

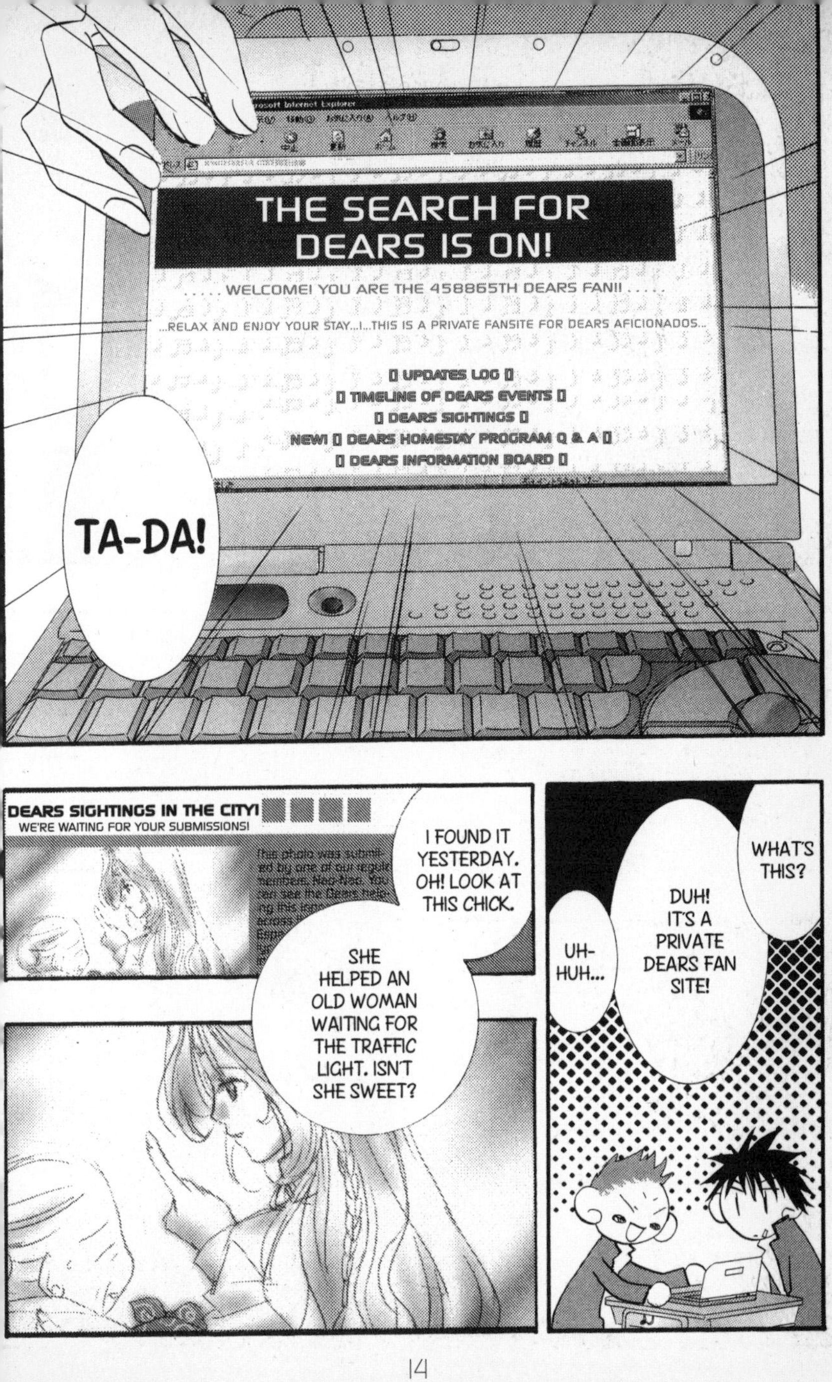
THE SEARCH FOR DEARS IS ON!
..... WELCOME! YOU ARE THE 458865TH DEARS FAN!! .....
...RELAX AND ENJOY YOUR STAY...!...THIS IS A PRIVATE FANSITE FOR DEARS AFICIONADOS...
[] UPDATES LOG []
[] TIMELINE OF DEARS EVENTS []
[] DEARS SIGHTINGS []
NEW! [] DEARS HOMESTAY PROGRAM Q & A []
[] DEARS INFORMATION BOARD []
TA-DA!
WHAT'S THIS?
DUH! IT'S A PRIVATE DEARS FAN SITE!
UH-HUH...
DEARS SIGHTINGS IN THE CITY!
WE'RE WAITING FOR YOUR SUBMISSIONS!
I FOUND IT YESTERDAY. OH! LOOK AT THIS CHICK.
SHE HELPED AN OLD WOMAN WAITING FOR THE TRAFFIC LIGHT. ISN'T SHE SWEET?

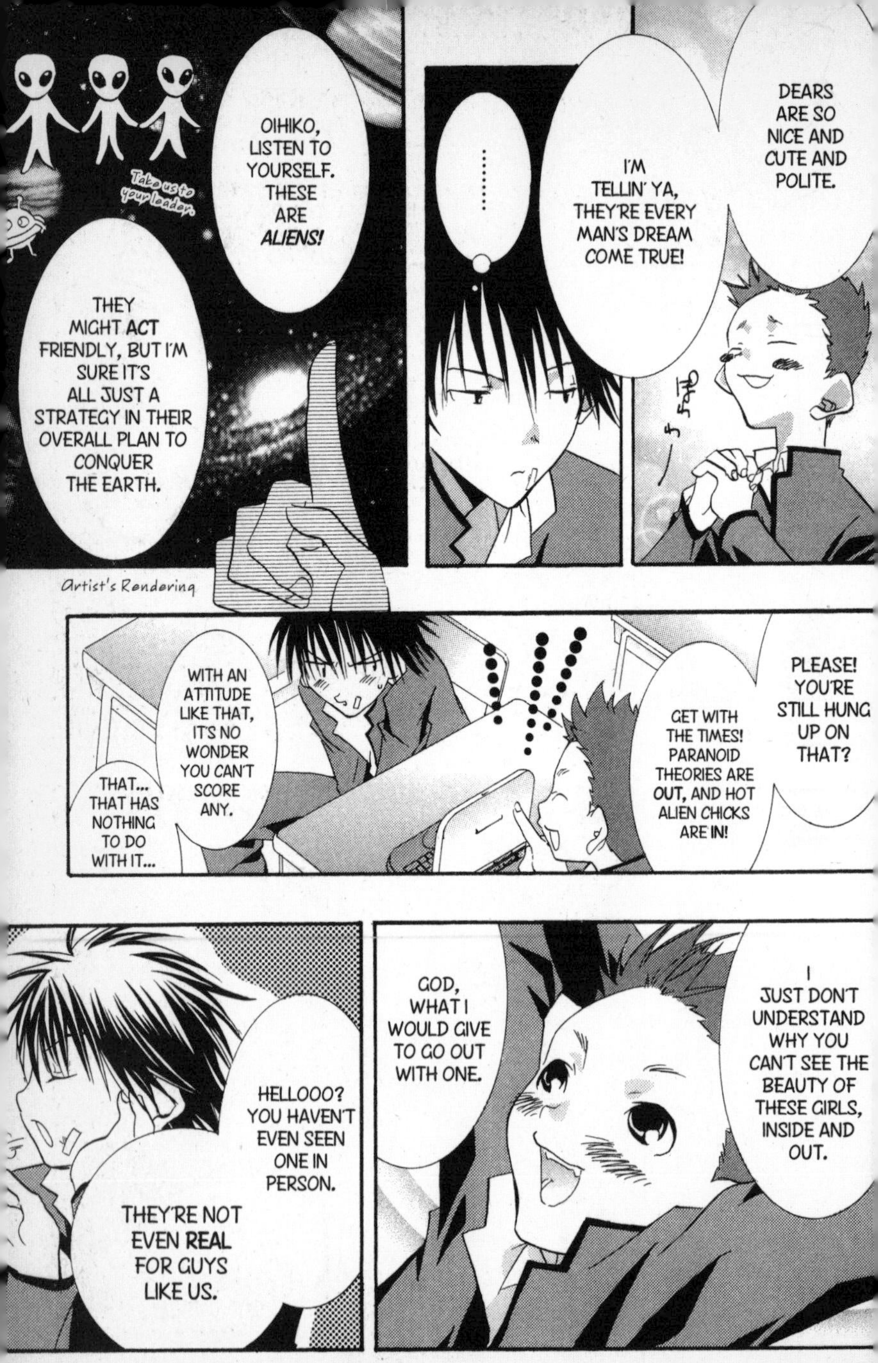
DEARS ARE SO NICE AND CUTE AND POLITE.
I'M TELLIN' YA, THEY'RE EVERY MAN'S DREAM COME TRUE!
......
OIHIKO, LISTEN TO YOURSELF. THESE ARE ALIENS!
Take us to your leader.
THEY MIGHT ACT FRIENDLY, BUT I'M SURE IT'S ALL JUST A STRATEGY IN THEIR OVERALL PLAN TO CONQUER THE EARTH.
Artist's Rendering
PLEASE! YOU'RE STILL HUNG UP ON THAT?
GET WITH THE TIMES! PARANOID THEORIES ARE OUT, AND HOT ALIEN CHICKS ARE IN!
WITH AN ATTITUDE LIKE THAT, IT'S NO WONDER YOU CAN'T SCORE ANY.
THAT... THAT HAS NOTHING TO DO WITH IT...
I JUST DON'T UNDERSTAND WHY YOU CAN'T SEE THE BEAUTY OF THESE GIRLS, INSIDE AND OUT.
GOD, WHAT I WOULD GIVE TO GO OUT WITH ONE.
HELLOOO? YOU HAVEN'T EVEN SEEN ONE IN PERSON.
THEY'RE NOT EVEN REAL FOR GUYS LIKE US.

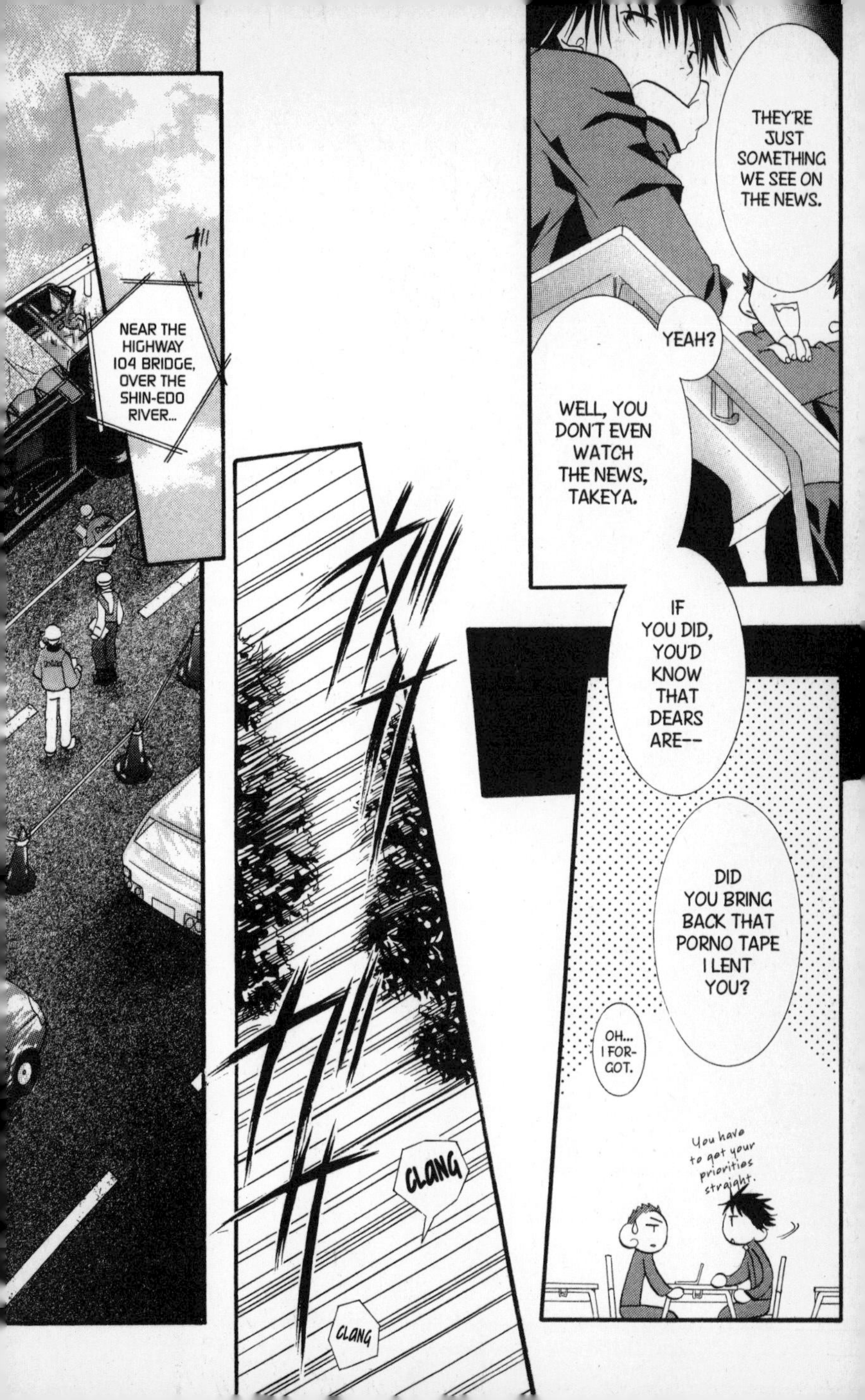

THEY'RE JUST SOMETHING WE SEE ON THE NEWS.
YEAH?
WELL, YOU DON'T EVEN WATCH THE NEWS, TAKEYA.
IF YOU DID, YOU'D KNOW THAT DEARS ARE--
DID YOU BRING BACK THAT PORNO TAPE I LENT YOU?
OH... I FOR-GOT.
You have to get your priorities straight.
CLANG
CLANG
NEAR THE HIGHWAY 104 BRIDGE, OVER THE SHIN-EDO RIVER...

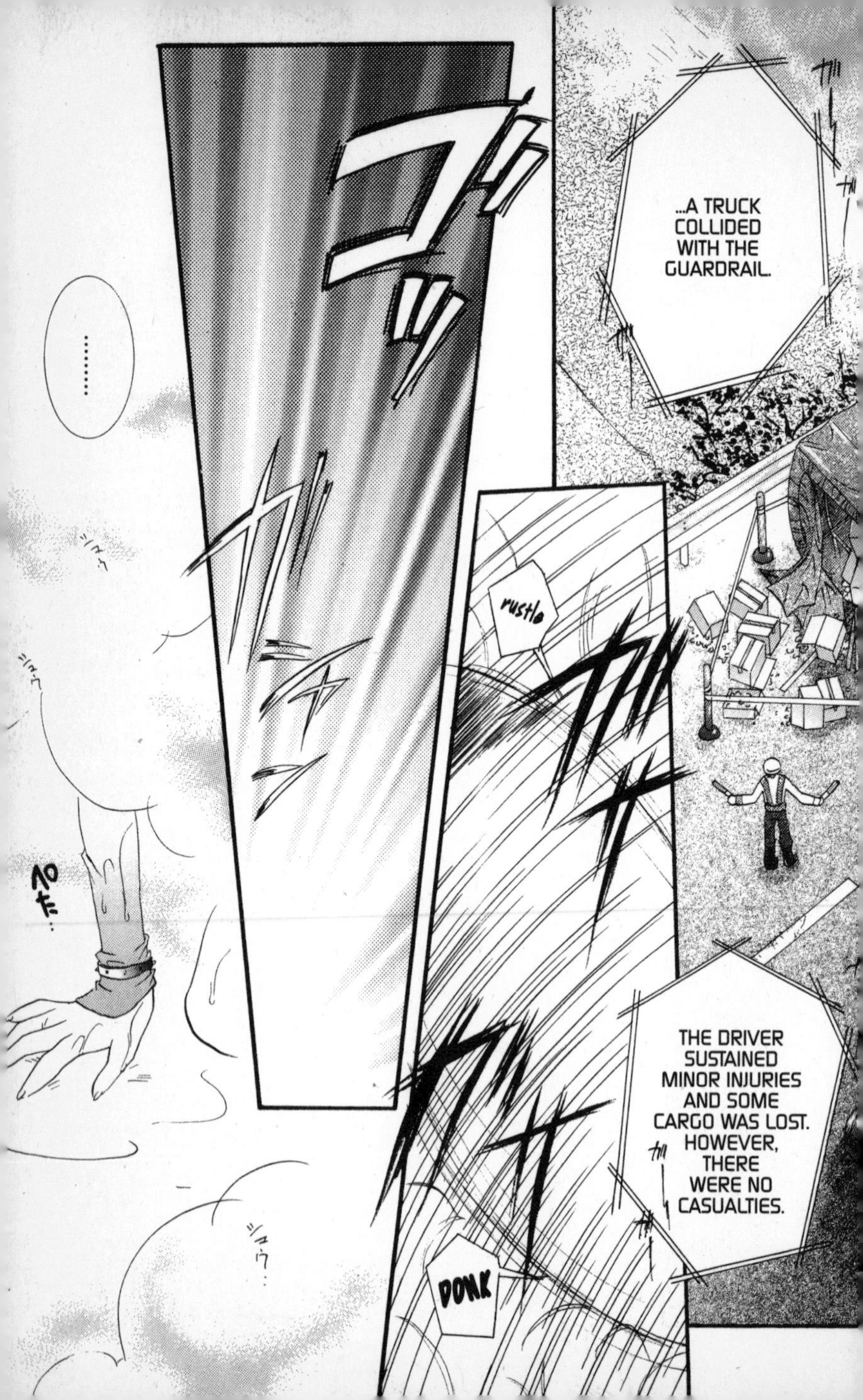
...A TRUCK COLLIDED WITH THE GUARDRAIL.
THE DRIVER SUSTAINED MINOR INJURIES AND SOME CARGO WAS LOST. HOWEVER, THERE WERE NO CASUALTIES.
rustle
DONK
......

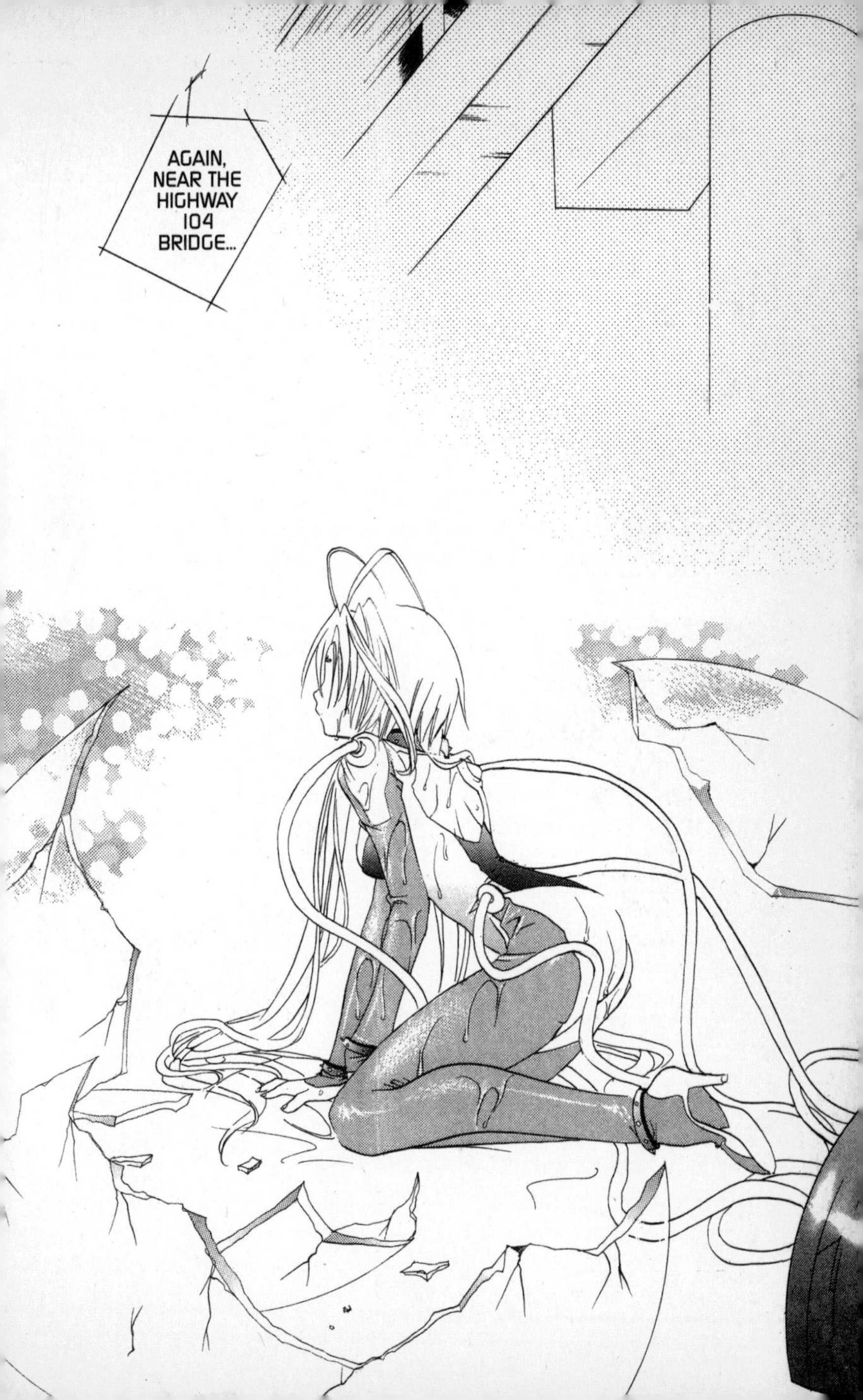
AGAIN, NEAR THE HIGHWAY 104 BRIDGE...

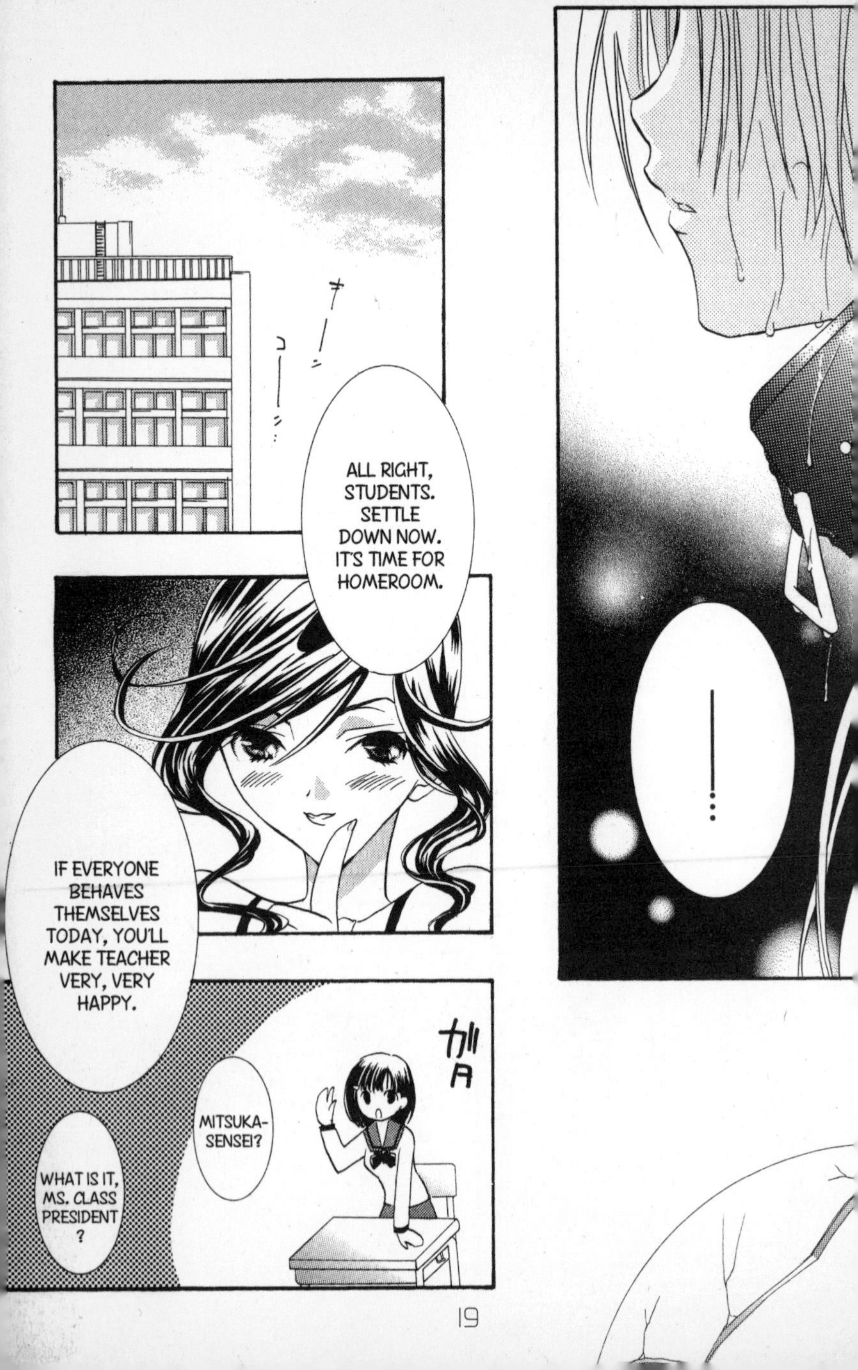
……
キーンコーン
ALL RIGHT, STUDENTS. SETTLE DOWN NOW. IT'S TIME FOR HOMEROOM.
IF EVERYONE BEHAVES THEMSELVES TODAY, YOU'LL MAKE TEACHER VERY, VERY HAPPY.
MITSUKA-SENSEI?
WHAT IS IT, MS. CLASS PRESIDENT?

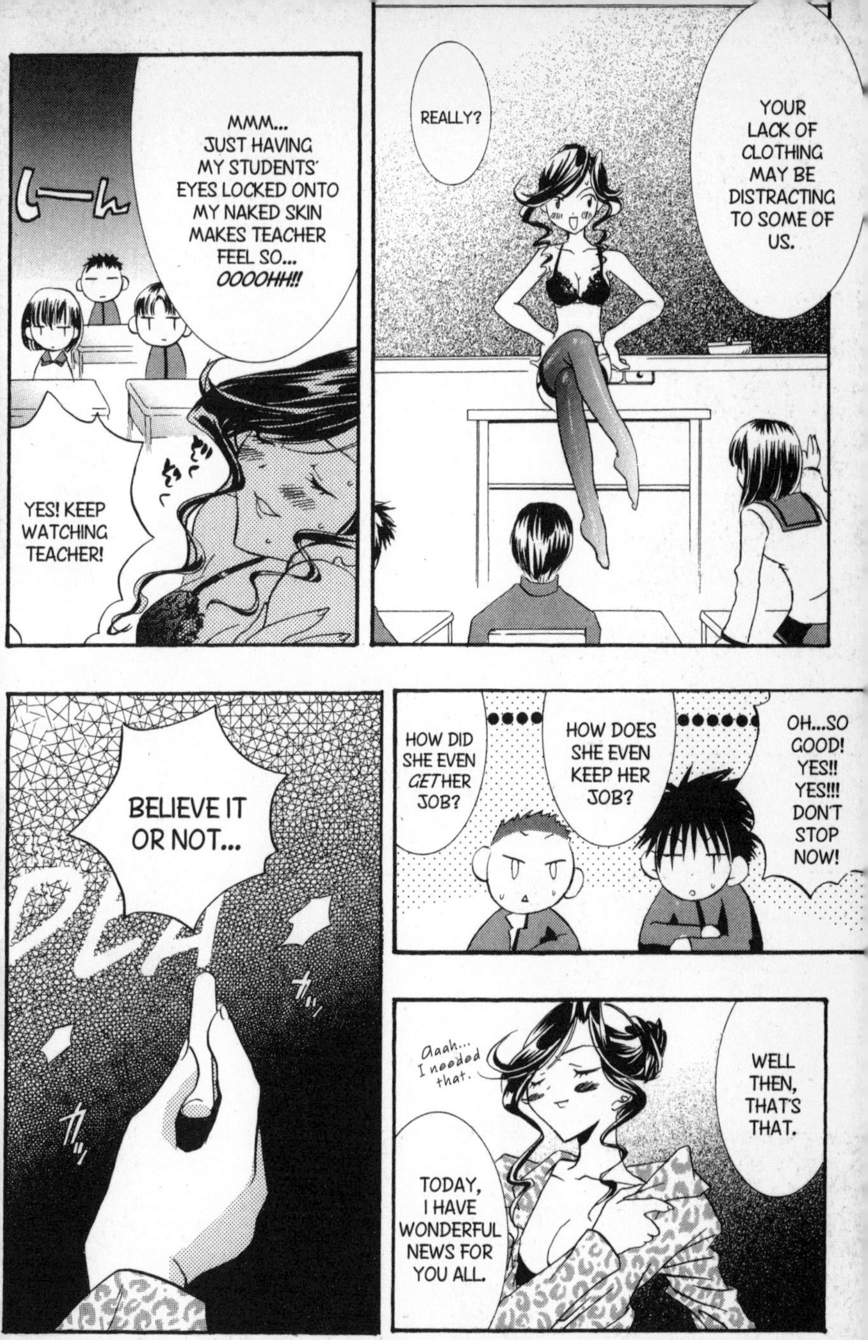
YOUR LACK OF CLOTHING MAY BE DISTRACTING TO SOME OF US.
REALLY?
MMM... JUST HAVING MY STUDENTS' EYES LOCKED ONTO MY NAKED SKIN MAKES TEACHER FEEL SO... *OOOOHH!!*
しーん
YES! KEEP WATCHING TEACHER!
OH...SO GOOD! YES!! YES!!! DON'T STOP NOW!
......
HOW DOES SHE EVEN KEEP HER JOB?
....
HOW DID SHE EVEN *GET* HER JOB?
WELL THEN, THAT'S THAT.
Aaah... I needed that.
TODAY, I HAVE WONDERFUL NEWS FOR YOU ALL.
BELIEVE IT OR NOT...

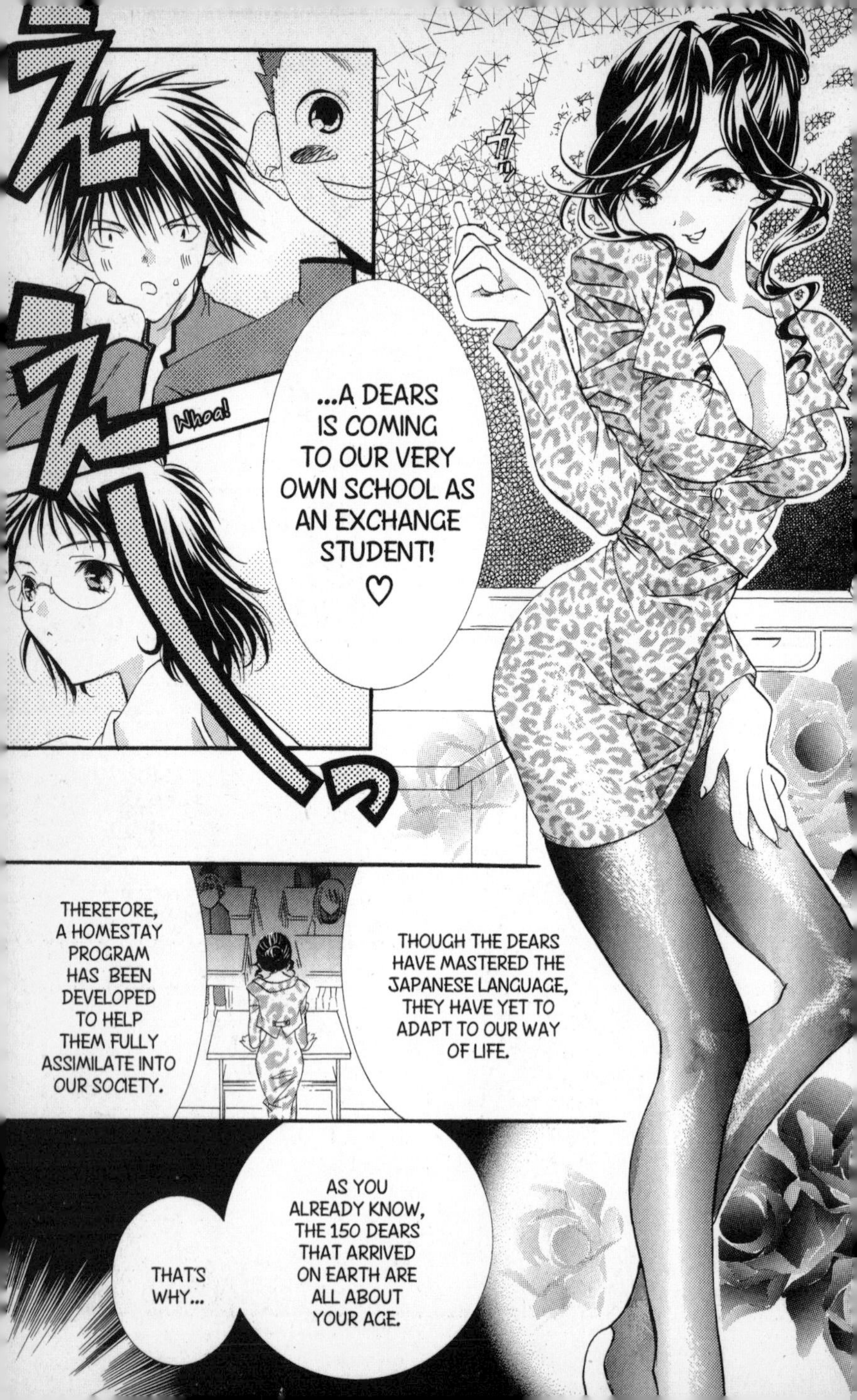
...A DEARS IS COMING TO OUR VERY OWN SCHOOL AS AN EXCHANGE STUDENT! ♡
えぇーっ
Whoa!
THOUGH THE DEARS HAVE MASTERED THE JAPANESE LANGUAGE, THEY HAVE YET TO ADAPT TO OUR WAY OF LIFE.
THEREFORE, A HOMESTAY PROGRAM HAS BEEN DEVELOPED TO HELP THEM FULLY ASSIMILATE INTO OUR SOCIETY.
AS YOU ALREADY KNOW, THE 150 DEARS THAT ARRIVED ON EARTH ARE ALL ABOUT YOUR AGE.
THAT'S WHY...

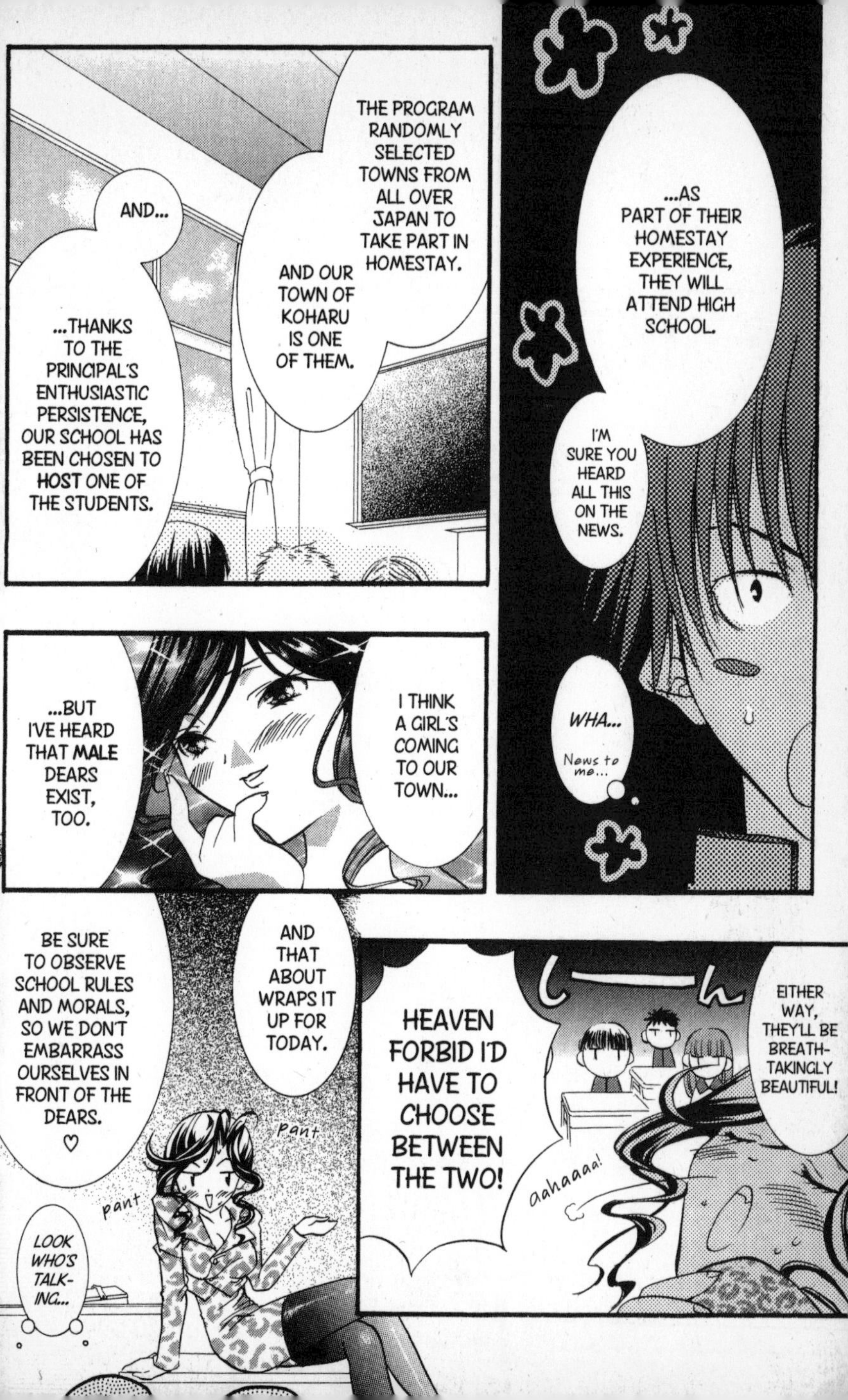
...AS PART OF THEIR HOMESTAY EXPERIENCE, THEY WILL ATTEND HIGH SCHOOL.
I'M SURE YOU HEARD ALL THIS ON THE NEWS.
WHA...
News to me...
THE PROGRAM RANDOMLY SELECTED TOWNS FROM ALL OVER JAPAN TO TAKE PART IN HOMESTAY.
AND OUR TOWN OF KOHARU IS ONE OF THEM.
AND...
...THANKS TO THE PRINCIPAL'S ENTHUSIASTIC PERSISTENCE, OUR SCHOOL HAS BEEN CHOSEN TO HOST ONE OF THE STUDENTS.
I THINK A GIRL'S COMING TO OUR TOWN...
...BUT I'VE HEARD THAT MALE DEARS EXIST, TOO.
EITHER WAY, THEY'LL BE BREATH-TAKINGLY BEAUTIFUL!
し—ん
HEAVEN FORBID I'D HAVE TO CHOOSE BETWEEN THE TWO!
aahaaaa!
AND THAT ABOUT WRAPS IT UP FOR TODAY.
BE SURE TO OBSERVE SCHOOL RULES AND MORALS, SO WE DON'T EMBARRASS OURSELVES IN FRONT OF THE DEARS. ♡
pant
pant
LOOK WHO'S TALK-ING...

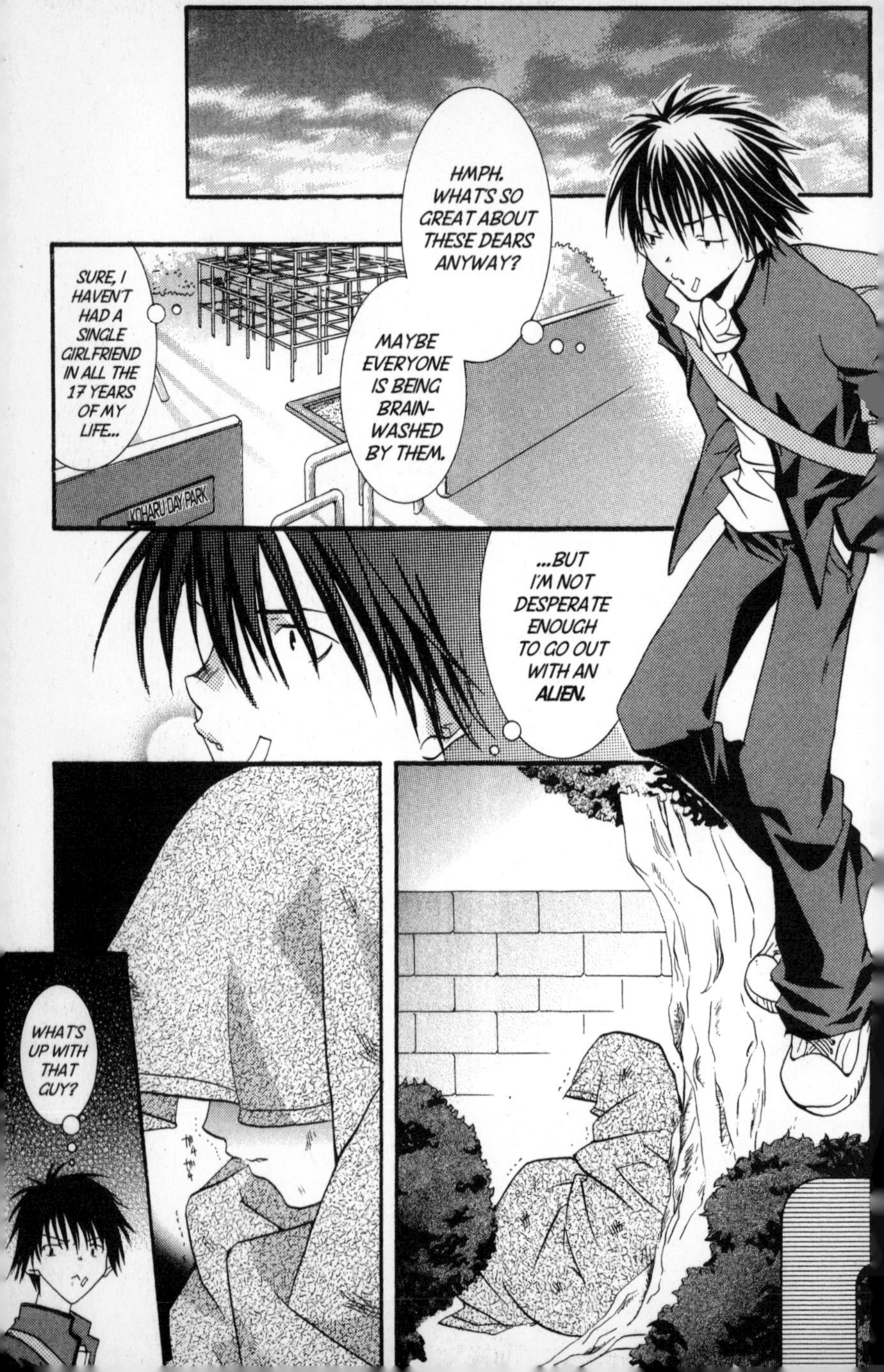
HMPH. WHAT'S SO GREAT ABOUT THESE DEARS ANYWAY?
MAYBE EVERYONE IS BEING BRAIN-WASHED BY THEM.
SURE, I HAVEN'T HAD A SINGLE GIRLFRIEND IN ALL THE 17 YEARS OF MY LIFE...
KOHARU DAY PARK
...BUT I'M NOT DESPERATE ENOUGH TO GO OUT WITH AN ALIEN.
WHAT'S UP WITH THAT GUY?

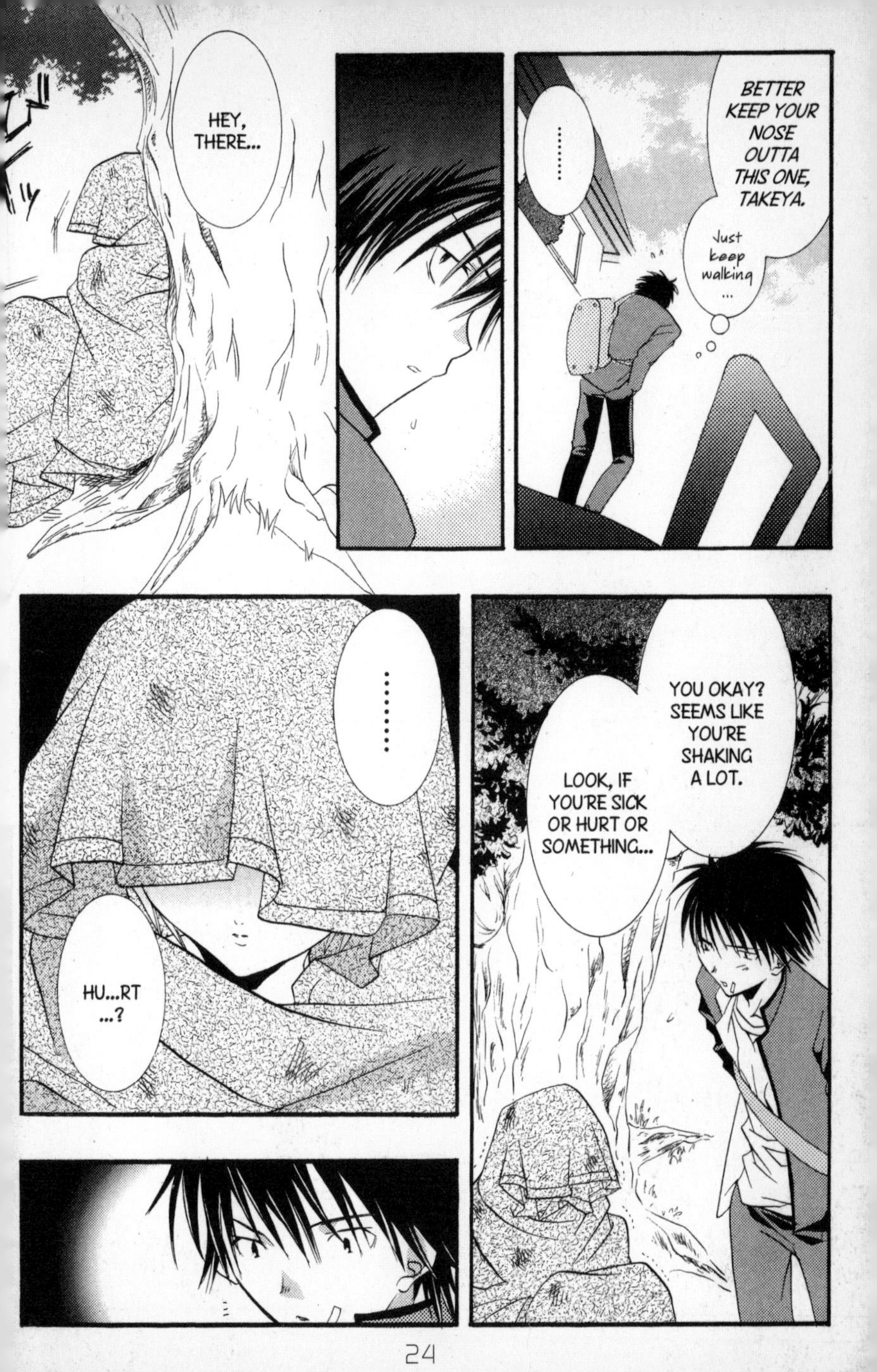
BETTER KEEP YOUR NOSE OUTTA THIS ONE, TAKEYA.
Just keep walking ...
......
HEY, THERE...
YOU OKAY? SEEMS LIKE YOU'RE SHAKING A LOT.
LOOK, IF YOU'RE SICK OR HURT OR SOMETHING...
....
HU...RT ...?

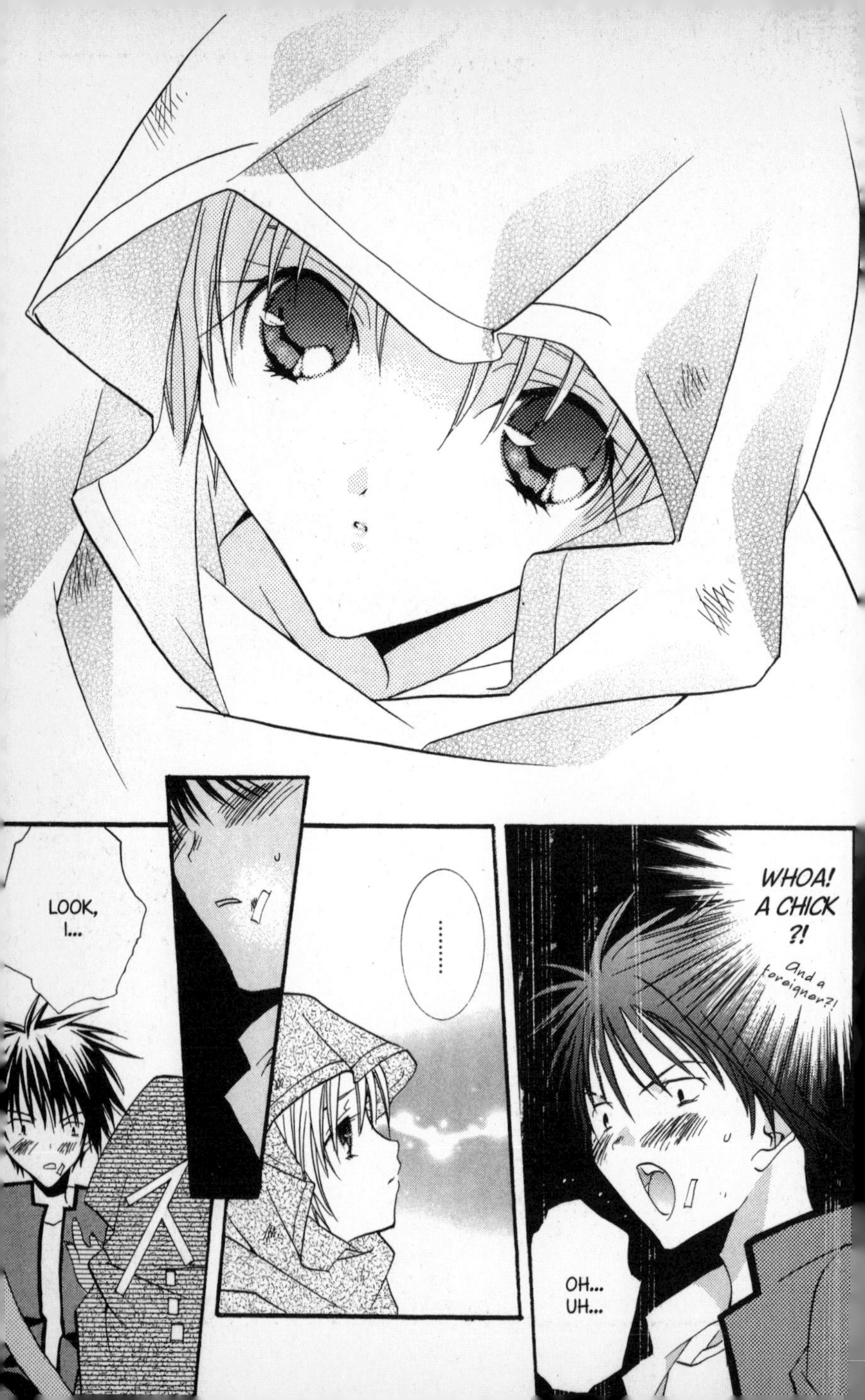
WHOA! A CHICK ?!
And a foreigner?!
OH... UH...
....
LOOK, I...

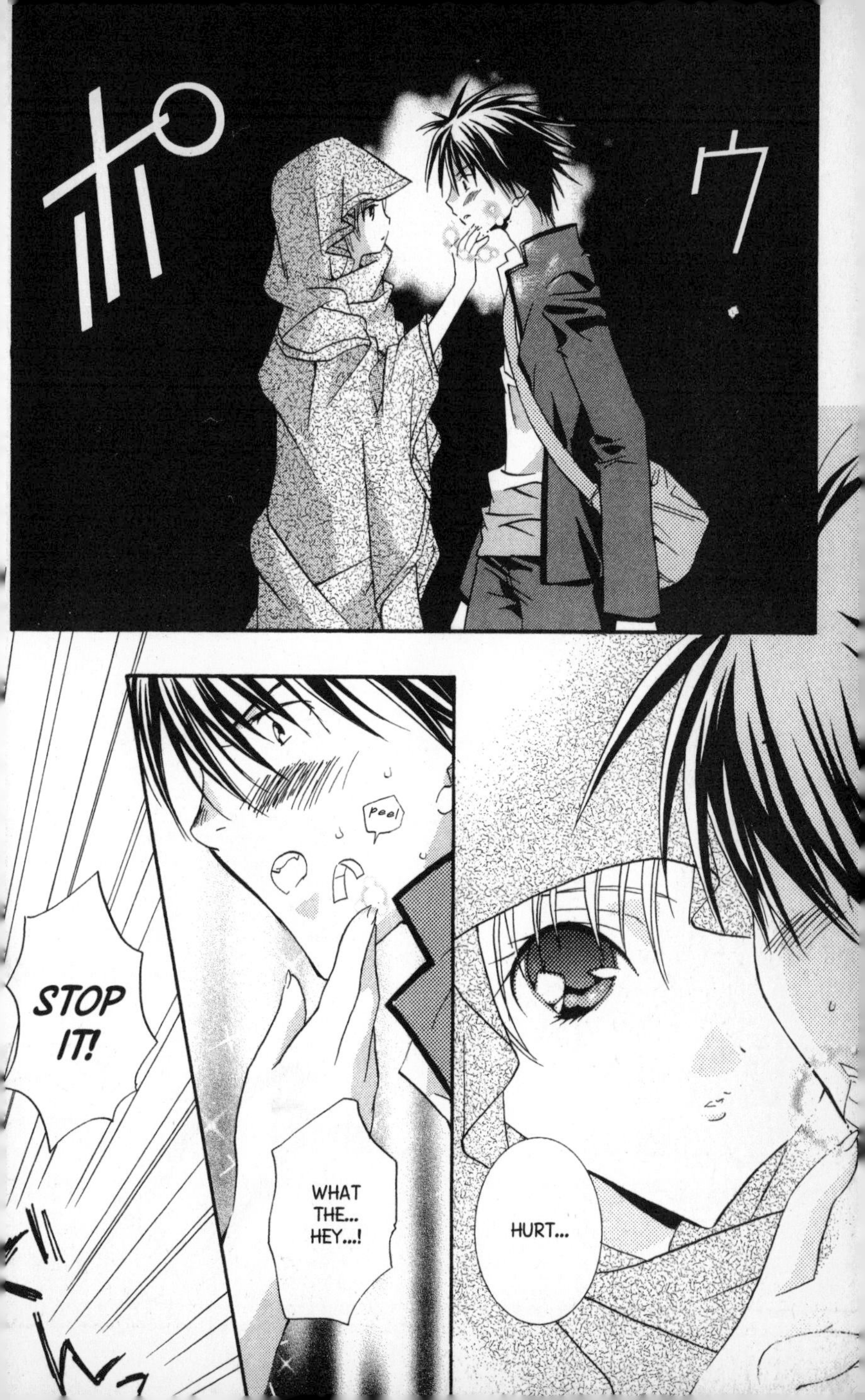
ポウ
HURT...
peel
WHAT THE... HEY...!
STOP IT!

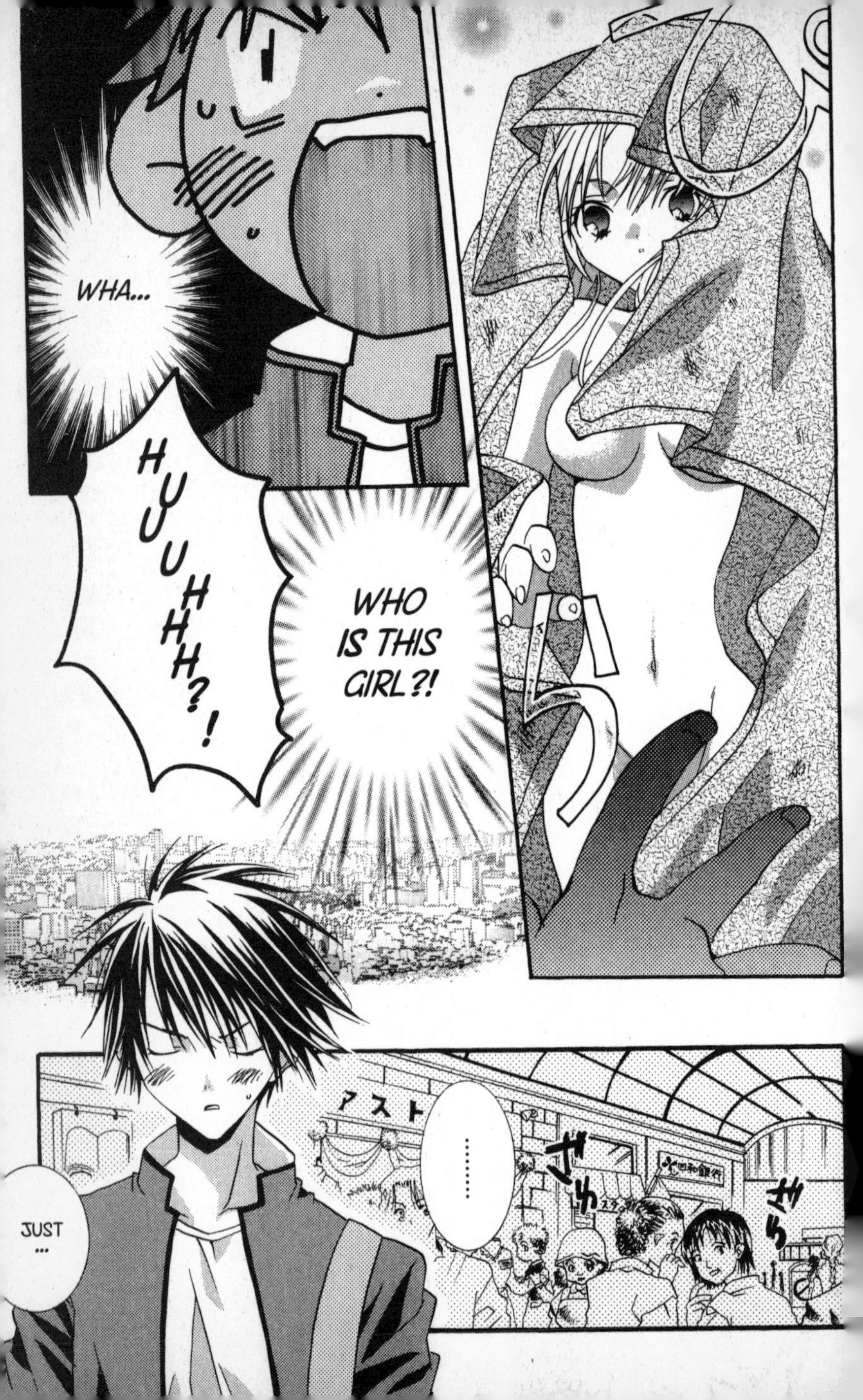

WHA...
HUUUHHHH?!
WHO IS THIS GIRL?!
アスト
ざわ
ざわ
....
JUST ...

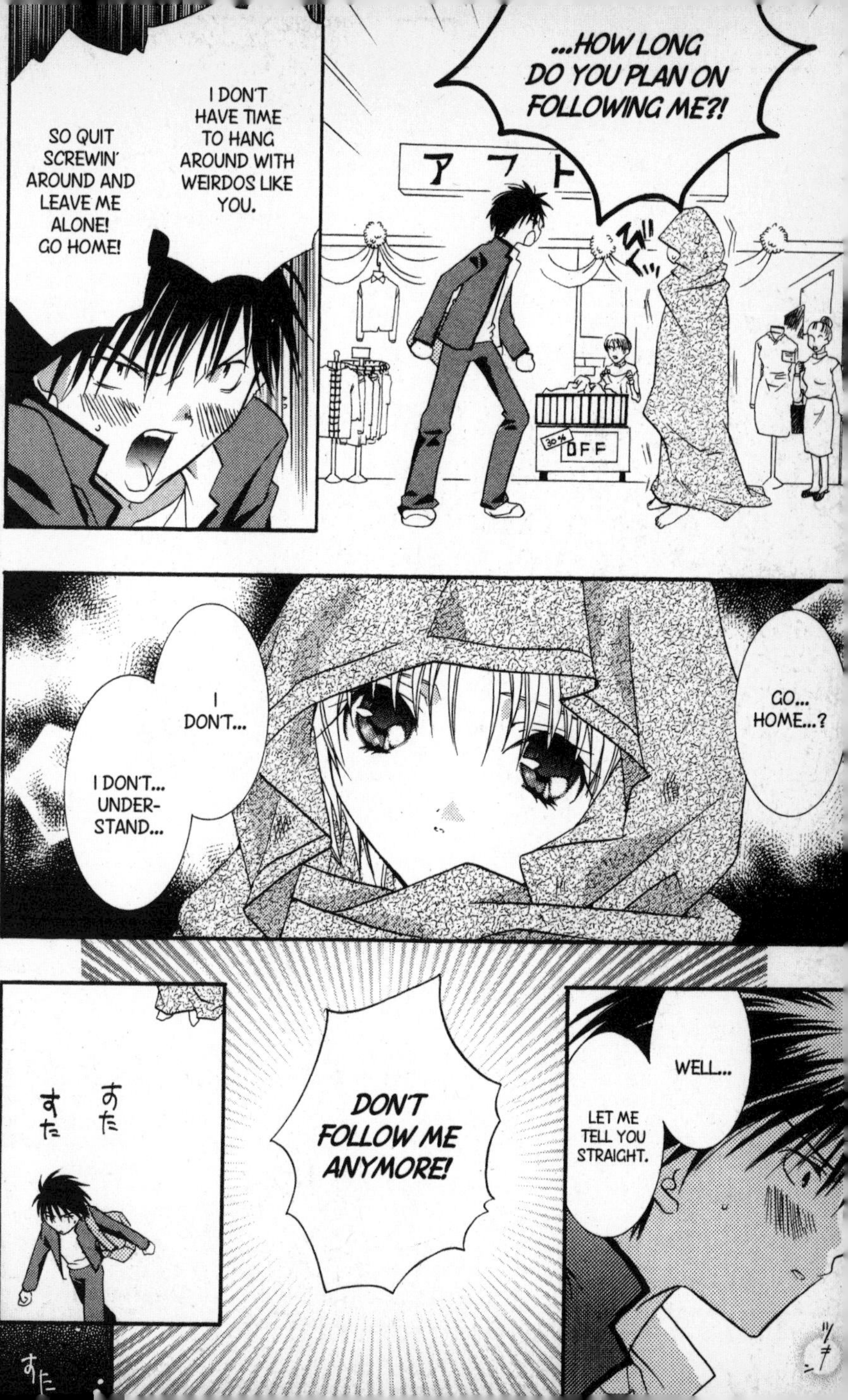
...HOW LONG DO YOU PLAN ON FOLLOWING ME?!
アフト
30%
OFF
I DON'T HAVE TIME TO HANG AROUND WITH WEIRDOS LIKE YOU.
SO QUIT SCREWIN' AROUND AND LEAVE ME ALONE! GO HOME!
GO... HOME...?
I DON'T...
I DON'T... UNDER-STAND...
WELL...
LET ME TELL YOU STRAIGHT.
DON'T FOLLOW ME ANYMORE!
すた すた
すた

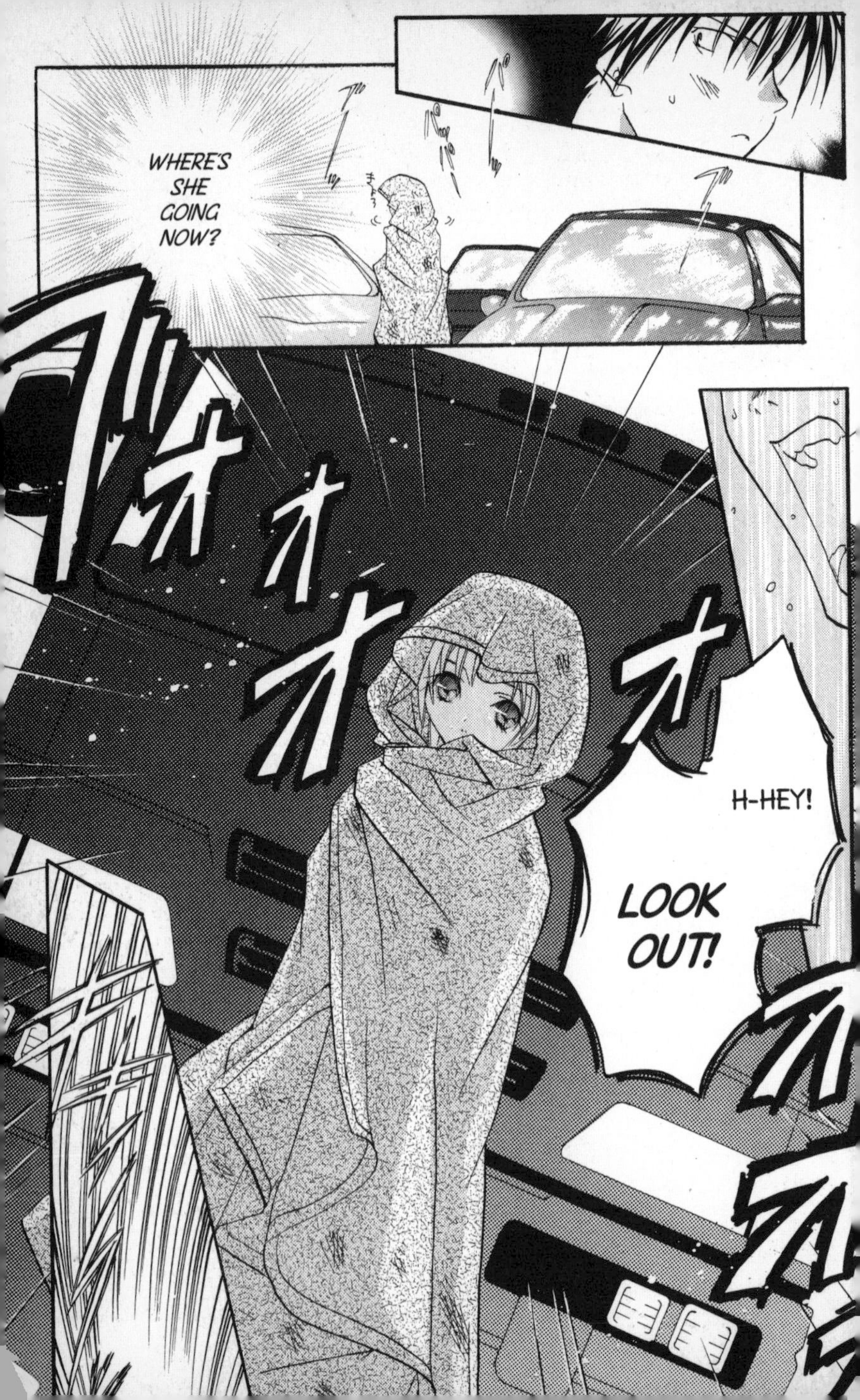
WHERE'S SHE GOING NOW?
H-HEY!
LOOK OUT!

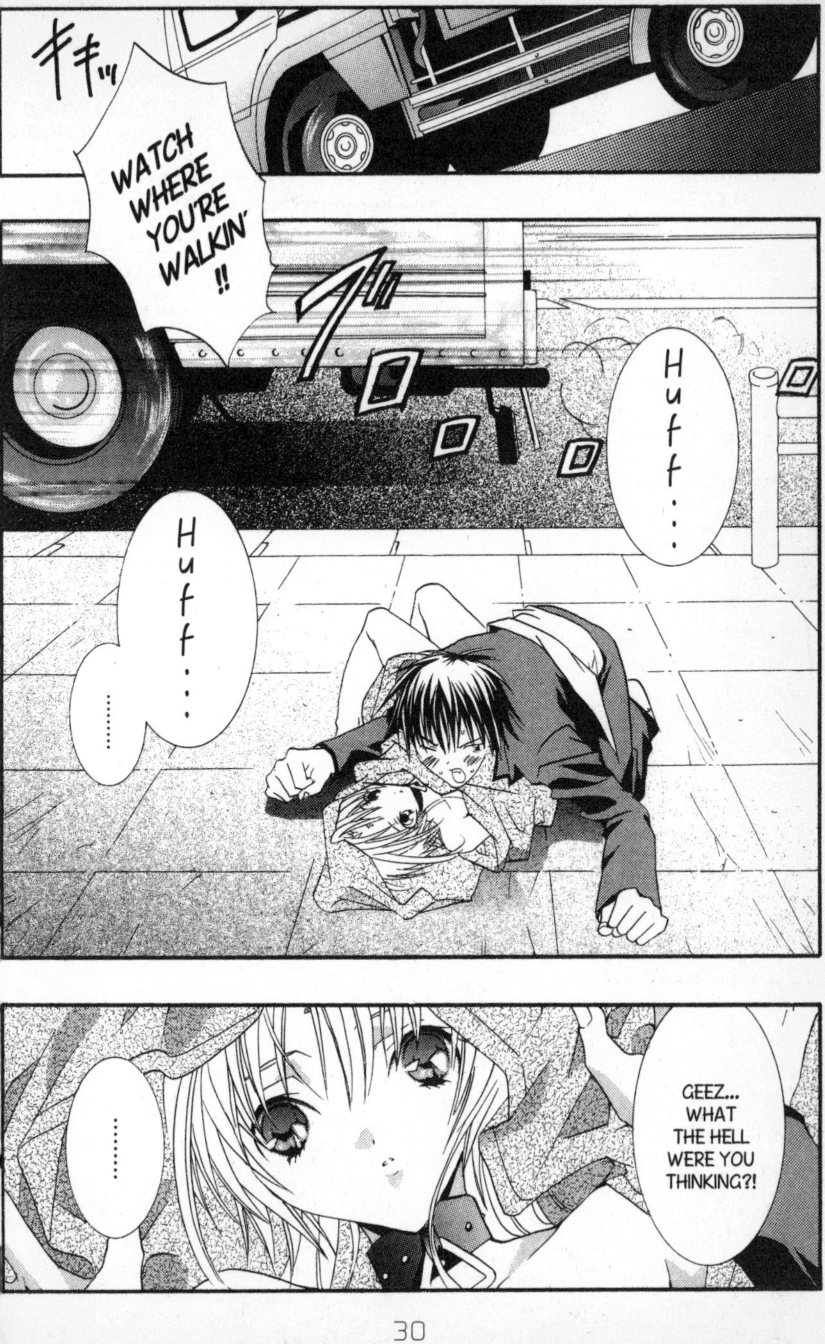
キキッ
WATCH WHERE YOU'RE WALKIN' !!
Huff...
Huff...
....
GEEZ... WHAT THE HELL WERE YOU THINKING?!
....

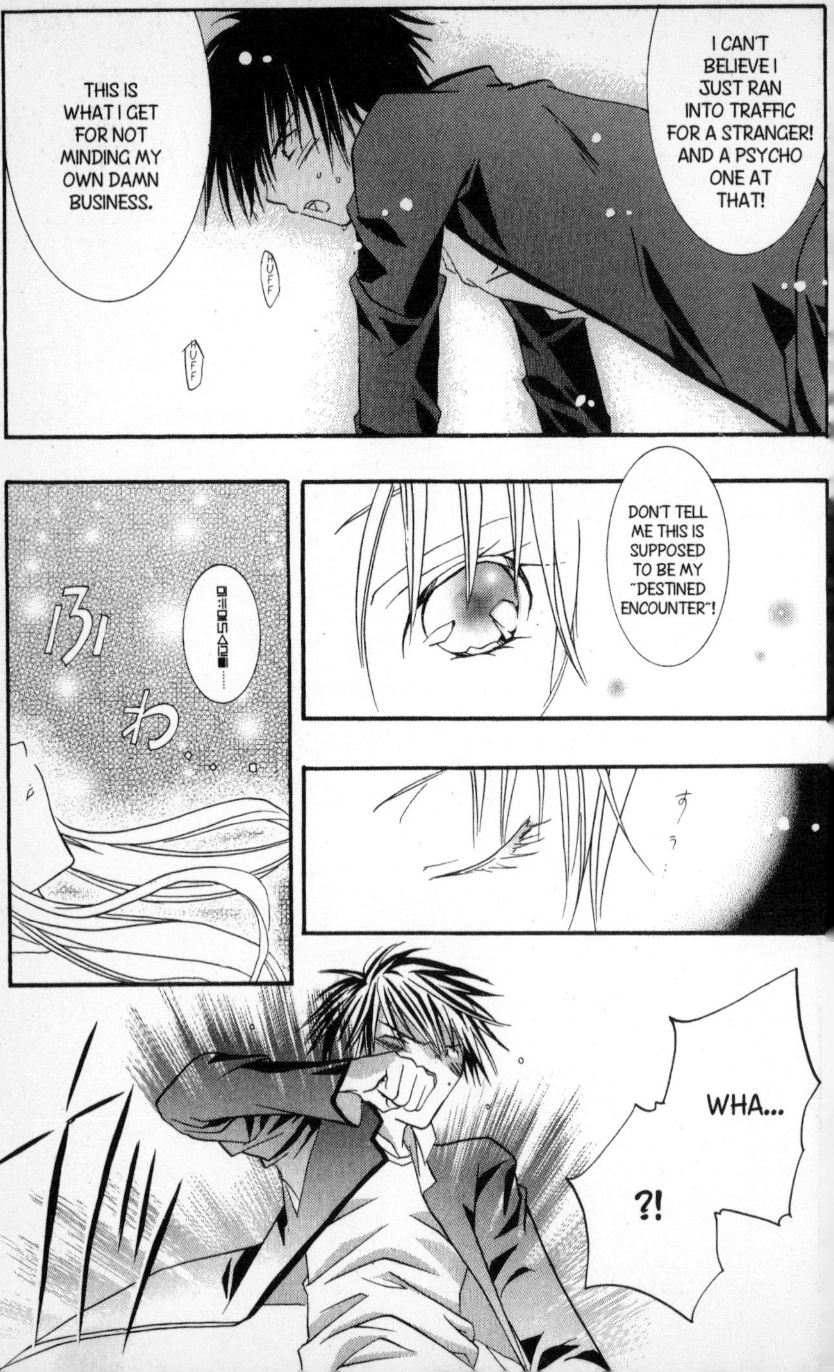
I CAN'T BELIEVE I JUST RAN INTO TRAFFIC FOR A STRANGER! AND A PSYCHO ONE AT THAT!
THIS IS WHAT I GET FOR NOT MINDING MY OWN DAMN BUSINESS.
HUFF
HUFF
DON'T TELL ME THIS IS SUPPOSED TO BE MY "DESTINED ENCOUNTER"!
ふわ
WHA...
?!

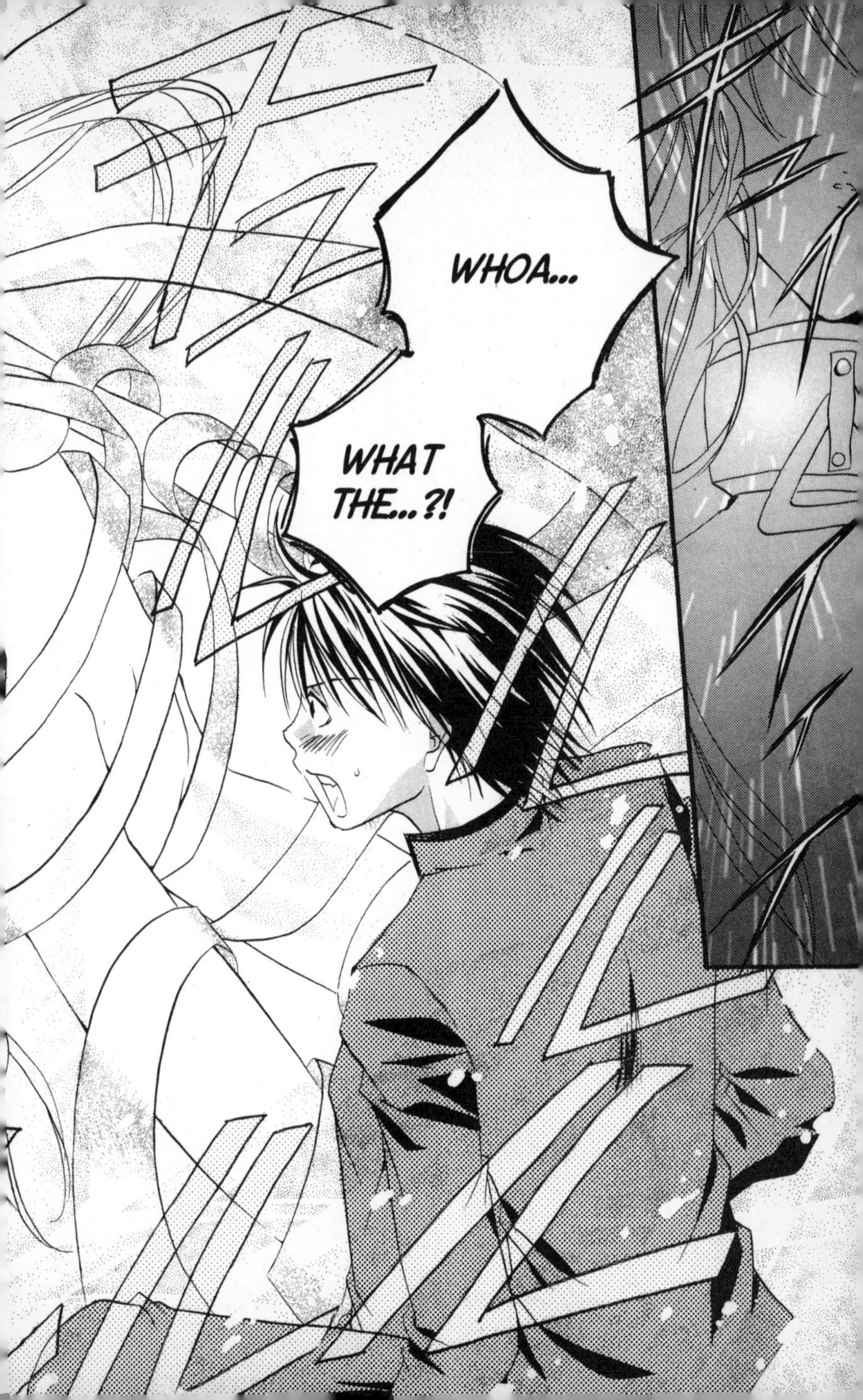
WHOA...
WHAT THE...?!

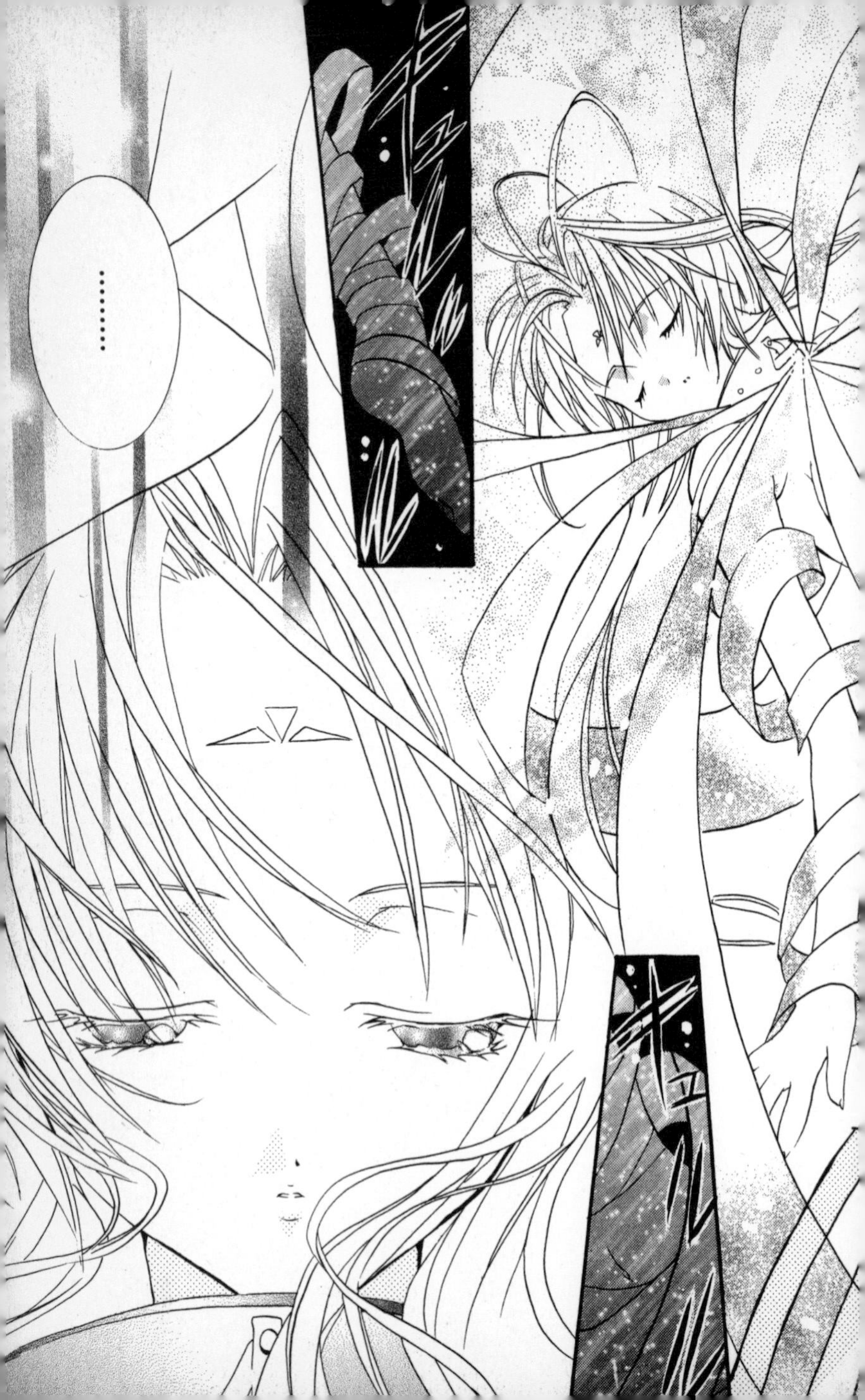
……

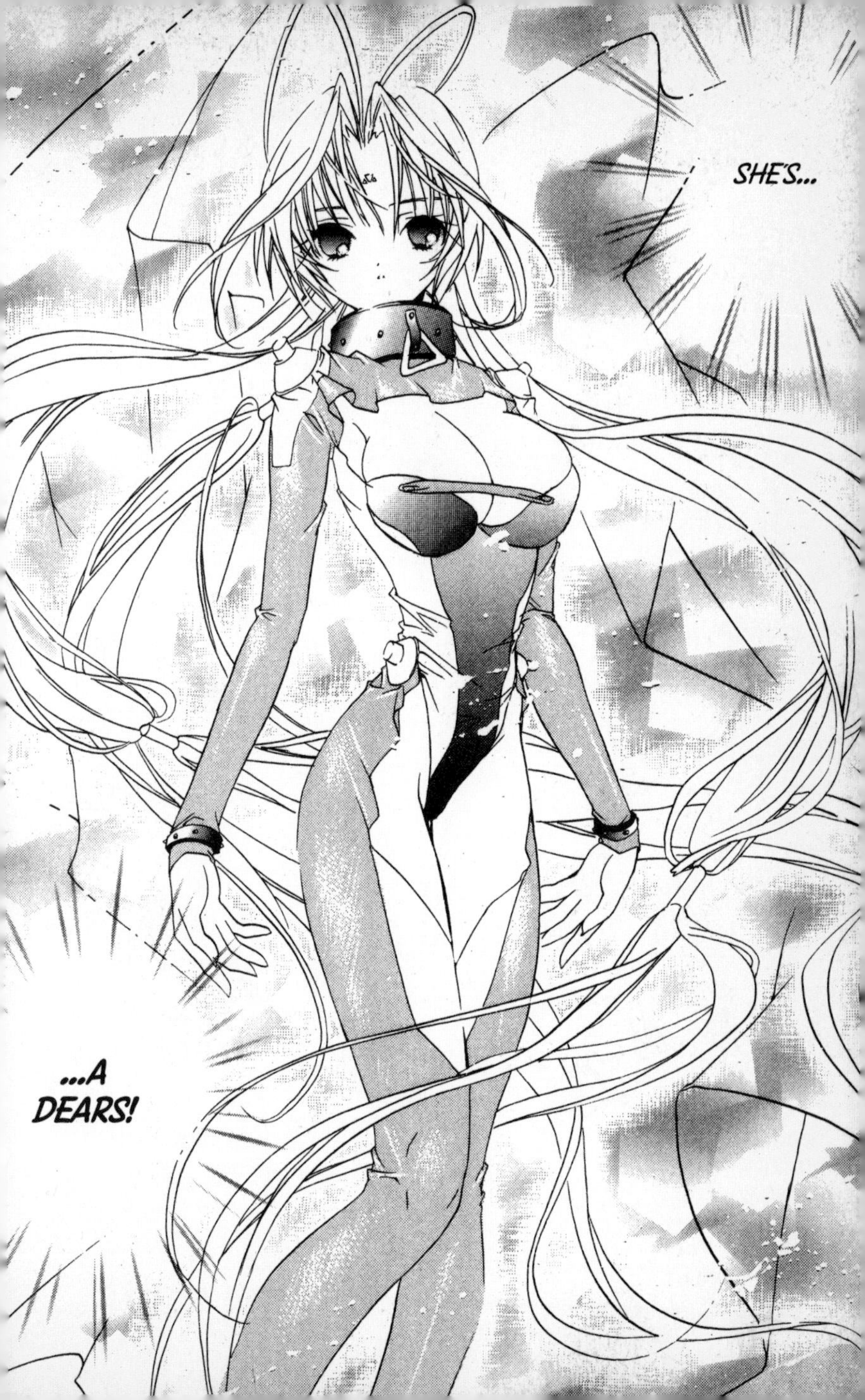
SHE'S...
...A DEARS!

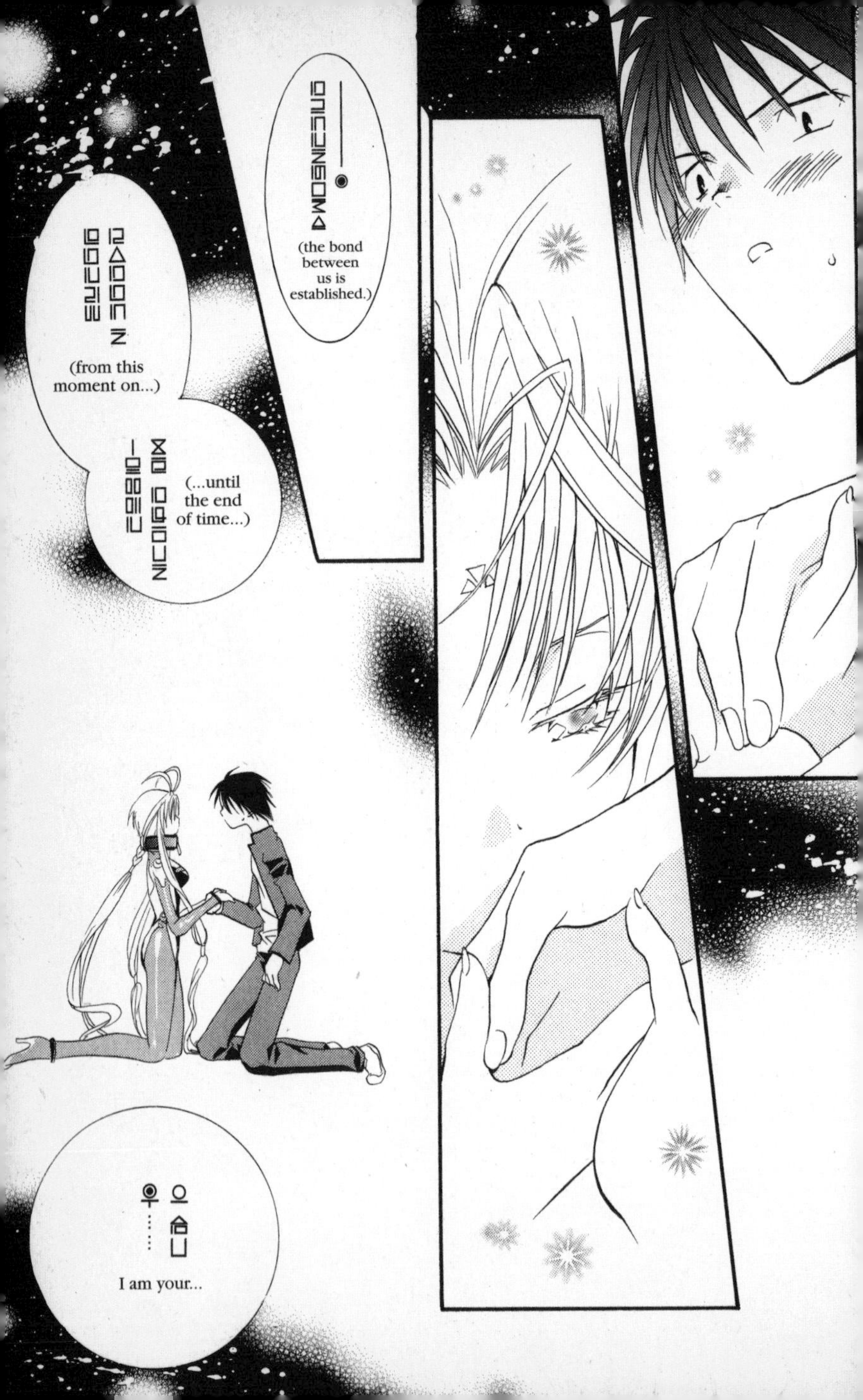

(the bond between us is established.)
(from this moment on...)
(...until the end of time...)
I am your...

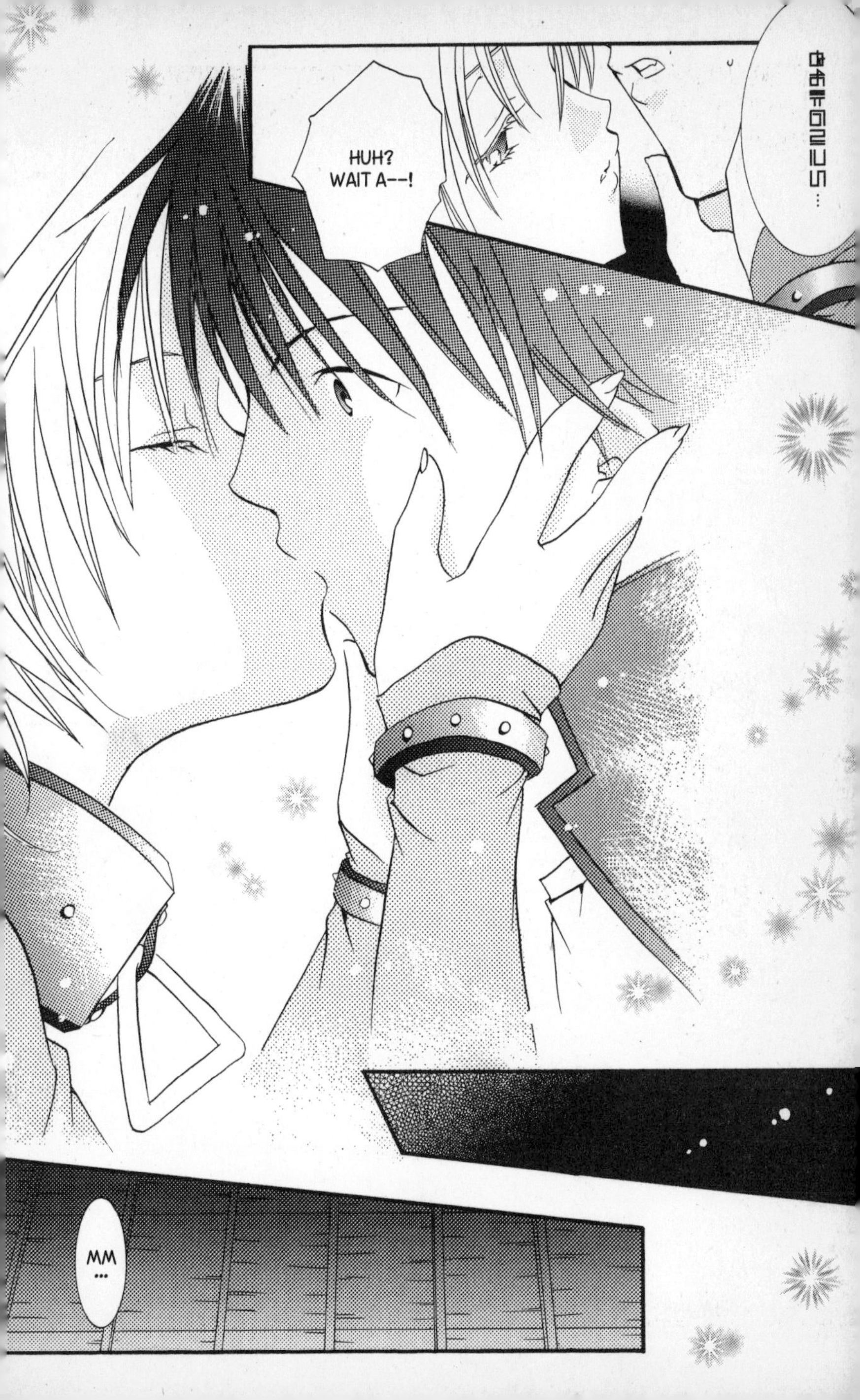

HUH? WAIT A--!
MM...

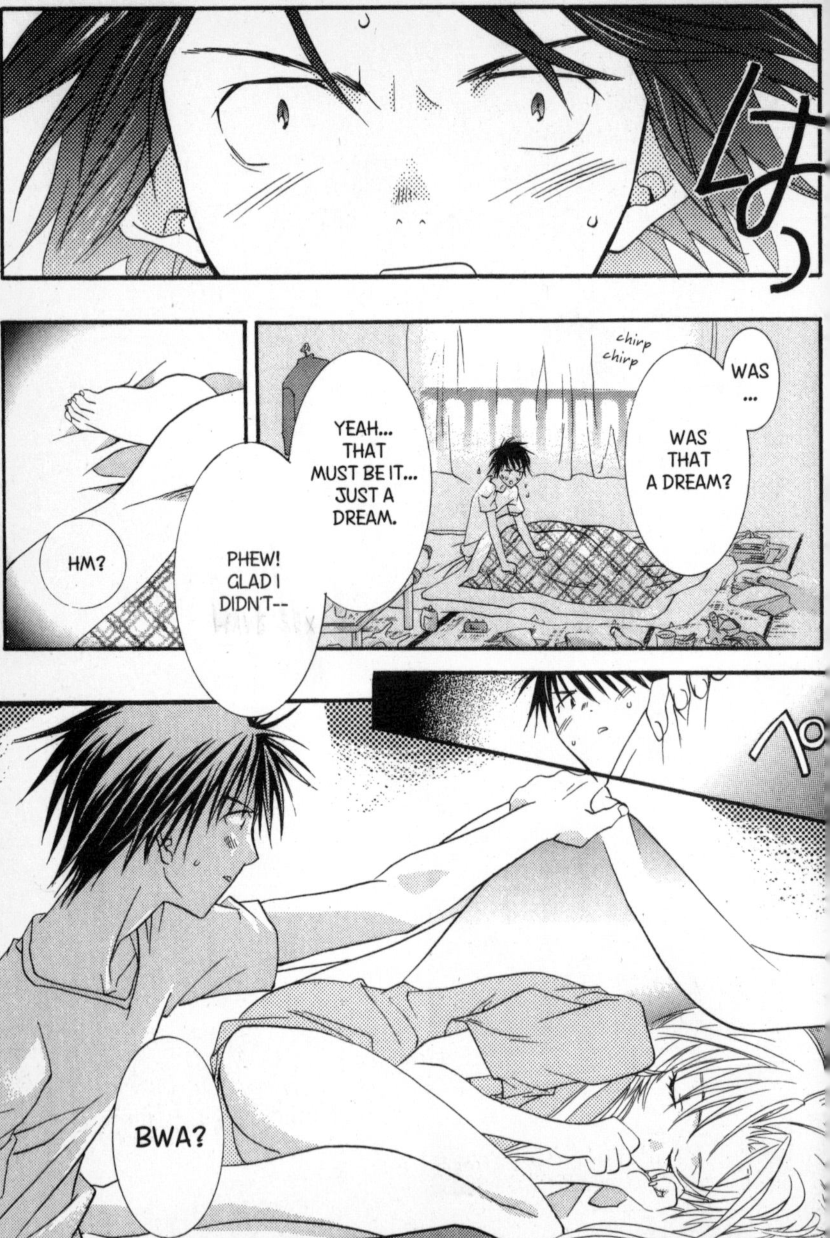
はっ
chirp chirp
WAS ...
WAS THAT A DREAM?
YEAH... THAT MUST BE IT... JUST A DREAM.
HM?
PHEW! GLAD I DIDN'T--
ぺ
BWA?

PEACE

ガリ ガサ
ガリ ガサ
ゴロゴロ・・・・
ガリッ
ゴロゴロ・・・
ボチャン
プカァ〜〜
END

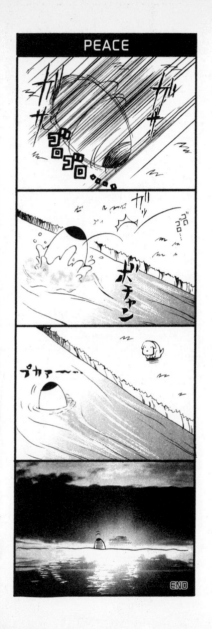

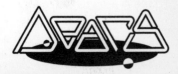

2nd Contact

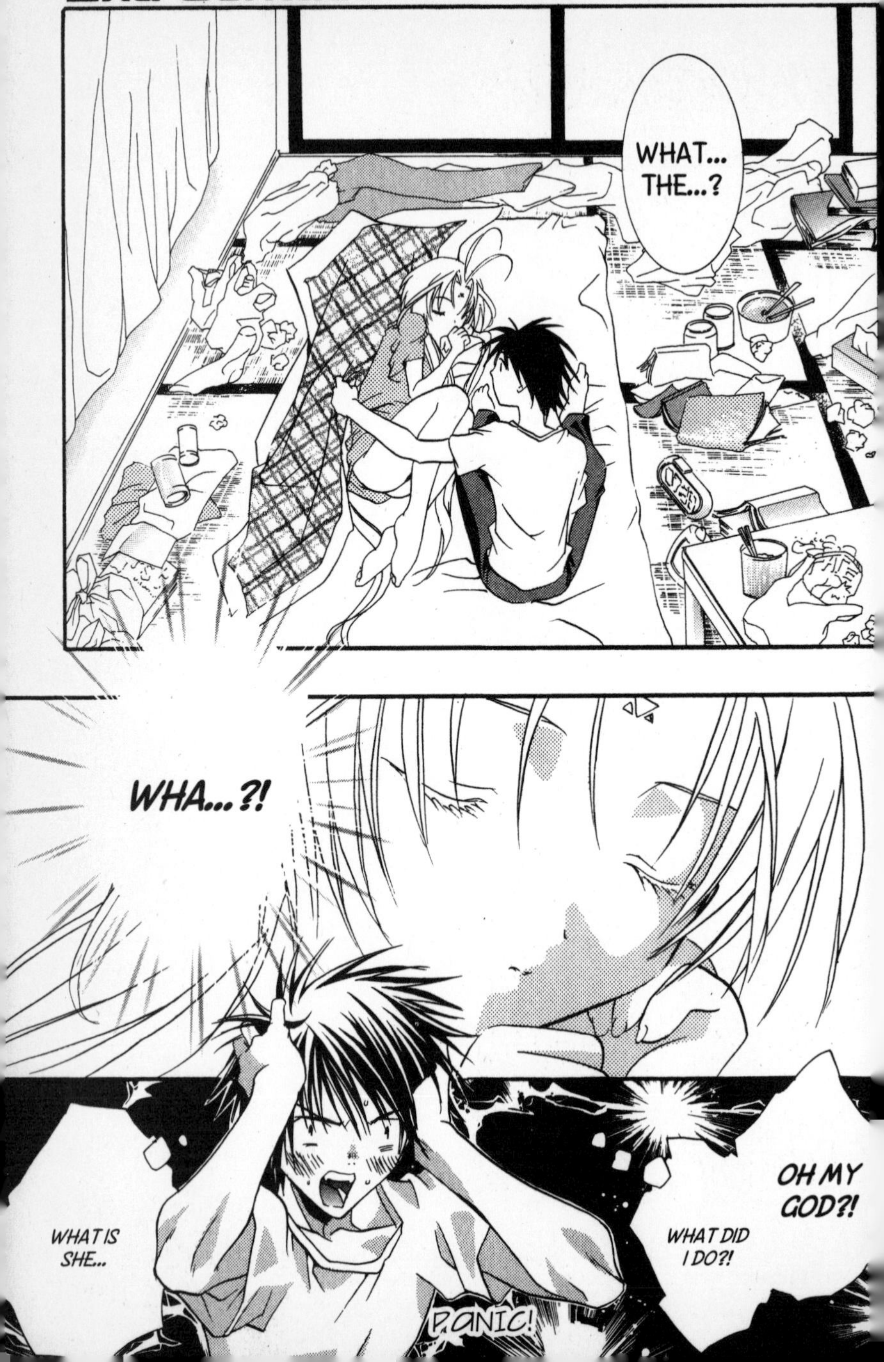
WHAT... THE...?
WHA...?!
OH MY GOD?!
WHAT DID I DO?!
WHAT IS SHE...
PANIC!

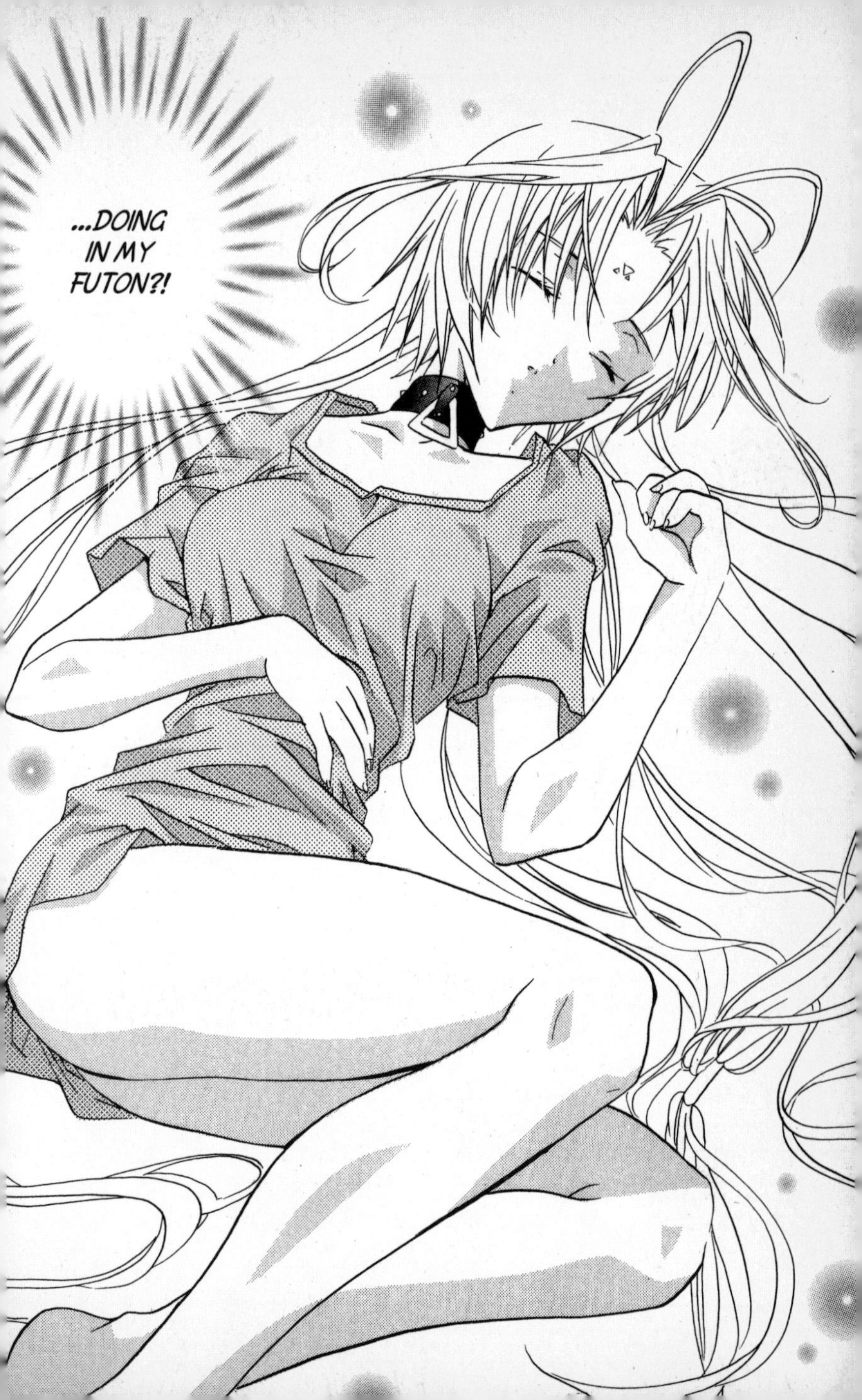
...DOING
IN MY
FUTON?!

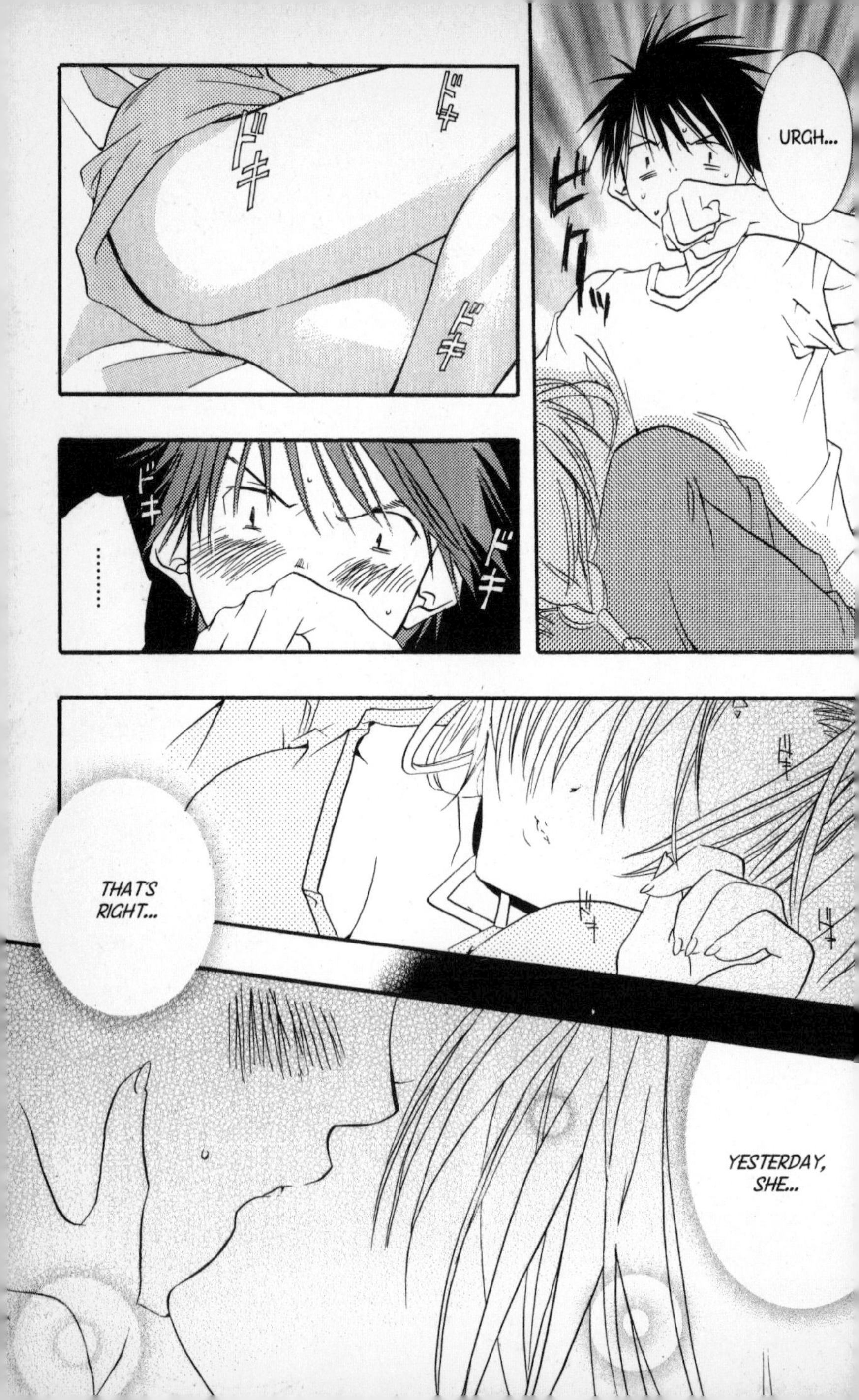
URGH...
ビクッ
ドキ
ドキ
ドキ
ドキ
ドキ
......
ドキ
THAT'S RIGHT...
YESTERDAY, SHE...

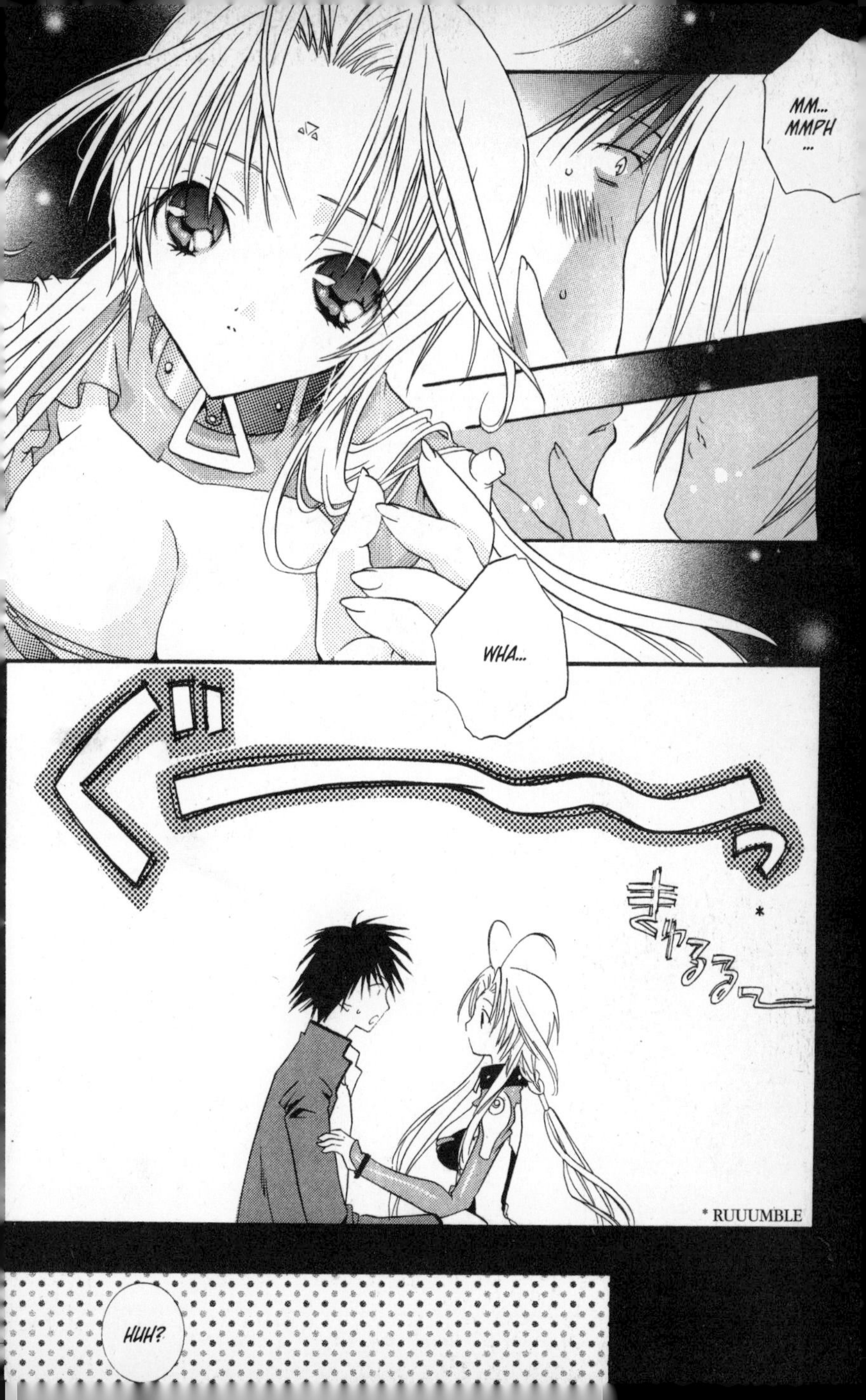
MM... MMPH ...
WHA...
ぐ〜〜っ
きゅるる〜*
* RUUUMBLE
HUH?

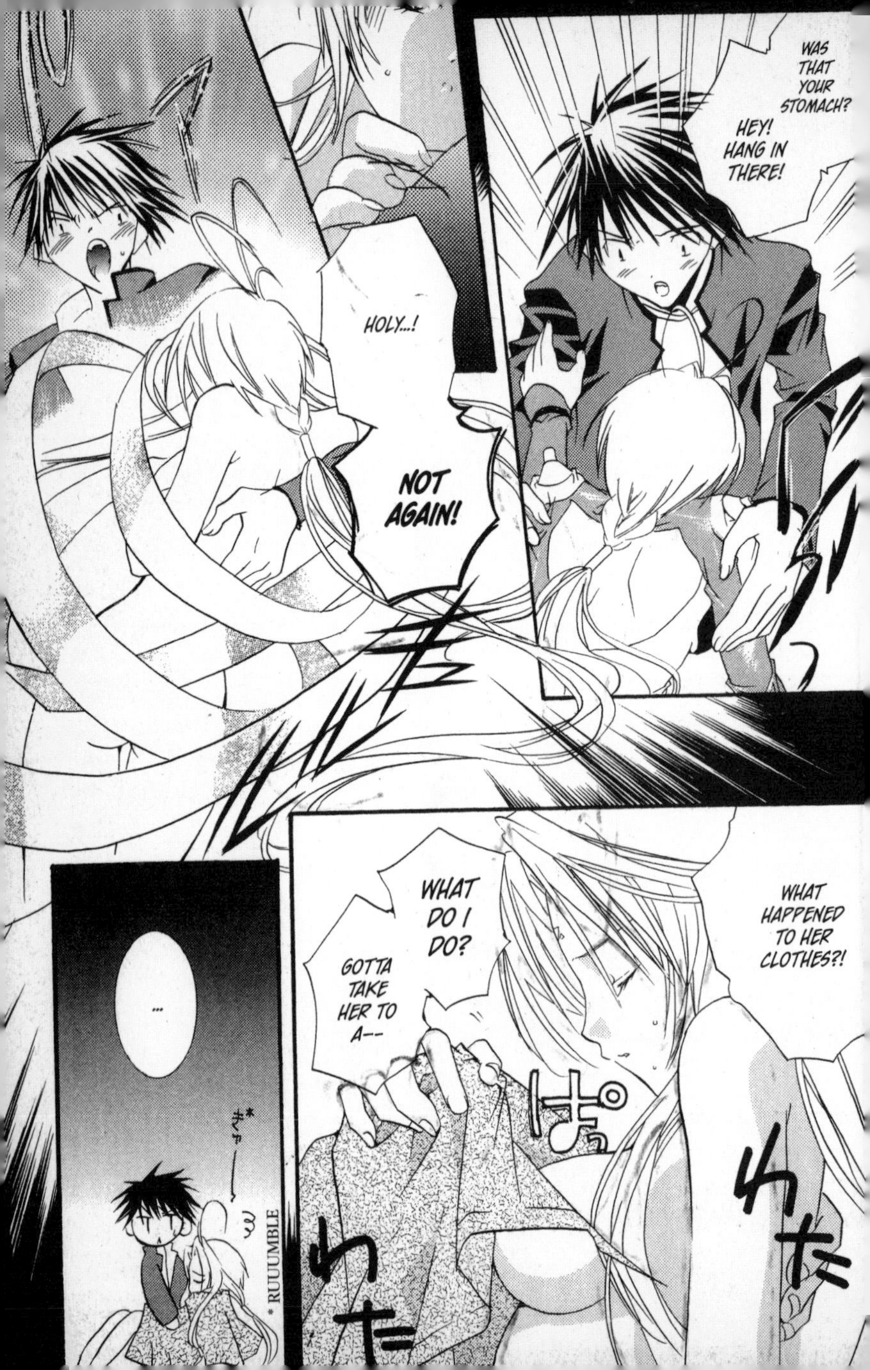
WAS THAT YOUR STOMACH?
HEY! HANG IN THERE!
HOLY...!
NOT AGAIN!
WHAT HAPPENED TO HER CLOTHES?!
WHAT DO I DO?
GOTTA TAKE HER TO A--
ぱっ
...
* RUUUMBLE

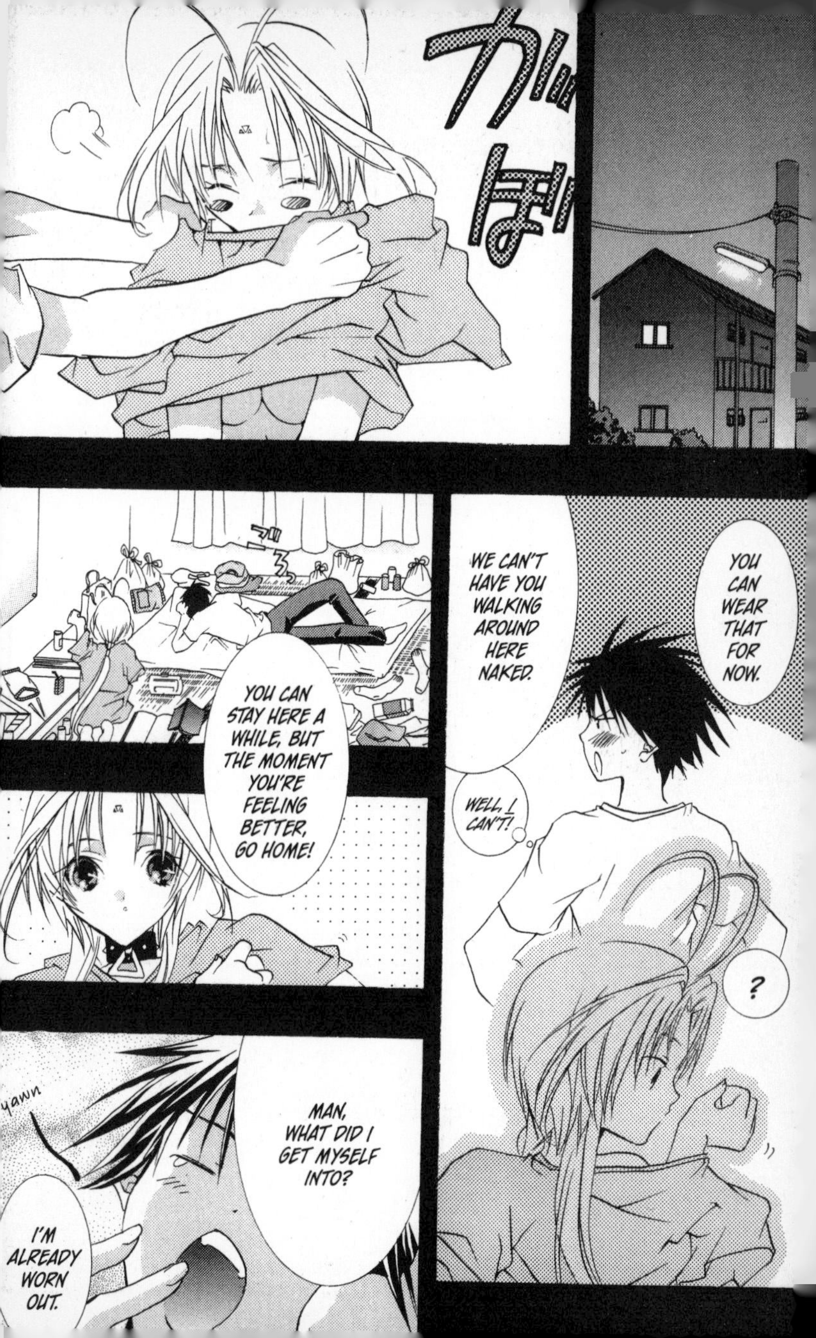
YOU CAN WEAR THAT FOR NOW.
WE CAN'T HAVE YOU WALKING AROUND HERE NAKED.
WELL, I CAN'T!
?
YOU CAN STAY HERE A WHILE, BUT THE MOMENT YOU'RE FEELING BETTER, GO HOME!
yawn
MAN, WHAT DID I GET MYSELF INTO?
I'M ALREADY WORN OUT.

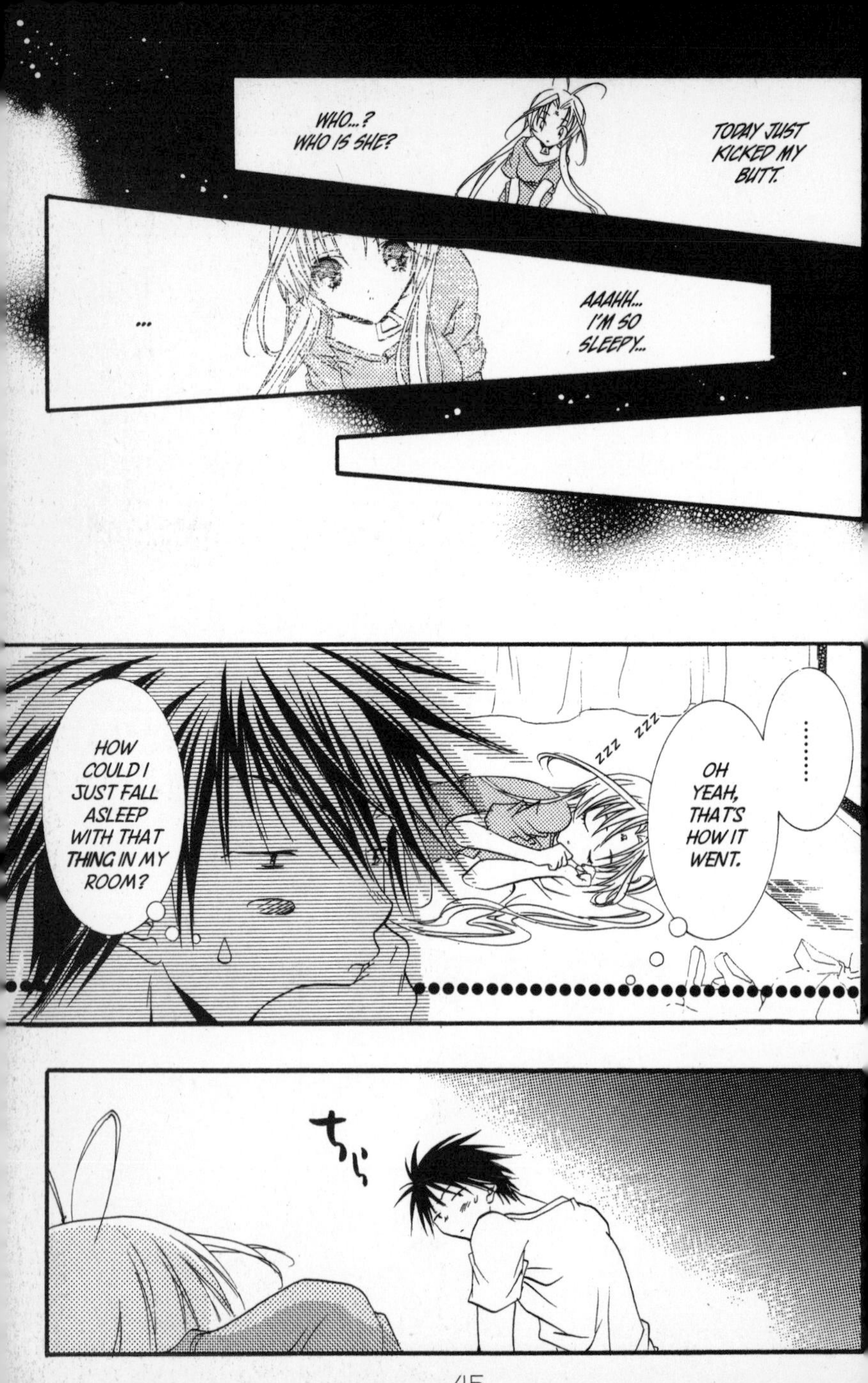
TODAY JUST KICKED MY BUTT.
WHO...? WHO IS SHE?
AAAHH... I'M SO SLEEPY...
...
......
OH YEAH, THAT'S HOW IT WENT.
ZZZ ZZZ
HOW COULD I JUST FALL ASLEEP WITH THAT THING IN MY ROOM?
ちら

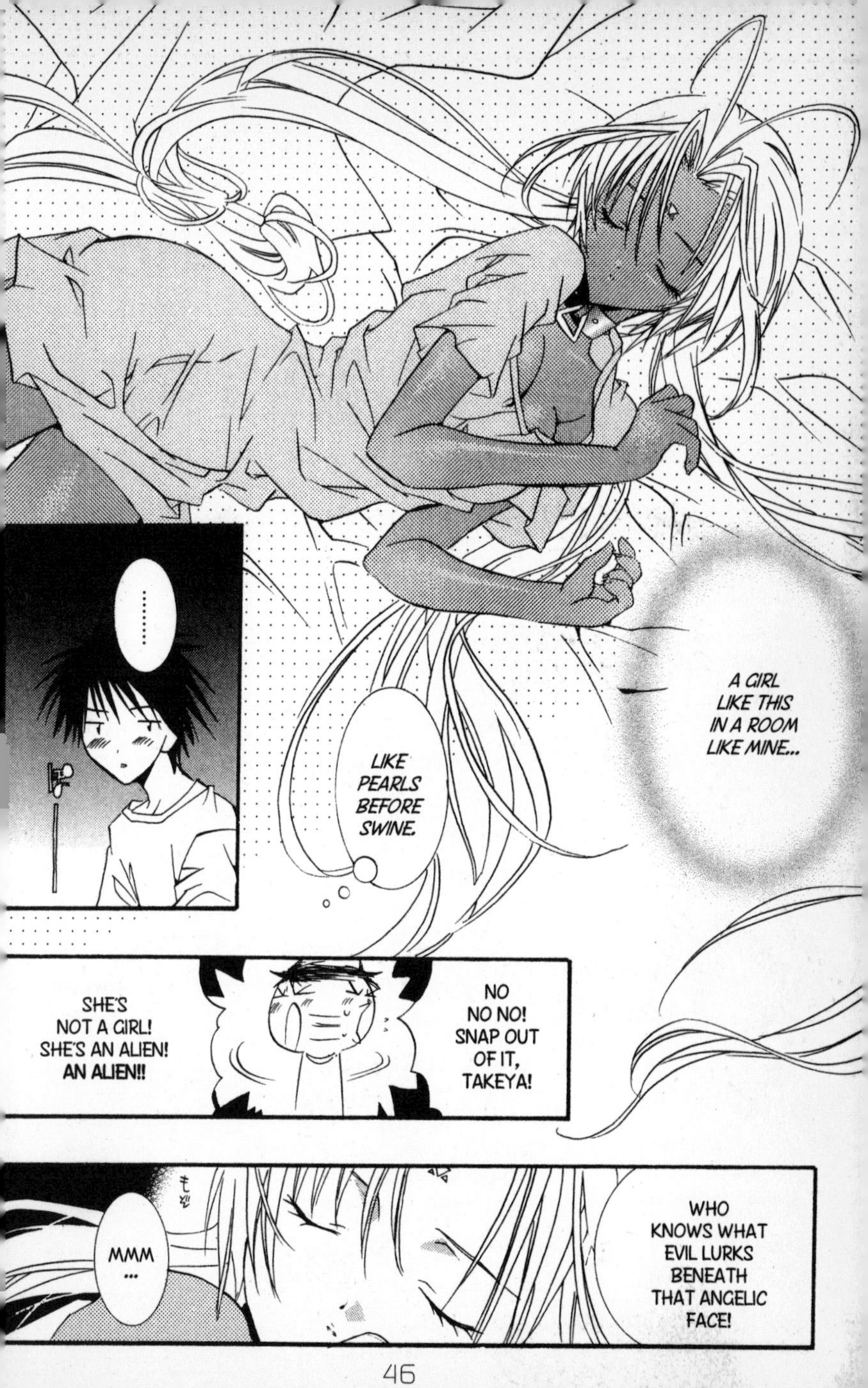
A GIRL LIKE THIS IN A ROOM LIKE MINE...
LIKE PEARLS BEFORE SWINE.
......
NO NO NO! SNAP OUT OF IT, TAKEYA!
SHE'S NOT A GIRL! SHE'S AN ALIEN! AN ALIEN!!
WHO KNOWS WHAT EVIL LURKS BENEATH THAT ANGELIC FACE!
MMM...

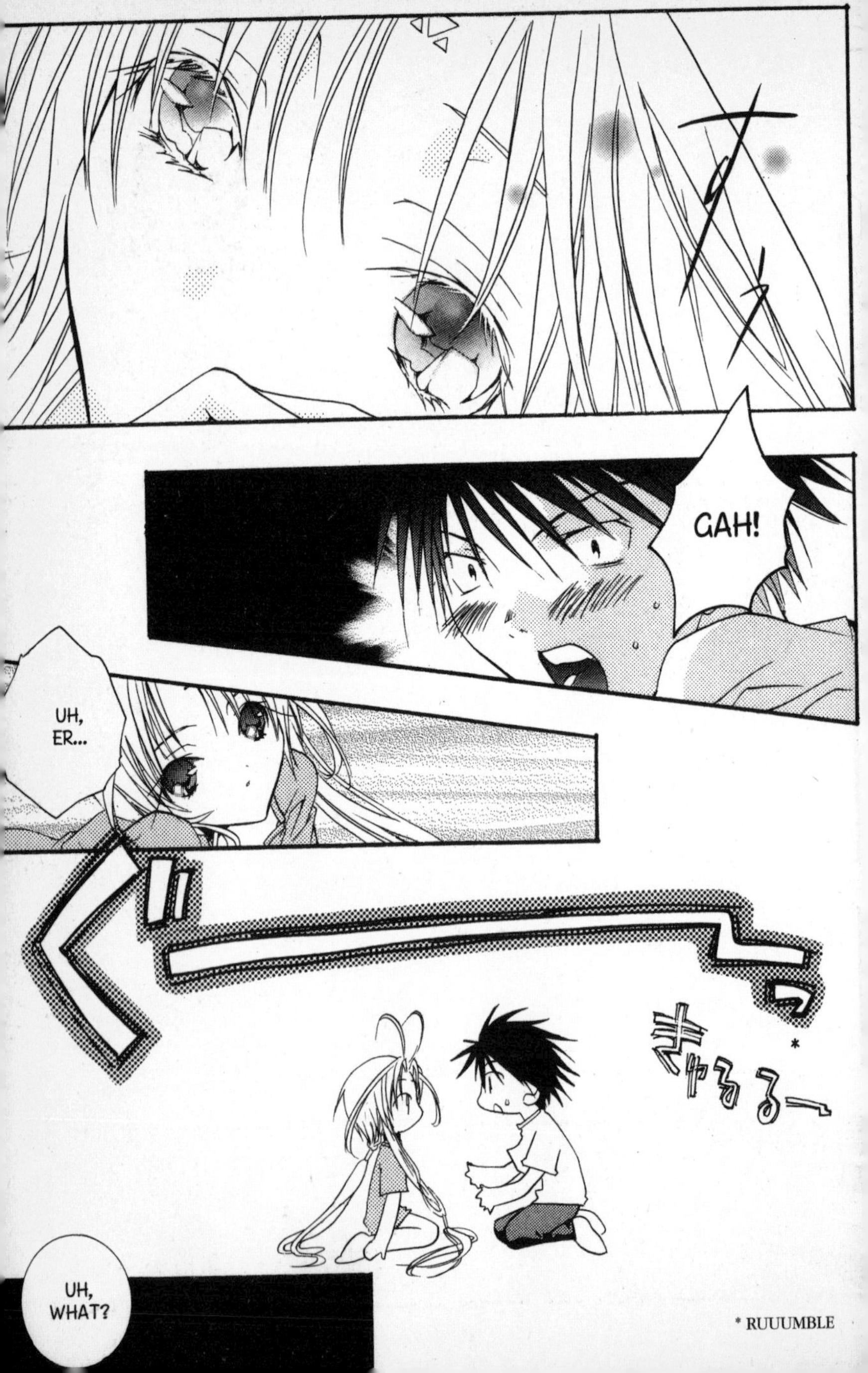
GAH!
UH, ER...
ぐーっ
きゅるるー*
UH, WHAT?

* RUUUMBLE

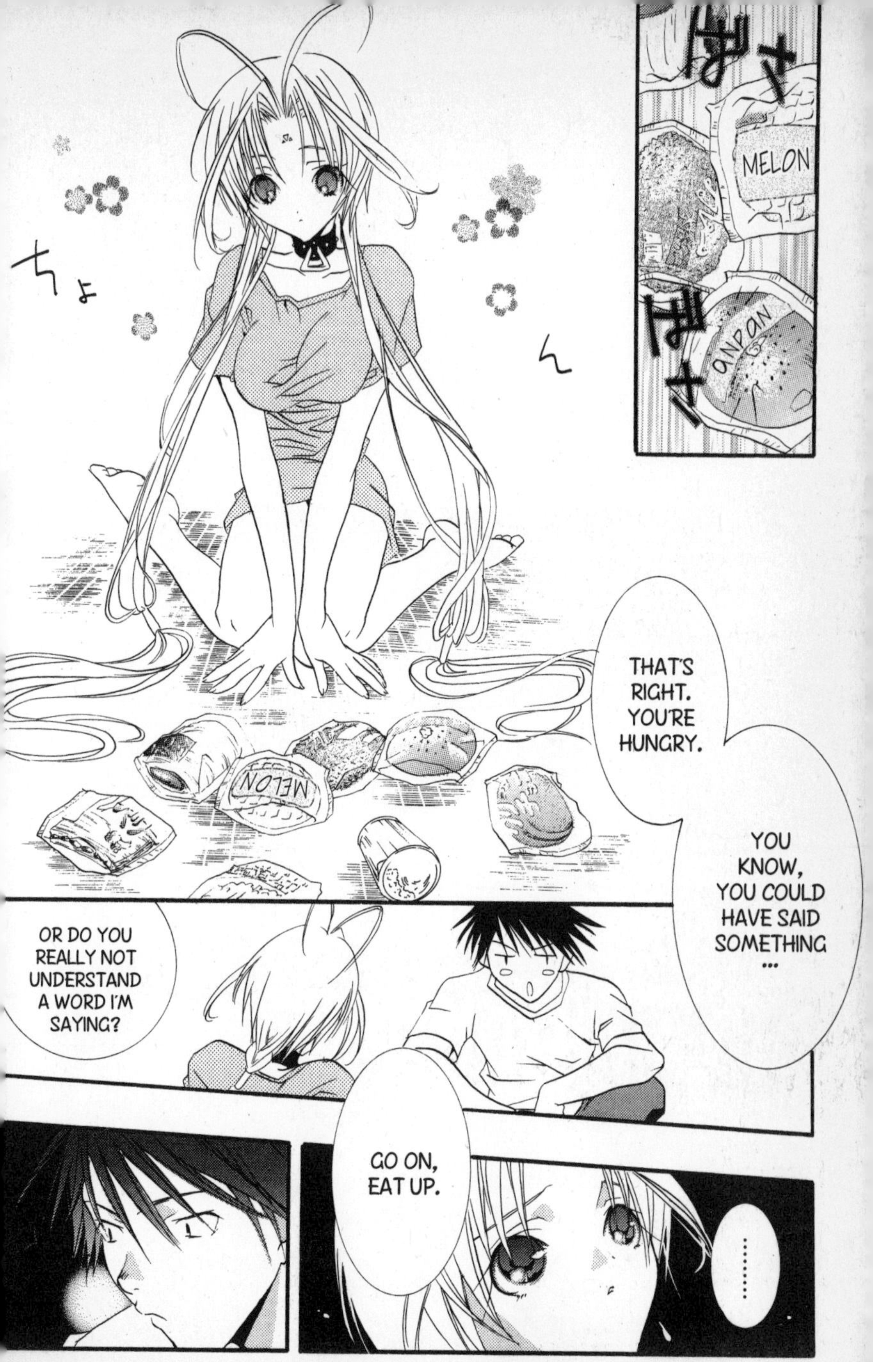

ぱさ
MELON
ぱさ
ANPAN
ちょん
MELON
THAT'S RIGHT. YOU'RE HUNGRY.
YOU KNOW, YOU COULD HAVE SAID SOMETHING...
OR DO YOU REALLY NOT UNDERSTAND A WORD I'M SAYING?
GO ON, EAT UP.
......

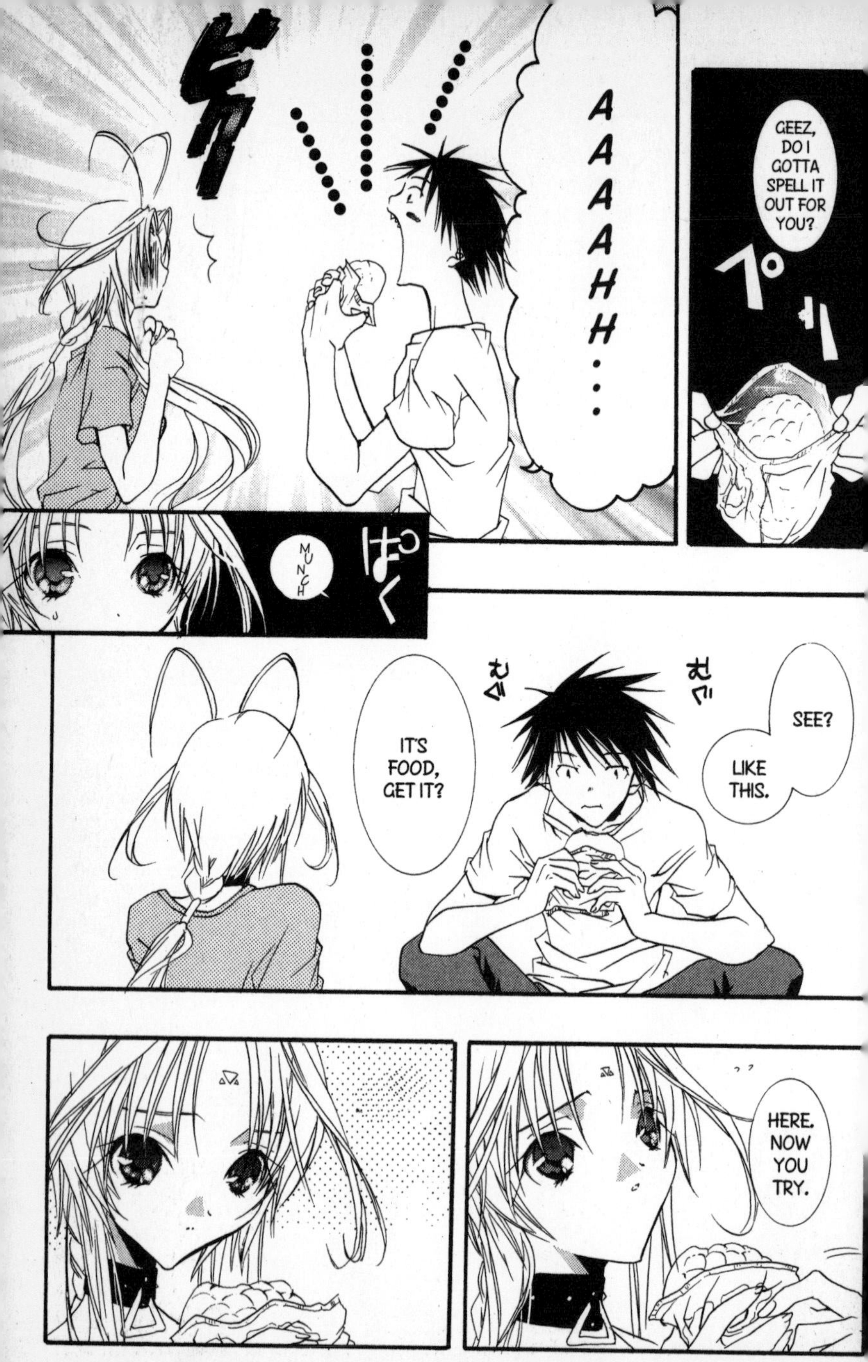
GEEZ, DO I GOTTA SPELL IT OUT FOR YOU?
AAAAAHH...
MUNCH
ぱく
SEE?
LIKE THIS.
むぐ
むぐ
IT'S FOOD, GET IT?
HERE. NOW YOU TRY.

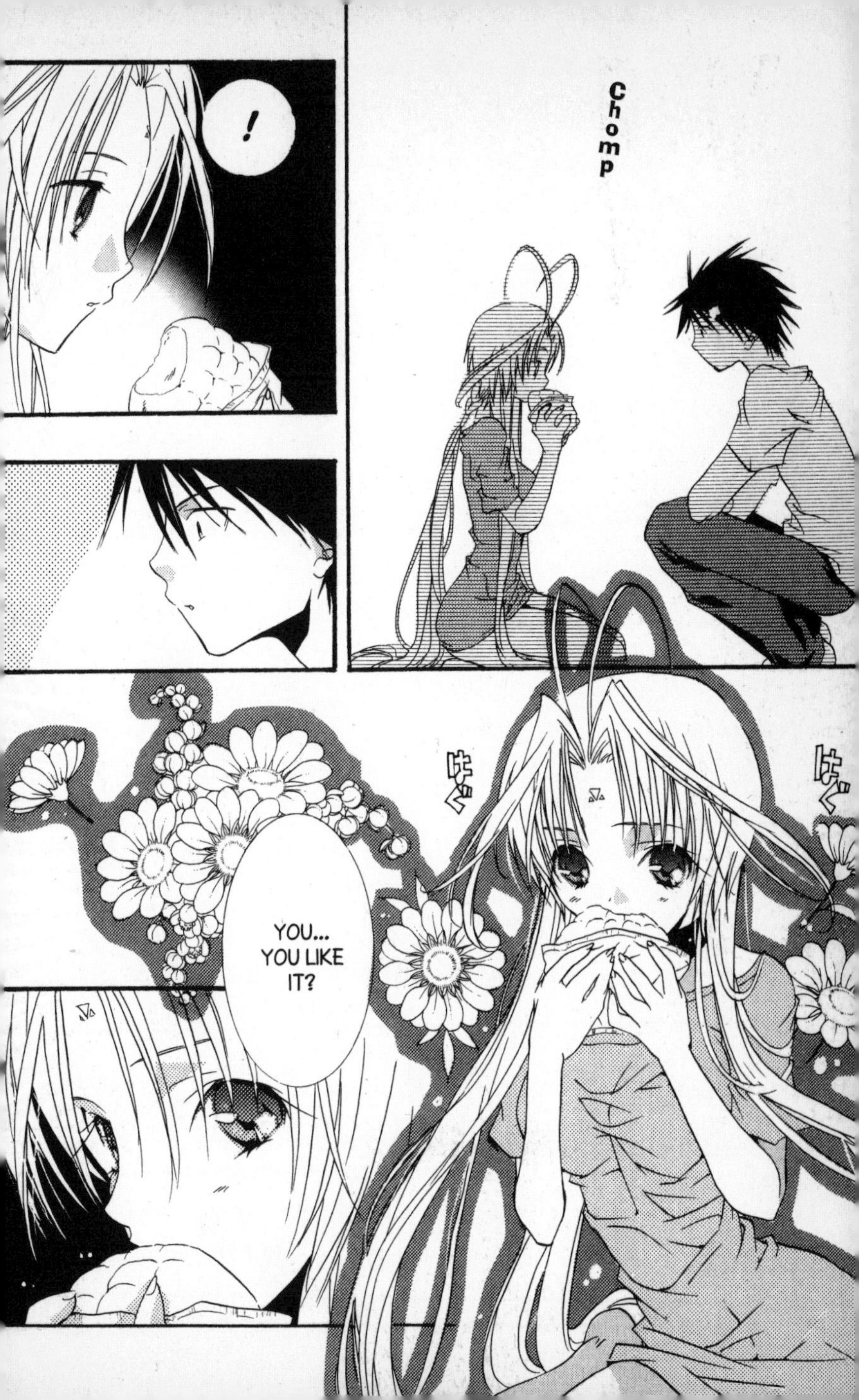
Chomp
!
はぐ
はぐ
YOU... YOU LIKE IT?

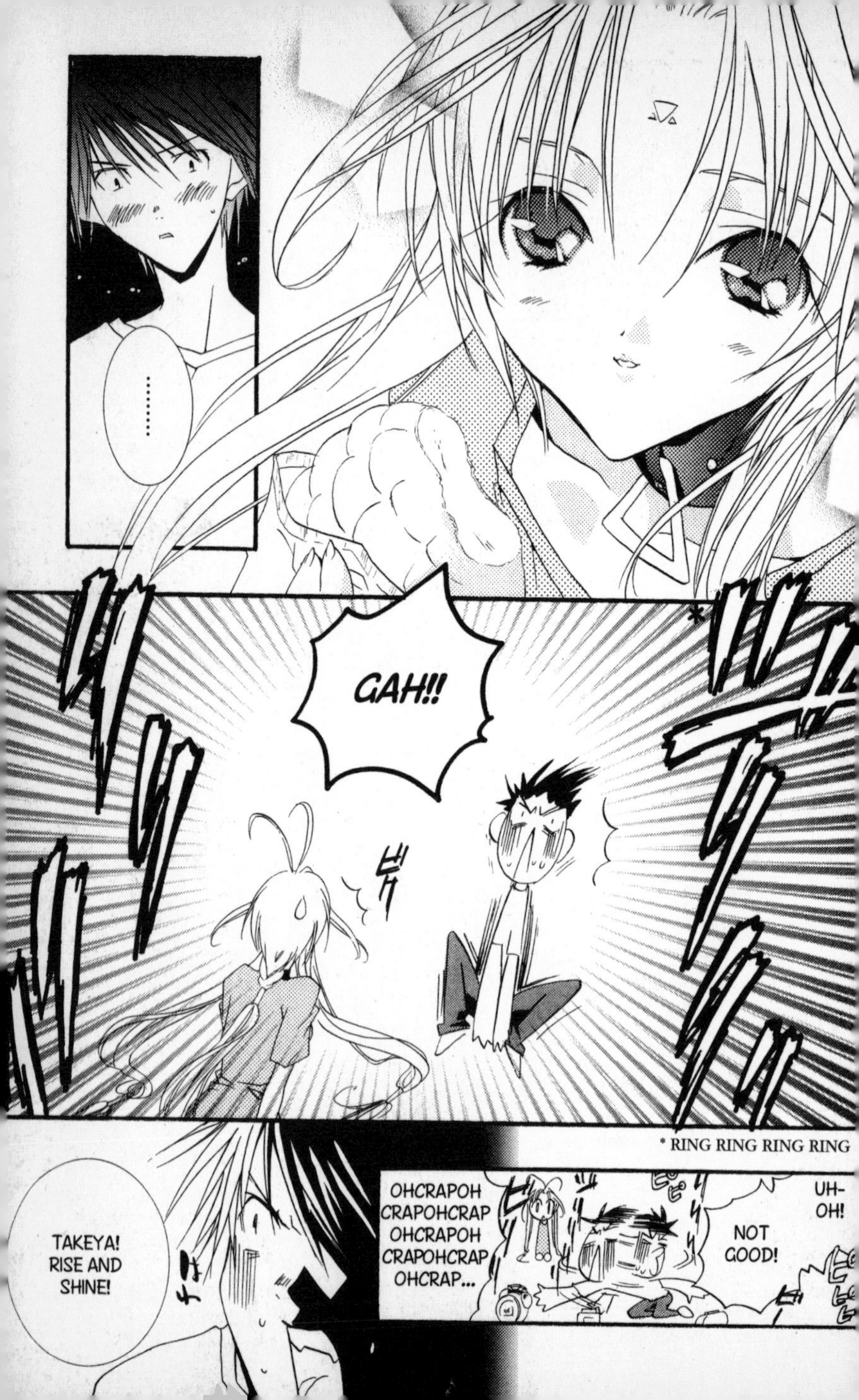
......
GAH!!
* RING RING RING RING
UH-OH!
NOT GOOD!
OHCRAPOH CRAPOHCRAP OHCRAPOH CRAPOHCRAP OHCRAP...
TAKEYA! RISE AND SHINE!

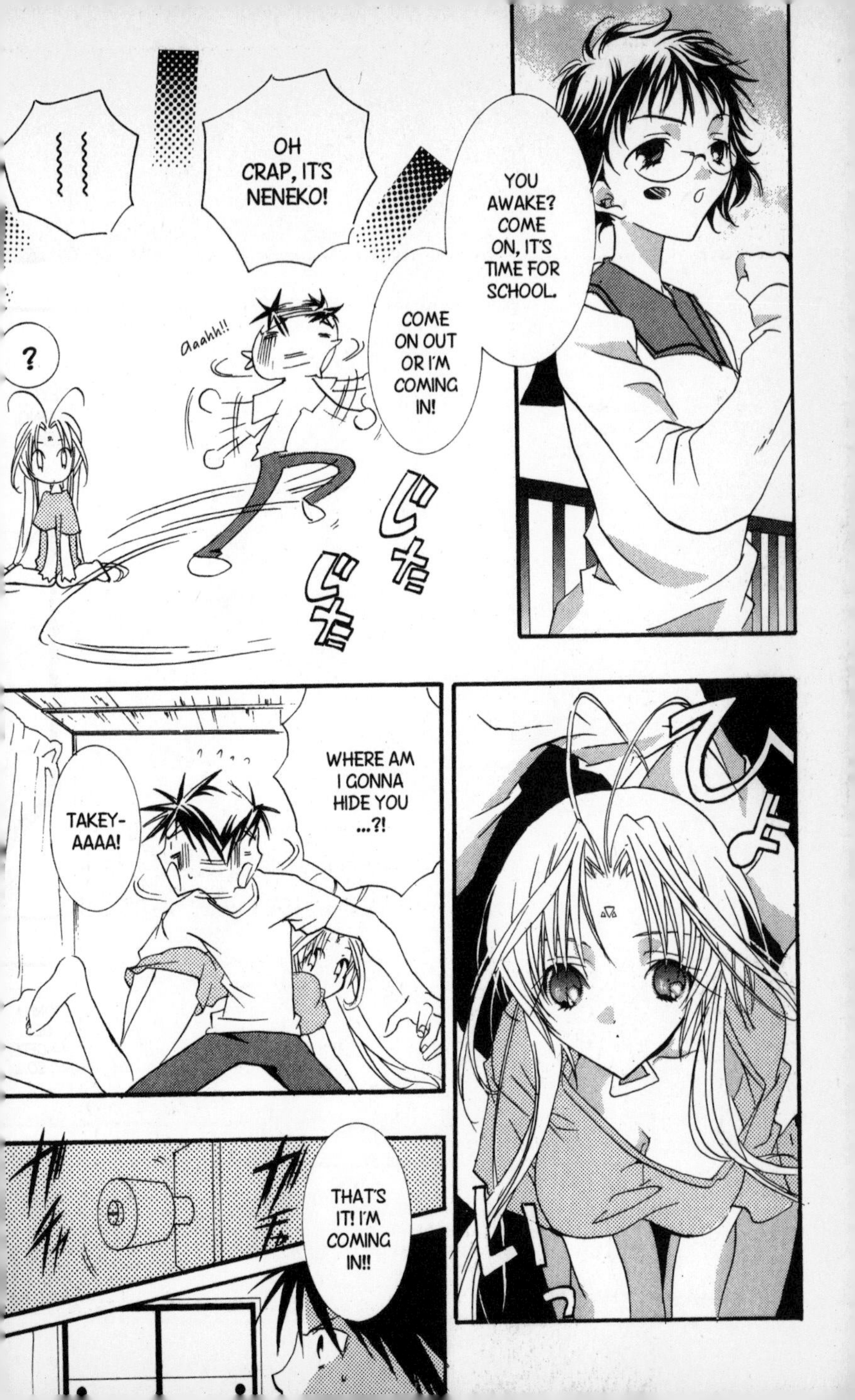
YOU AWAKE? COME ON, IT'S TIME FOR SCHOOL.
COME ON OUT OR I'M COMING IN!
じた じた
OH CRAP, IT'S NENEKO!
Aaahh!!
?
WHERE AM I GONNA HIDE YOU ...?!
TAKEY-AAAA!
THAT'S IT! I'M COMING IN!!

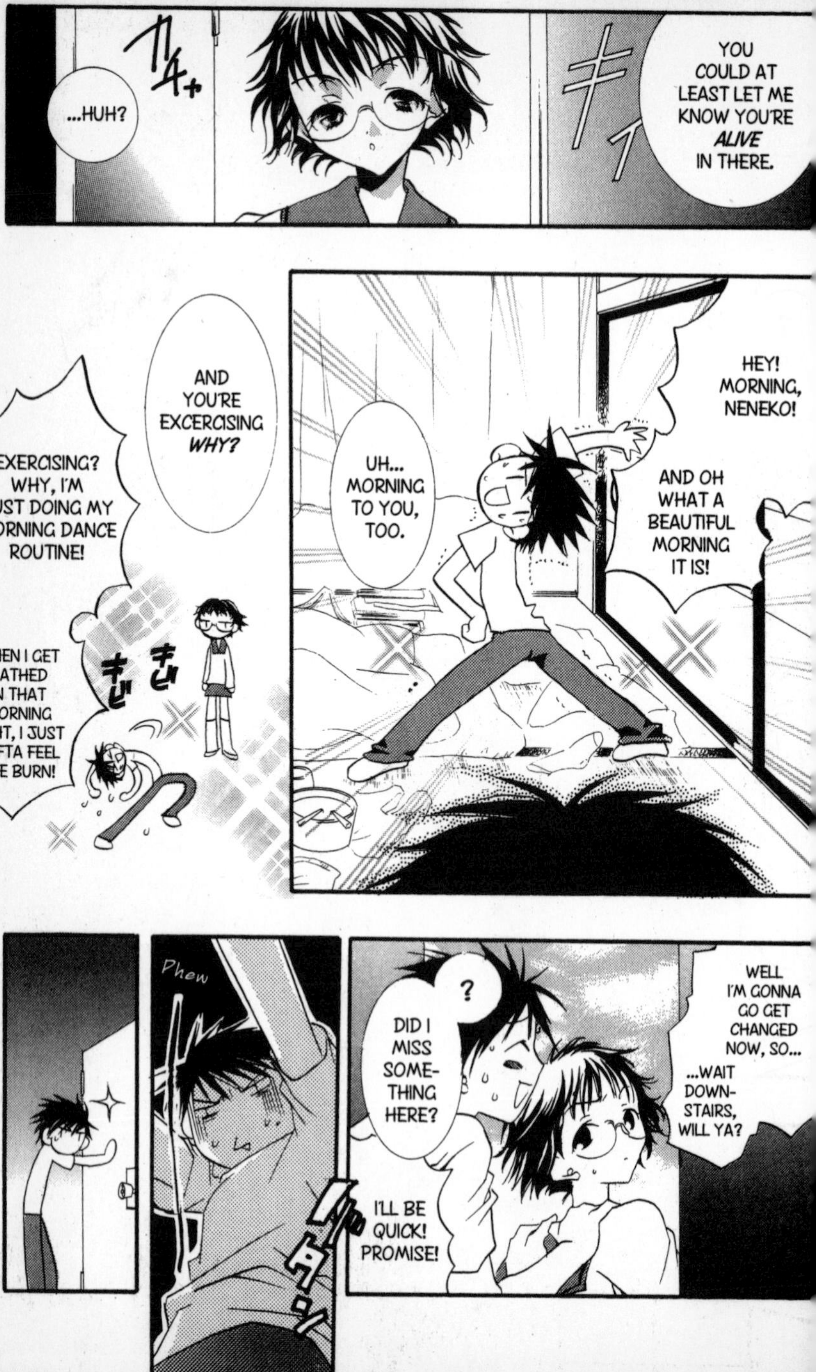
YOU COULD AT LEAST LET ME KNOW YOU'RE *ALIVE* IN THERE.
...HUH?
HEY! MORNING, NENEKO!
AND OH WHAT A BEAUTIFUL MORNING IT IS!
UH... MORNING TO YOU, TOO.
AND YOU'RE EXCERCISING *WHY?*
EXERCISING? WHY, I'M JUST DOING MY MORNING DANCE ROUTINE!
WHEN I GET BATHED IN THAT MORNING LIGHT, I JUST HAFTA FEEL THE BURN!
WELL I'M GONNA GO GET CHANGED NOW, SO...
...WAIT DOWN-STAIRS, WILL YA?
?
DID I MISS SOME-THING HERE?
I'LL BE QUICK! PROMISE!
Phew

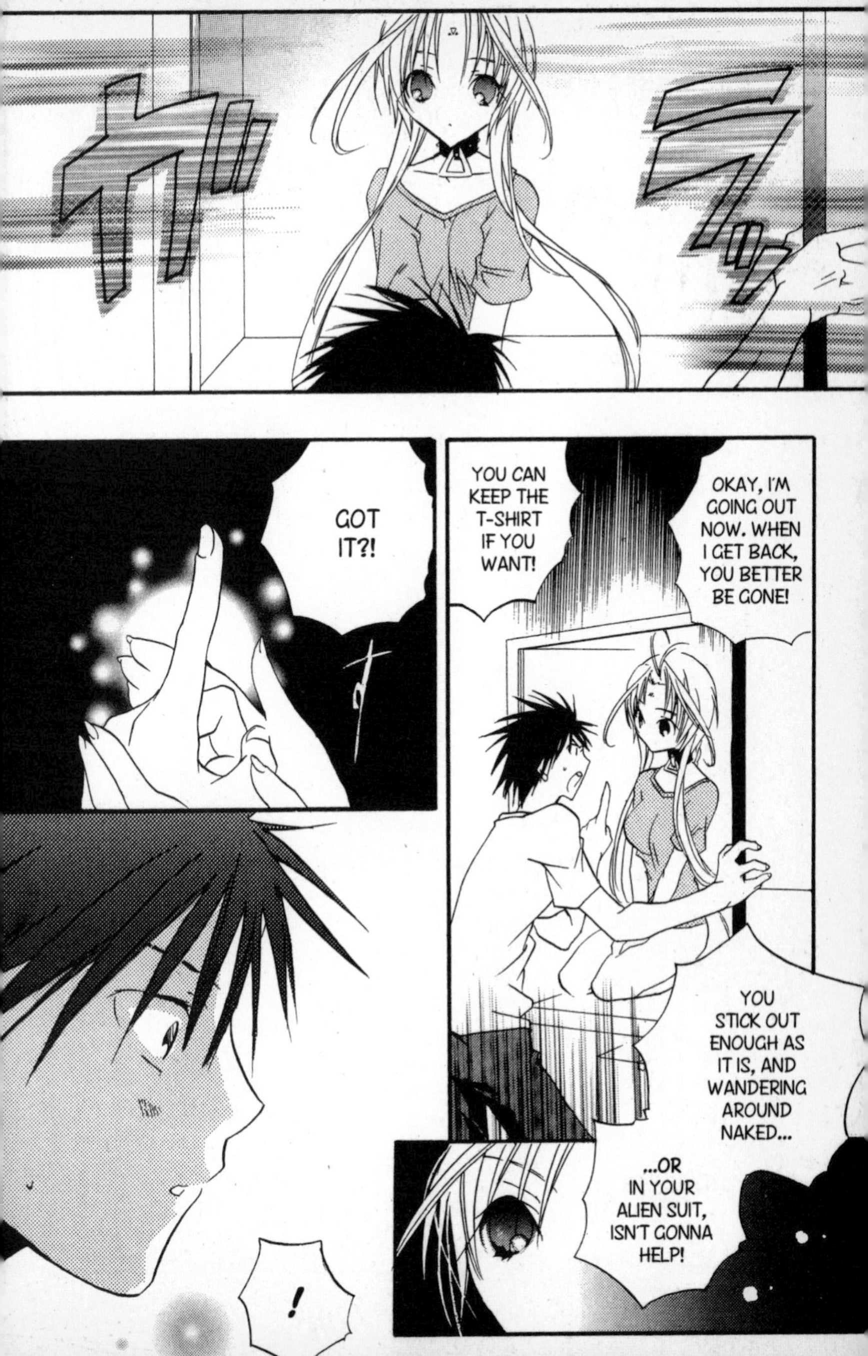
OKAY, I'M GOING OUT NOW. WHEN I GET BACK, YOU BETTER BE GONE!
YOU CAN KEEP THE T-SHIRT IF YOU WANT!
YOU STICK OUT ENOUGH AS IT IS, AND WANDERING AROUND NAKED...
...OR IN YOUR ALIEN SUIT, ISN'T GONNA HELP!
GOT IT?!
!

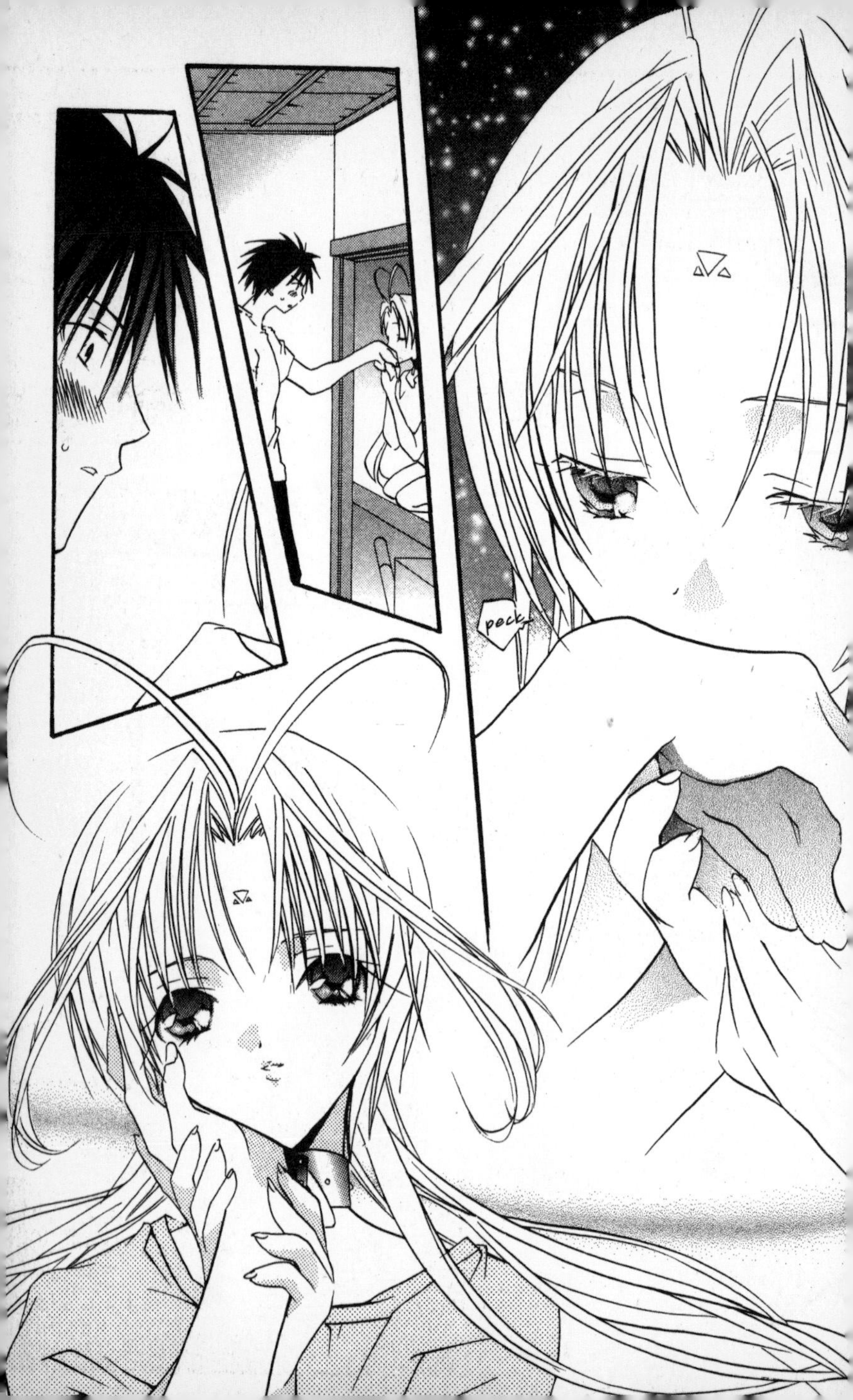
peck

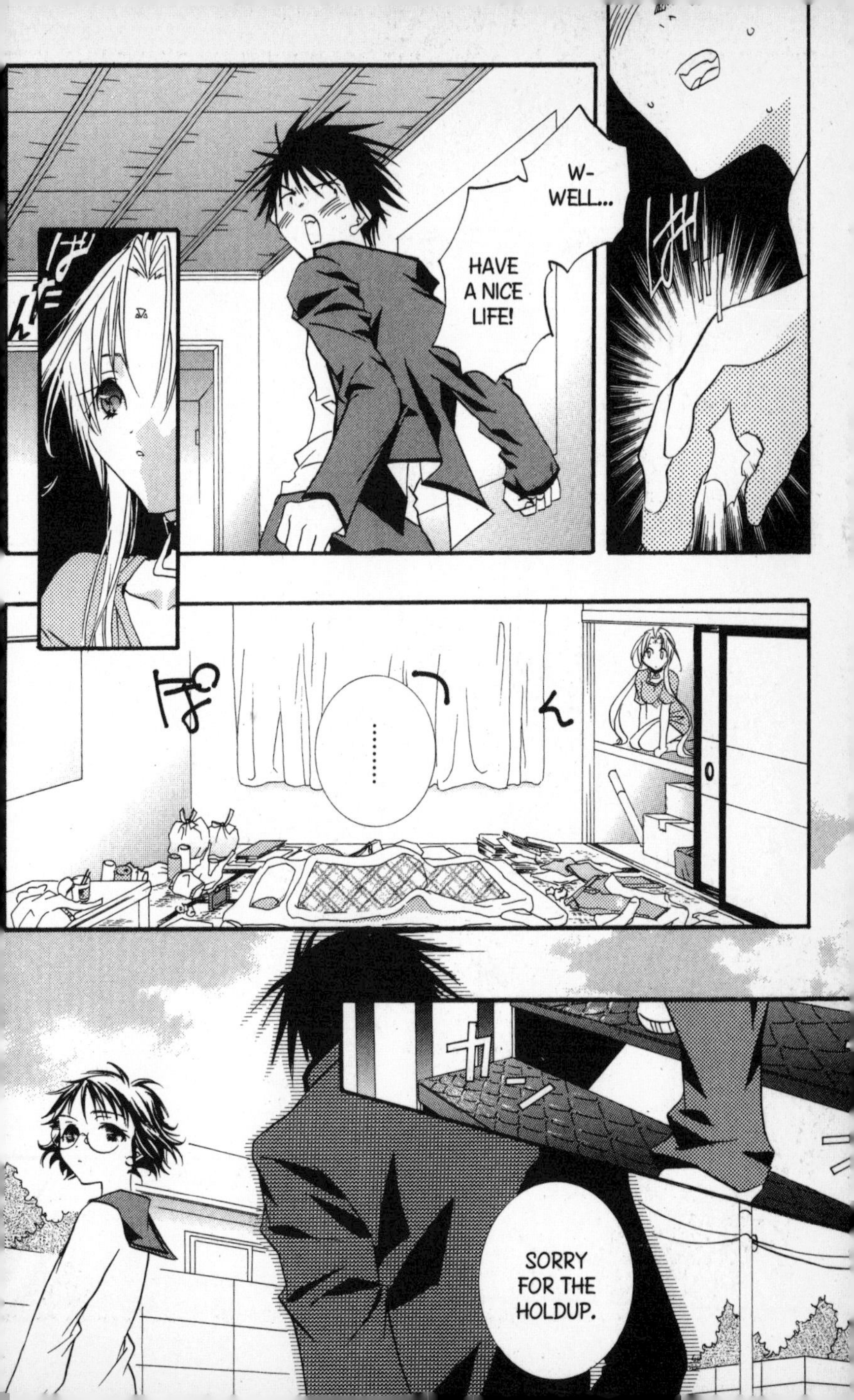
W- WELL...
HAVE A NICE LIFE!
ぽつん
......
SORRY FOR THE HOLDUP.

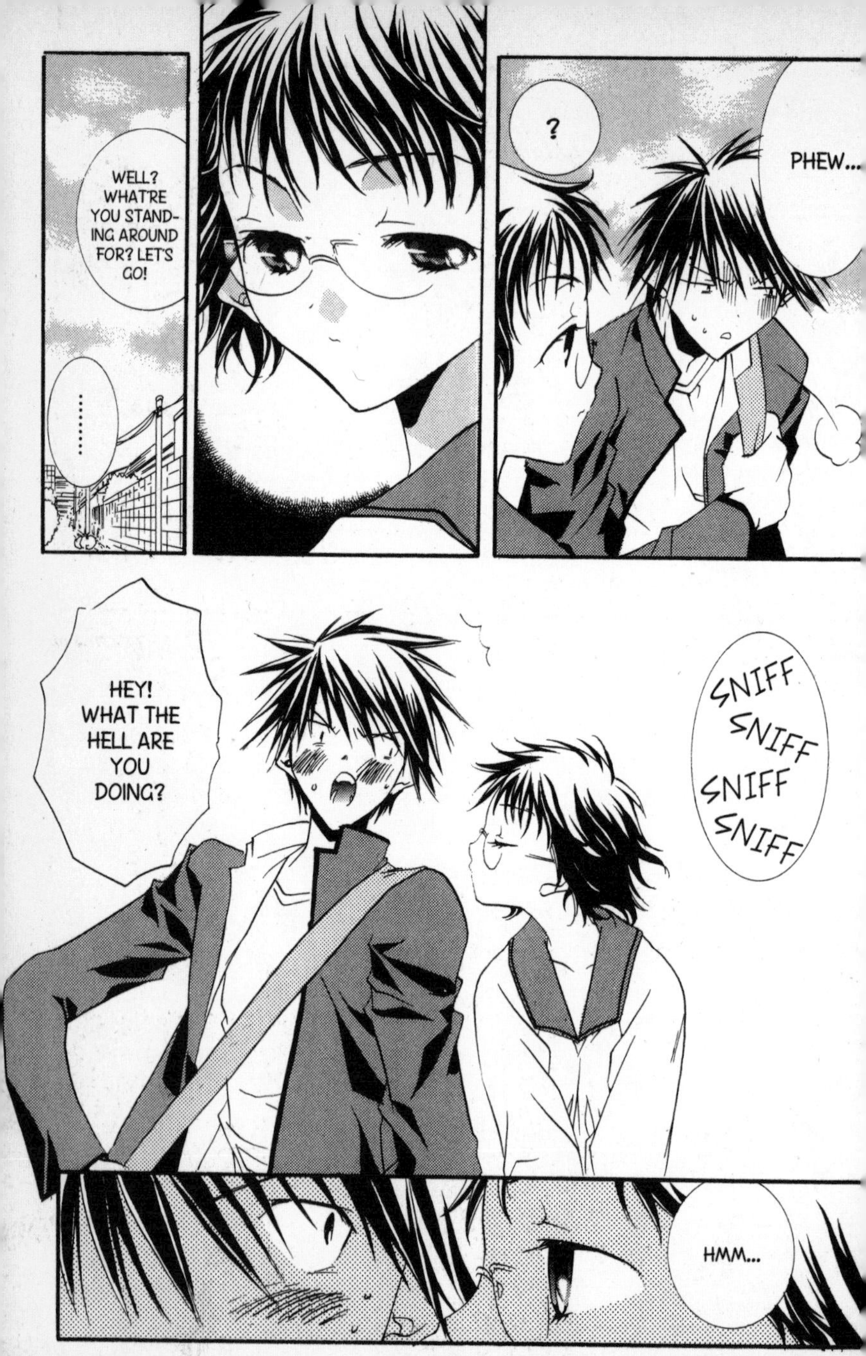
PHEW...
?
WELL? WHAT'RE YOU STANDING AROUND FOR? LET'S GO!
....
SNIFF SNIFF SNIFF SNIFF
HEY! WHAT THE HELL ARE YOU DOING?
HMM...

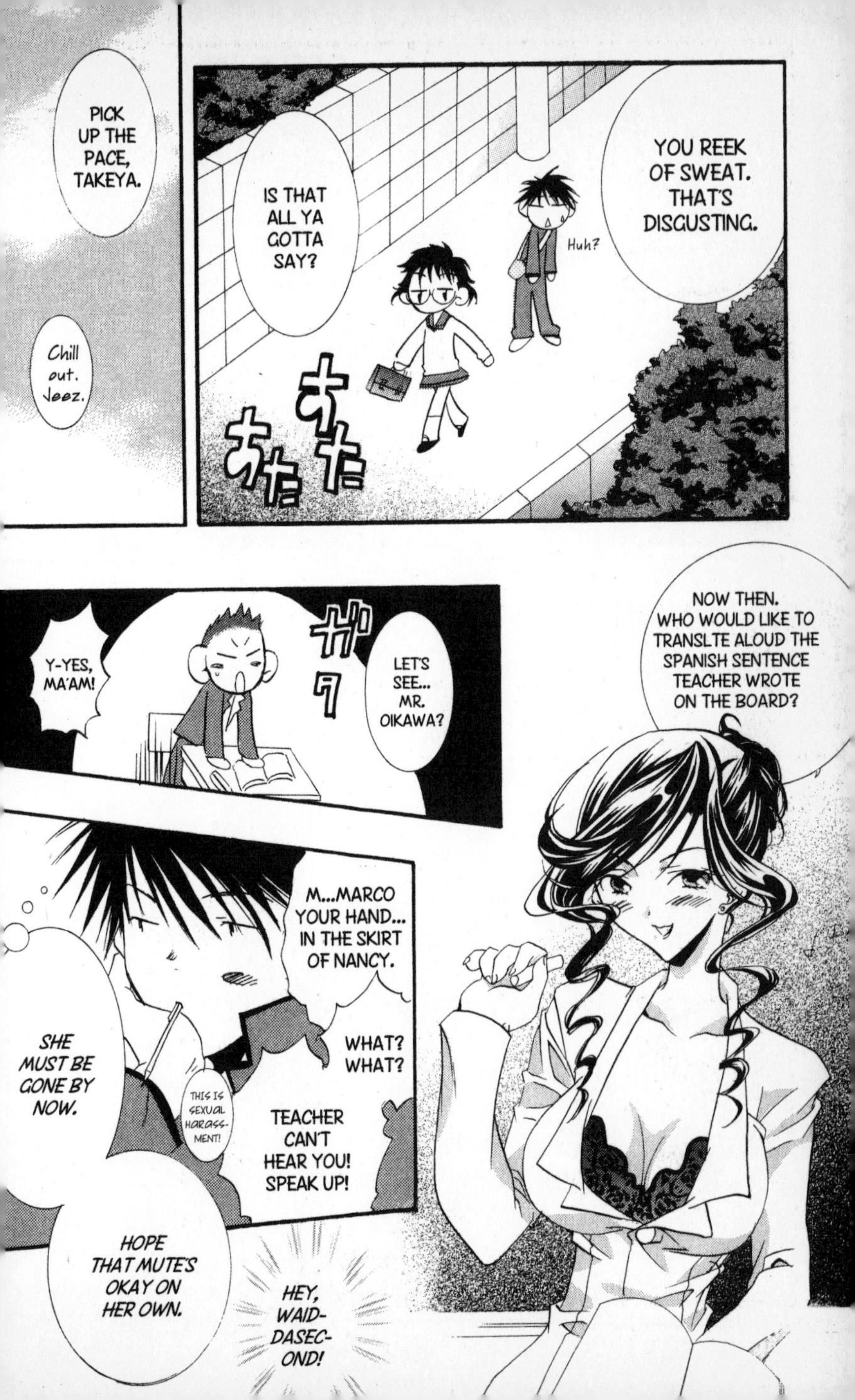
YOU REEK OF SWEAT. THAT'S DISGUSTING.
Huh?
IS THAT ALL YA GOTTA SAY?
PICK UP THE PACE, TAKEYA.
Chill out. Jeez.
NOW THEN. WHO WOULD LIKE TO TRANSLTE ALOUD THE SPANISH SENTENCE TEACHER WROTE ON THE BOARD?
LET'S SEE... MR. OIKAWA?
ガタ
Y-YES, MA'AM!
M...MARCO YOUR HAND... IN THE SKIRT OF NANCY.
WHAT? WHAT?
TEACHER CAN'T HEAR YOU! SPEAK UP!
THIS IS SEXUAL HARASS-MENT!
SHE MUST BE GONE BY NOW.
HOPE THAT MUTE'S OKAY ON HER OWN.
HEY, WAID-DASEC-OND!

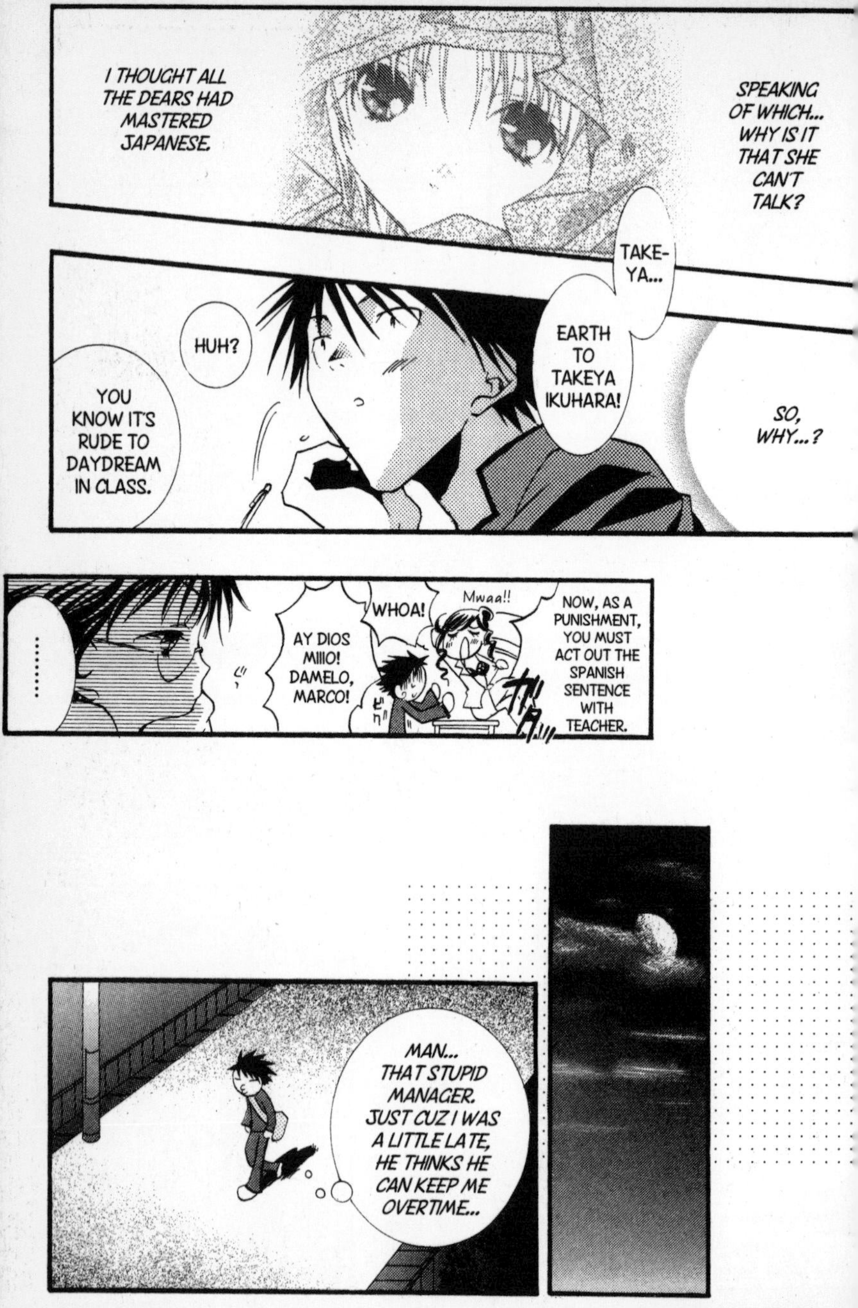
SPEAKING OF WHICH... WHY IS IT THAT SHE CAN'T TALK?
I THOUGHT ALL THE DEARS HAD MASTERED JAPANESE.
SO, WHY...?
TAKE-YA...
EARTH TO TAKEYA IKUHARA!
HUH?
YOU KNOW IT'S RUDE TO DAYDREAM IN CLASS.
NOW, AS A PUNISHMENT, YOU MUST ACT OUT THE SPANISH SENTENCE WITH TEACHER.
Mwaa!!
WHOA!
AY DIOS MIIIO! DAMELO, MARCO!
......
MAN... THAT STUPID MANAGER. JUST CUZ I WAS A LITTLE LATE, HE THINKS HE CAN KEEP ME OVERTIME...

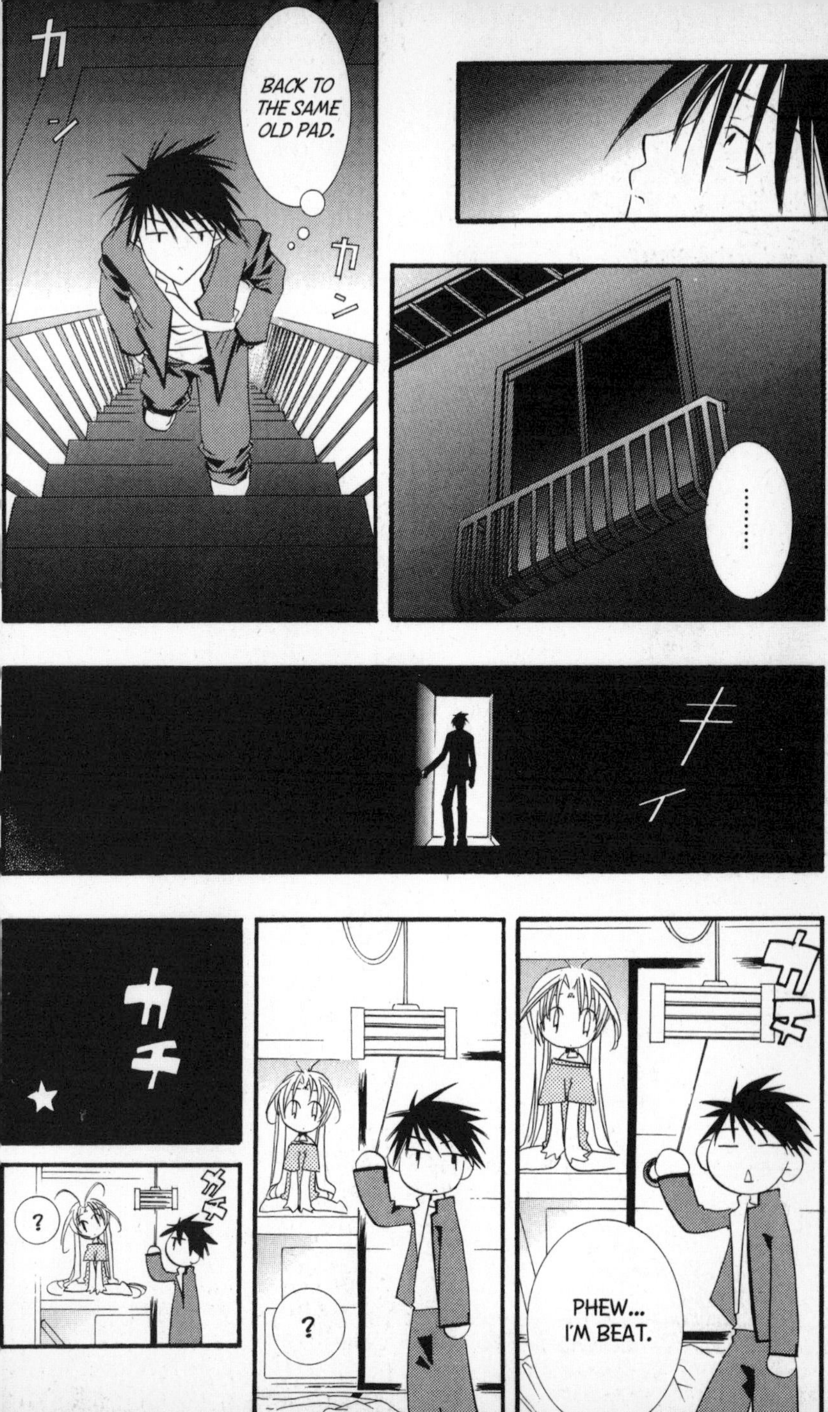
......
カーン
BACK TO THE SAME OLD PAD.
カン
キィ
カチカチ
PHEW... I'M BEAT.
?
カチ☆
?
カチ

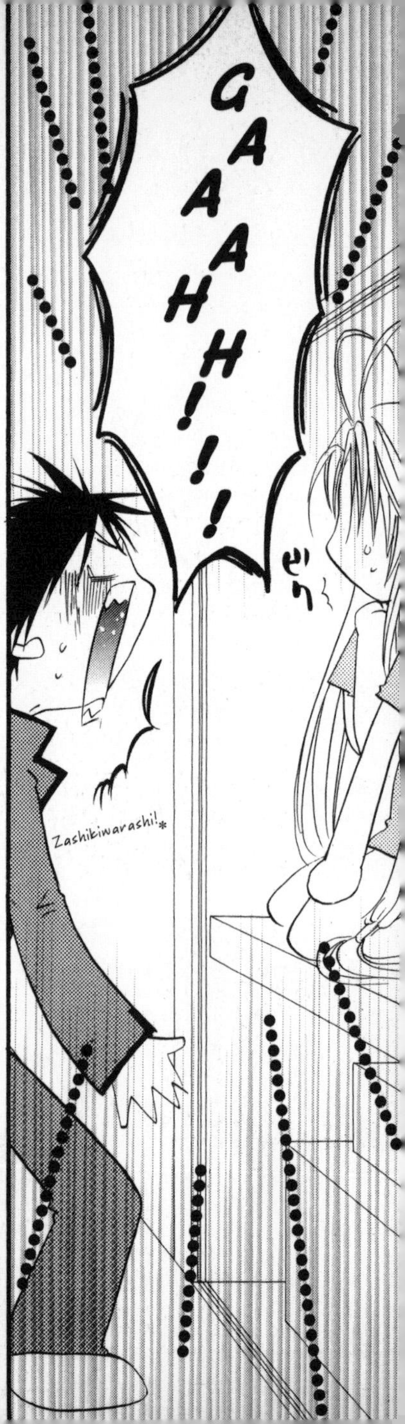
GAAAHH!!!!
ビク
Zashikiwarashi!*

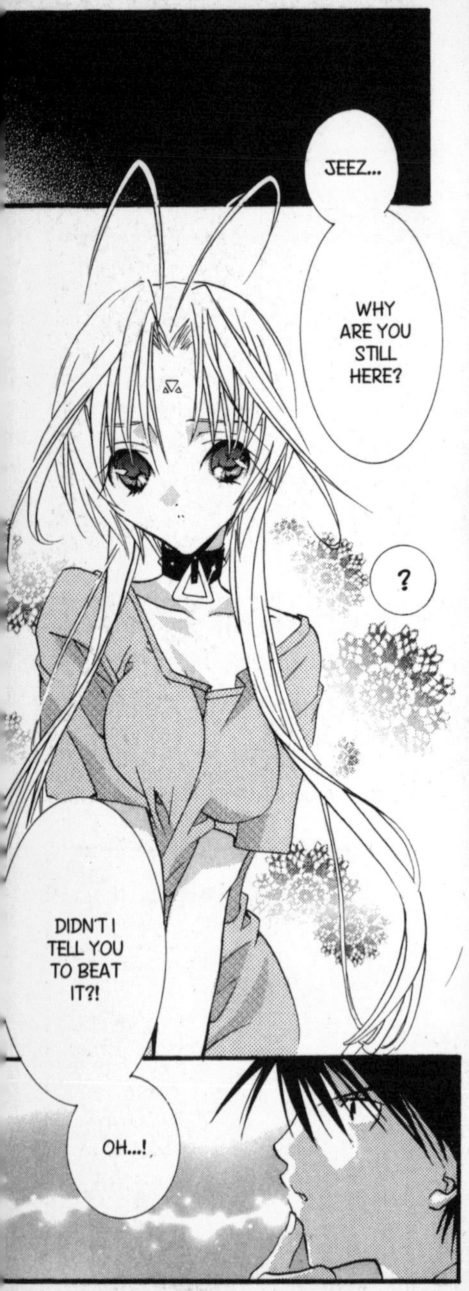
JEEZ...
WHY ARE YOU STILL HERE?
?
DIDN'T I TELL YOU TO BEAT IT?!
OH...!

* MISCHIEVOUS JAPANESE SPIRIT FOUND IN INNS THAT GETS INTO PEOPLE'S STUFF.

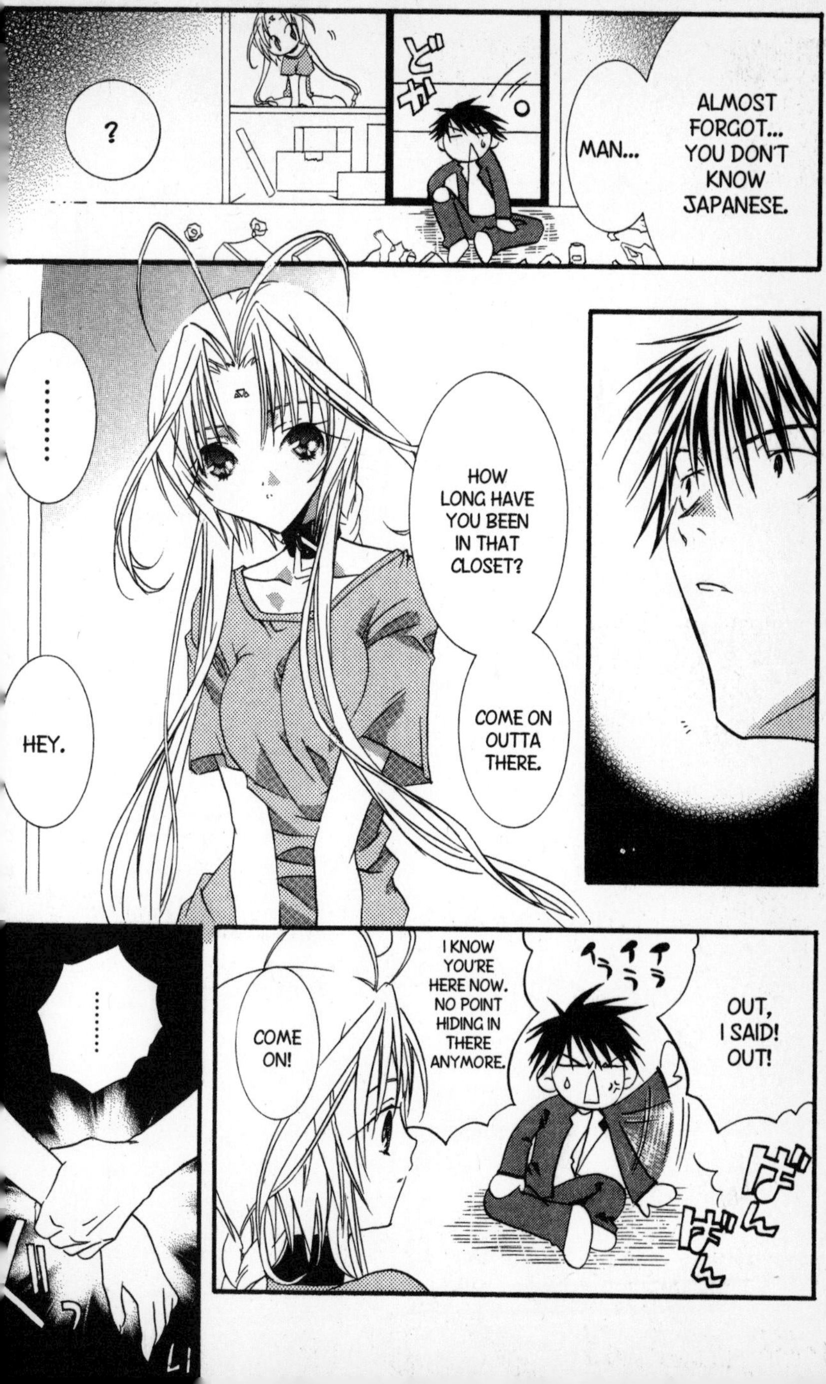
ALMOST FORGOT... YOU DON'T KNOW JAPANESE.
MAN...
どか
?
HOW LONG HAVE YOU BEEN IN THAT CLOSET?
COME ON OUTTA THERE.
....
HEY.
OUT, I SAID! OUT!
イライライラ
I KNOW YOU'RE HERE NOW. NO POINT HIDING IN THERE ANYMORE.
COME ON!
ばんばん
....

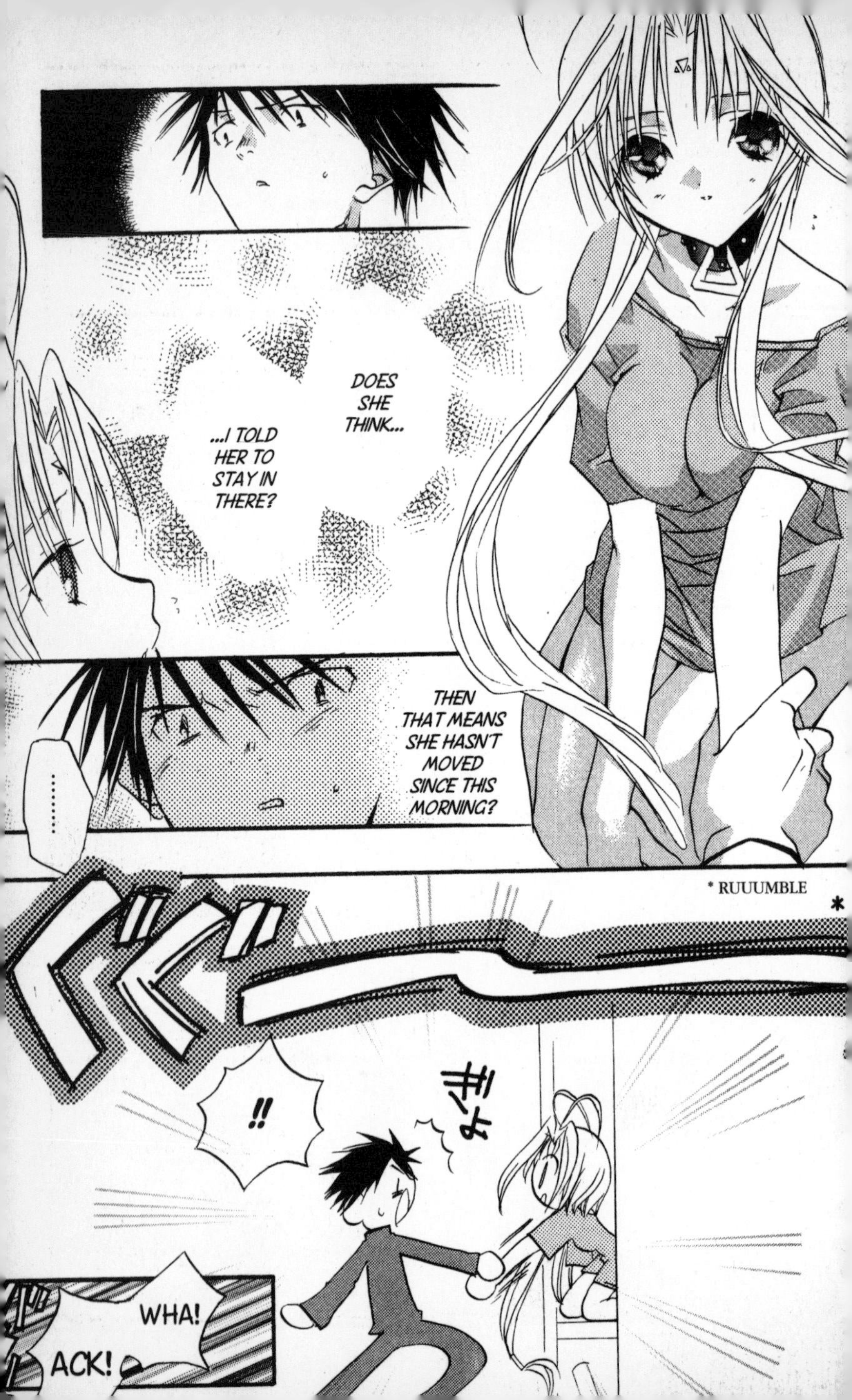
DOES SHE THINK...
...I TOLD HER TO STAY IN THERE?
THEN THAT MEANS SHE HASN'T MOVED SINCE THIS MORNING?
......
* RUUUMBLE
!!
WHA!
ACK!

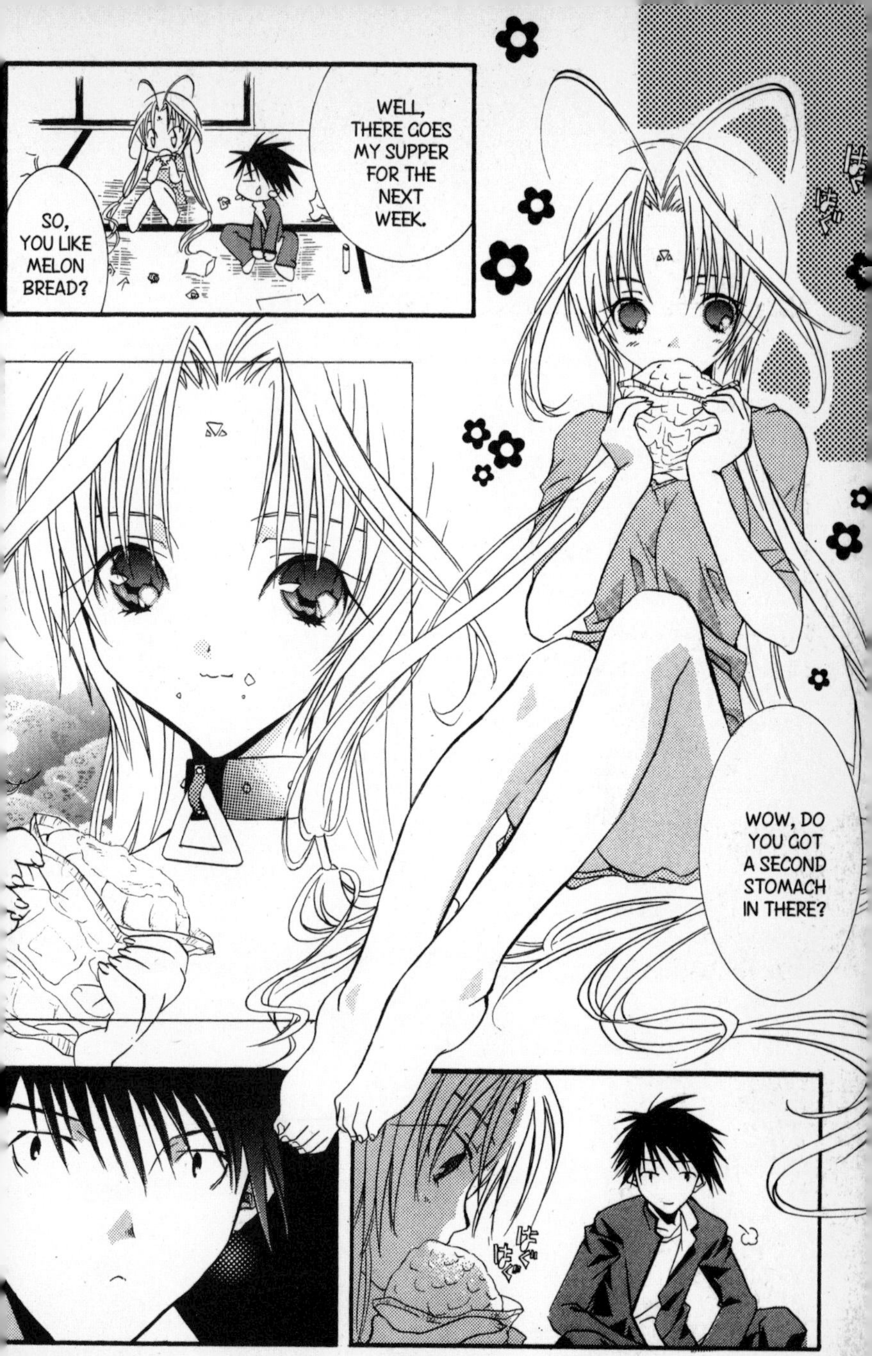
WELL, THERE GOES MY SUPPER FOR THE NEXT WEEK.
SO, YOU LIKE MELON BREAD?
はぐ はぐ
WOW, DO YOU GOT A SECOND STOMACH IN THERE?
はぐ はぐ

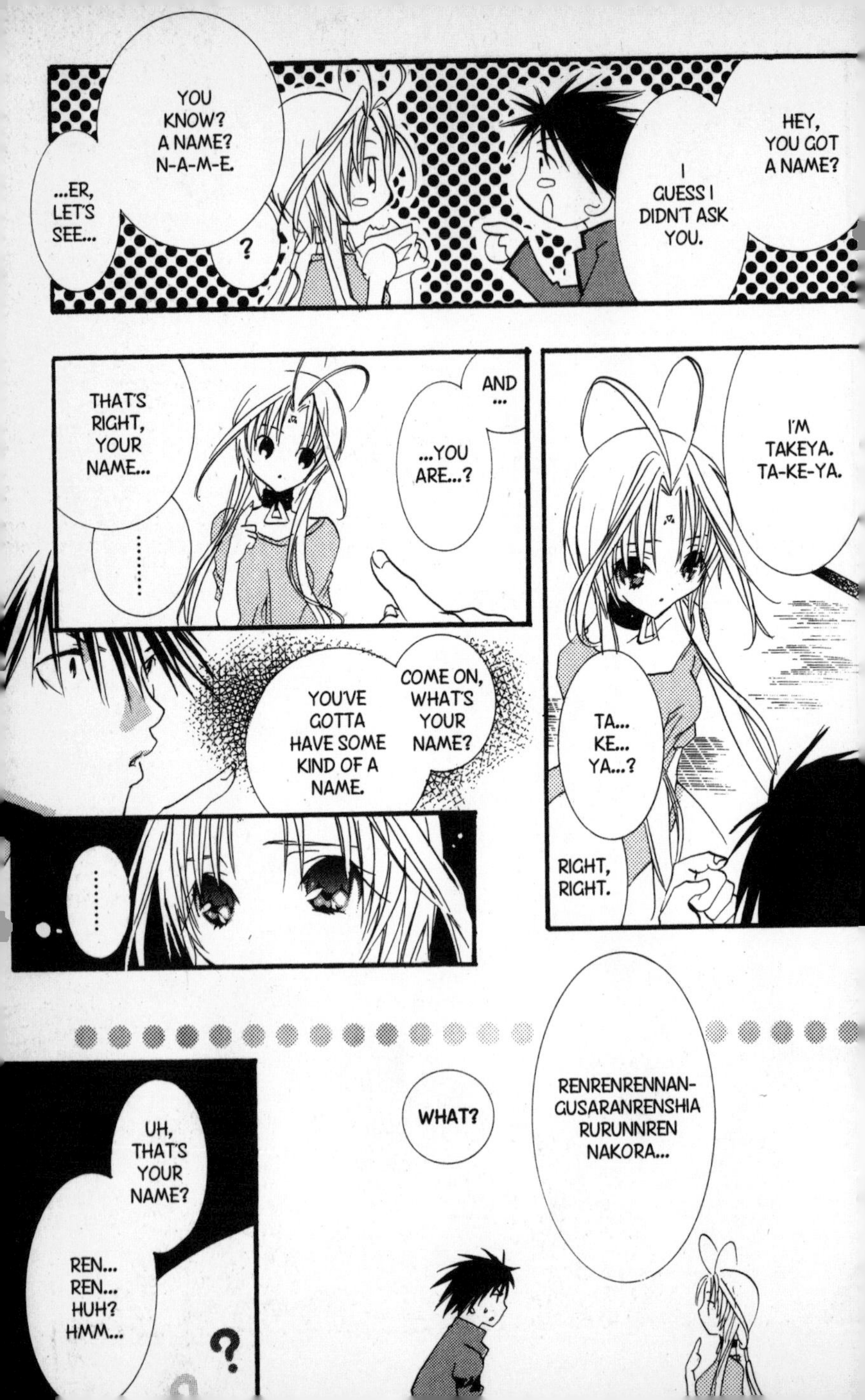
HEY, YOU GOT A NAME?
I GUESS I DIDN'T ASK YOU.
?
YOU KNOW? A NAME? N-A-M-E.
...ER, LET'S SEE...
I'M TAKEYA. TA-KE-YA.
TA... KE... YA...?
RIGHT, RIGHT.
AND ...
...YOU ARE...?
THAT'S RIGHT, YOUR NAME...
....
COME ON, WHAT'S YOUR NAME?
YOU'VE GOTTA HAVE SOME KIND OF A NAME.
....
RENRENRENNAN-GUSARANRENSHIA RURUNNREN NAKORA...
WHAT?
UH, THAT'S YOUR NAME?
REN... REN... HUH? HMM...
?

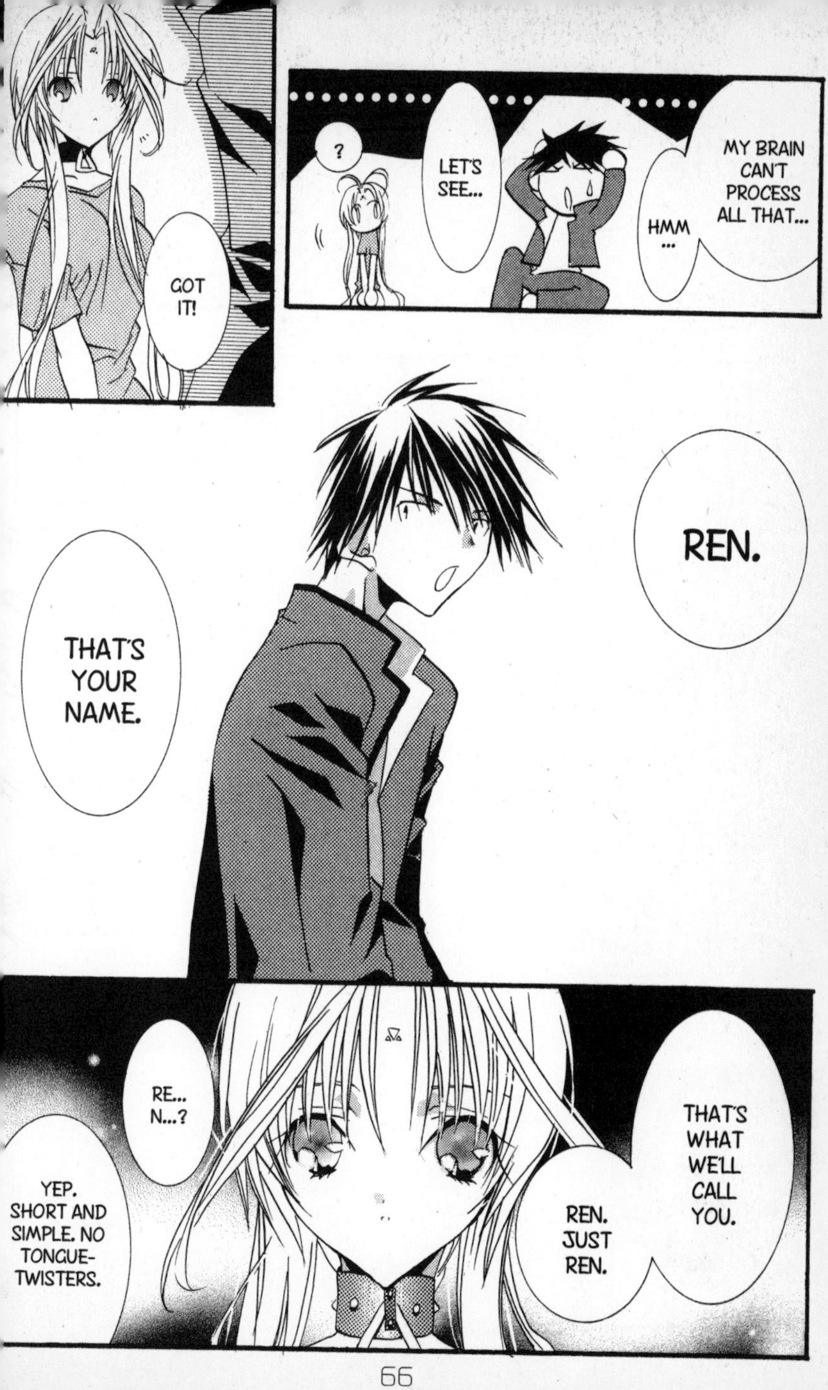
MY BRAIN CAN'T PROCESS ALL THAT...
HMM...
LET'S SEE...
?
GOT IT!
REN.
THAT'S YOUR NAME.
THAT'S WHAT WE'LL CALL YOU.
REN. JUST REN.
RE... N...?
YEP. SHORT AND SIMPLE. NO TONGUE-TWISTERS.

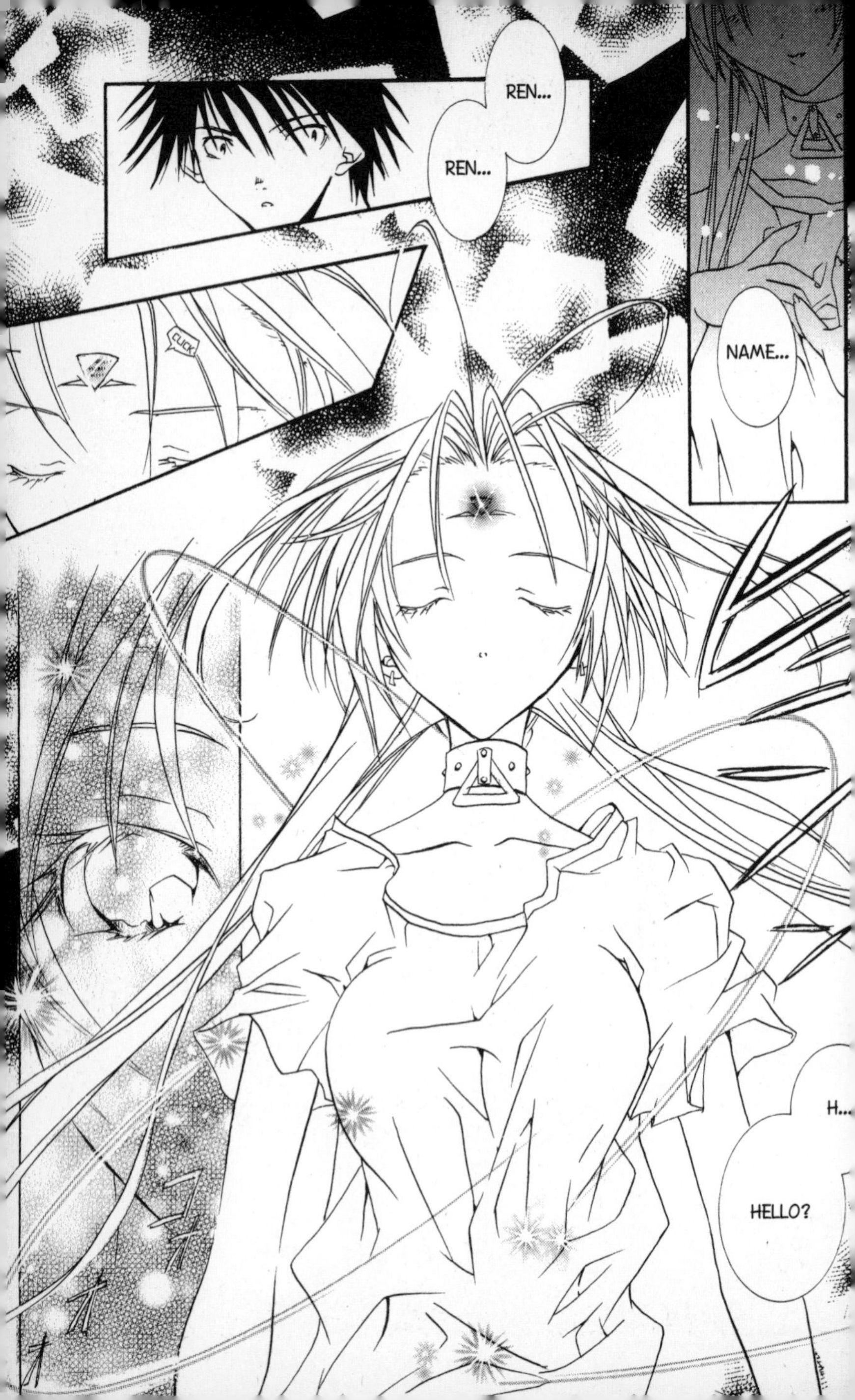
NAME...
REN...
REN...
CLICK
H...
HELLO?

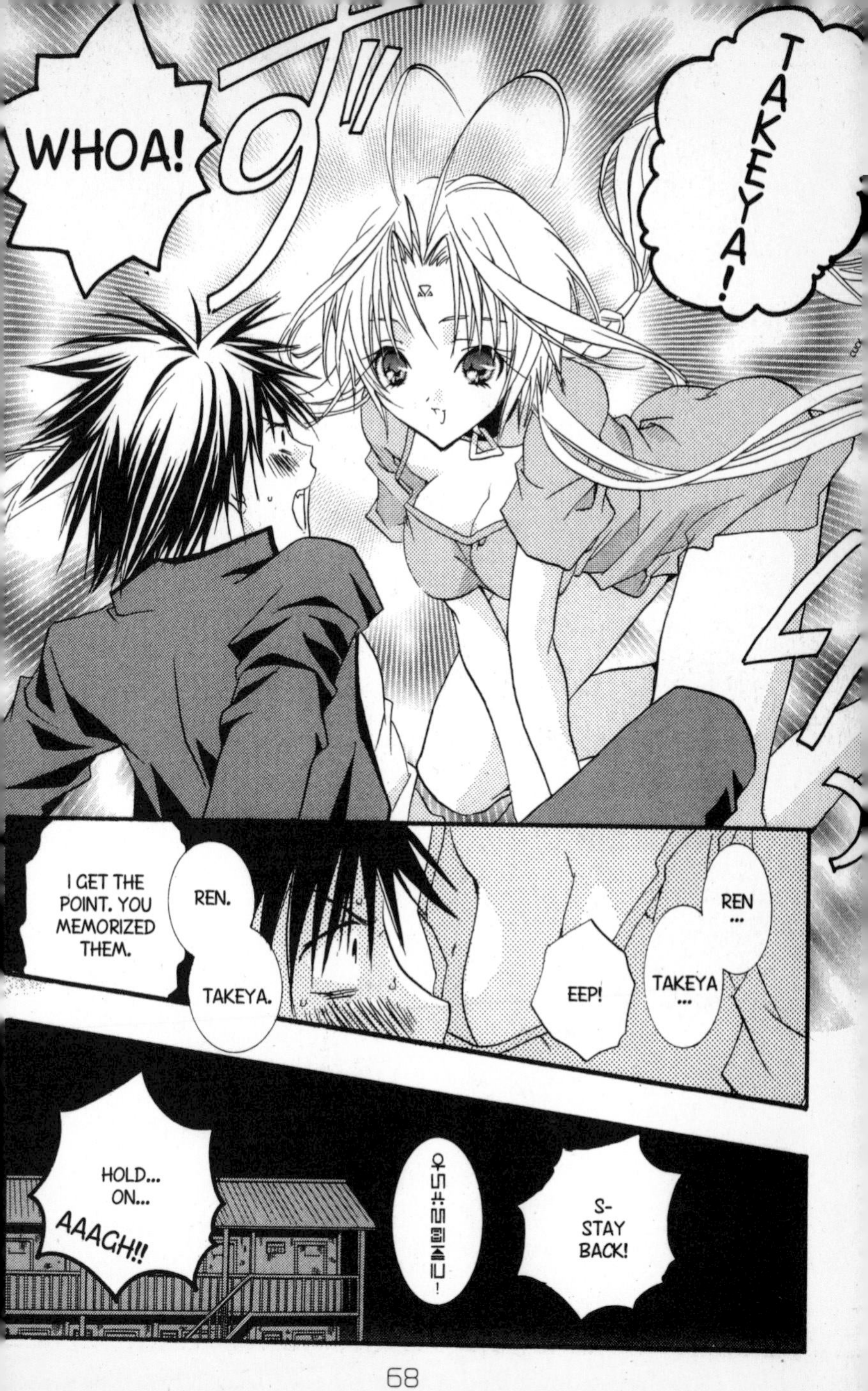
TAKEYA!
WHOA!
REN...
TAKEYA...
EEP!
REN.
TAKEYA.
I GET THE POINT. YOU MEMORIZED THEM.
S-STAY BACK!
HOLD... ON...
AAAGH!!

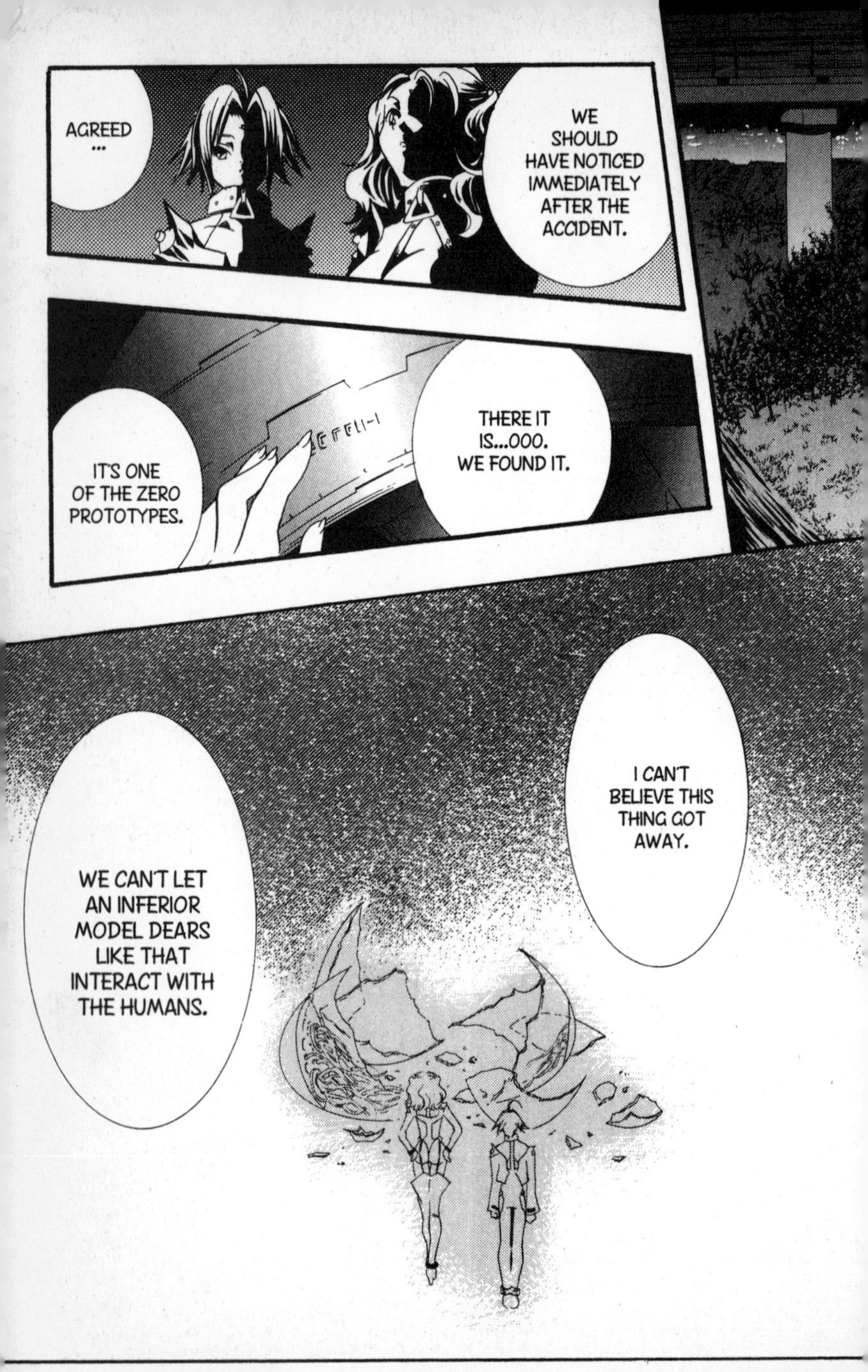
WE SHOULD HAVE NOTICED IMMEDIATELY AFTER THE ACCIDENT.
AGREED ...
THERE IT IS...000. WE FOUND IT.
IT'S ONE OF THE ZERO PROTOTYPES.
I CAN'T BELIEVE THIS THING GOT AWAY.
WE CAN'T LET AN INFERIOR MODEL DEARS LIKE THAT INTERACT WITH THE HUMANS.

?
?
カチ
カチ★
ぱっ
カチ
!?
カチ
カチ
It's mooorning...!!
ぱ
カチ
カチ
......
......

DearS ディアーズ

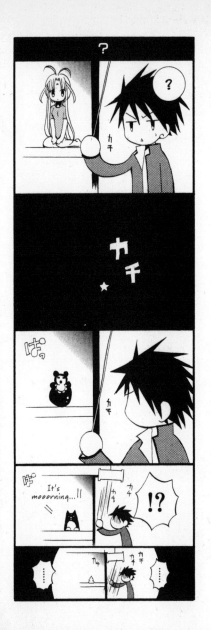

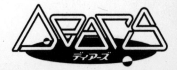

3rd Contact

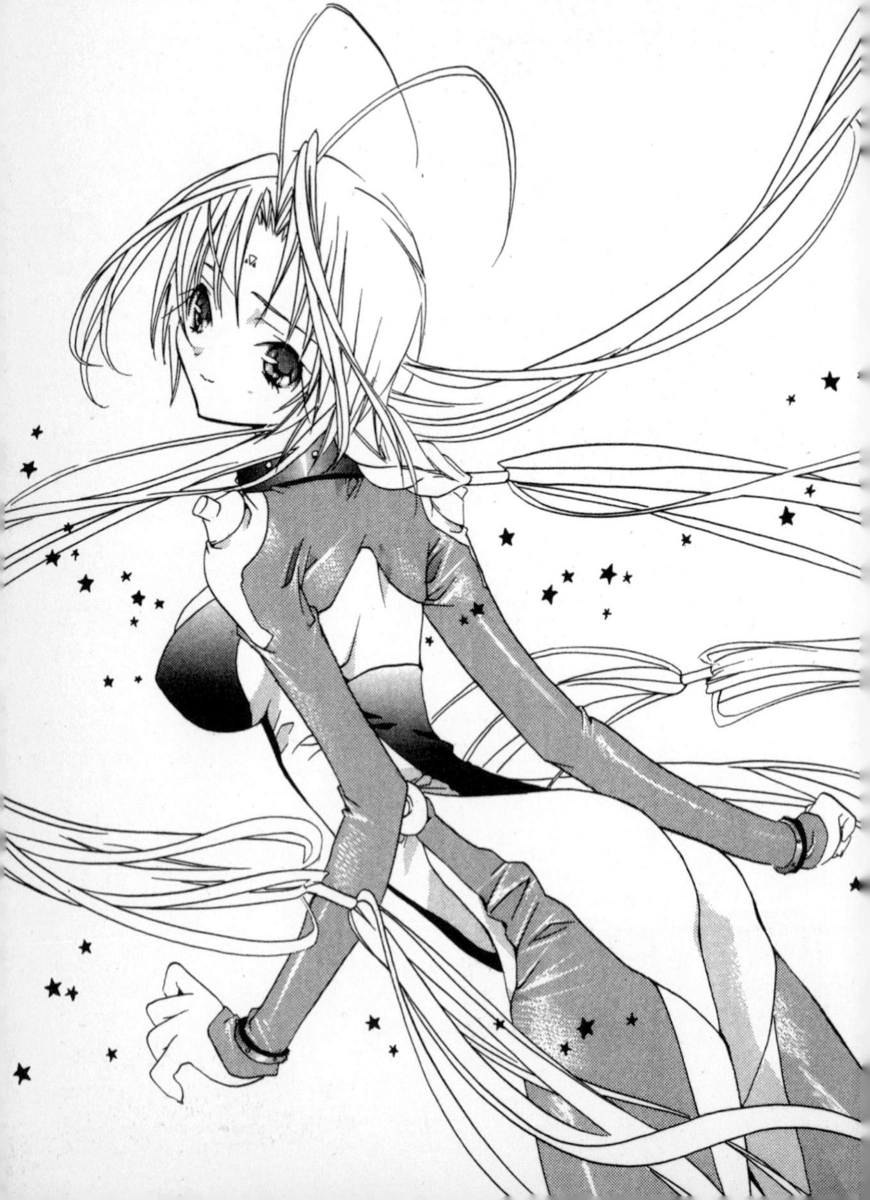

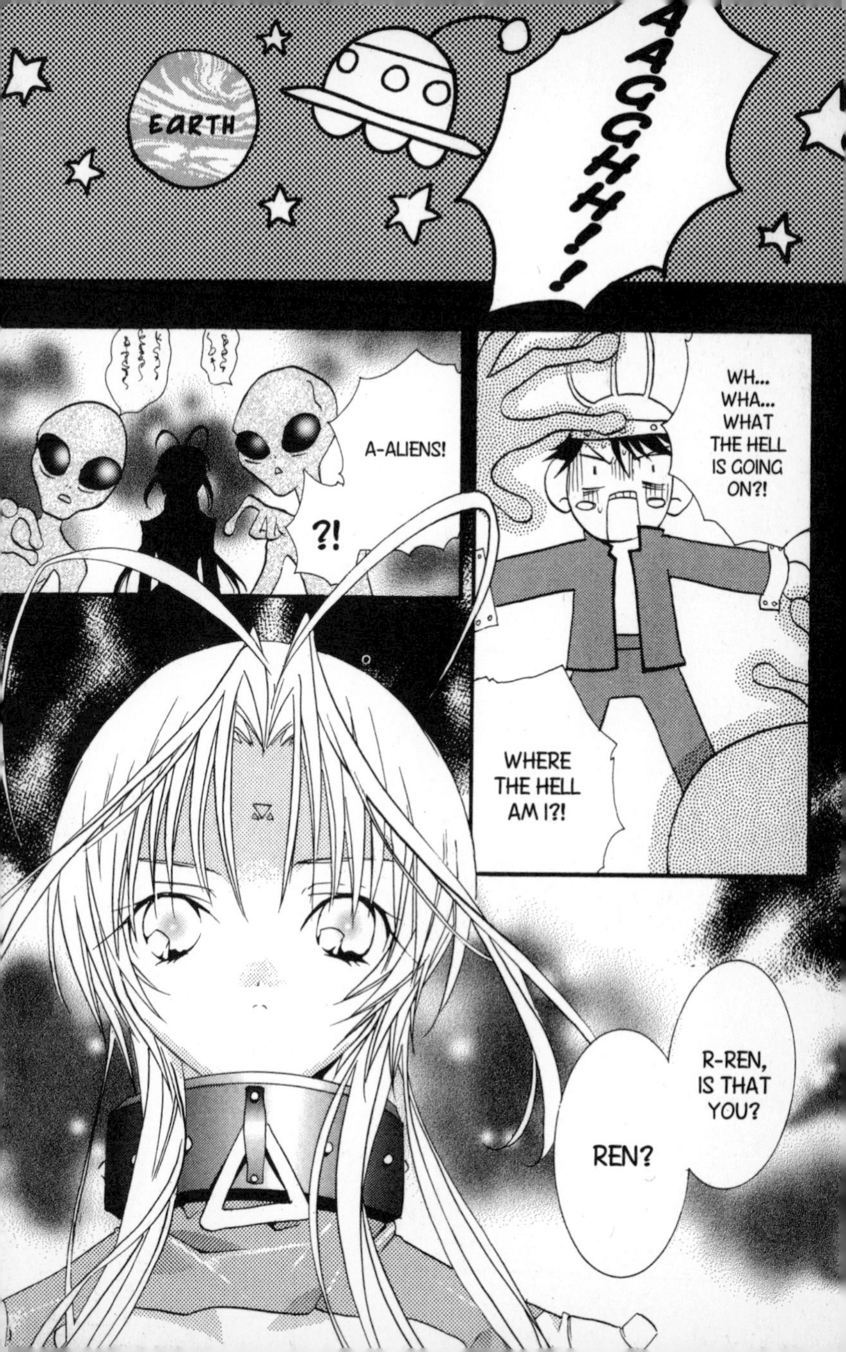
AAGGHH!!
EARTH
WH... WHA... WHAT THE HELL IS GOING ON?!
WHERE THE HELL AM I?!
A-ALIENS!
?!
R-REN, IS THAT YOU?
REN?

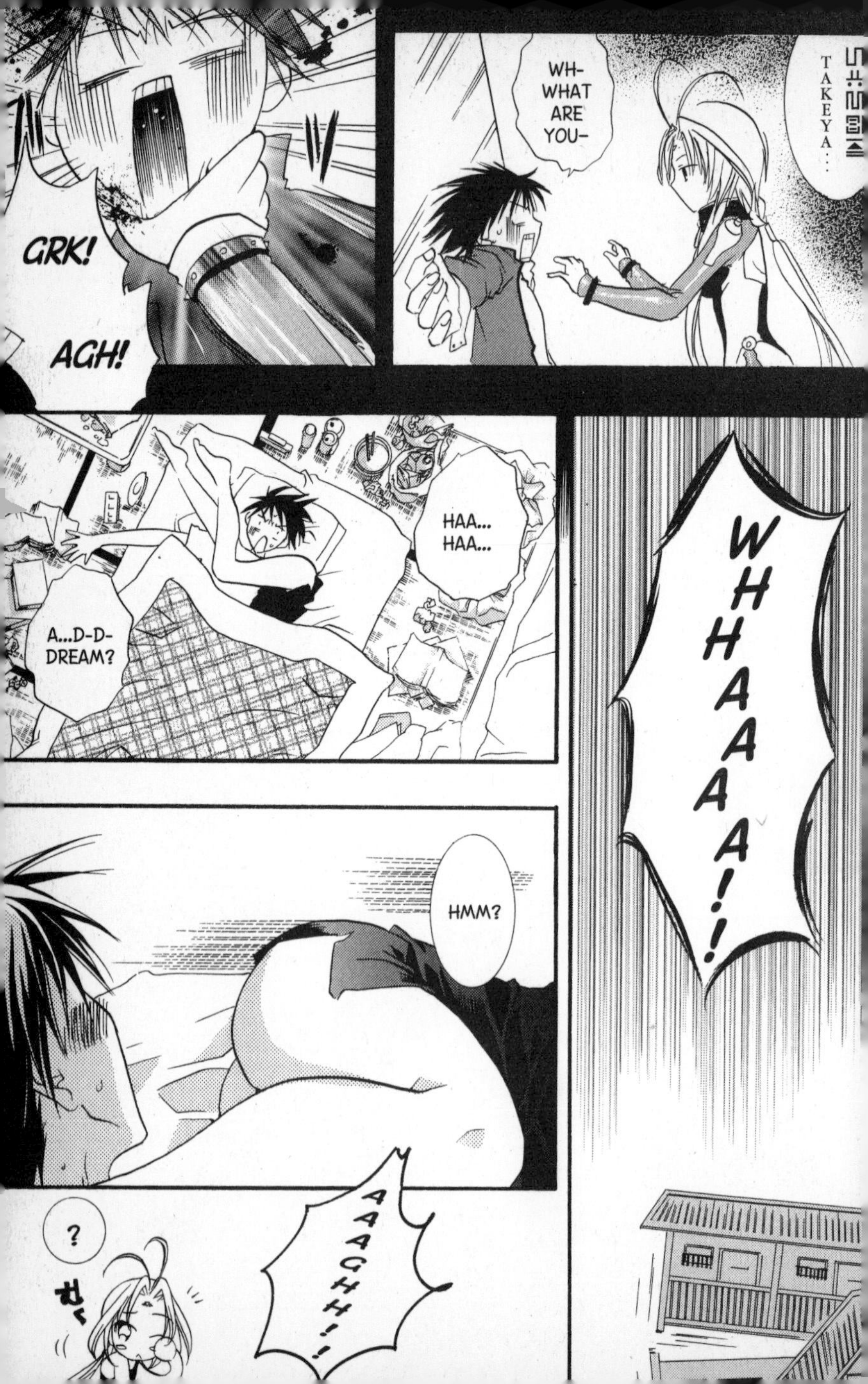
TAKEYA...
WH- WHAT ARE YOU-
GRK!
AGH!
WHHAAAAA!!!
HAA... HAA...
A...D-D-DREAM?
HMM?
AAAAGHH!!
?

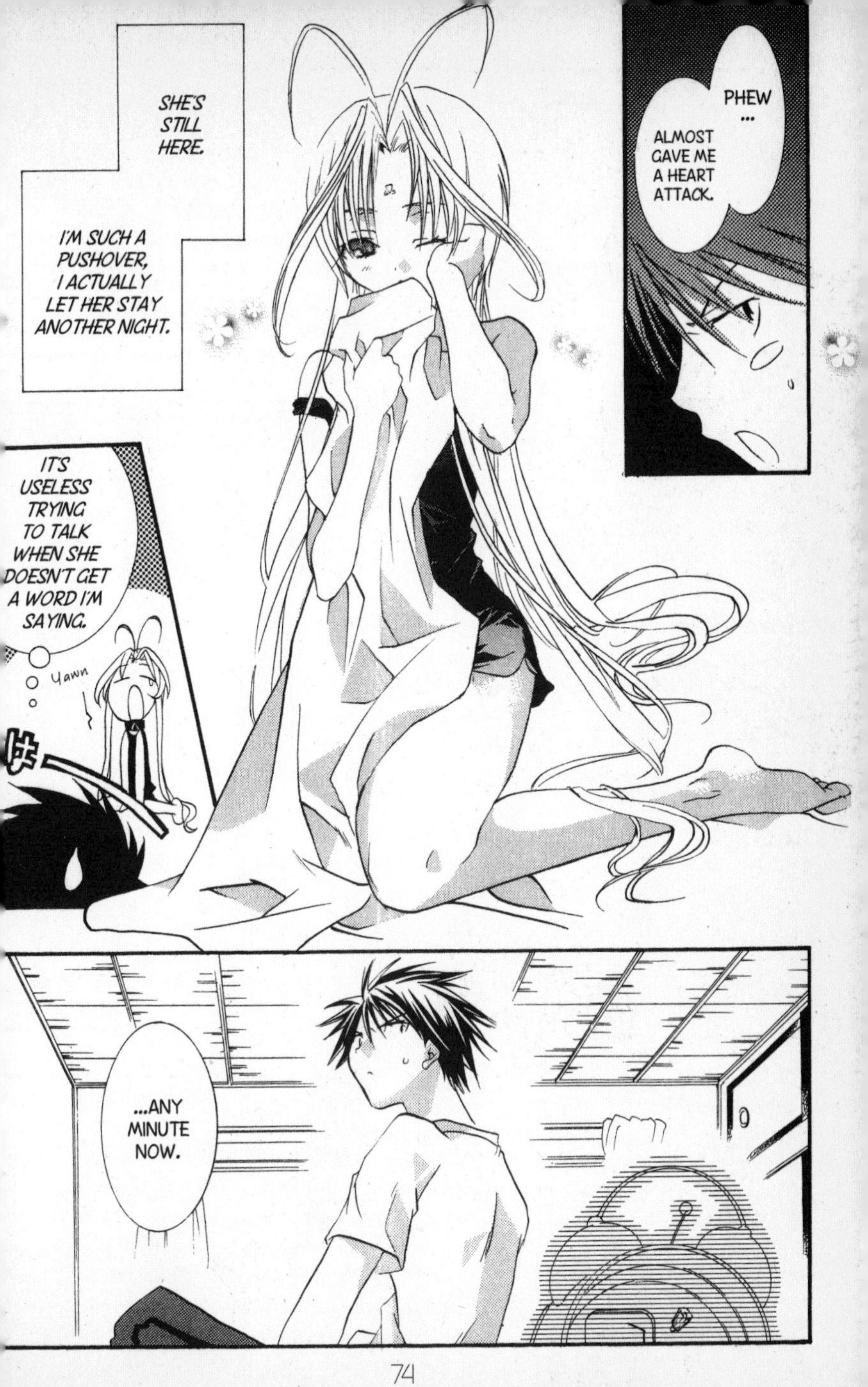
PHEW... ALMOST GAVE ME A HEART ATTACK.
SHE'S STILL HERE.
I'M SUCH A PUSHOVER, I ACTUALLY LET HER STAY ANOTHER NIGHT.
IT'S USELESS TRYING TO TALK WHEN SHE DOESN'T GET A WORD I'M SAYING.
Yawn
...ANY MINUTE NOW.

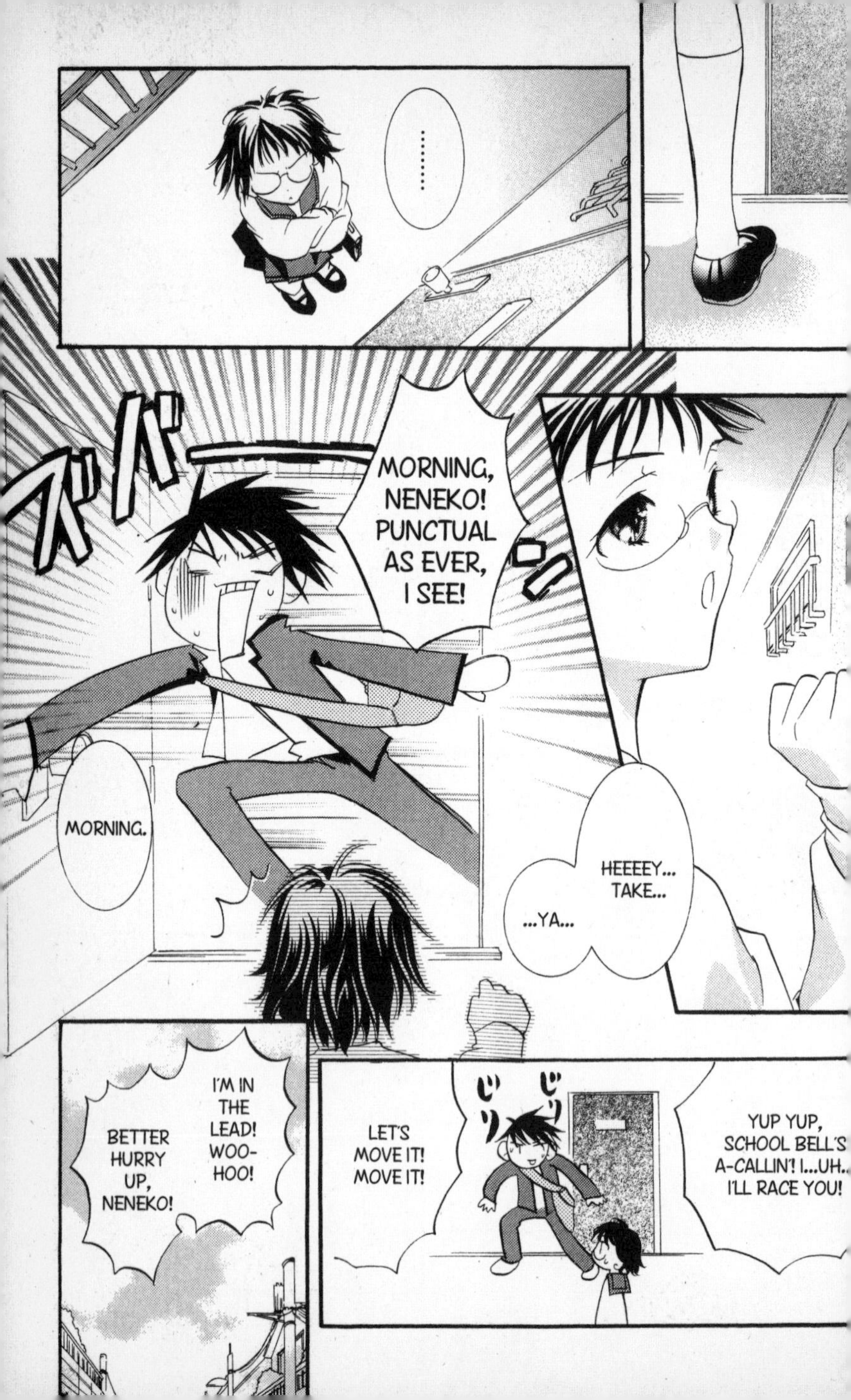
......
HEEEEY... TAKE...
...YA...
MORNING, NENEKO! PUNCTUAL AS EVER, I SEE!
ズバー
MORNING.
YUP YUP, SCHOOL BELL'S A-CALLIN'! I...UH... I'LL RACE YOU!
じりっ じりっ
LET'S MOVE IT! MOVE IT!
I'M IN THE LEAD! WOO-HOO!
BETTER HURRY UP, NENEKO!

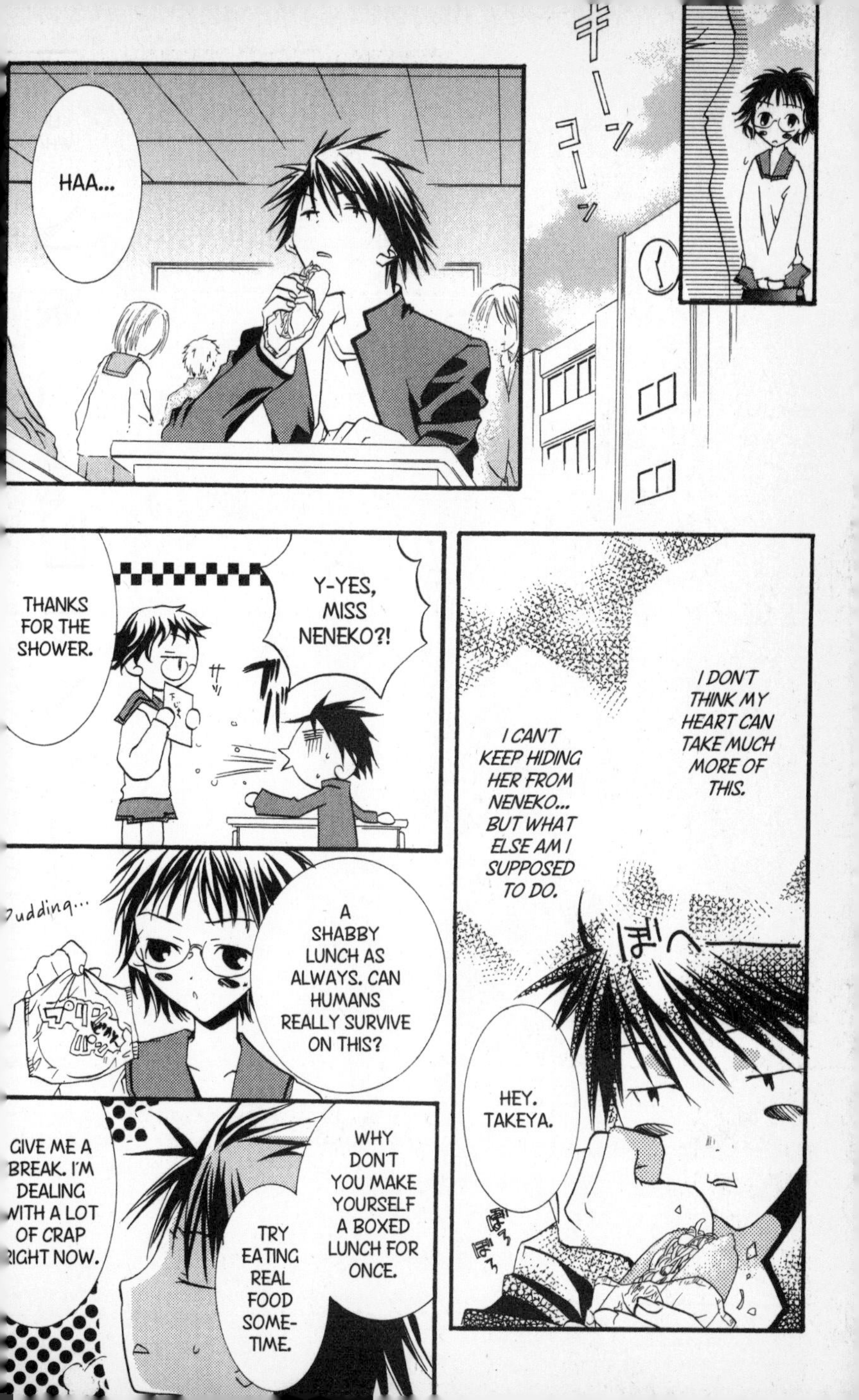

キーンコーン
HAA...
I DON'T THINK MY HEART CAN TAKE MUCH MORE OF THIS.
I CAN'T KEEP HIDING HER FROM NENEKO... BUT WHAT ELSE AM I SUPPOSED TO DO.
HEY. TAKEYA.
Y-YES, MISS NENEKO?!
THANKS FOR THE SHOWER.
A SHABBY LUNCH AS ALWAYS. CAN HUMANS REALLY SURVIVE ON THIS?
udding...
WHY DON'T YOU MAKE YOURSELF A BOXED LUNCH FOR ONCE.
TRY EATING REAL FOOD SOME-TIME.
GIVE ME A BREAK. I'M DEALING WITH A LOT OF CRAP RIGHT NOW.

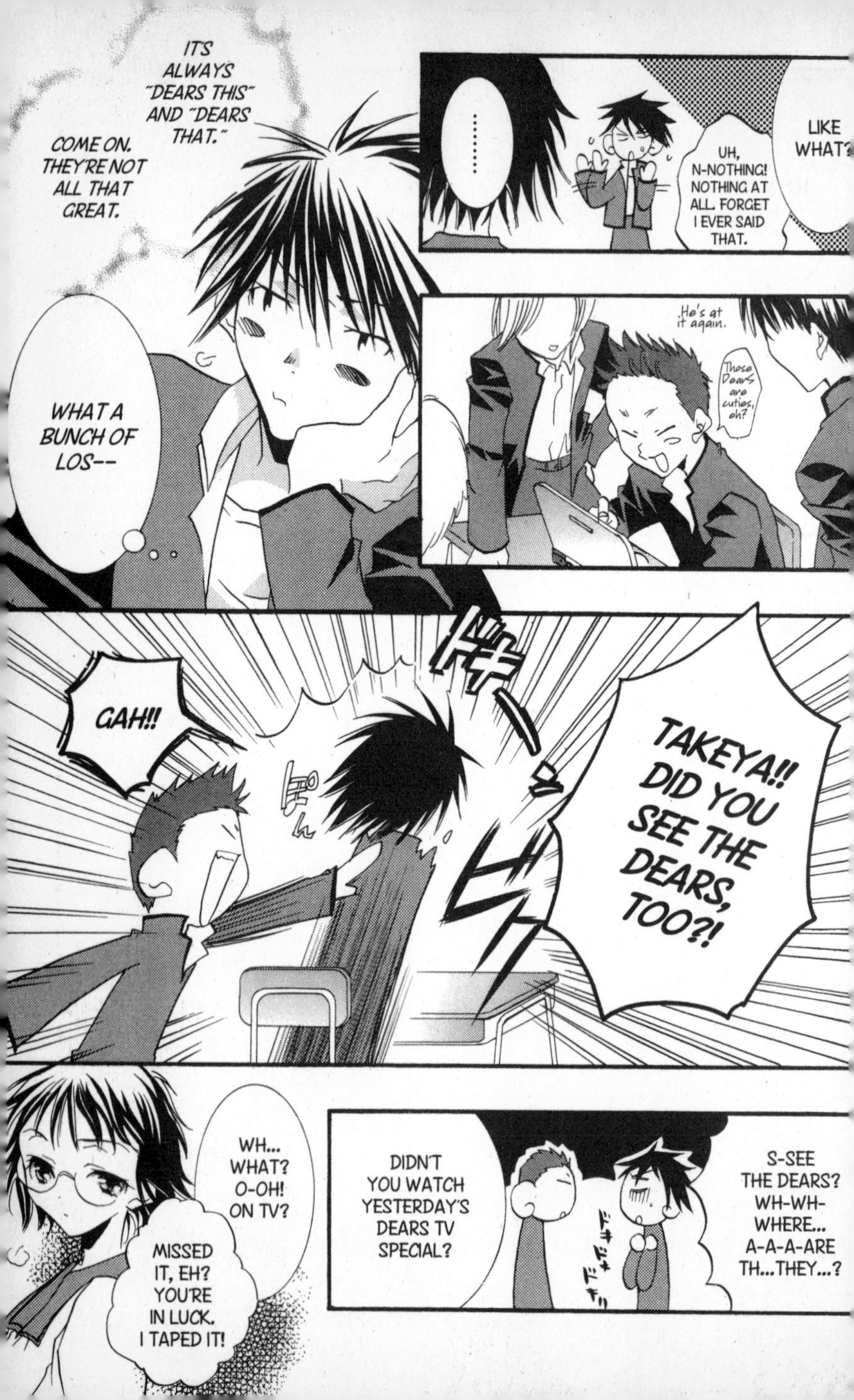

LIKE WHAT?
UH, N-NOTHING! NOTHING AT ALL. FORGET I EVER SAID THAT.
......
He's at it again.
Those Dears are cuties, eh?
IT'S ALWAYS "DEARS THIS" AND "DEARS THAT."
COME ON. THEY'RE NOT ALL THAT GREAT.
WHAT A BUNCH OF LOS--
TAKEYA!! DID YOU SEE THE DEARS, TOO?!
GAH!!
S-SEE THE DEARS? WH-WH-WHERE... A-A-A-ARE TH...THEY...?
DIDN'T YOU WATCH YESTERDAY'S DEARS TV SPECIAL?
WH... WHAT? O-OH! ON TV?
MISSED IT, EH? YOU'RE IN LUCK. I TAPED IT!

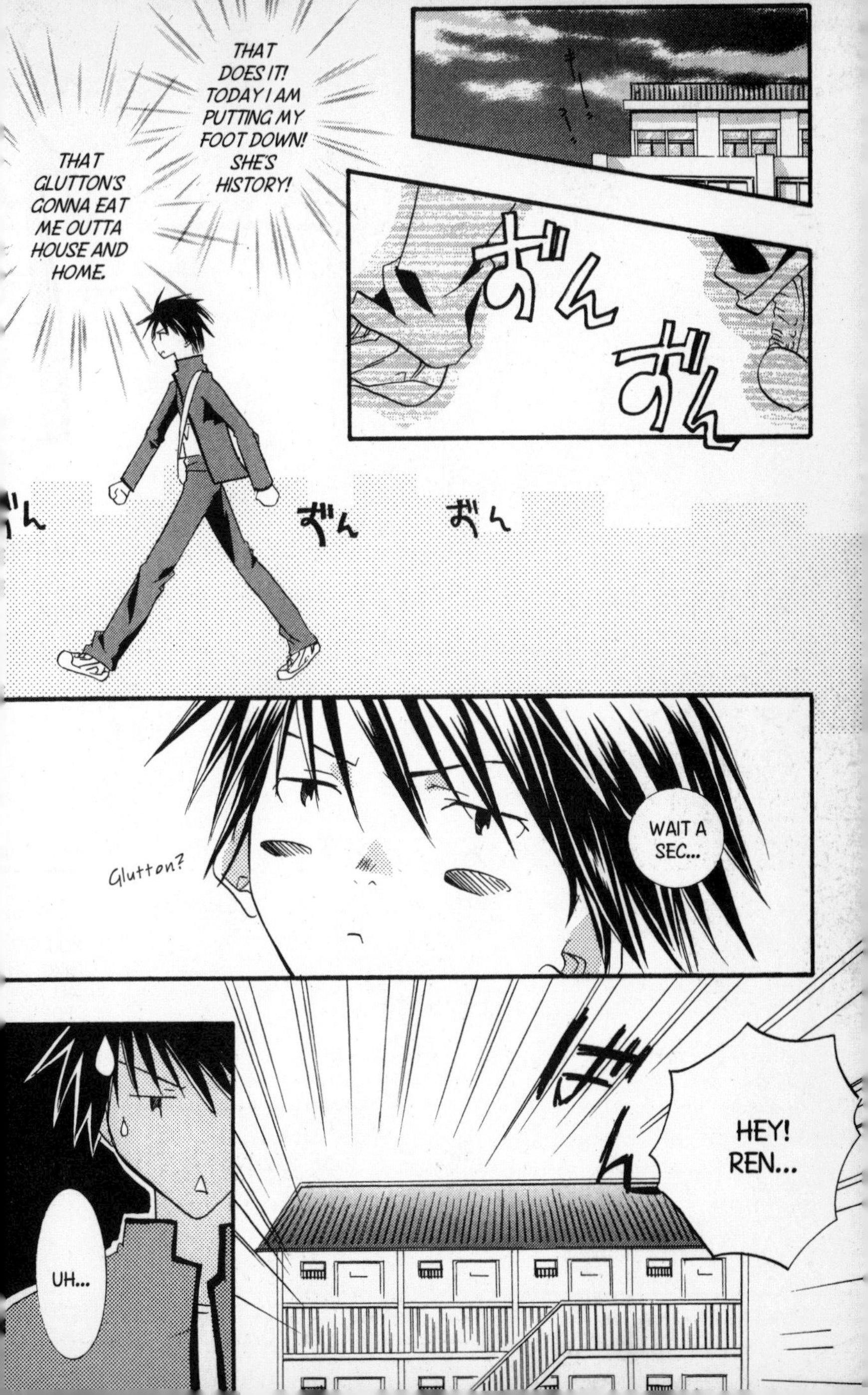

ずん
ずん
THAT DOES IT! TODAY I AM PUTTING MY FOOT DOWN! SHE'S HISTORY!
THAT GLUTTON'S GONNA EAT ME OUTTA HOUSE AND HOME.
ずん
ずん
WAIT A SEC...
Glutton?
HEY! REN...
UH...

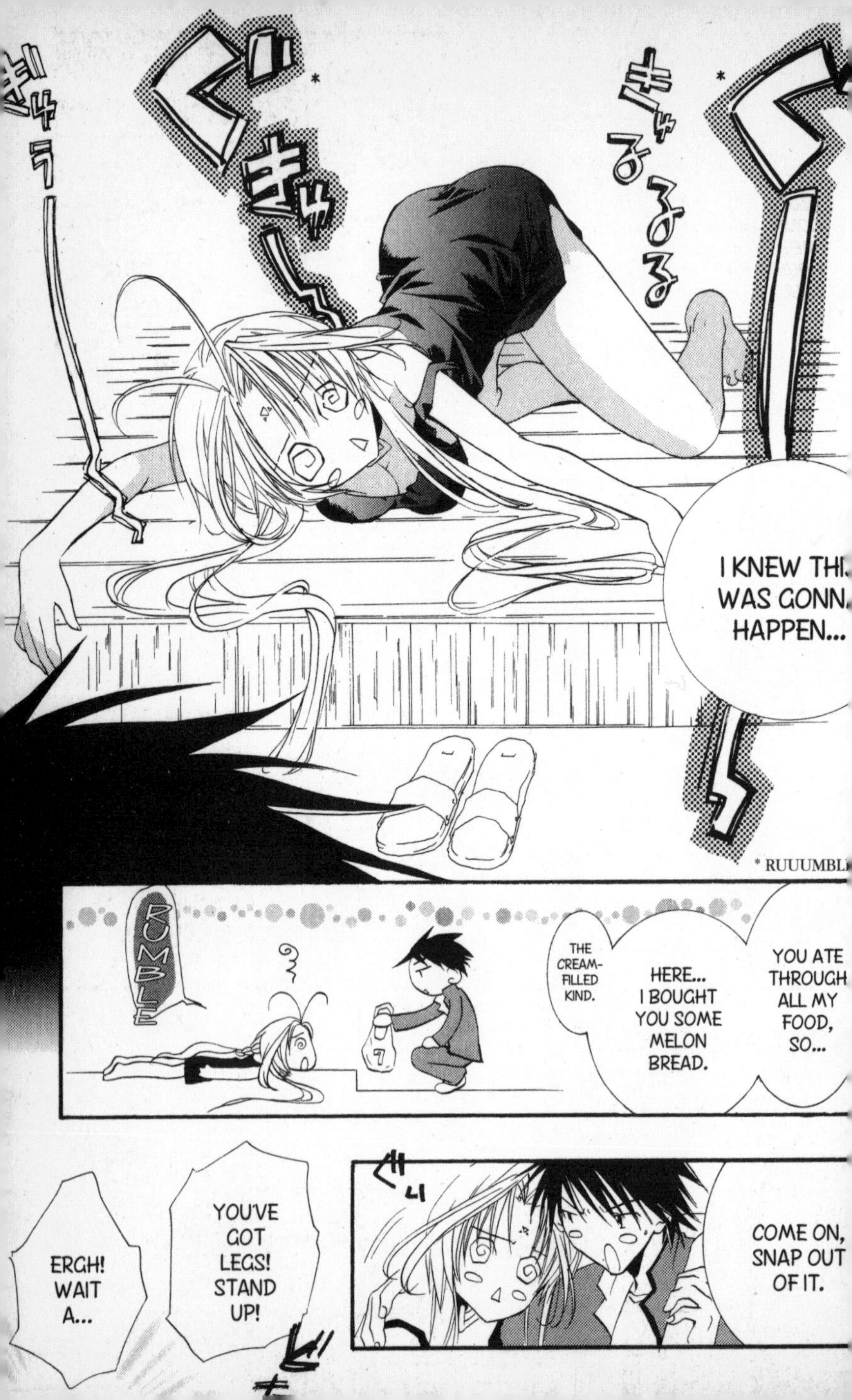
I KNEW THI WAS GONN HAPPEN...
* RUUUMBL
YOU ATE THROUGH ALL MY FOOD, SO...
HERE... I BOUGHT YOU SOME MELON BREAD.
THE CREAM-FILLED KIND.
RUMBLE
COME ON, SNAP OUT OF IT.
YOU'VE GOT LEGS! STAND UP!
ERGH! WAIT A...

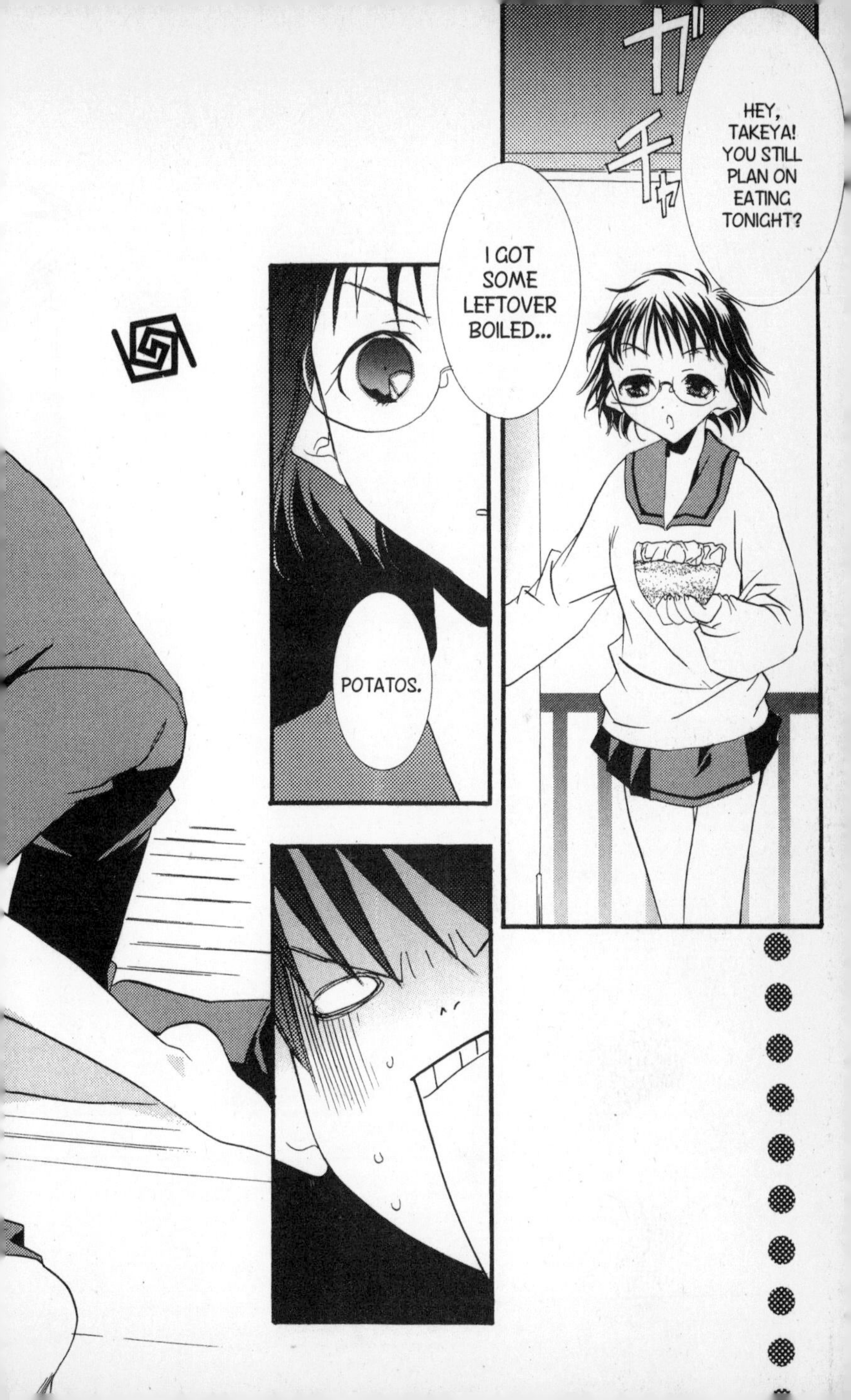
ガチャ
HEY, TAKEYA! YOU STILL PLAN ON EATING TONIGHT?
I GOT SOME LEFTOVER BOILED...
POTATOS.

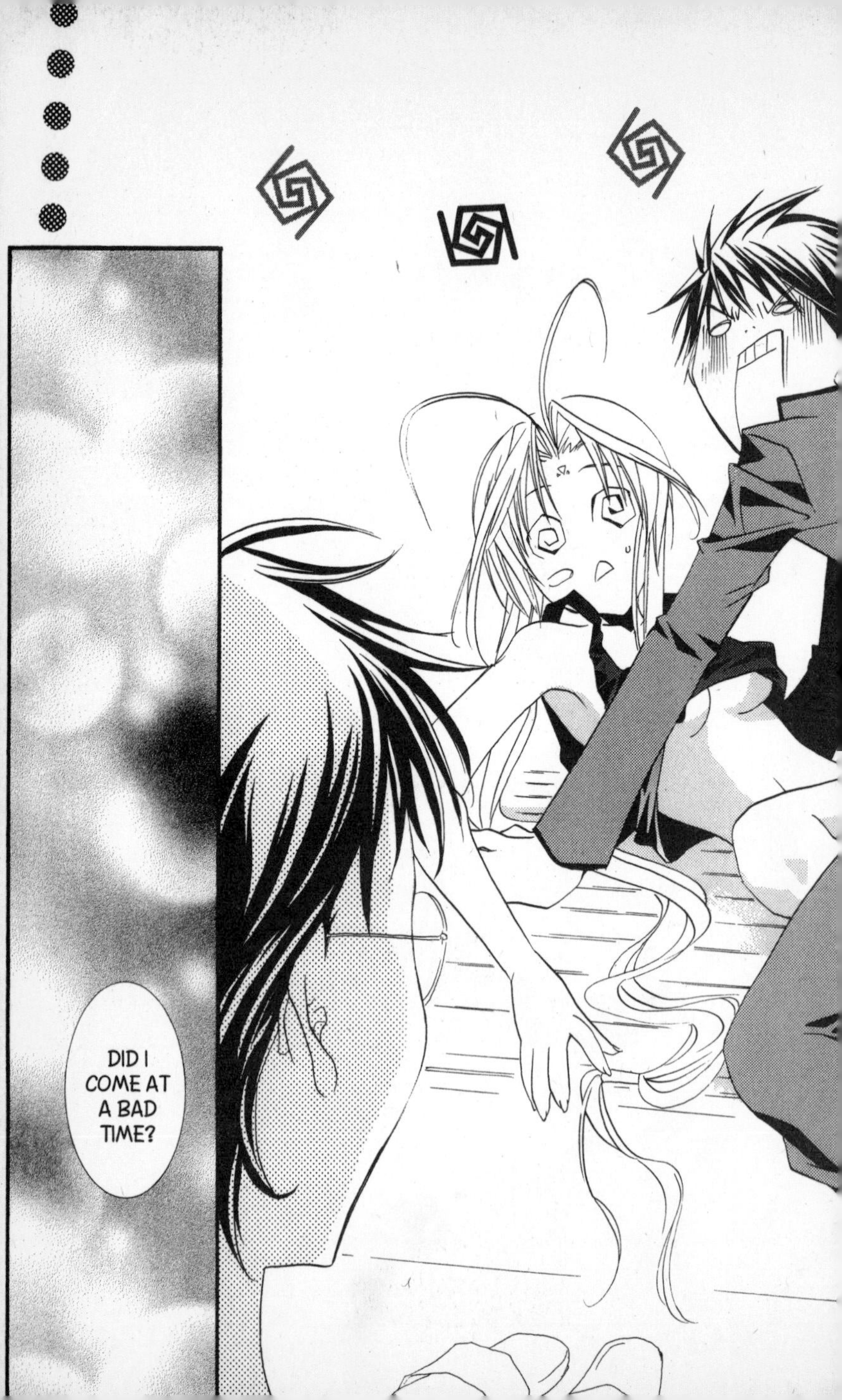
DID I COME AT A BAD TIME?

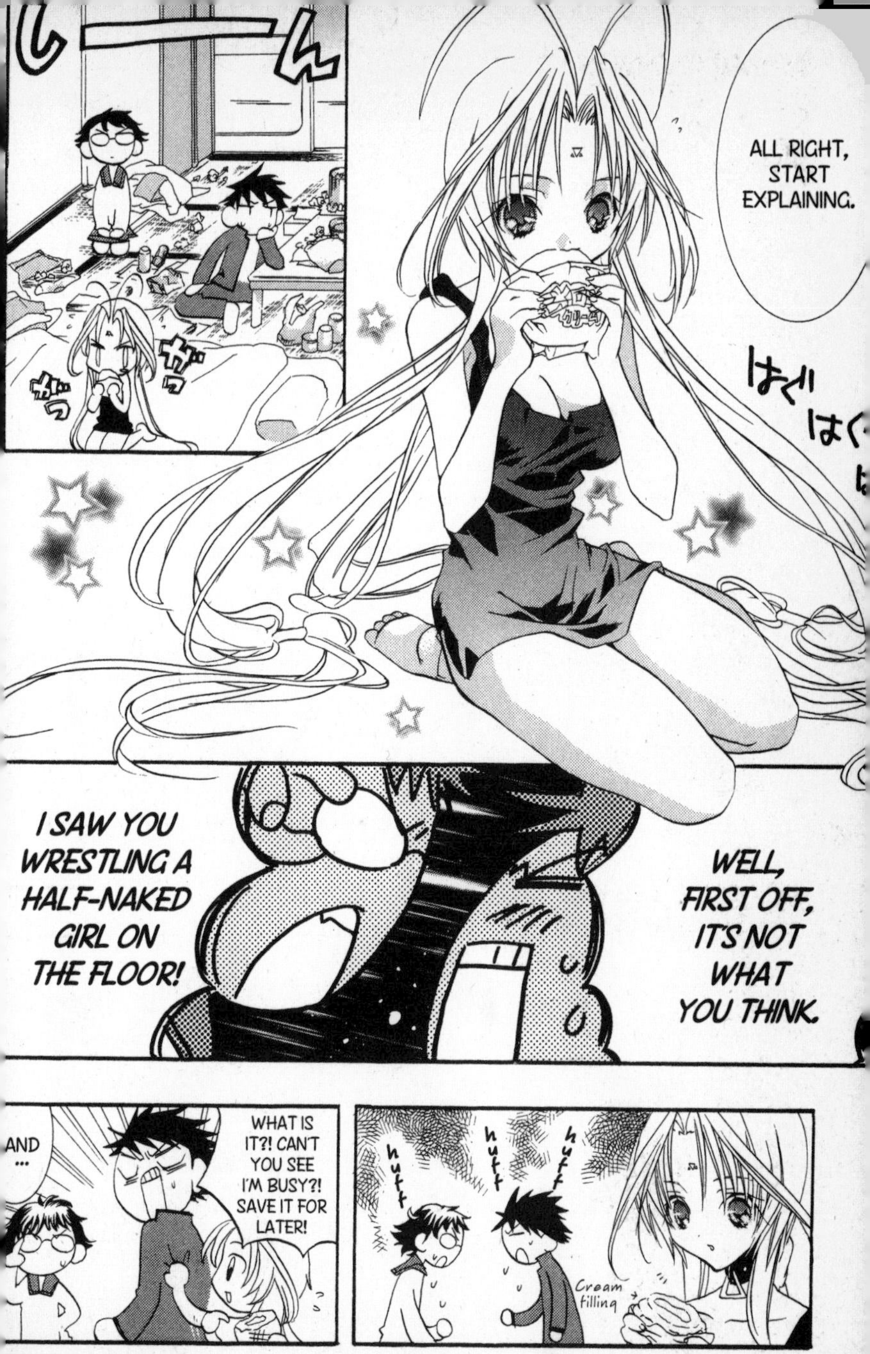
ALL RIGHT, START EXPLAINING.
はぐ
はぐ
しーーん
がつ
がつ
WELL, FIRST OFF, IT'S NOT WHAT YOU THINK.
I SAW YOU WRESTLING A HALF-NAKED GIRL ON THE FLOOR!
huff
huff
Cream filling
WHAT IS IT?! CAN'T YOU SEE I'M BUSY?! SAVE IT FOR LATER!
AND ...

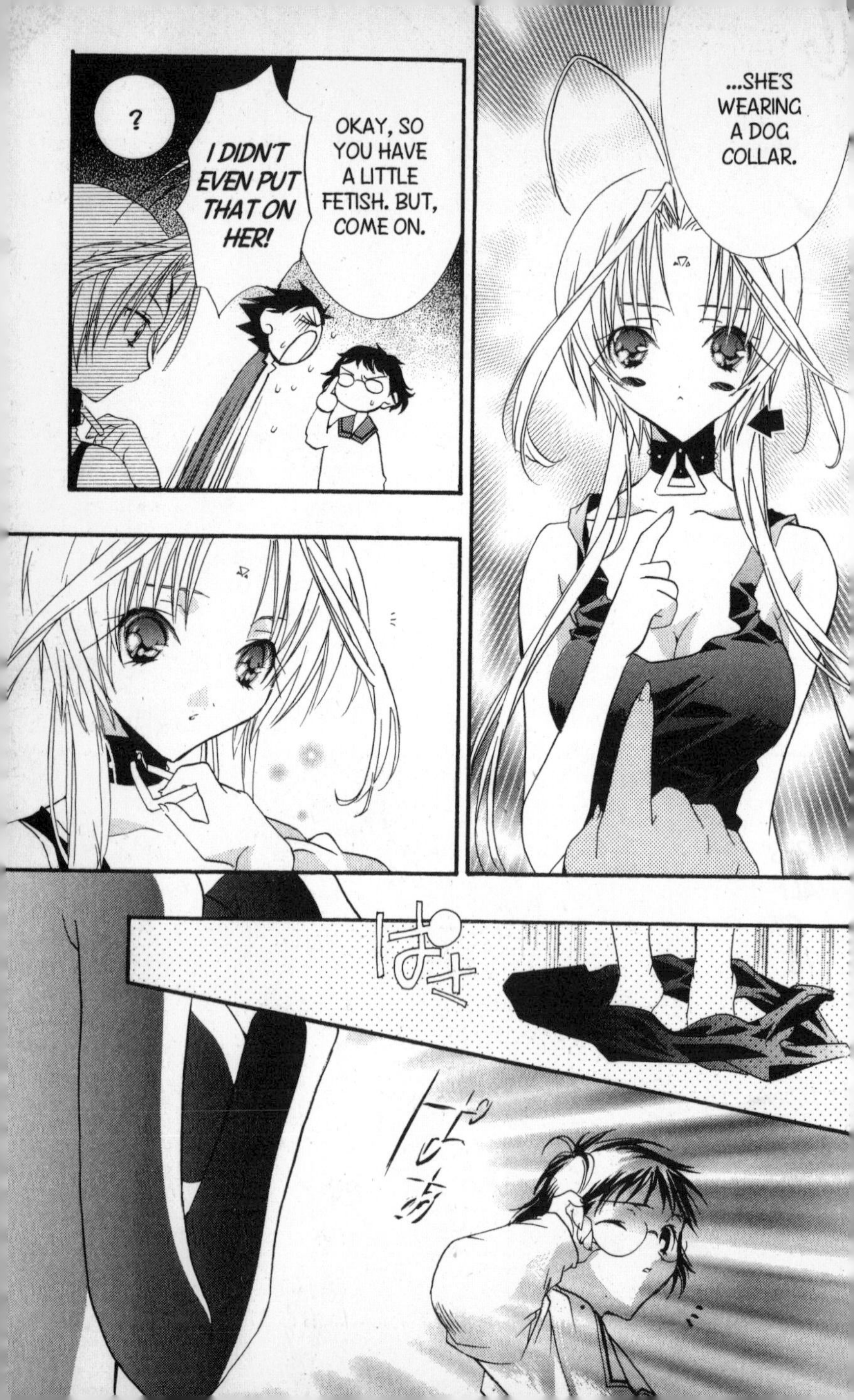
...SHE'S WEARING A DOG COLLAR.
OKAY, SO YOU HAVE A LITTLE FETISH. BUT, COME ON.
I DIDN'T EVEN PUT THAT ON HER!
?

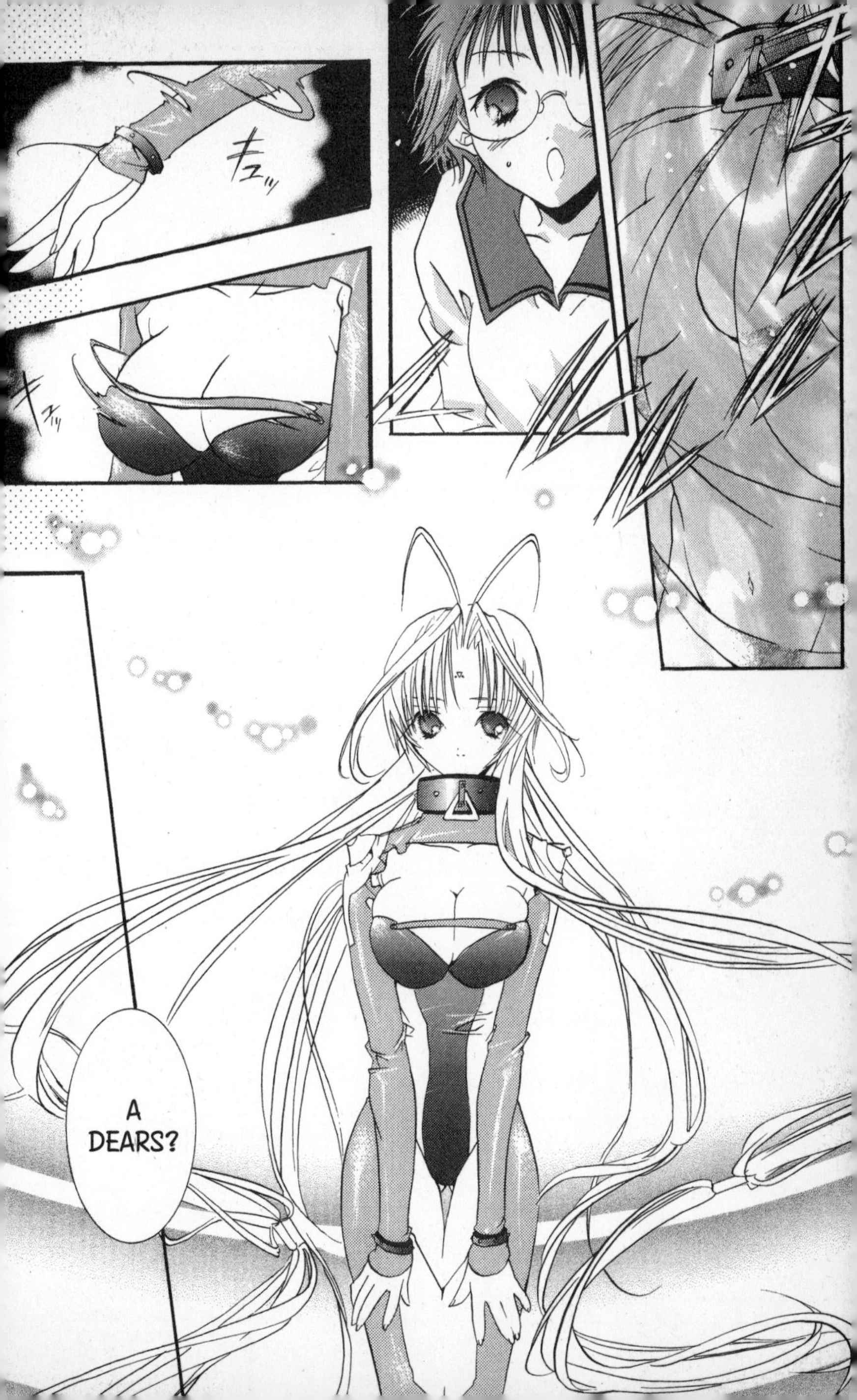
キュッ
キュッ
A DEARS?

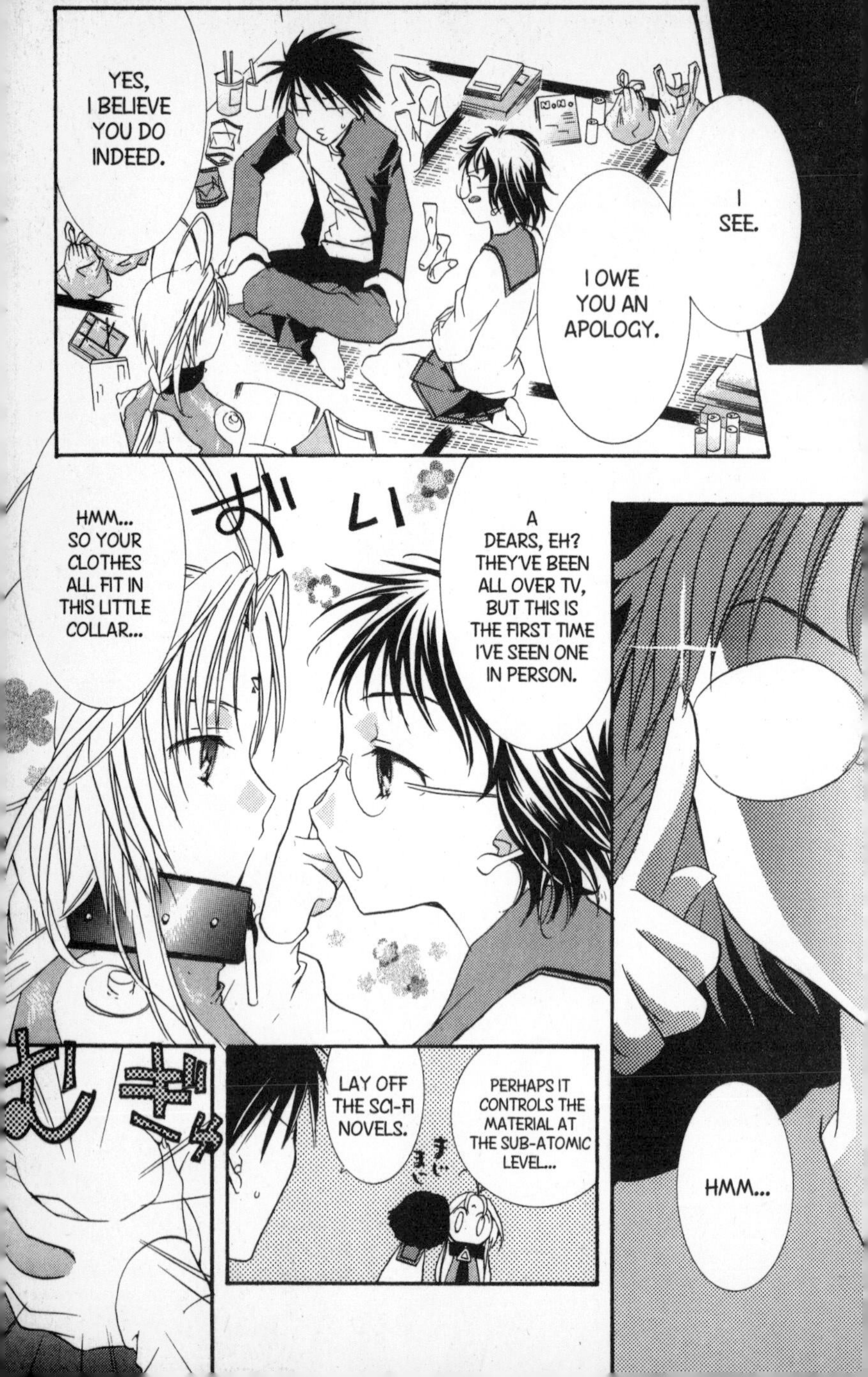
I SEE.
I OWE YOU AN APOLOGY.
YES, I BELIEVE YOU DO INDEED.
HMM...
A DEARS, EH? THEY'VE BEEN ALL OVER TV, BUT THIS IS THE FIRST TIME I'VE SEEN ONE IN PERSON.
ずい
HMM... SO YOUR CLOTHES ALL FIT IN THIS LITTLE COLLAR...
PERHAPS IT CONTROLS THE MATERIAL AT THE SUB-ATOMIC LEVEL...
LAY OFF THE SCI-FI NOVELS.
むぎゅ

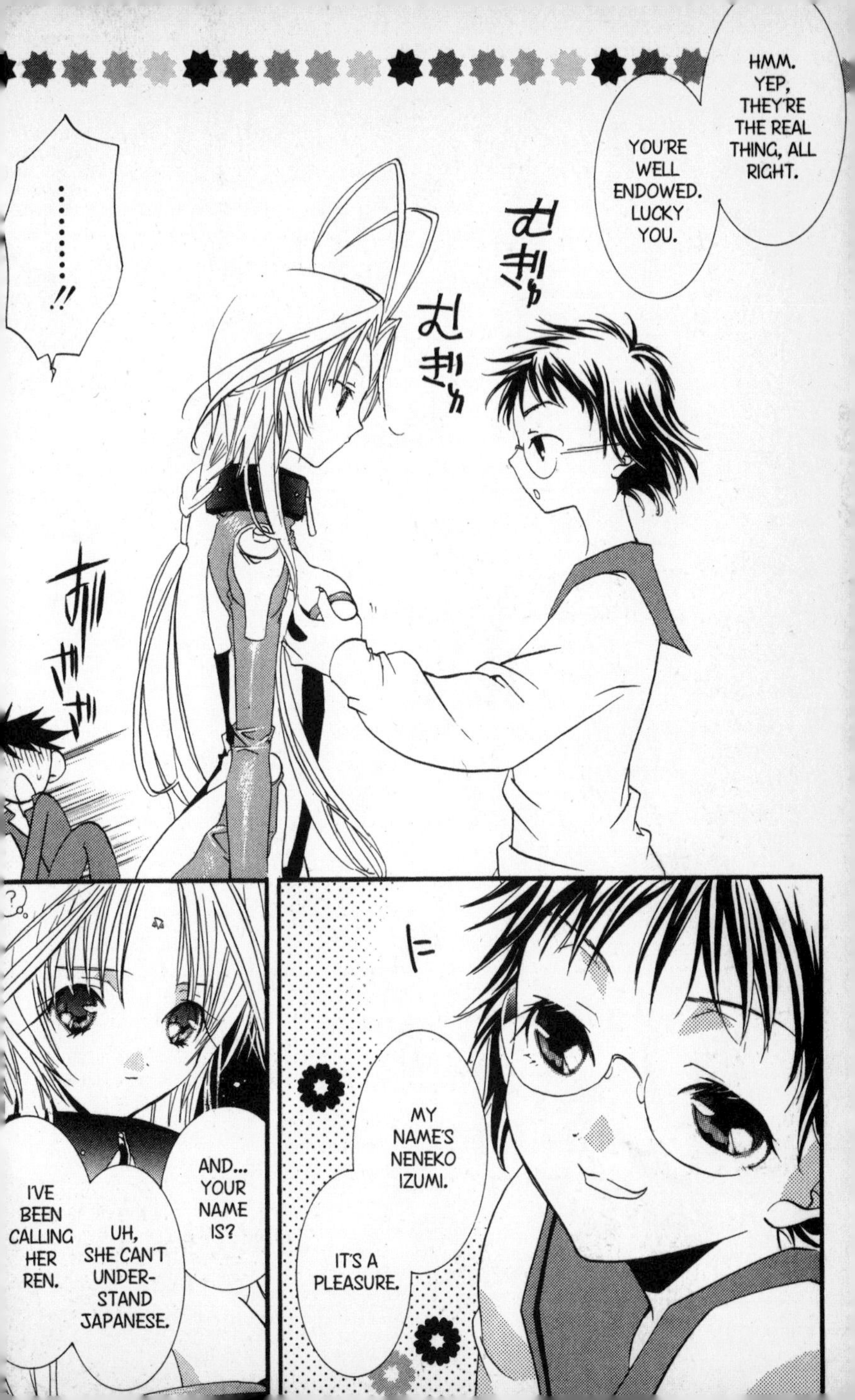
HMM. YEP, THEY'RE THE REAL THING, ALL RIGHT.
YOU'RE WELL ENDOWED. LUCKY YOU.
......!!
MY NAME'S NENEKO IZUMI.
IT'S A PLEASURE.
AND... YOUR NAME IS?
UH, SHE CAN'T UNDER-STAND JAPANESE.
I'VE BEEN CALLING HER REN.

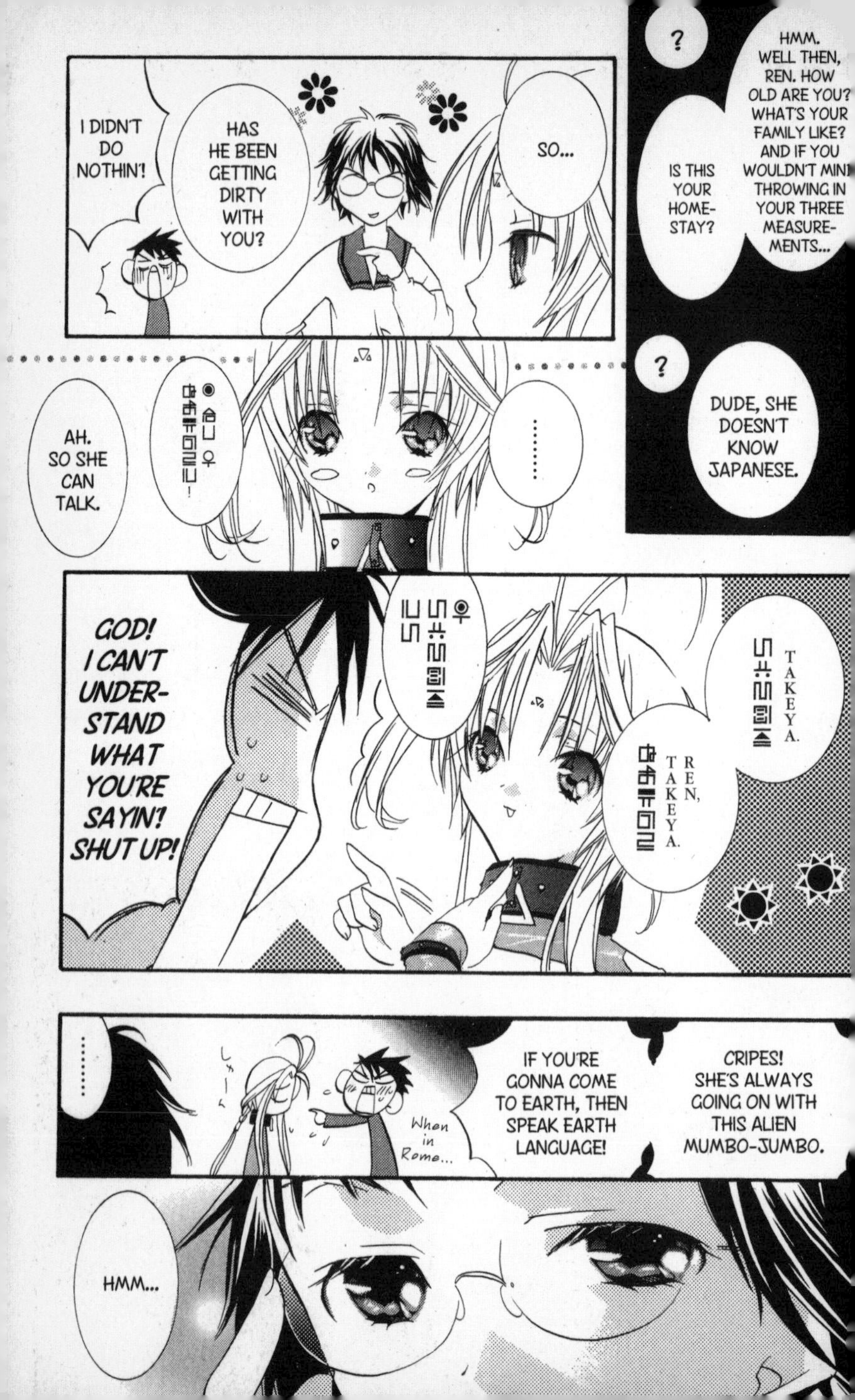
?
HMM. WELL THEN, REN. HOW OLD ARE YOU? WHAT'S YOUR FAMILY LIKE? AND IF YOU WOULDN'T MIN THROWING IN YOUR THREE MEASURE-MENTS...
IS THIS YOUR HOME-STAY?
SO...
HAS HE BEEN GETTING DIRTY WITH YOU?
I DIDN'T DO NOTHIN'!
?
DUDE, SHE DOESN'T KNOW JAPANESE.
....
AH. SO SHE CAN TALK.
TAKEYA.
REN, TAKEYA.
GOD! I CAN'T UNDERSTAND WHAT YOU'RE SAYIN'! SHUT UP!
CRIPES! SHE'S ALWAYS GOING ON WITH THIS ALIEN MUMBO-JUMBO.
IF YOU'RE GONNA COME TO EARTH, THEN SPEAK EARTH LANGUAGE!
When in Rome...
....
HMM...

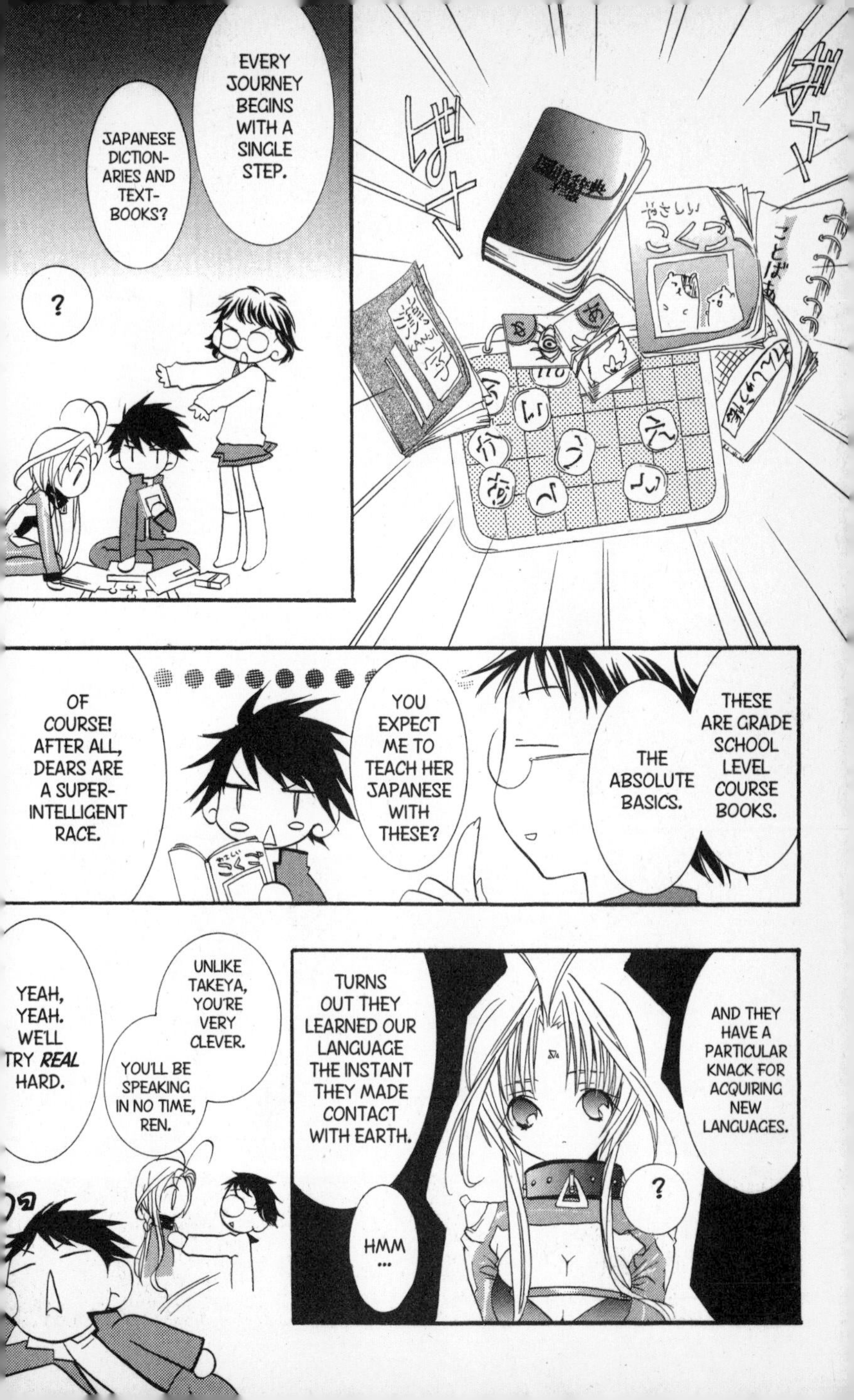
やさしいこくご
KANJI
EVERY JOURNEY BEGINS WITH A SINGLE STEP.
JAPANESE DICTIONARIES AND TEXTBOOKS?
?
THESE ARE GRADE SCHOOL LEVEL COURSE BOOKS.
THE ABSOLUTE BASICS.
YOU EXPECT ME TO TEACH HER JAPANESE WITH THESE?
OF COURSE! AFTER ALL, DEARS ARE A SUPER-INTELLIGENT RACE.
AND THEY HAVE A PARTICULAR KNACK FOR ACQUIRING NEW LANGUAGES.
?
TURNS OUT THEY LEARNED OUR LANGUAGE THE INSTANT THEY MADE CONTACT WITH EARTH.
HMM...
UNLIKE TAKEYA, YOU'RE VERY CLEVER.
YOU'LL BE SPEAKING IN NO TIME, REN.
YEAH, YEAH. WE'LL TRY *REAL* HARD.

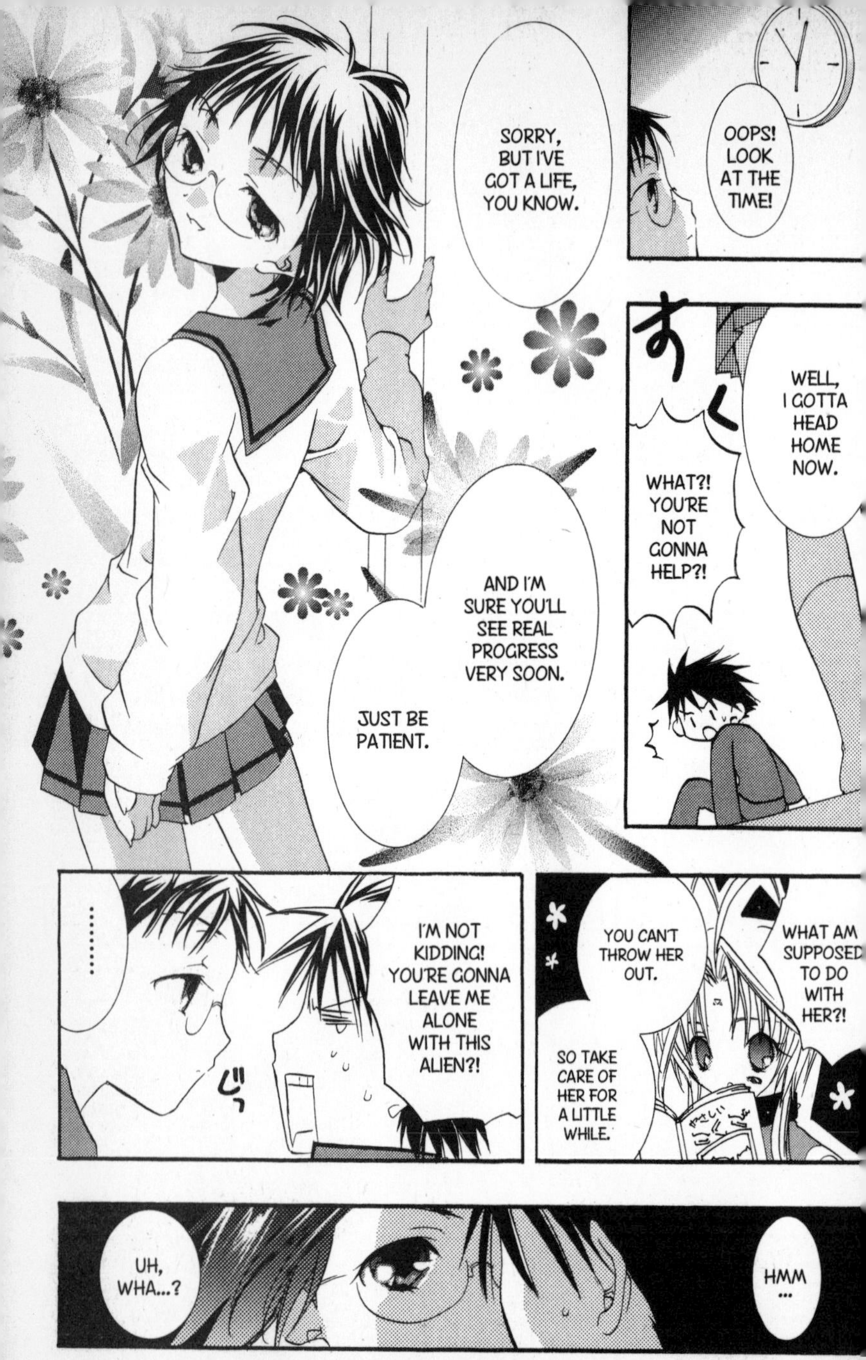
OOPS! LOOK AT THE TIME!
すく
WELL, I GOTTA HEAD HOME NOW.
WHAT?! YOU'RE NOT GONNA HELP?!
SORRY, BUT I'VE GOT A LIFE, YOU KNOW.
AND I'M SURE YOU'LL SEE REAL PROGRESS VERY SOON.
JUST BE PATIENT.
WHAT AM SUPPOSED TO DO WITH HER?!
YOU CAN'T THROW HER OUT.
SO TAKE CARE OF HER FOR A LITTLE WHILE.
I'M NOT KIDDING! YOU'RE GONNA LEAVE ME ALONE WITH THIS ALIEN?!
......
ぐっ
HMM...
UH, WHA...?

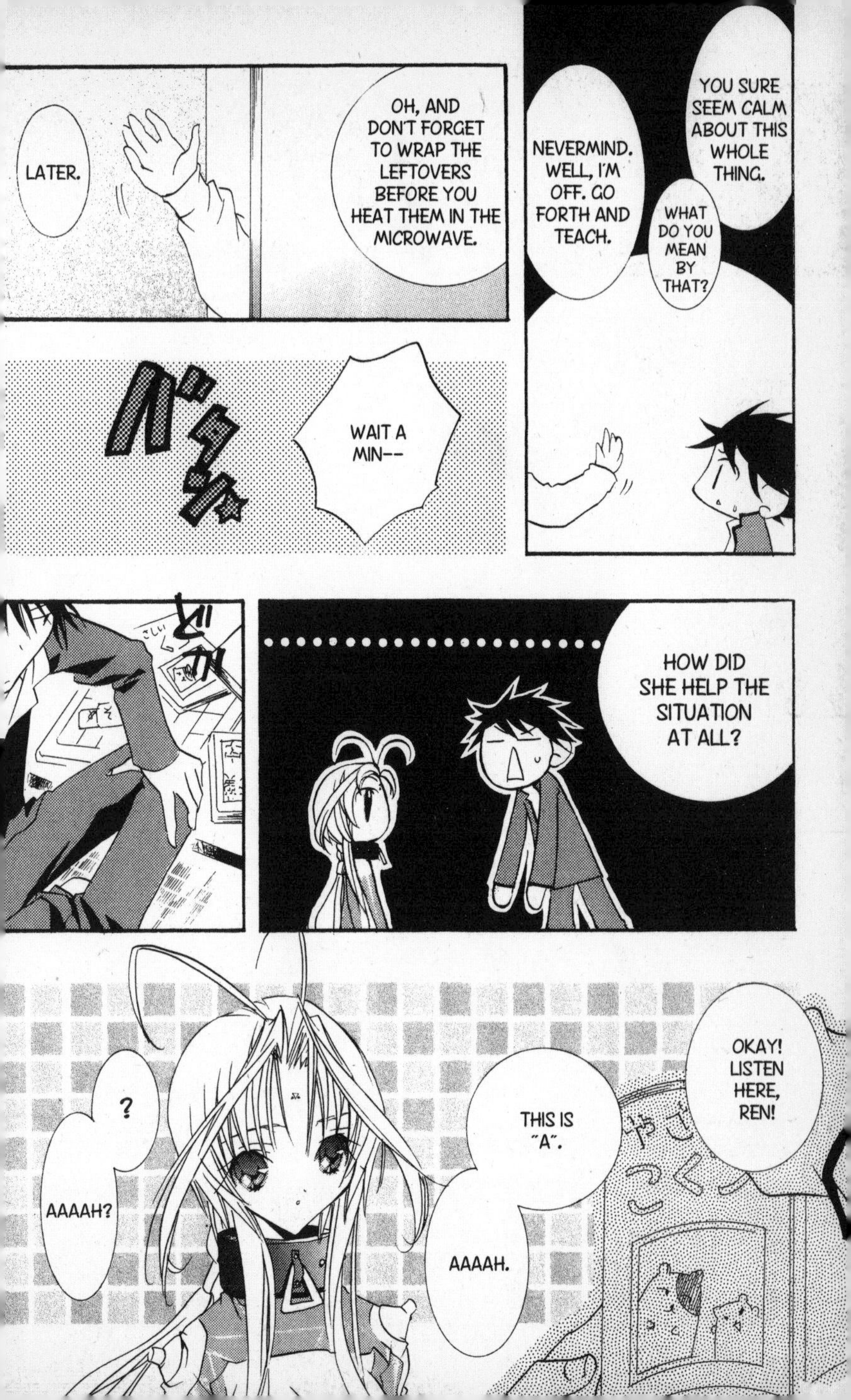
YOU SURE SEEM CALM ABOUT THIS WHOLE THING.
WHAT DO YOU MEAN BY THAT?
NEVERMIND. WELL, I'M OFF. GO FORTH AND TEACH.
OH, AND DON'T FORGET TO WRAP THE LEFTOVERS BEFORE YOU HEAT THEM IN THE MICROWAVE.
LATER.
WAIT A MIN--
バタン
....
HOW DID SHE HELP THE SITUATION AT ALL?
OKAY! LISTEN HERE, REN!
THIS IS "A".
AAAAH.
?
AAAAH?

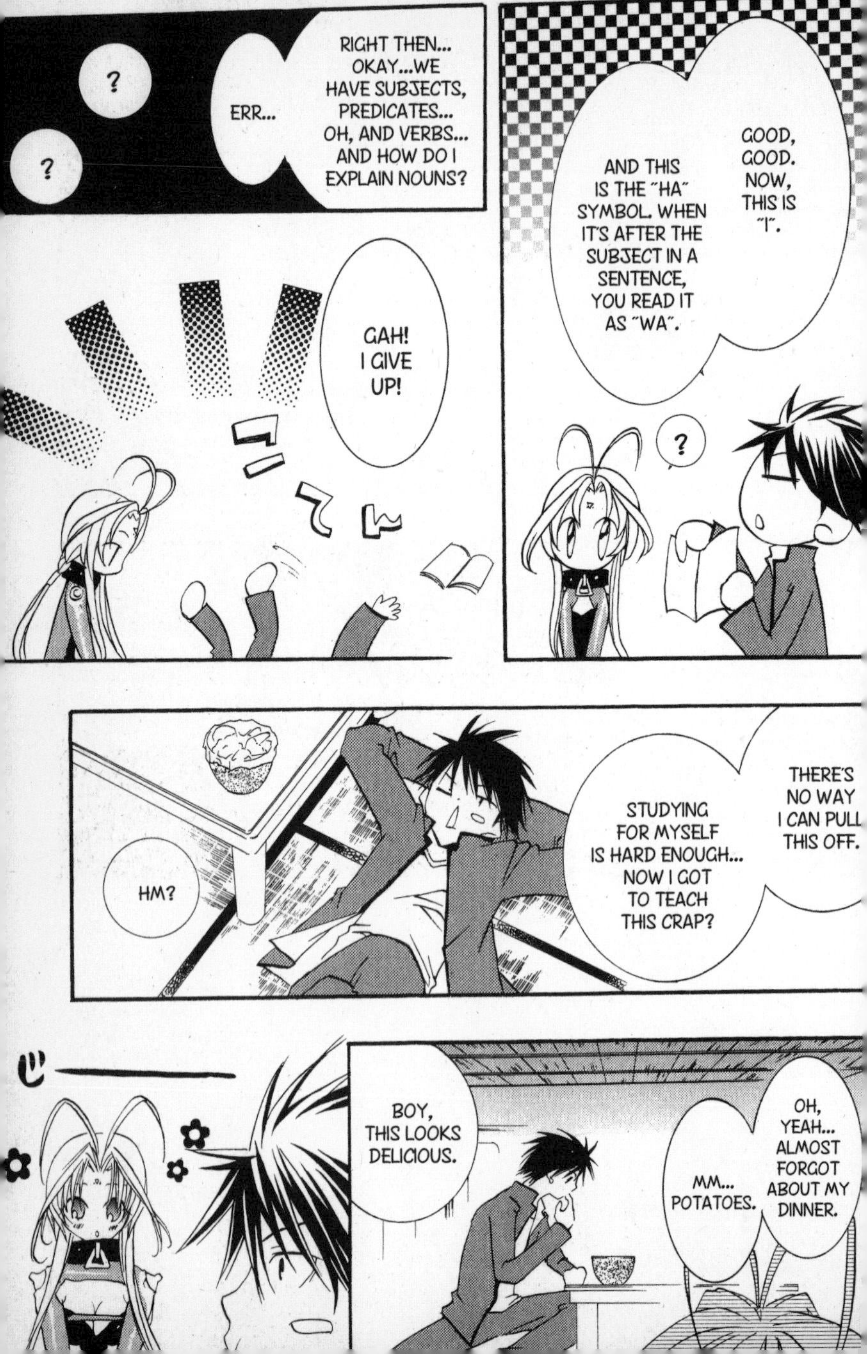
GOOD, GOOD. NOW, THIS IS "I".
AND THIS IS THE "HA" SYMBOL. WHEN IT'S AFTER THE SUBJECT IN A SENTENCE, YOU READ IT AS "WA".
?
RIGHT THEN... OKAY...WE HAVE SUBJECTS, PREDICATES... OH, AND VERBS... AND HOW DO I EXPLAIN NOUNS?
ERR...
?
?
GAH! I GIVE UP!
THERE'S NO WAY I CAN PULL THIS OFF.
STUDYING FOR MYSELF IS HARD ENOUGH... NOW I GOT TO TEACH THIS CRAP?
HM?
OH, YEAH... ALMOST FORGOT ABOUT MY DINNER.
MM... POTATOES.
BOY, THIS LOOKS DELICIOUS.
じ

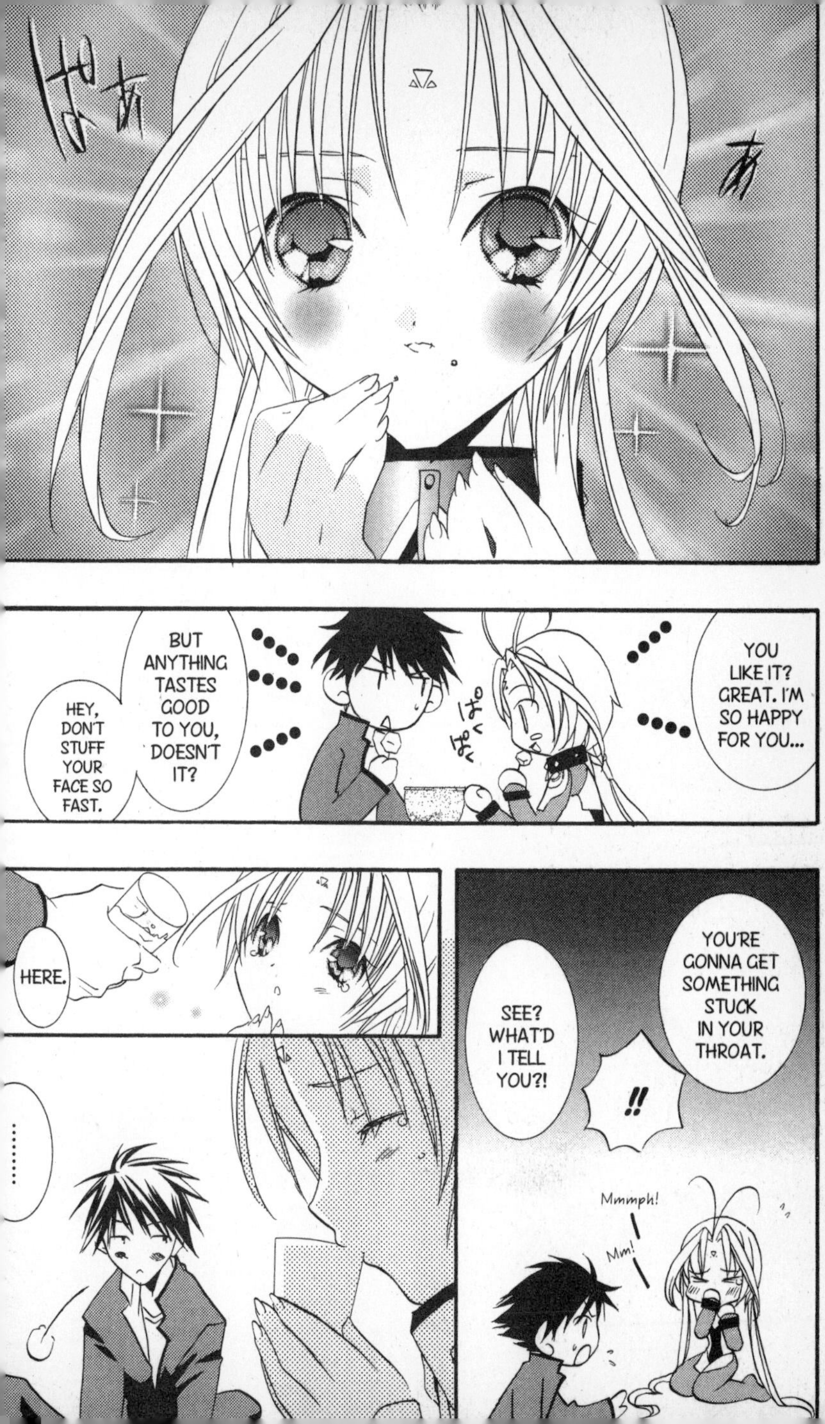
ぱぁ
あ
YOU LIKE IT? GREAT. I'M SO HAPPY FOR YOU...
ぱくぱく
BUT ANYTHING TASTES GOOD TO YOU, DOESN'T IT?
HEY, DON'T STUFF YOUR FACE SO FAST.
YOU'RE GONNA GET SOMETHING STUCK IN YOUR THROAT.
!!
SEE? WHAT'D I TELL YOU?!
Mmmph!
Mm!
HERE.
......

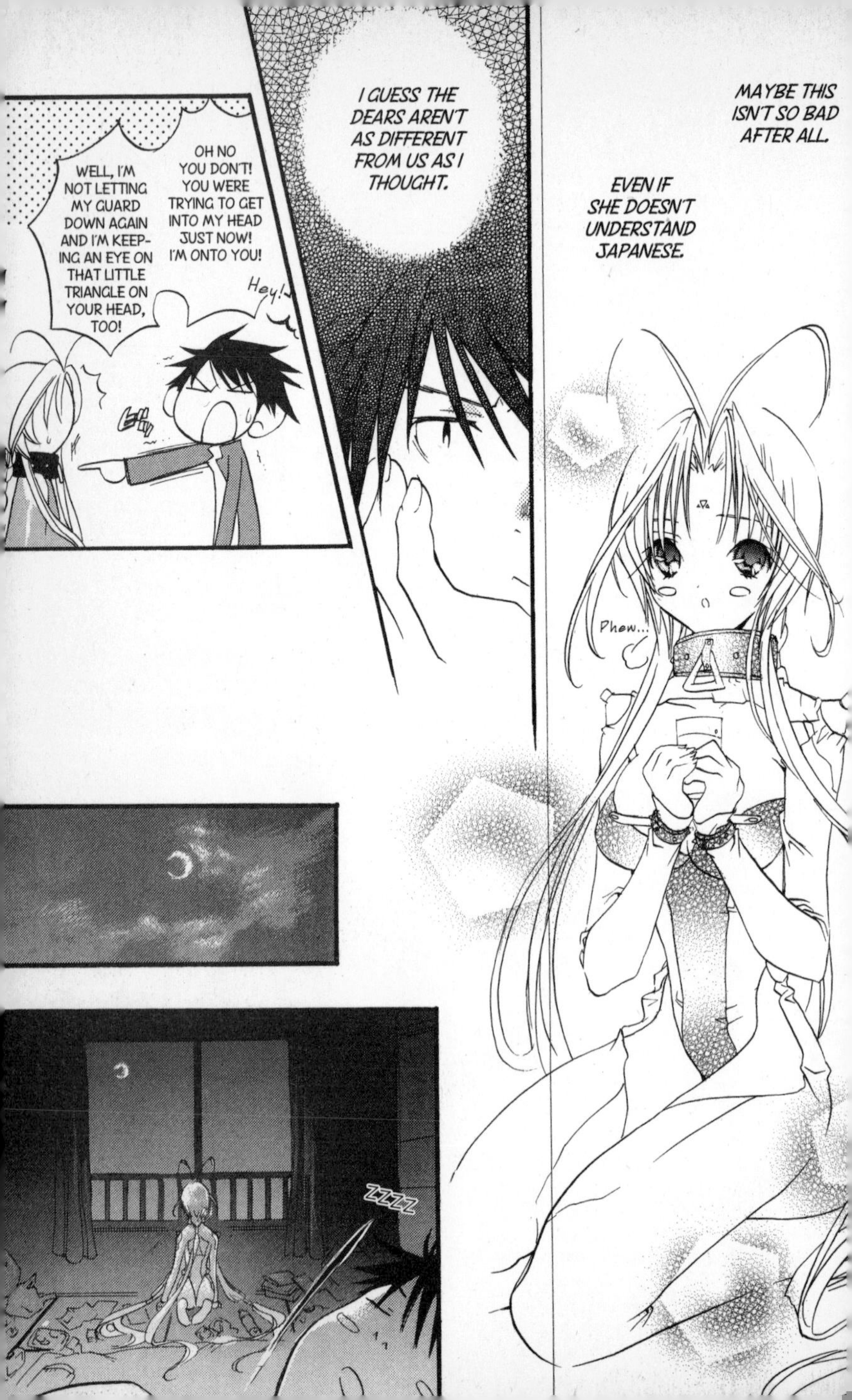
MAYBE THIS ISN'T SO BAD AFTER ALL.
EVEN IF SHE DOESN'T UNDERSTAND JAPANESE.
Phew...
I GUESS THE DEARS AREN'T AS DIFFERENT FROM US AS I THOUGHT.
OH NO YOU DON'T! YOU WERE TRYING TO GET INTO MY HEAD JUST NOW! I'M ONTO YOU!
WELL, I'M NOT LETTING MY GUARD DOWN AGAIN AND I'M KEEPING AN EYE ON THAT LITTLE TRIANGLE ON YOUR HEAD, TOO!
Hey!
ZZZZ

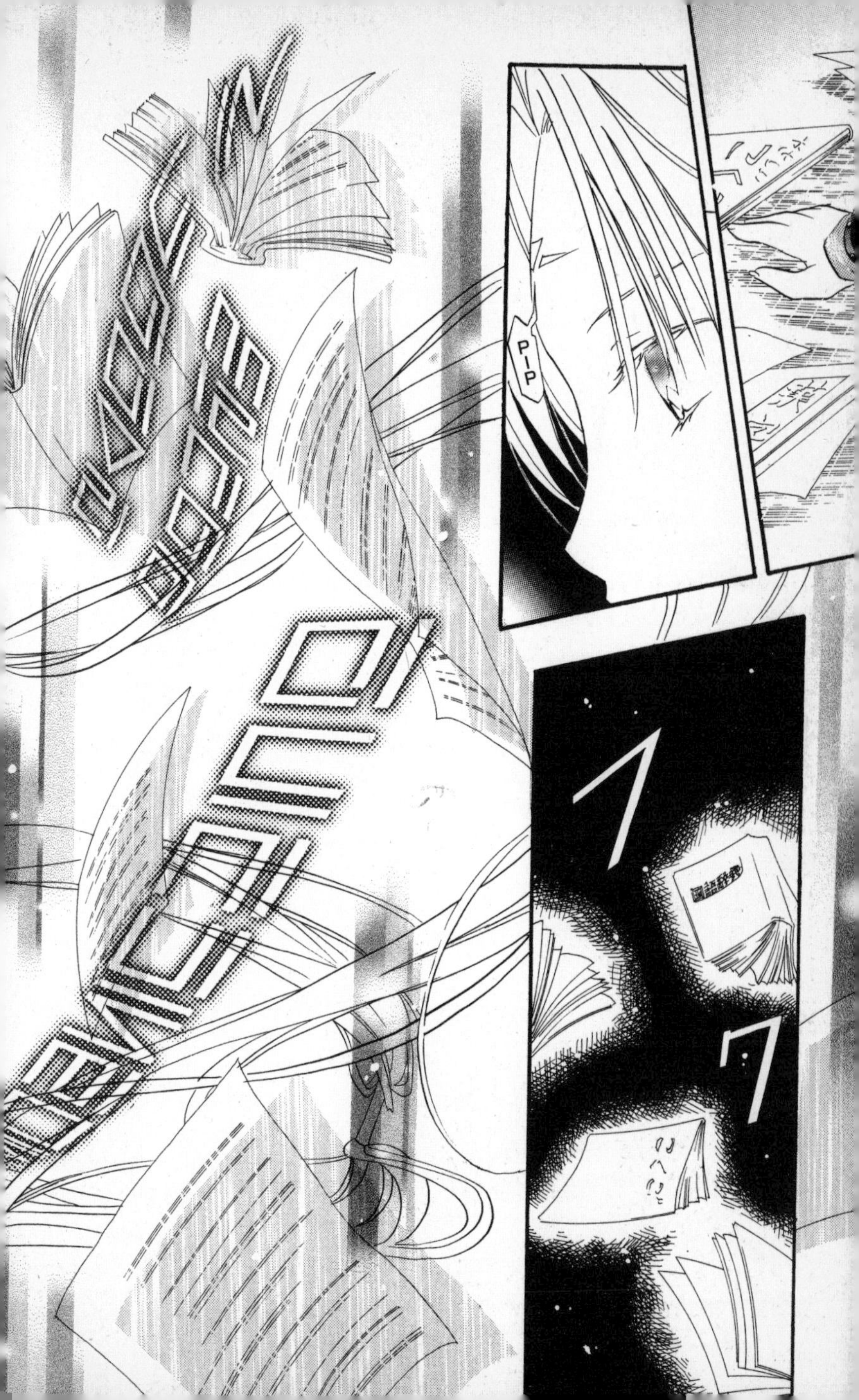
PIP

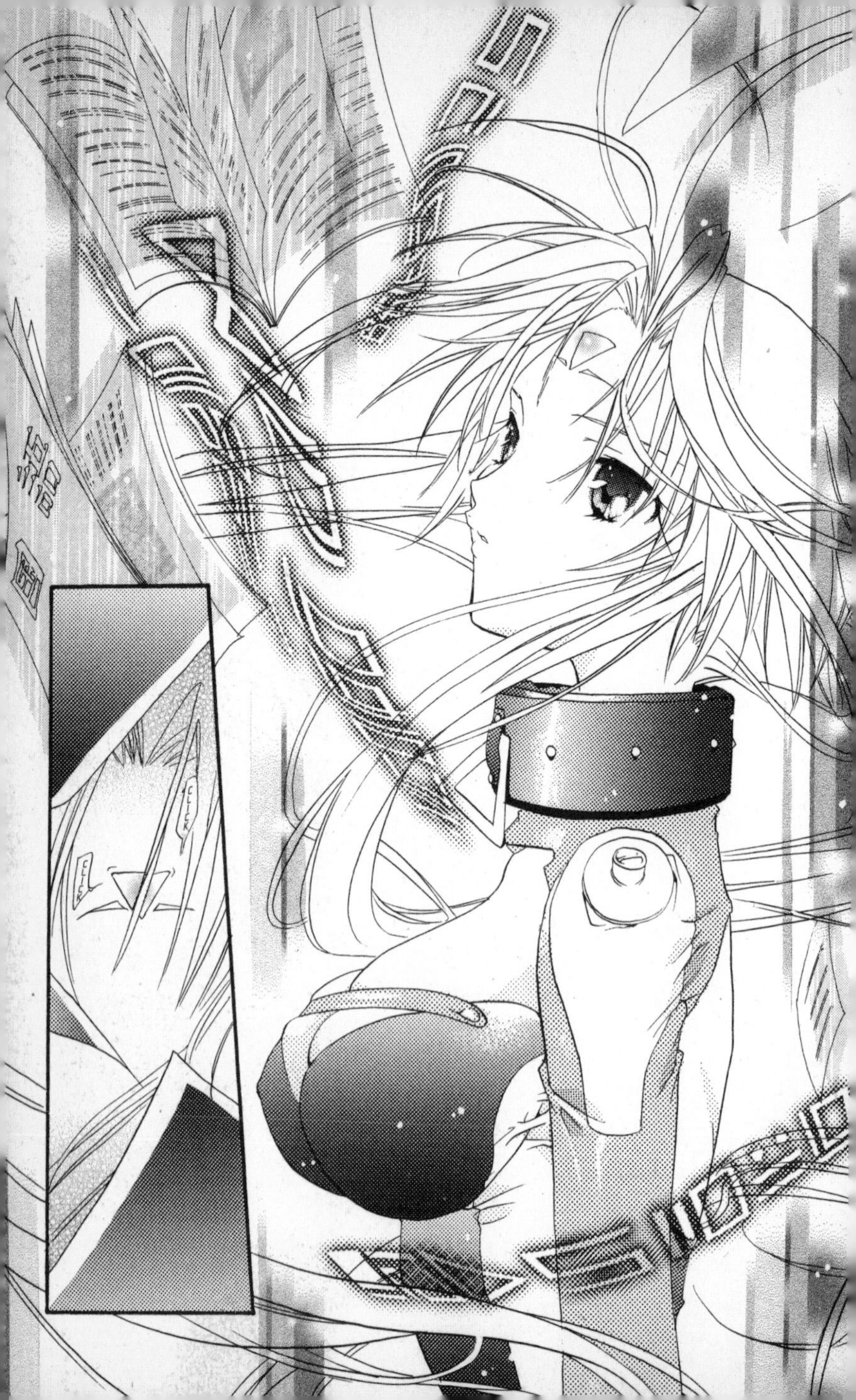
CLICK
CLICK

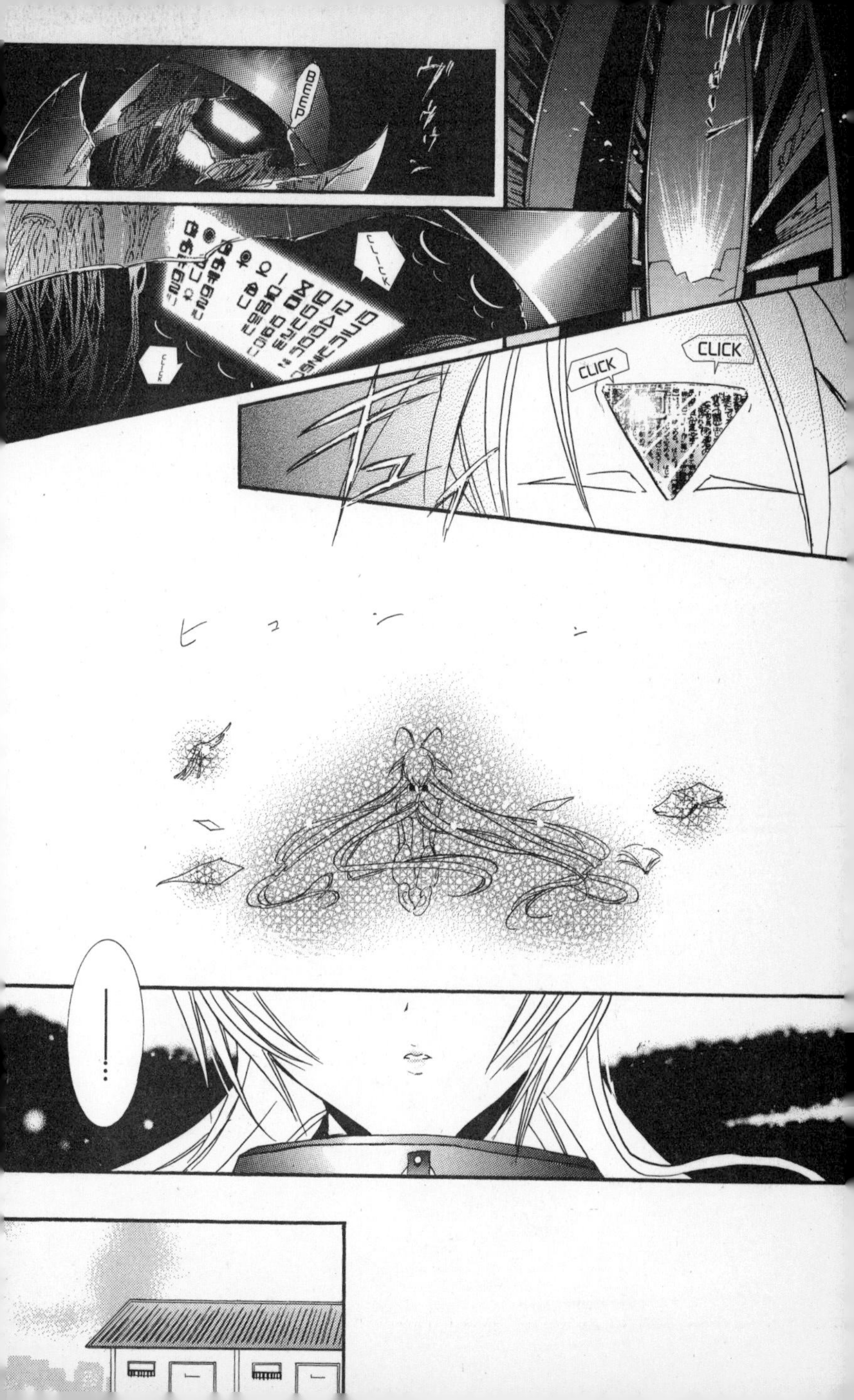
BEEP
CLICK
CLICK
CLICK
CLICK
—!...

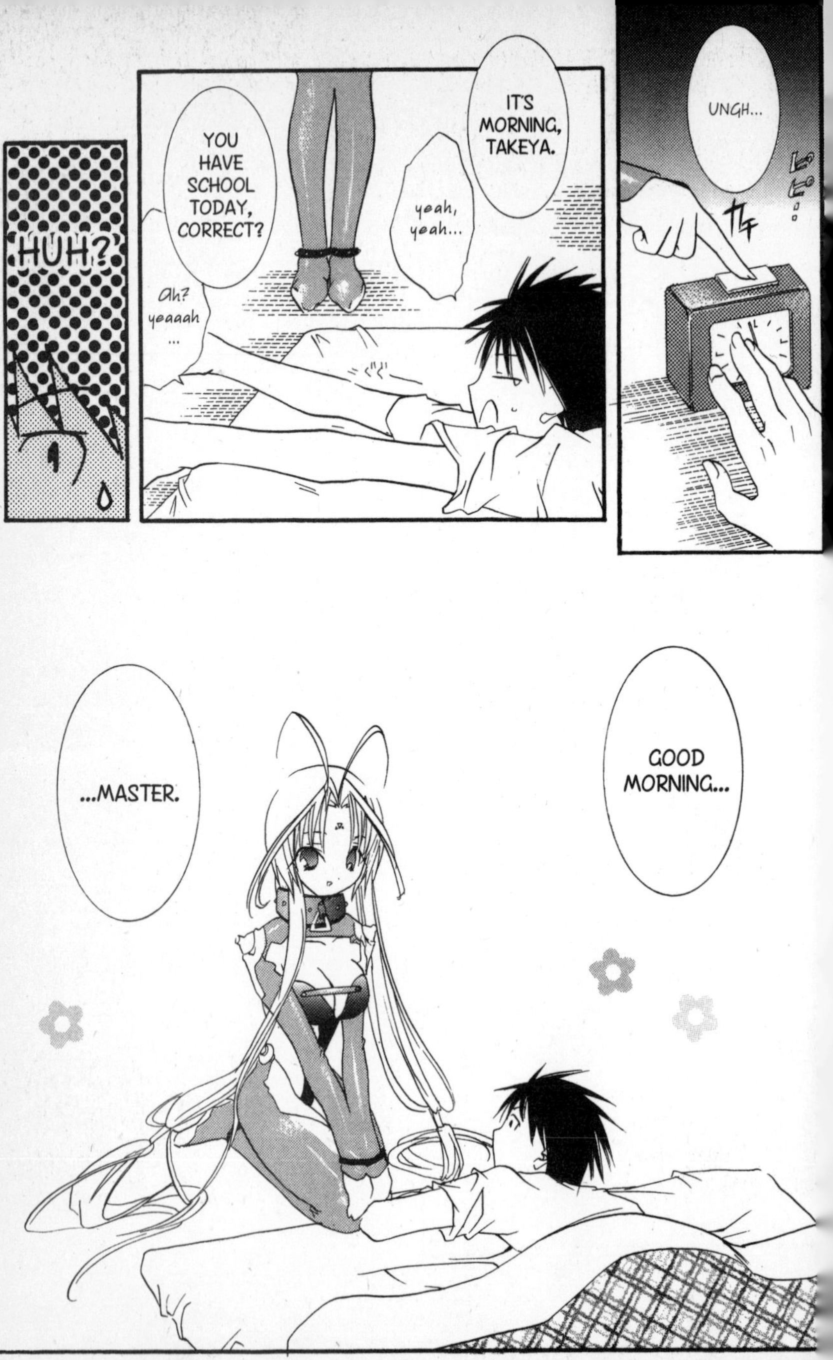
UNGH...
IT'S MORNING, TAKEYA.
yeah, yeah...
YOU HAVE SCHOOL TODAY, CORRECT?
ah? yeaaah ...
HUH?
GOOD MORNING...
...MASTER.

INSTALL

パ
TRASHY DETECTIVE STORY
N-NO WAY! YOU LEARNED OUR LANGUAGE IN ONE NIGHT?!
Master!
UH, SAY SOMETHING *ELSE* THAT YOU'VE LEARNED.
I'LL SHOW YOU *MY* EVIDENCE IF YOU SHOW ME *YOURS.*

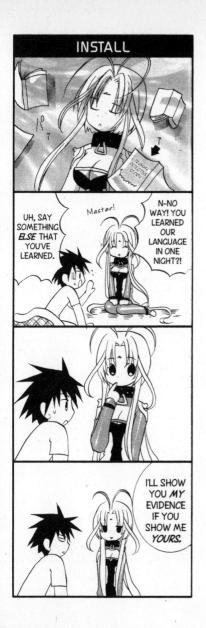

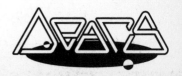

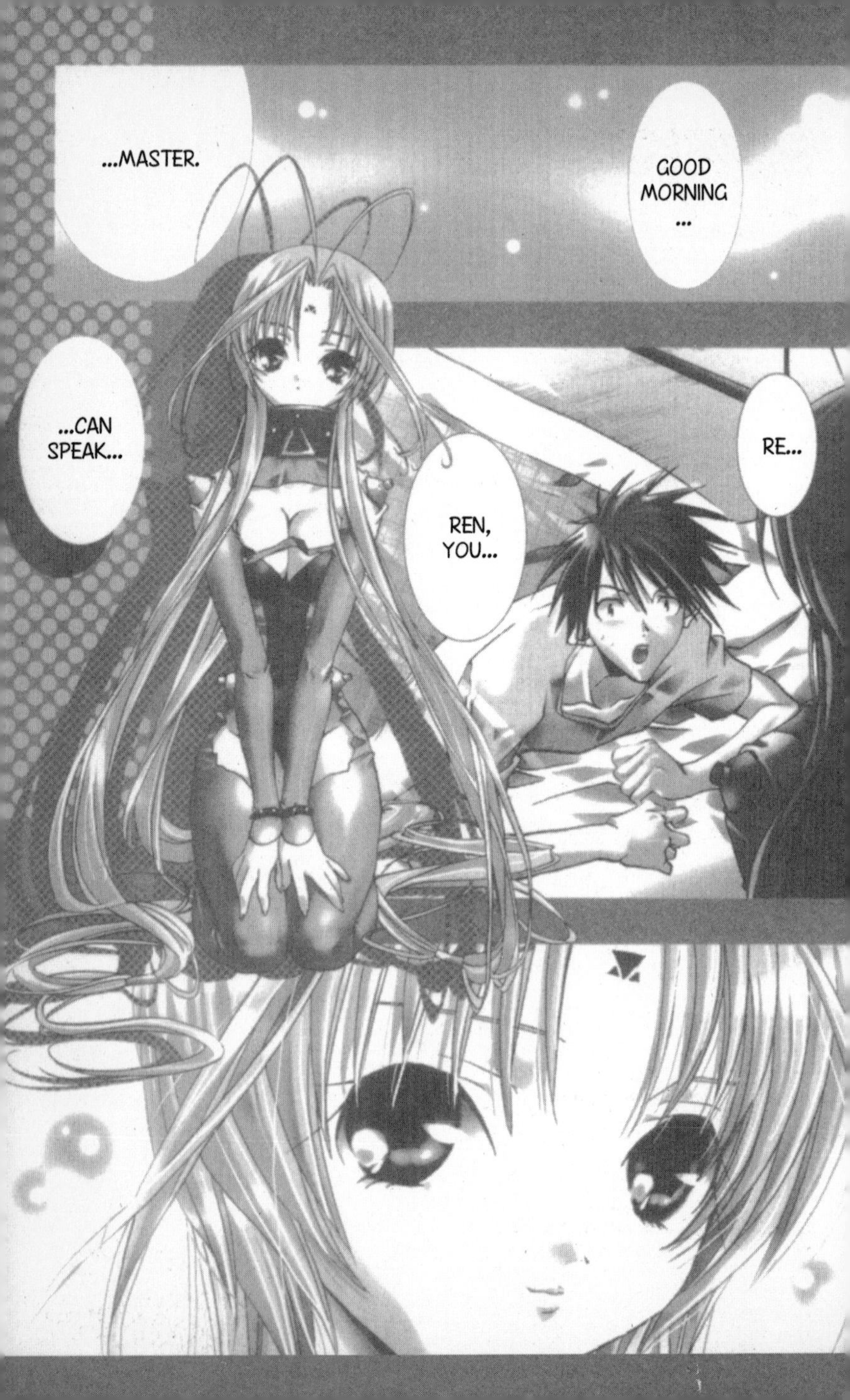
GOOD MORNING ...
...MASTER.
RE...
REN, YOU...
...CAN SPEAK...

4th Contact

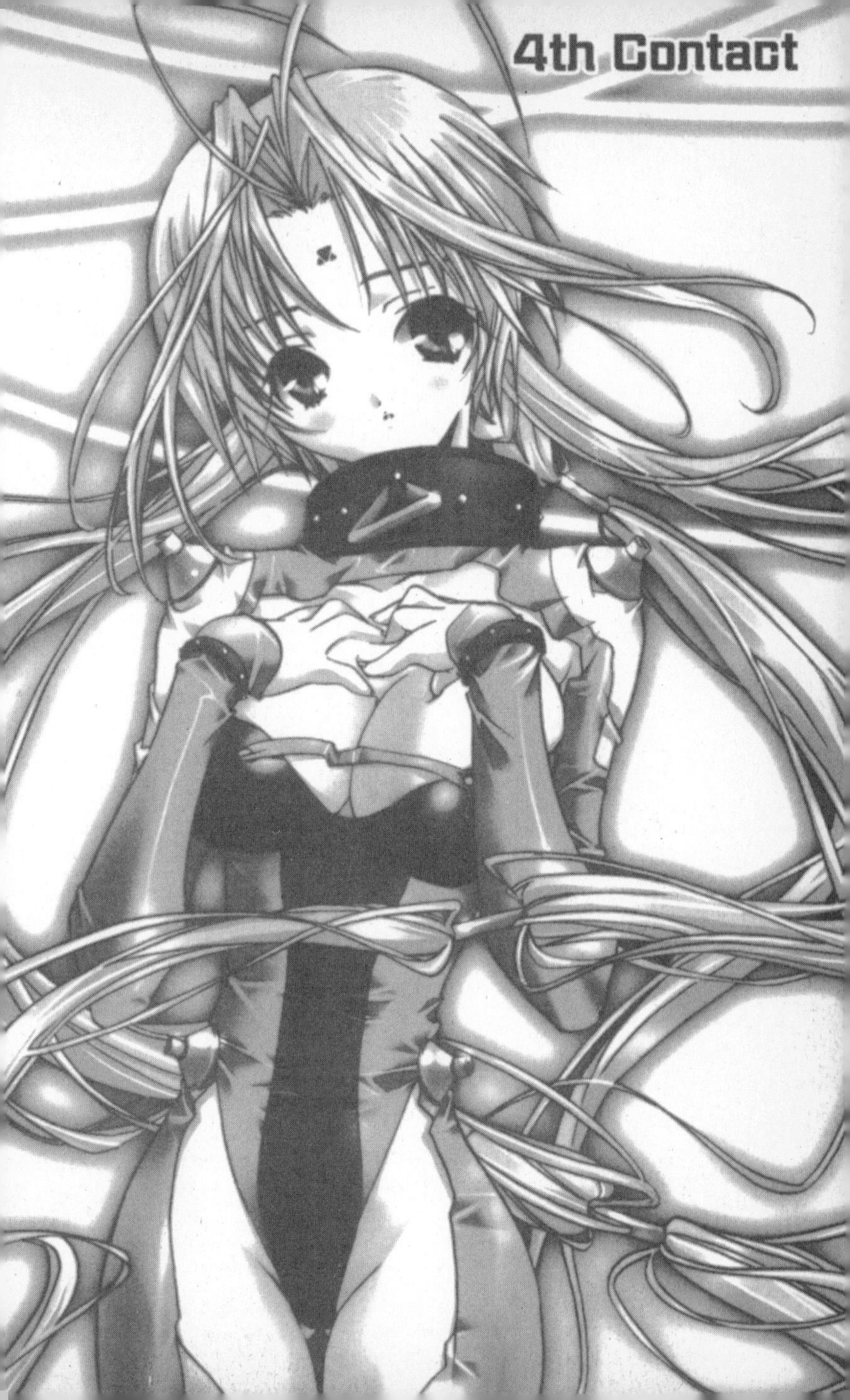

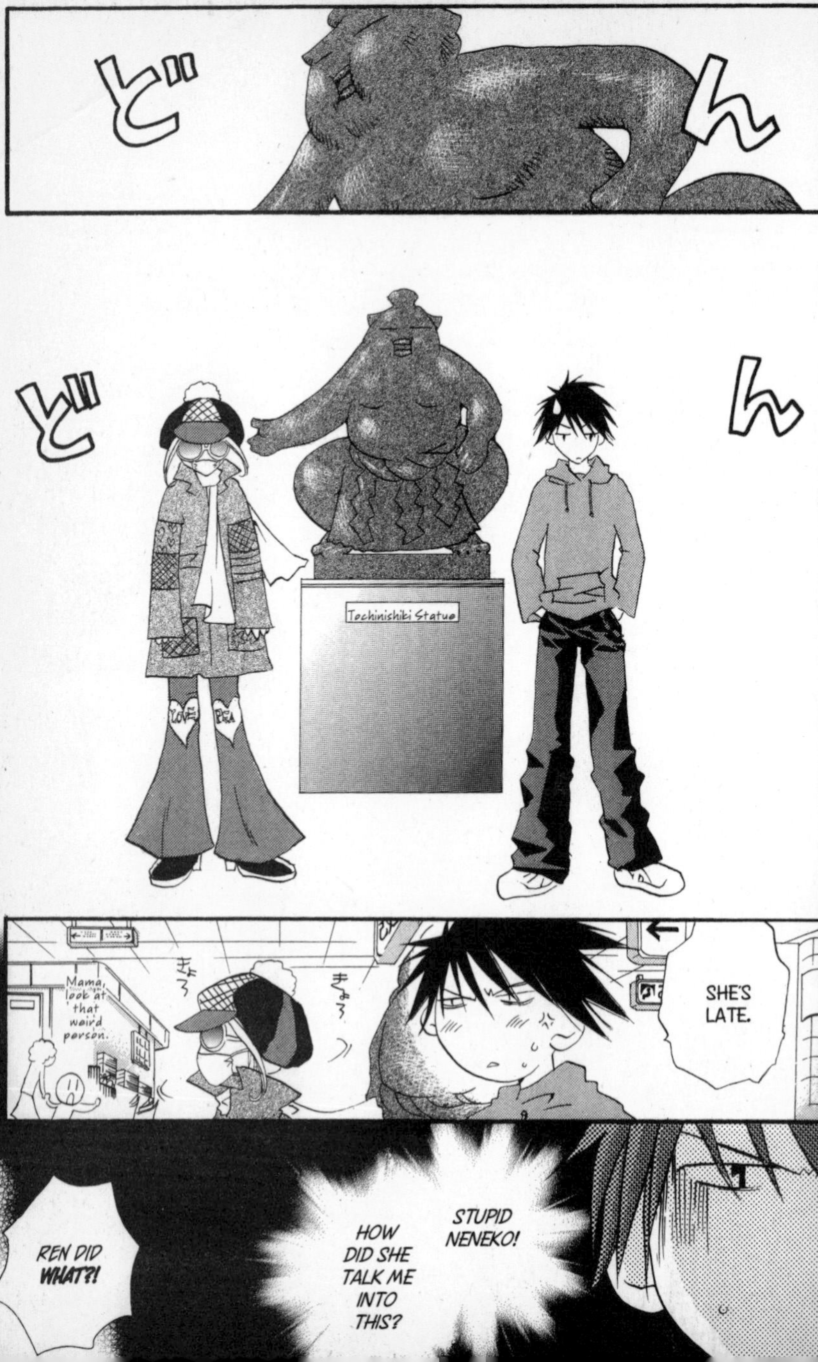
どん
どん
Tochinishiki Statue
SHE'S LATE.
きょろ
きょろ
Mama, look at that weird person.
STUPID NENEKO!
HOW DID SHE TALK ME INTO THIS?
REN DID WHAT?!

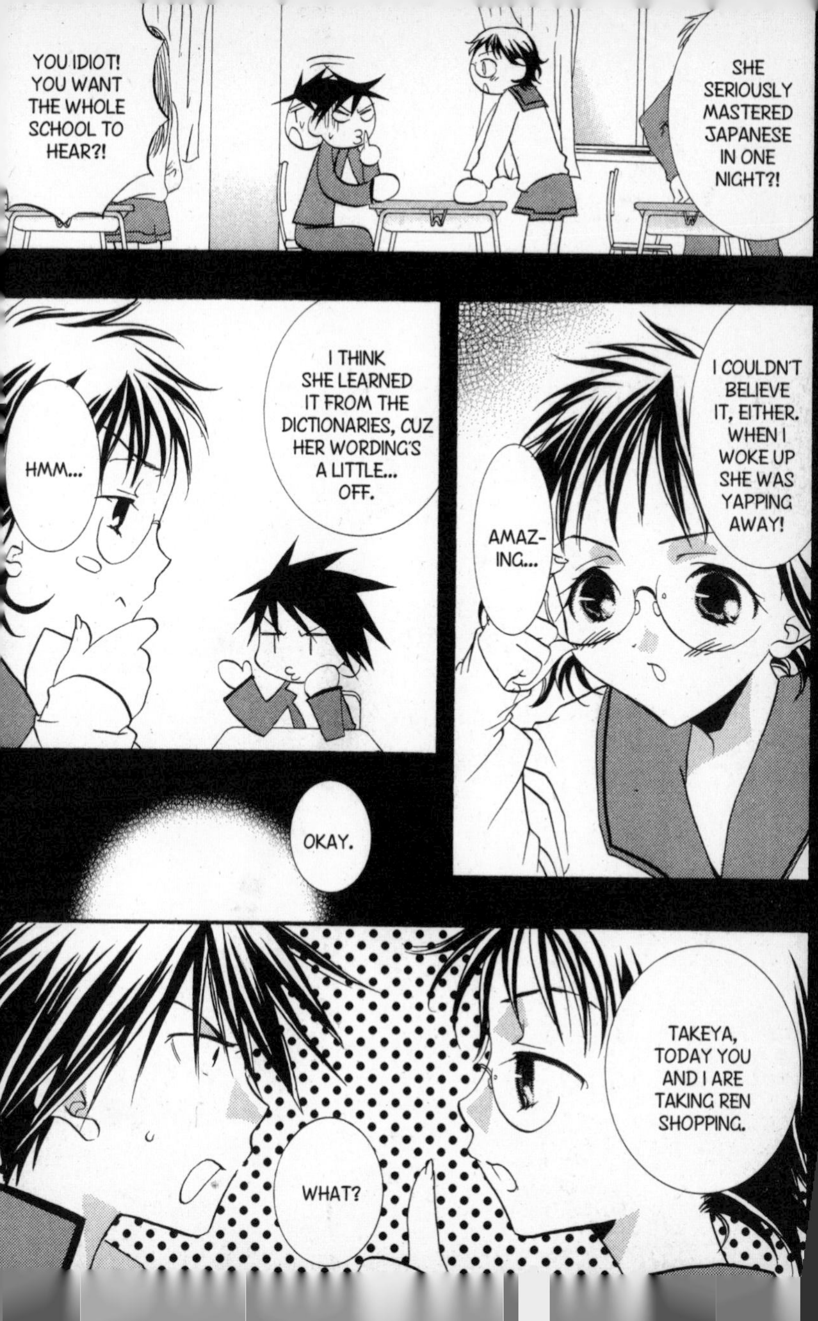
SHE SERIOUSLY MASTERED JAPANESE IN ONE NIGHT?!
YOU IDIOT! YOU WANT THE WHOLE SCHOOL TO HEAR?!
I COULDN'T BELIEVE IT, EITHER. WHEN I WOKE UP SHE WAS YAPPING AWAY!
AMAZ-ING...
I THINK SHE LEARNED IT FROM THE DICTIONARIES, CUZ HER WORDING'S A LITTLE... OFF.
HMM...
OKAY.
TAKEYA, TODAY YOU AND I ARE TAKING REN SHOPPING.
WHAT?

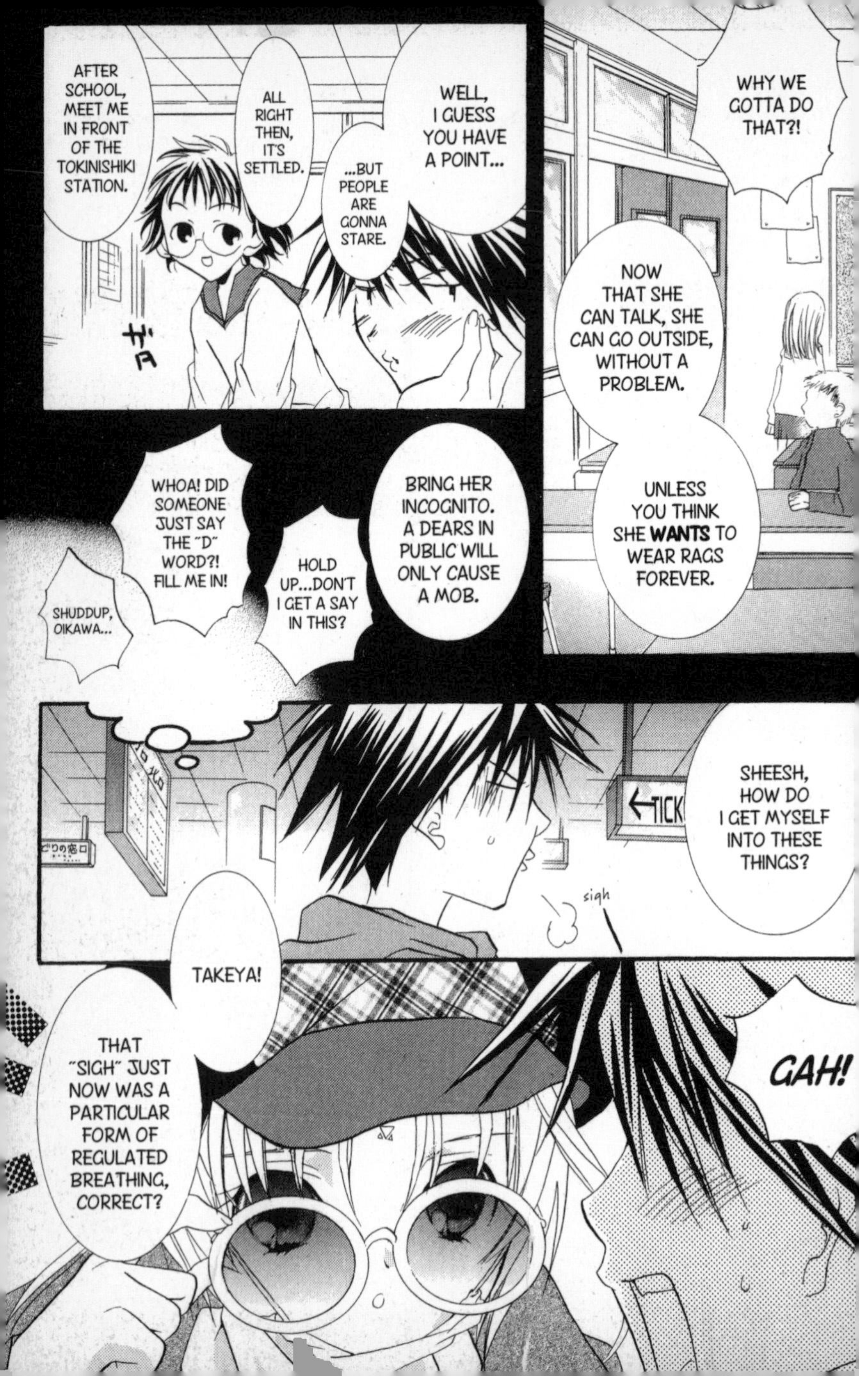
WHY WE GOTTA DO THAT?!
NOW THAT SHE CAN TALK, SHE CAN GO OUTSIDE, WITHOUT A PROBLEM.
UNLESS YOU THINK SHE **WANTS** TO WEAR RAGS FOREVER.
WELL, I GUESS YOU HAVE A POINT...
...BUT PEOPLE ARE GONNA STARE.
ALL RIGHT THEN, IT'S SETTLED.
AFTER SCHOOL, MEET ME IN FRONT OF THE TOKINISHIKI STATION.
ガタ
BRING HER INCOGNITO. A DEARS IN PUBLIC WILL ONLY CAUSE A MOB.
HOLD UP...DON'T I GET A SAY IN THIS?
WHOA! DID SOMEONE JUST SAY THE "D" WORD?! FILL ME IN!
SHUDDUP, OIKAWA...
SHEESH, HOW DO I GET MYSELF INTO THESE THINGS?
←TICK
sigh
TAKEYA!
GAH!
THAT "SIGH" JUST NOW WAS A PARTICULAR FORM OF REGULATED BREATHING, CORRECT?

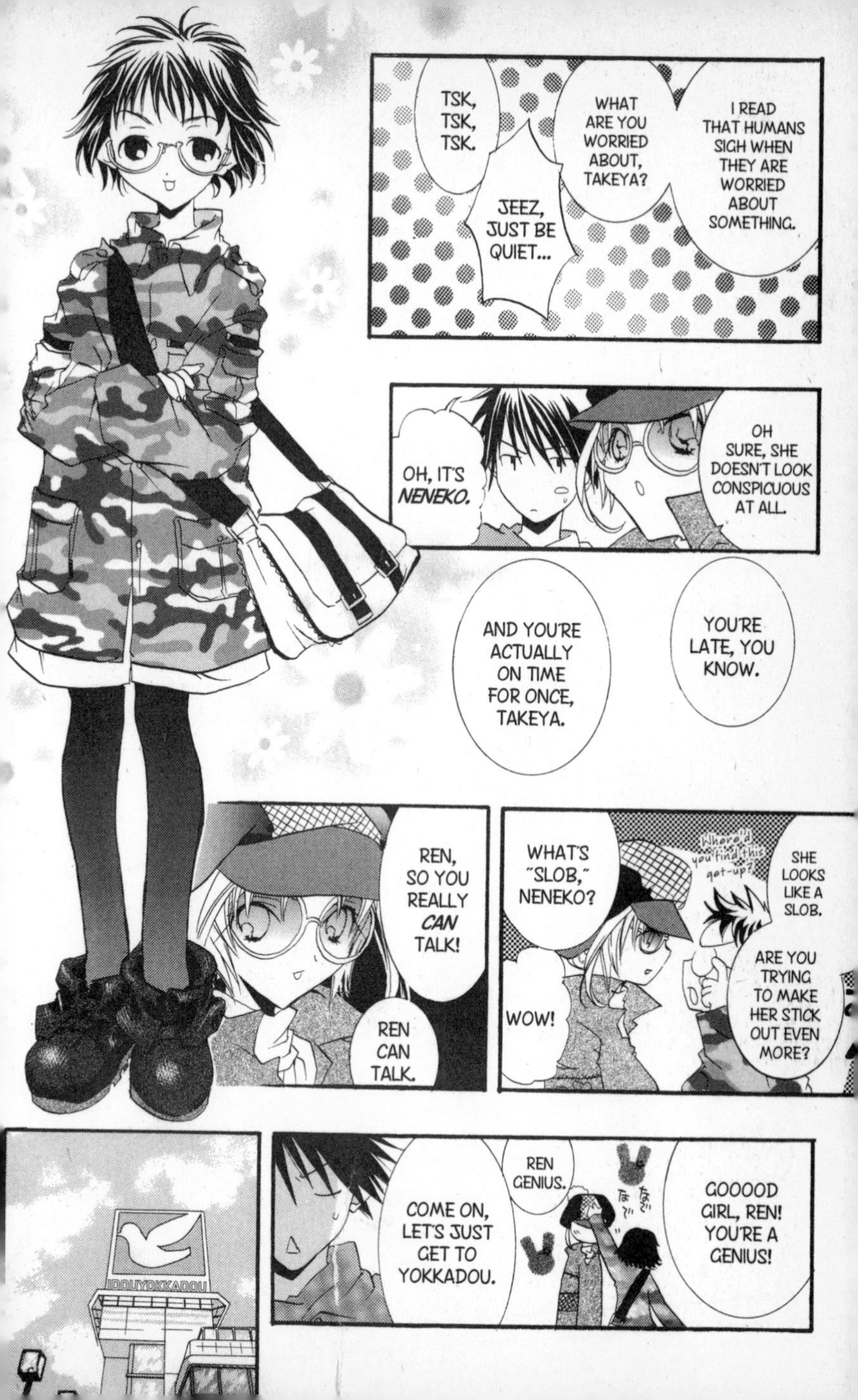
I READ THAT HUMANS SIGH WHEN THEY ARE WORRIED ABOUT SOMETHING.
WHAT ARE YOU WORRIED ABOUT, TAKEYA?
JEEZ, JUST BE QUIET...
TSK, TSK, TSK.
OH SURE, SHE DOESN'T LOOK CONSPICUOUS AT ALL.
OH, IT'S *NENEKO.*
YOU'RE LATE, YOU KNOW.
AND YOU'RE ACTUALLY ON TIME FOR ONCE, TAKEYA.
SHE LOOKS LIKE A SLOB.
Where'd you find this get-up?
ARE YOU TRYING TO MAKE HER STICK OUT EVEN MORE?
WHAT'S "SLOB," NENEKO?
WOW!
REN, SO YOU REALLY *CAN* TALK!
REN CAN TALK.
GOOOOD GIRL, REN! YOU'RE A GENIUS!
REN GENIUS.
COME ON, LET'S JUST GET TO YOKKADOU.
IDOUYOKKADOU

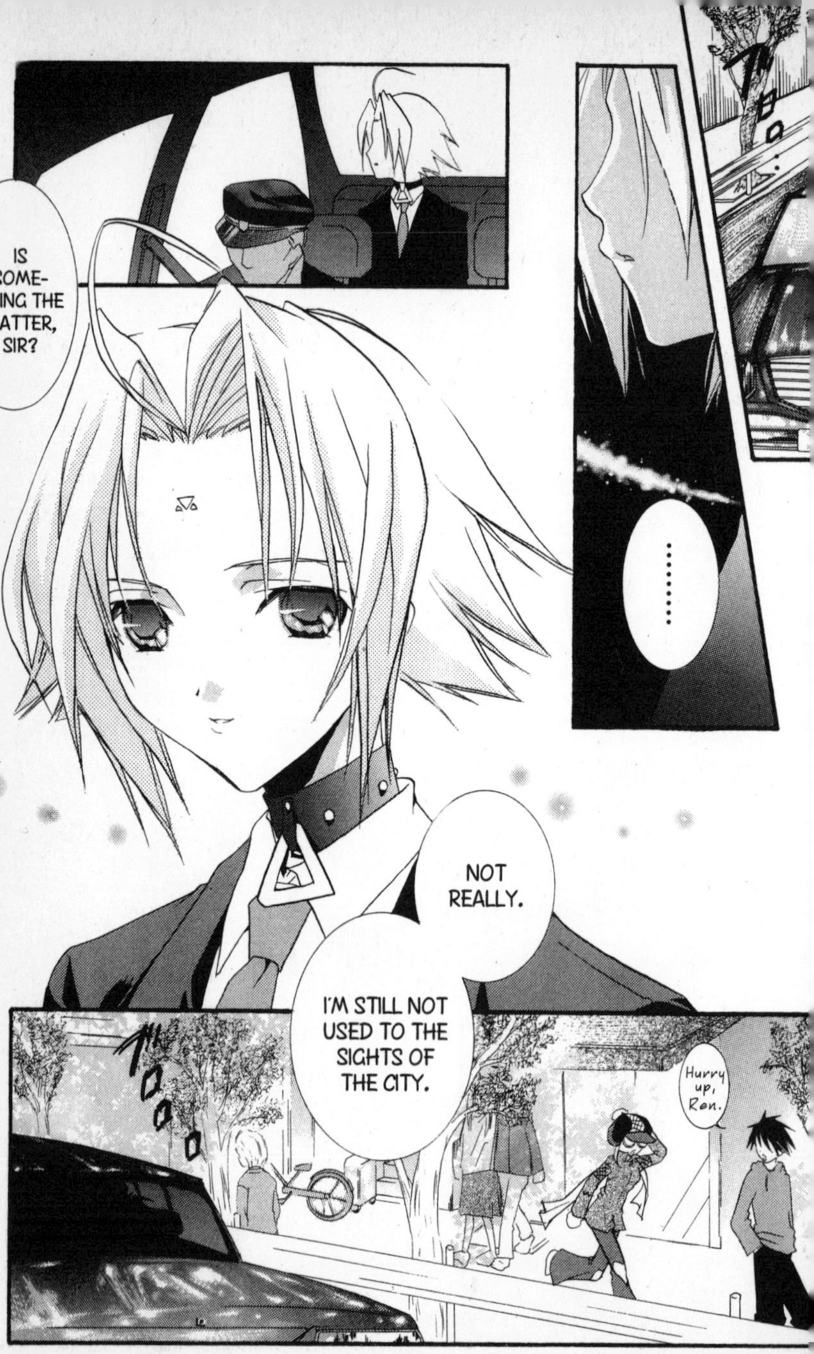
......
IS SOMETHING THE MATTER, SIR?
NOT REALLY.
I'M STILL NOT USED TO THE SIGHTS OF THE CITY.
Hurry up, Ren.

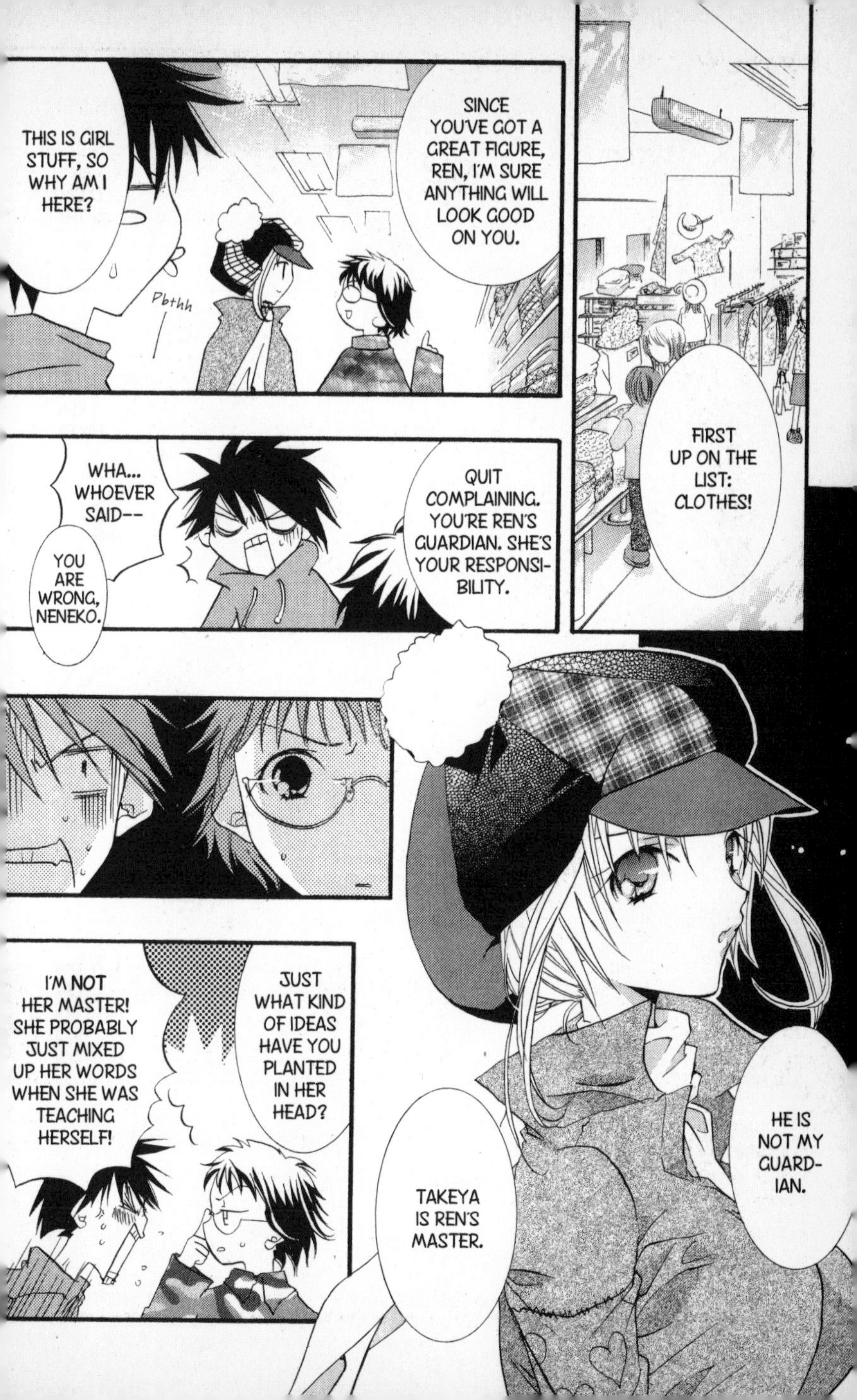
FIRST UP ON THE LIST: CLOTHES!
SINCE YOU'VE GOT A GREAT FIGURE, REN, I'M SURE ANYTHING WILL LOOK GOOD ON YOU.
THIS IS GIRL STUFF, SO WHY AM I HERE?
Pbthh
QUIT COMPLAINING. YOU'RE REN'S GUARDIAN. SHE'S YOUR RESPONSI-BILITY.
WHA... WHOEVER SAID--
YOU ARE WRONG, NENEKO.
HE IS NOT MY GUARD-IAN.
TAKEYA IS REN'S MASTER.
JUST WHAT KIND OF IDEAS HAVE YOU PLANTED IN HER HEAD?
I'M **NOT** HER MASTER! SHE PROBABLY JUST MIXED UP HER WORDS WHEN SHE WAS TEACHING HERSELF!

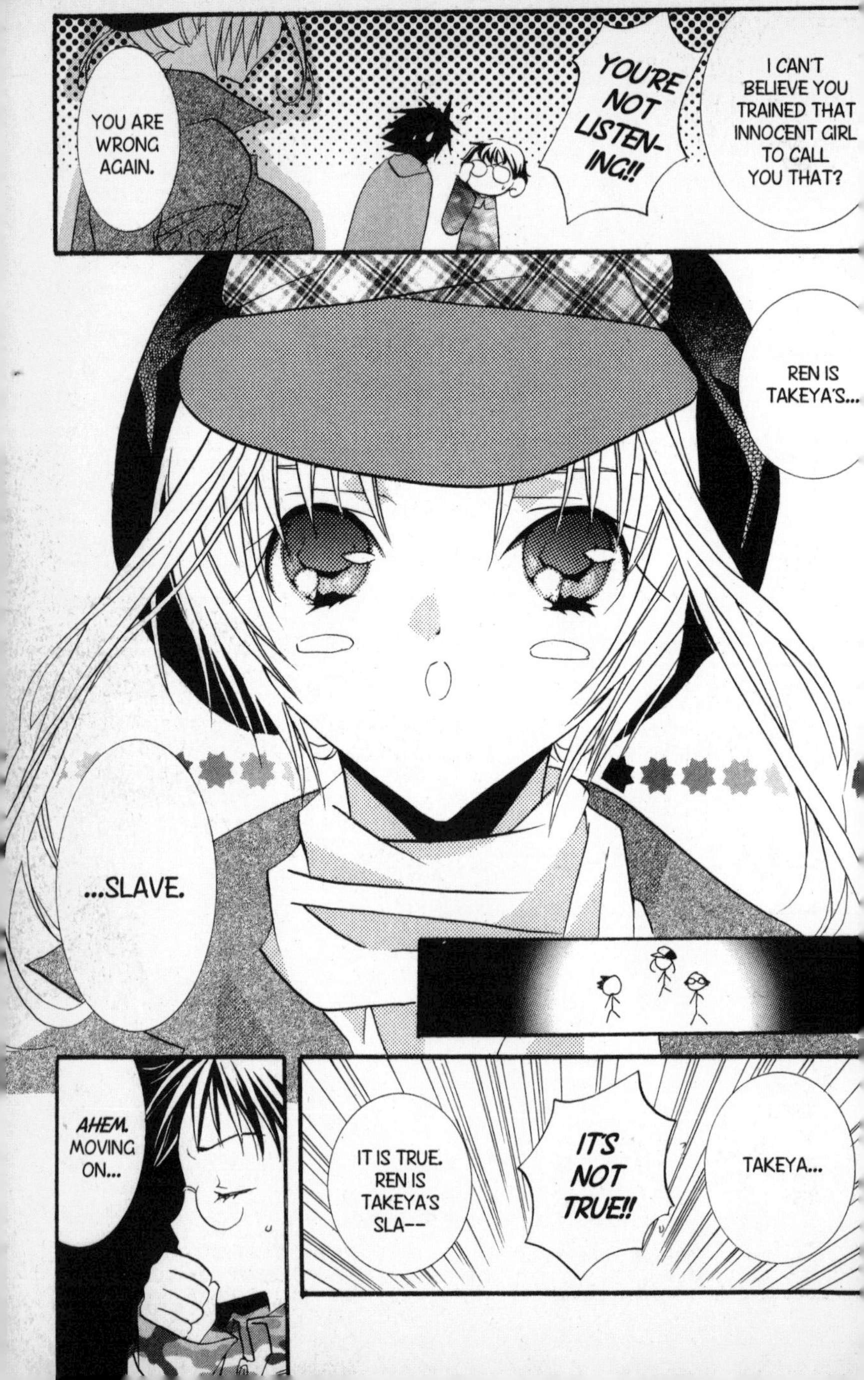
I CAN'T BELIEVE YOU TRAINED THAT INNOCENT GIRL TO CALL YOU THAT?
YOU'RE NOT LISTEN-ING!!
YOU ARE WRONG AGAIN.
REN IS TAKEYA'S...
...SLAVE.
TAKEYA...
IT'S NOT TRUE!!
IT IS TRUE. REN IS TAKEYA'S SLA--
AHEM. MOVING ON...

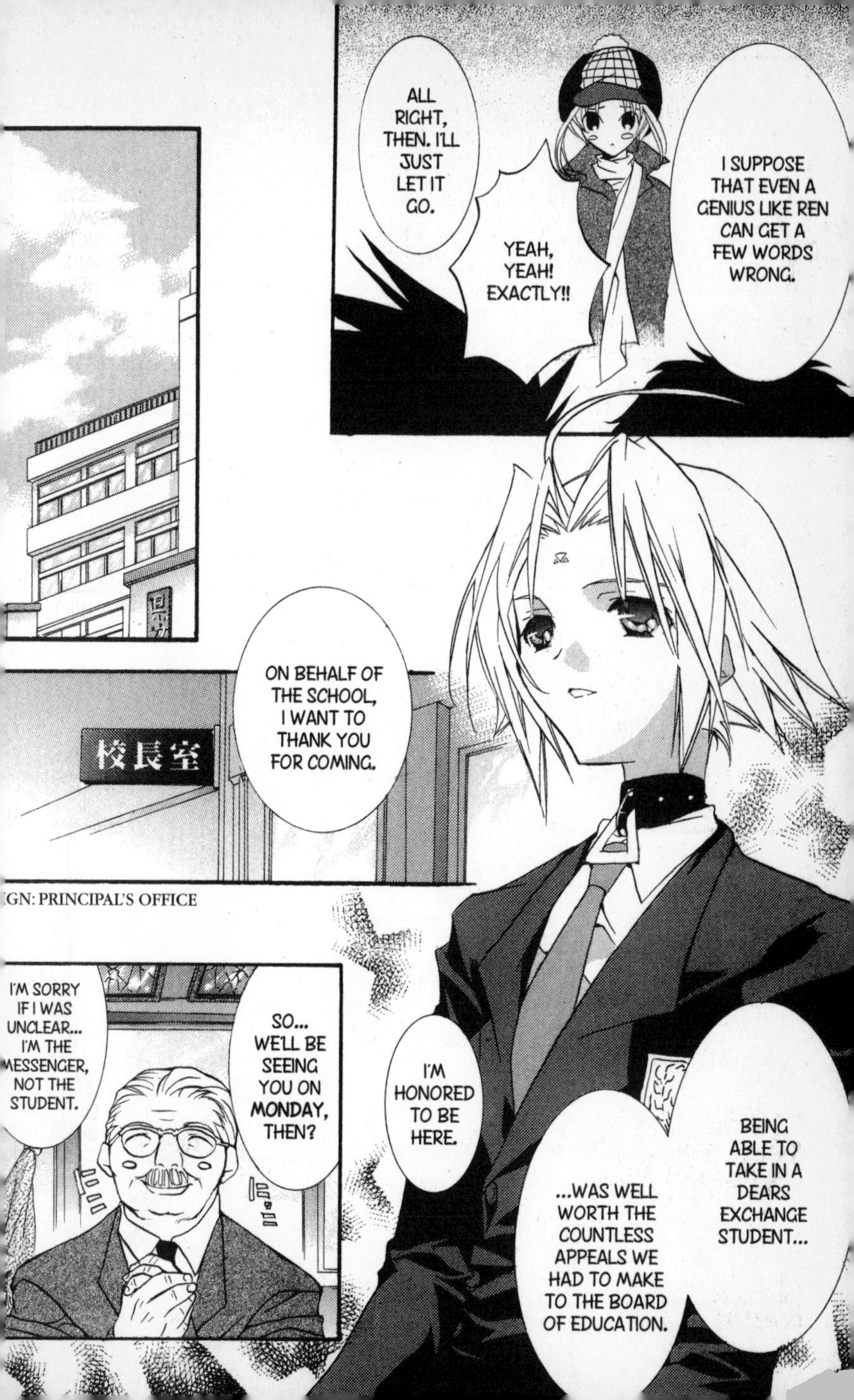
I SUPPOSE THAT EVEN A GENIUS LIKE REN CAN GET A FEW WORDS WRONG.
YEAH, YEAH! EXACTLY!!
ALL RIGHT, THEN. I'LL JUST LET IT GO.
校長室
ON BEHALF OF THE SCHOOL, I WANT TO THANK YOU FOR COMING.
BEING ABLE TO TAKE IN A DEARS EXCHANGE STUDENT...
...WAS WELL WORTH THE COUNTLESS APPEALS WE HAD TO MAKE TO THE BOARD OF EDUCATION.
I'M HONORED TO BE HERE.
SO... WE'LL BE SEEING YOU ON MONDAY, THEN?
I'M SORRY IF I WAS UNCLEAR... I'M THE MESSENGER, NOT THE STUDENT.
IGN: PRINCIPAL'S OFFICE

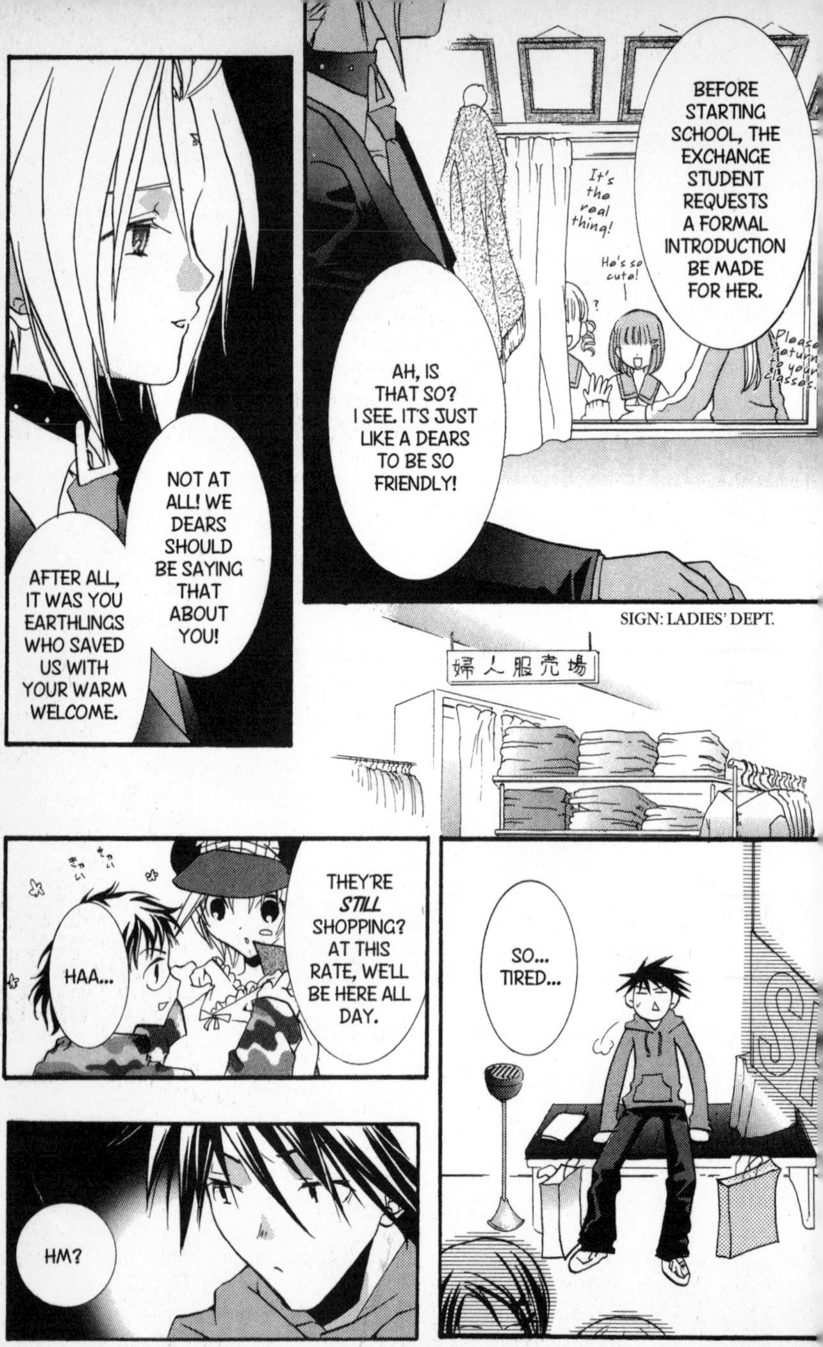
BEFORE STARTING SCHOOL, THE EXCHANGE STUDENT REQUESTS A FORMAL INTRODUCTION BE MADE FOR HER.
It's the real thing!
He's so cute!
?
Please return to your classes.
AH, IS THAT SO? I SEE. IT'S JUST LIKE A DEARS TO BE SO FRIENDLY!
NOT AT ALL! WE DEARS SHOULD BE SAYING THAT ABOUT YOU!
AFTER ALL, IT WAS YOU EARTHLINGS WHO SAVED US WITH YOUR WARM WELCOME.
SIGN: LADIES' DEPT.
婦人服売場
SO... TIRED...
きゃい きゃい
THEY'RE *STILL* SHOPPING? AT THIS RATE, WE'LL BE HERE ALL DAY.
HAA...
HM?

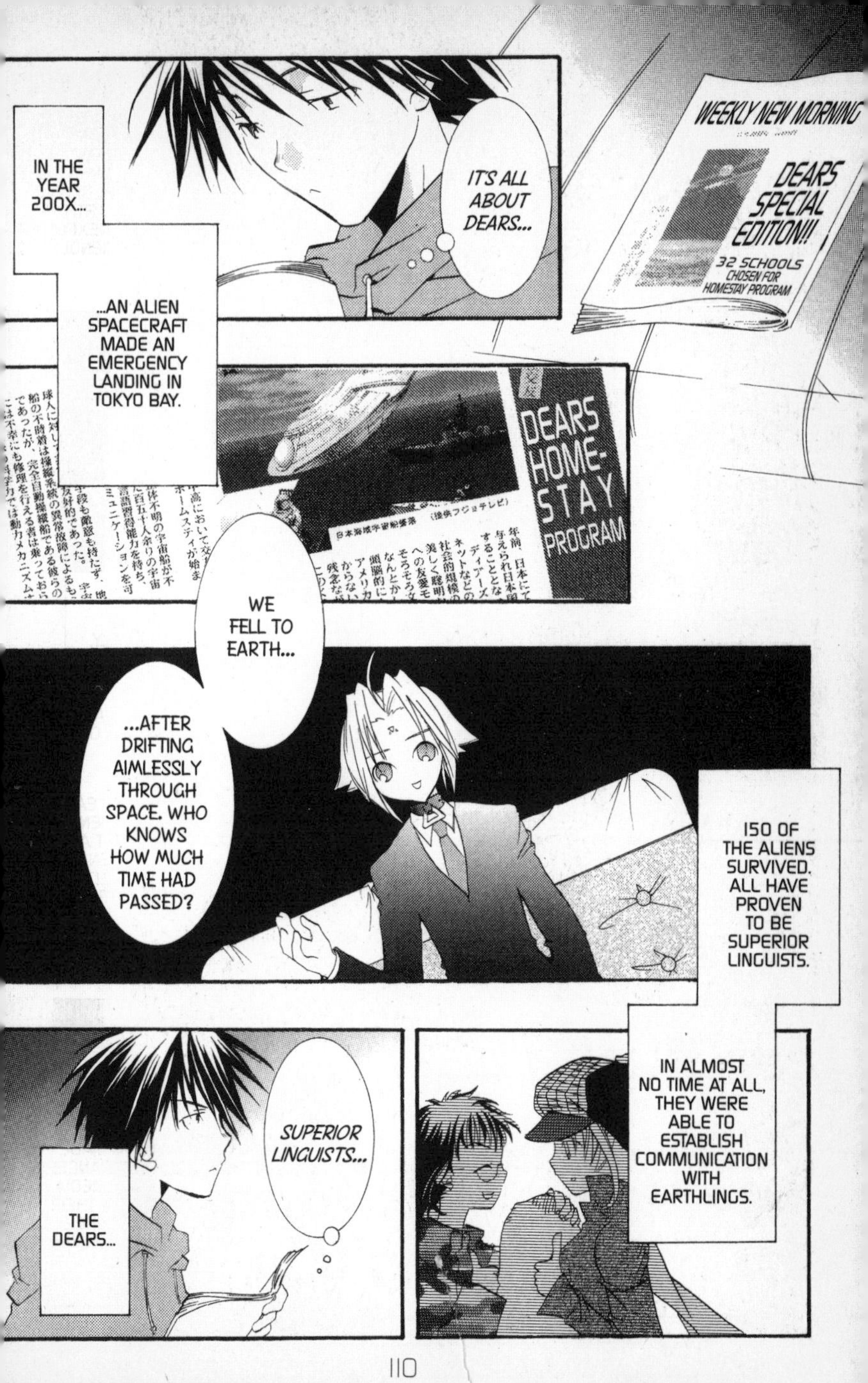
WEEKLY NEW MORNING
DEARS SPECIAL EDITION!!
32 SCHOOLS CHOSEN FOR HOMESTAY PROGRAM
IT'S ALL ABOUT DEARS...
IN THE YEAR 200X...
...AN ALIEN SPACECRAFT MADE AN EMERGENCY LANDING IN TOKYO BAY.
DEARS HOME-STAY PROGRAM
WE FELL TO EARTH...
...AFTER DRIFTING AIMLESSLY THROUGH SPACE. WHO KNOWS HOW MUCH TIME HAD PASSED?
150 OF THE ALIENS SURVIVED. ALL HAVE PROVEN TO BE SUPERIOR LINGUISTS.
IN ALMOST NO TIME AT ALL, THEY WERE ABLE TO ESTABLISH COMMUNICATION WITH EARTHLINGS.
SUPERIOR LINGUISTS...
THE DEARS...

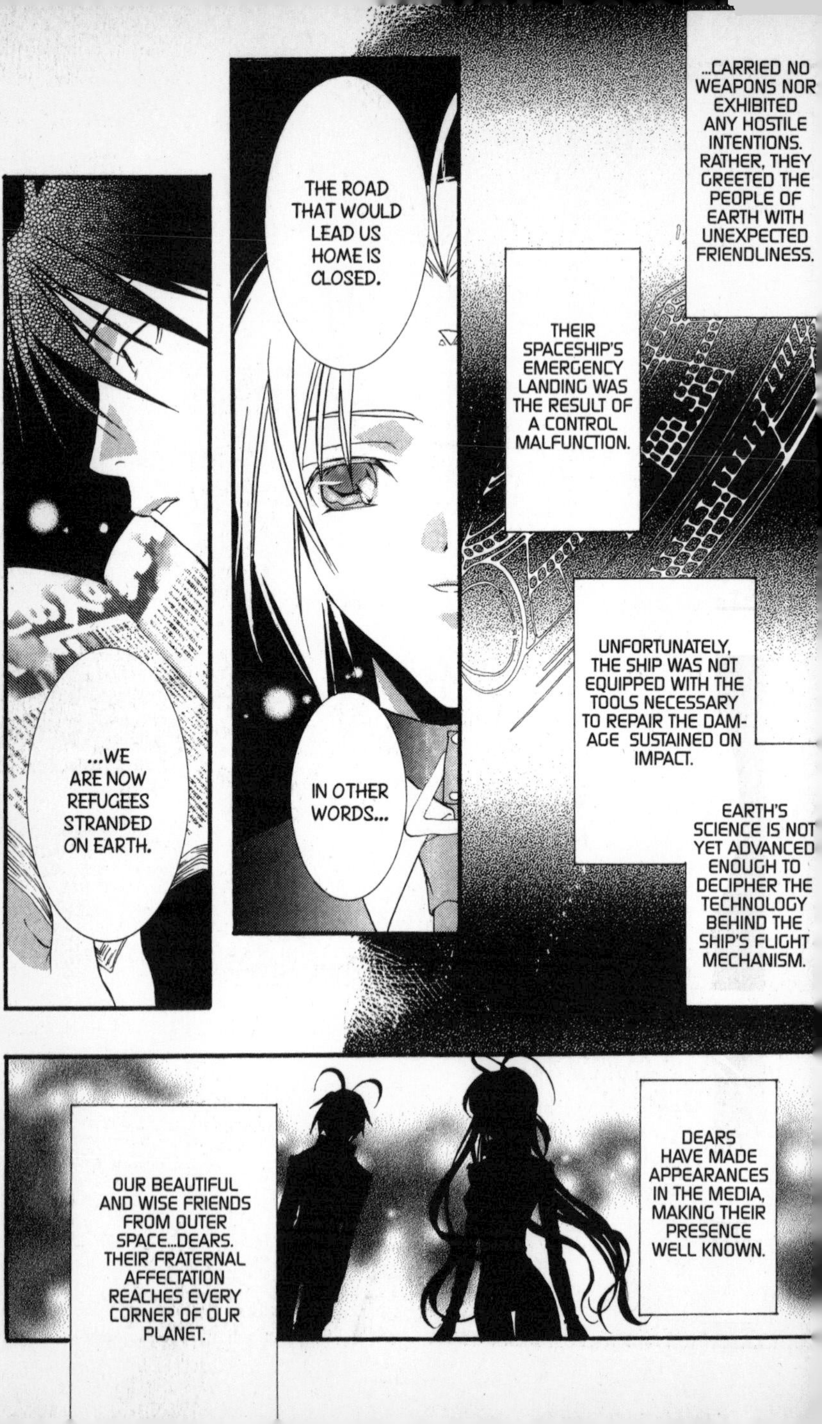
...CARRIED NO WEAPONS NOR EXHIBITED ANY HOSTILE INTENTIONS. RATHER, THEY GREETED THE PEOPLE OF EARTH WITH UNEXPECTED FRIENDLINESS.
THEIR SPACESHIP'S EMERGENCY LANDING WAS THE RESULT OF A CONTROL MALFUNCTION.
UNFORTUNATELY, THE SHIP WAS NOT EQUIPPED WITH THE TOOLS NECESSARY TO REPAIR THE DAM-AGE SUSTAINED ON IMPACT.
EARTH'S SCIENCE IS NOT YET ADVANCED ENOUGH TO DECIPHER THE TECHNOLOGY BEHIND THE SHIP'S FLIGHT MECHANISM.
THE ROAD THAT WOULD LEAD US HOME IS CLOSED.
IN OTHER WORDS...
...WE ARE NOW REFUGEES STRANDED ON EARTH.
DEARS HAVE MADE APPEARANCES IN THE MEDIA, MAKING THEIR PRESENCE WELL KNOWN.
OUR BEAUTIFUL AND WISE FRIENDS FROM OUTER SPACE...DEARS. THEIR FRATERNAL AFFECTATION REACHES EVERY CORNER OF OUR PLANET.

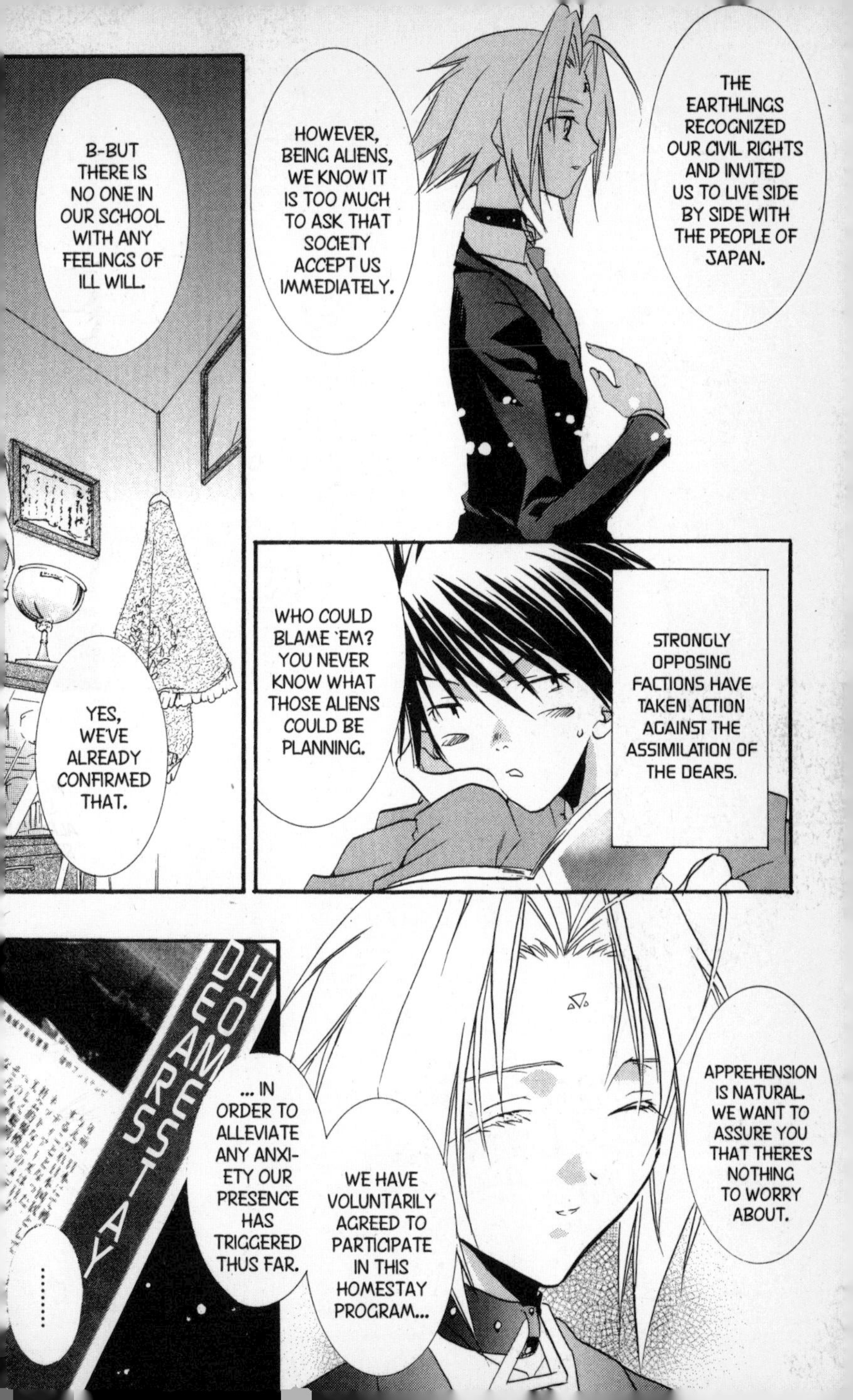
THE EARTHLINGS RECOGNIZED OUR CIVIL RIGHTS AND INVITED US TO LIVE SIDE BY SIDE WITH THE PEOPLE OF JAPAN.
HOWEVER, BEING ALIENS, WE KNOW IT IS TOO MUCH TO ASK THAT SOCIETY ACCEPT US IMMEDIATELY.
STRONGLY OPPOSING FACTIONS HAVE TAKEN ACTION AGAINST THE ASSIMILATION OF THE DEARS.
WHO COULD BLAME `EM? YOU NEVER KNOW WHAT THOSE ALIENS COULD BE PLANNING.
B-BUT THERE IS NO ONE IN OUR SCHOOL WITH ANY FEELINGS OF ILL WILL.
YES, WE'VE ALREADY CONFIRMED THAT.
APPREHENSION IS NATURAL. WE WANT TO ASSURE YOU THAT THERE'S NOTHING TO WORRY ABOUT.
WE HAVE VOLUNTARILY AGREED TO PARTICIPATE IN THIS HOMESTAY PROGRAM...
... IN ORDER TO ALLEVIATE ANY ANXI-ETY OUR PRESENCE HAS TRIGGERED THUS FAR.
HOMESTAY
......

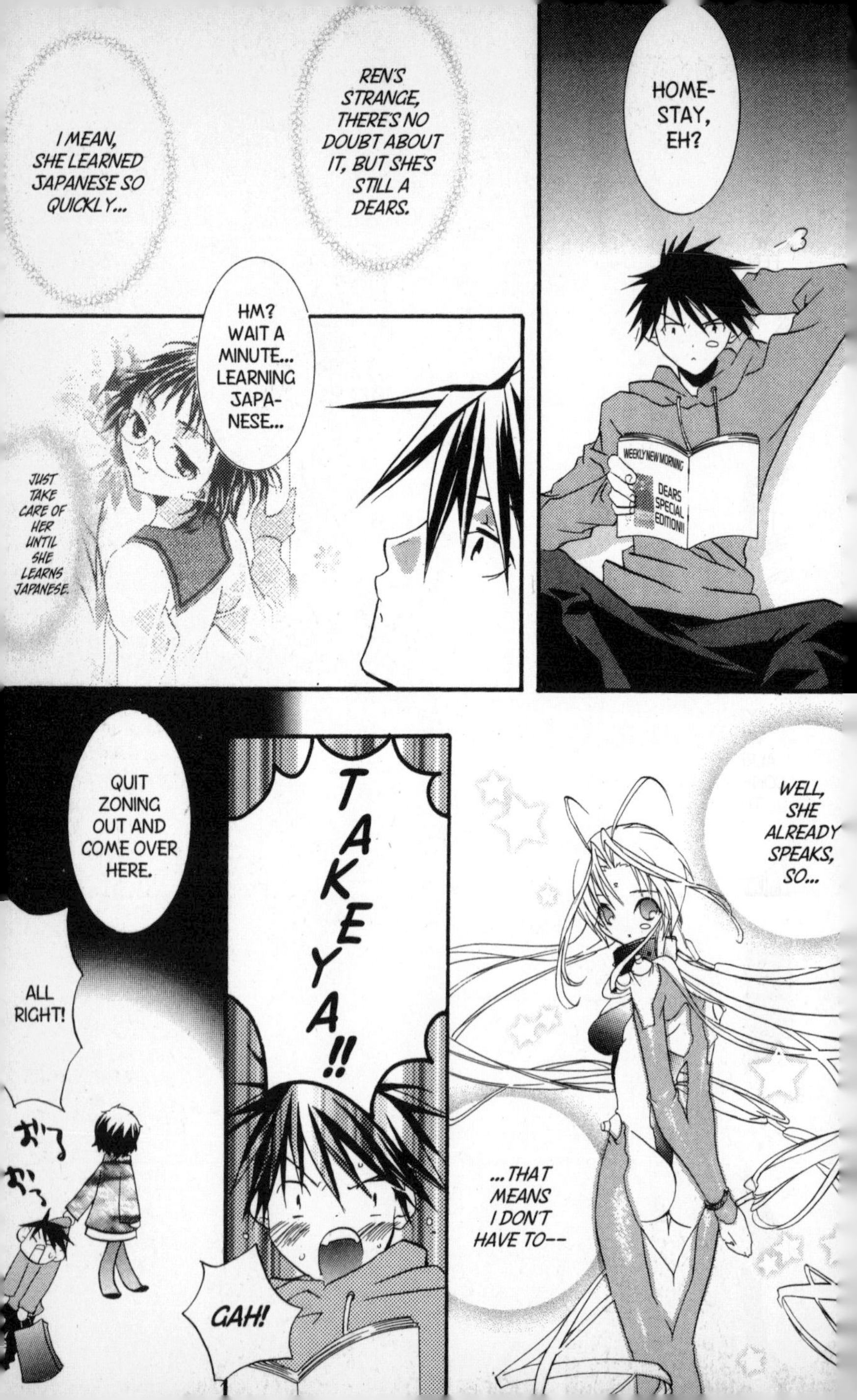
HOME-STAY, EH?
WEEKLY NEW MORNING
DEARS SPECIAL EDITION!!
REN'S STRANGE, THERE'S NO DOUBT ABOUT IT, BUT SHE'S STILL A DEARS.
I MEAN, SHE LEARNED JAPANESE SO QUICKLY...
HM? WAIT A MINUTE... LEARNING JAPA-NESE...
JUST TAKE CARE OF HER UNTIL SHE LEARNS JAPANESE.
WELL, SHE ALREADY SPEAKS, SO...
...THAT MEANS I DON'T HAVE TO--
TAKEYA!!
GAH!
QUIT ZONING OUT AND COME OVER HERE.
ALL RIGHT!

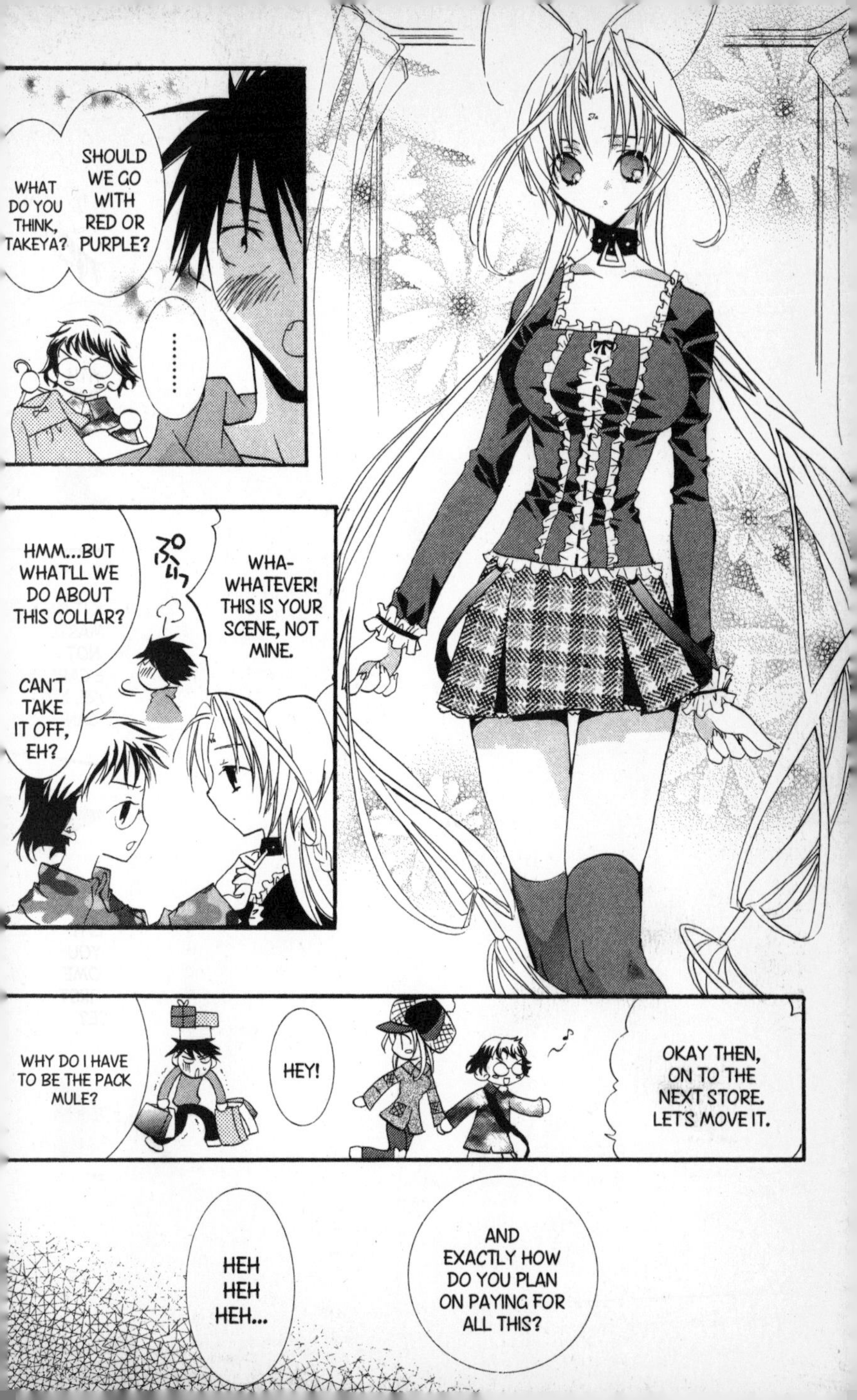
SHOULD WE GO WITH RED OR PURPLE?
WHAT DO YOU THINK, TAKEYA?
....
WHA-WHATEVER! THIS IS YOUR SCENE, NOT MINE.
ぷいっ
HMM...BUT WHAT'LL WE DO ABOUT THIS COLLAR?
CAN'T TAKE IT OFF, EH?
OKAY THEN, ON TO THE NEXT STORE. LET'S MOVE IT.
HEY!
WHY DO I HAVE TO BE THE PACK MULE?
AND EXACTLY HOW DO YOU PLAN ON PAYING FOR ALL THIS?
HEH HEH HEH...

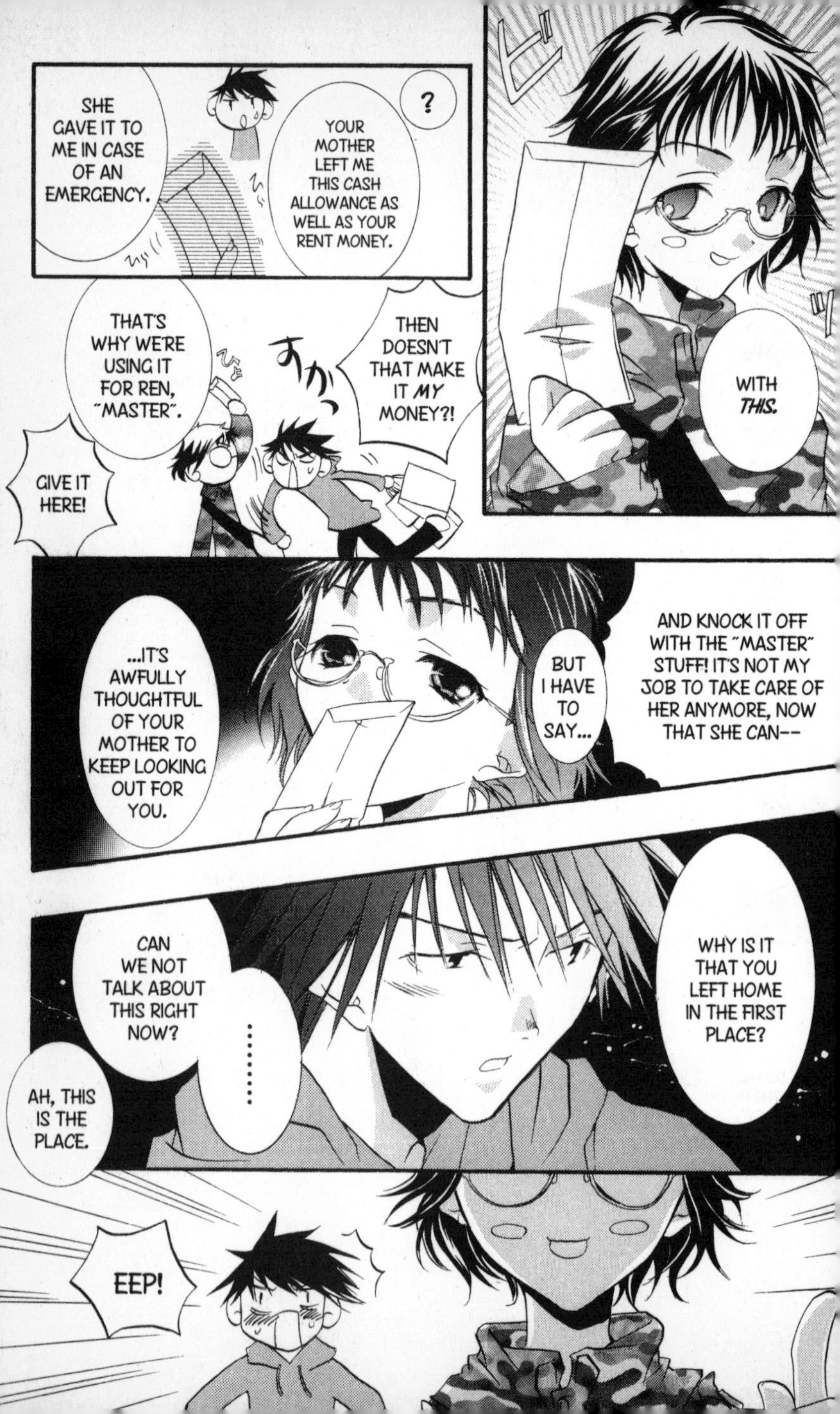

WITH THIS.
?
YOUR MOTHER LEFT ME THIS CASH ALLOWANCE AS WELL AS YOUR RENT MONEY.
SHE GAVE IT TO ME IN CASE OF AN EMERGENCY.
THEN DOESN'T THAT MAKE IT MY MONEY?!
THAT'S WHY WE'RE USING IT FOR REN, "MASTER".
GIVE IT HERE!
AND KNOCK IT OFF WITH THE "MASTER" STUFF! IT'S NOT MY JOB TO TAKE CARE OF HER ANYMORE, NOW THAT SHE CAN--
BUT I HAVE TO SAY...
...IT'S AWFULLY THOUGHTFUL OF YOUR MOTHER TO KEEP LOOKING OUT FOR YOU.
WHY IS IT THAT YOU LEFT HOME IN THE FIRST PLACE?
......
CAN WE NOT TALK ABOUT THIS RIGHT NOW?
AH, THIS IS THE PLACE.
EEP!

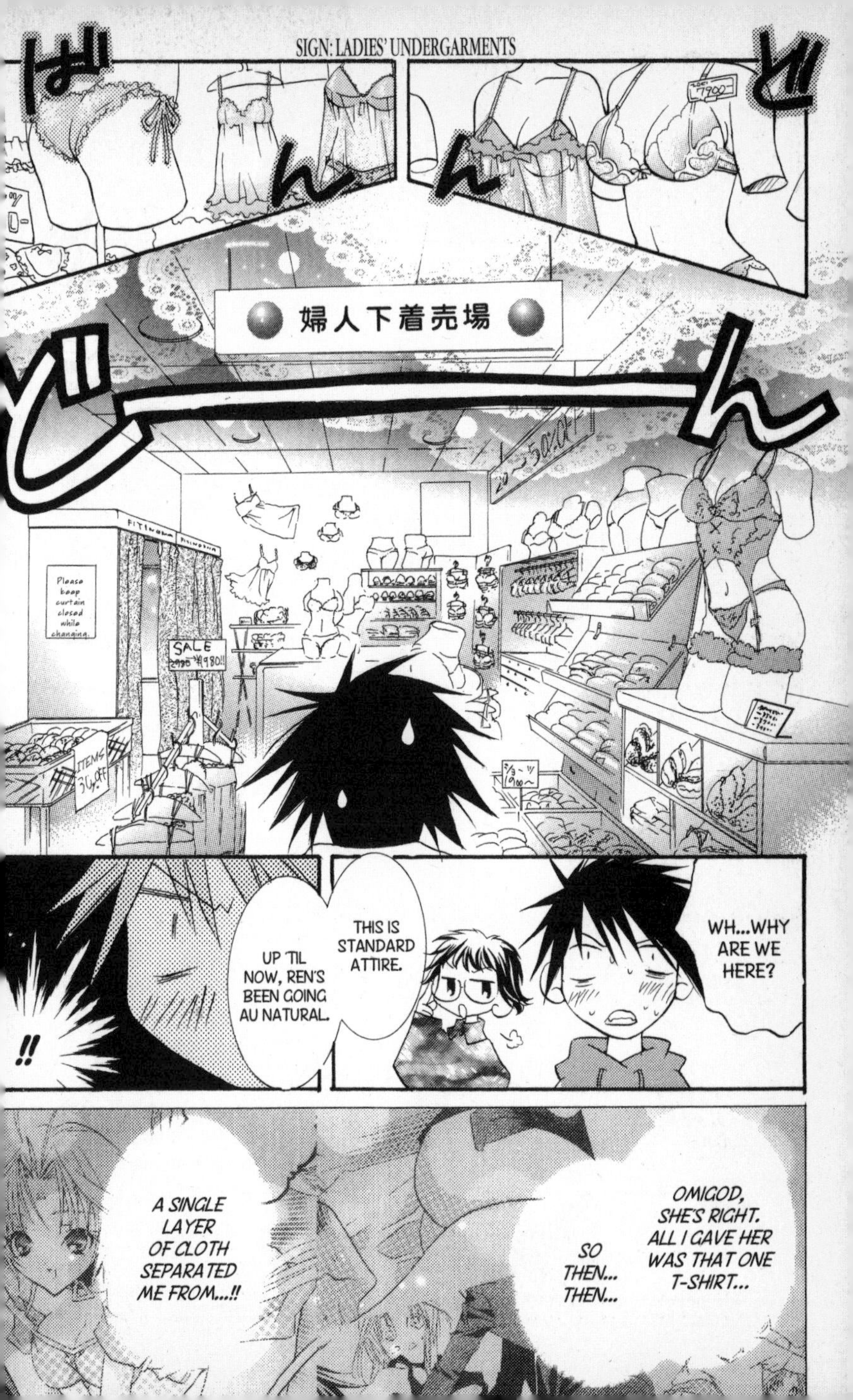

SIGN: LADIES' UNDERGARMENTS
どん
ばん
婦人下着売場
どーん
Please keep curtain closed while changing.
SALE ¥980!!
ITEMS 30% OFF
WH...WHY ARE WE HERE?
THIS IS STANDARD ATTIRE.
UP 'TIL NOW, REN'S BEEN GOING AU NATURAL.
!!
OMIGOD, SHE'S RIGHT. ALL I GAVE HER WAS THAT ONE T-SHIRT...
SO THEN... THEN...
A SINGLE LAYER OF CLOTH SEPARATED ME FROM...!!

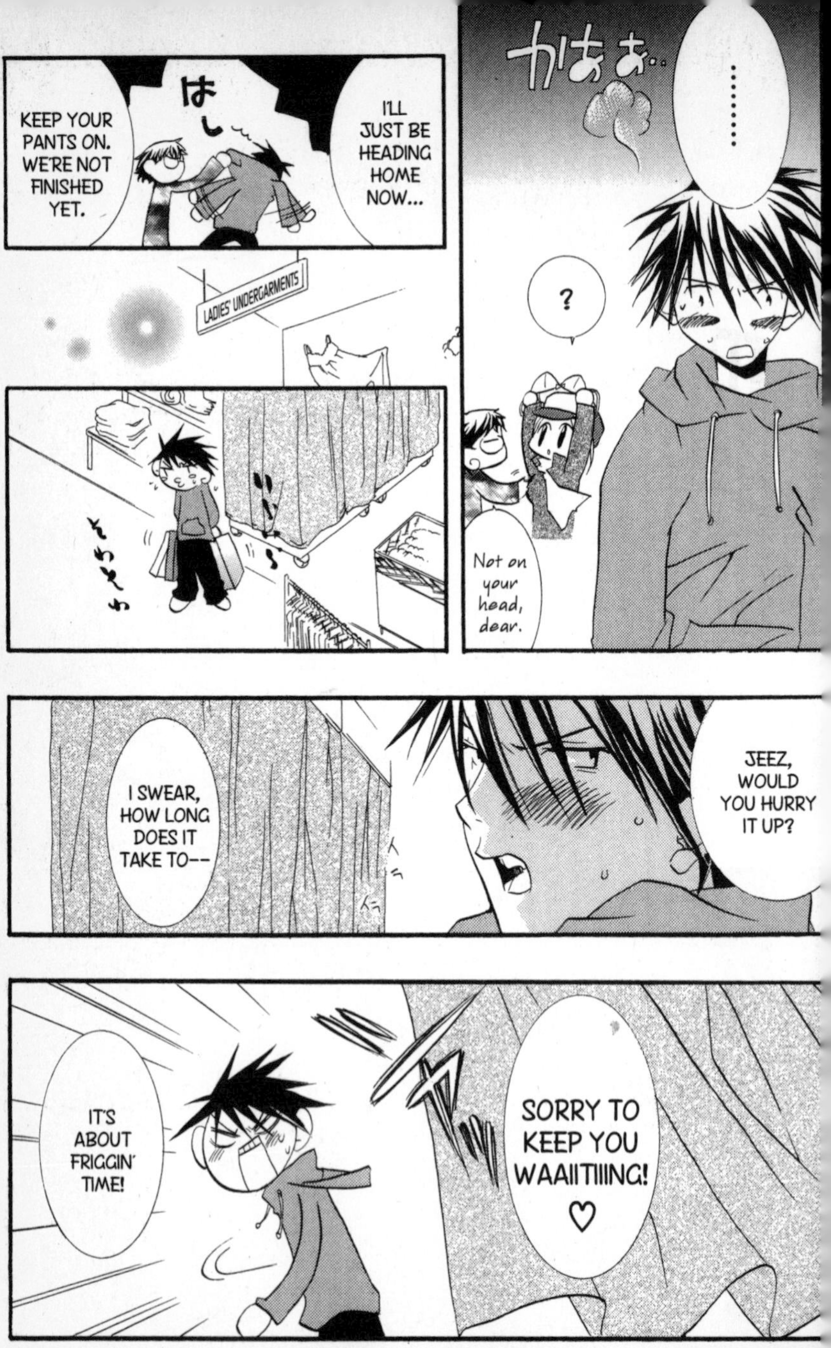
......
?
Not on your head, dear.
I'LL JUST BE HEADING HOME NOW...
はし
KEEP YOUR PANTS ON. WE'RE NOT FINISHED YET.
LADIES' UNDERGARMENTS
JEEZ, WOULD YOU HURRY IT UP?
I SWEAR, HOW LONG DOES IT TAKE TO--
SORRY TO KEEP YOU WAAIITIIING! ♡
IT'S ABOUT FRIGGIN' TIME!

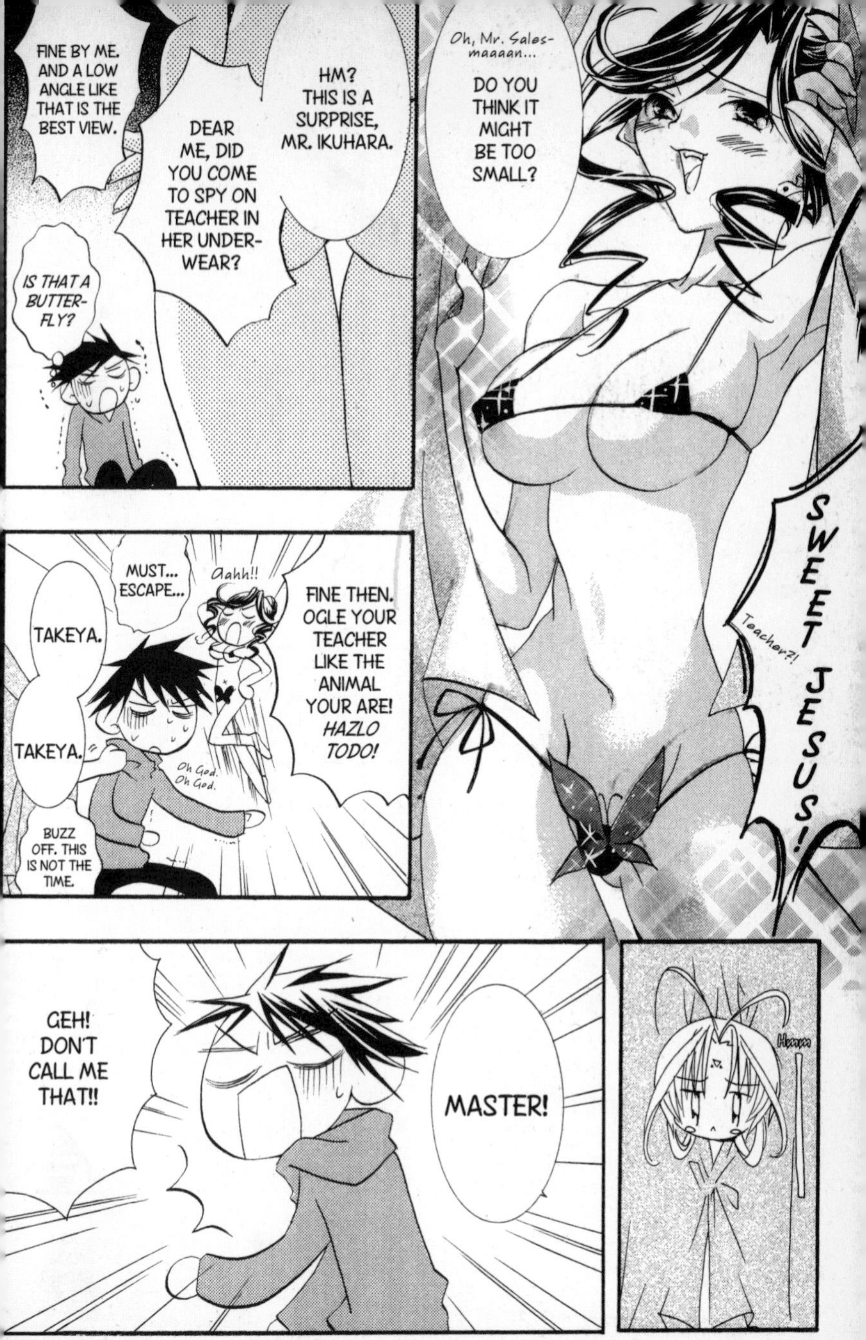

Oh, Mr. Sales-maaaan...
DO YOU THINK IT MIGHT BE TOO SMALL?
SWEET JESUS!!
Teacher?!
HM? THIS IS A SURPRISE, MR. IKUHARA.
DEAR ME, DID YOU COME TO SPY ON TEACHER IN HER UNDER-WEAR?
FINE BY ME. AND A LOW ANGLE LIKE THAT IS THE BEST VIEW.
IS THAT A BUTTER-FLY?
FINE THEN. OGLE YOUR TEACHER LIKE THE ANIMAL YOUR ARE! HAZLO TODO!
Aahh!!
MUST... ESCAPE...
TAKEYA.
TAKEYA.
Oh God. Oh God.
BUZZ OFF. THIS IS NOT THE TIME.
Hmm
MASTER!
GEH! DON'T CALL ME THAT!!

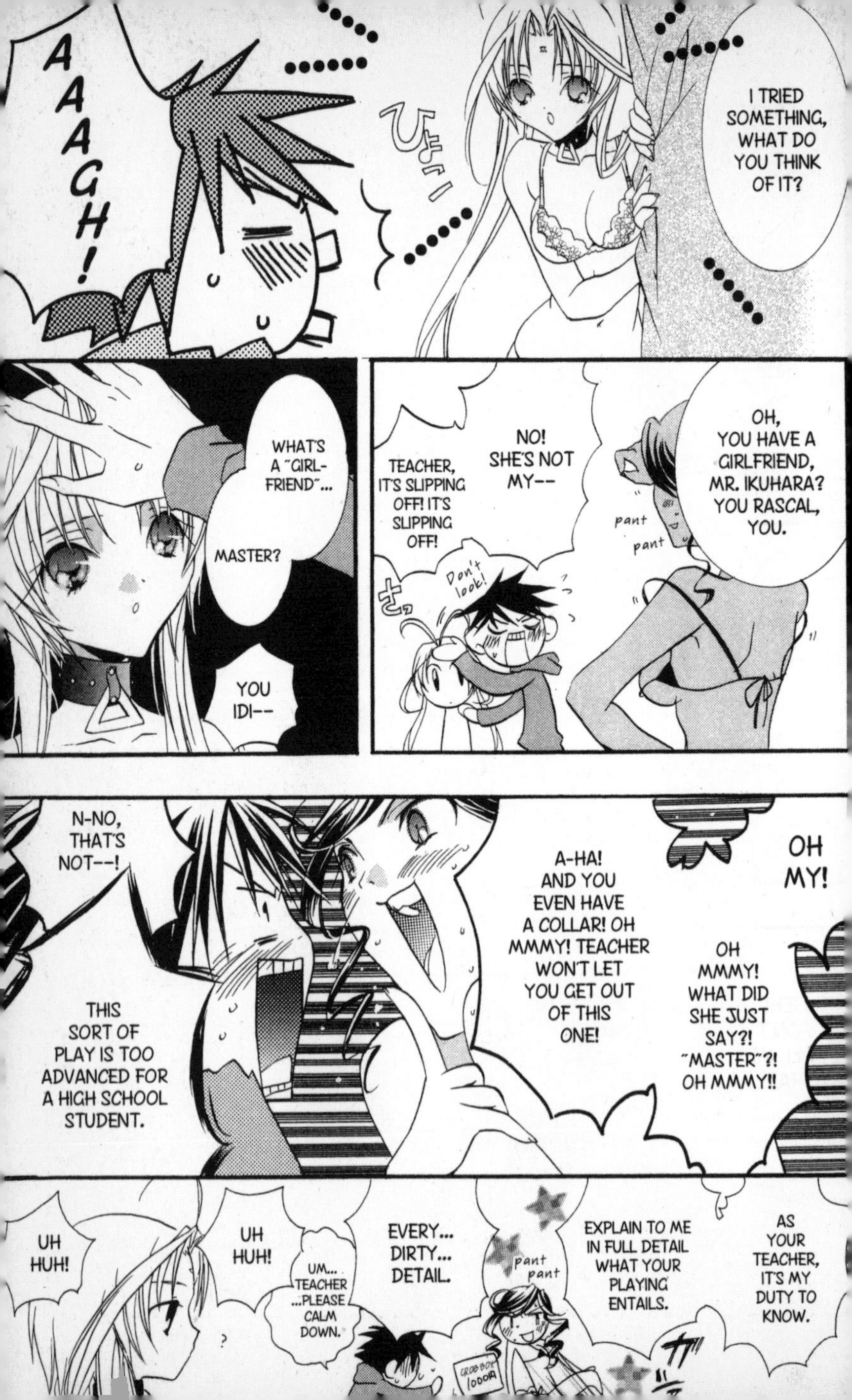

......
I TRIED SOMETHING, WHAT DO YOU THINK OF IT?
......
......
......
......
AAAGH!
OH, YOU HAVE A GIRLFRIEND, MR. IKUHARA? YOU RASCAL, YOU.
pant
pant
NO! SHE'S NOT MY--
TEACHER, IT'S SLIPPING OFF! IT'S SLIPPING OFF!
Don't look!
WHAT'S A "GIRL-FRIEND"...
MASTER?
YOU IDI--
OH MY!
A-HA! AND YOU EVEN HAVE A COLLAR! OH MMMY! TEACHER WON'T LET YOU GET OUT OF THIS ONE!
OH MMMY! WHAT DID SHE JUST SAY?! "MASTER"?! OH MMMY!!
N-NO, THAT'S NOT--!
THIS SORT OF PLAY IS TOO ADVANCED FOR A HIGH SCHOOL STUDENT.
AS YOUR TEACHER, IT'S MY DUTY TO KNOW.
EXPLAIN TO ME IN FULL DETAIL WHAT YOUR PLAYING ENTAILS.
pant pant
EVERY... DIRTY... DETAIL.
UM... TEACHER ...PLEASE CALM DOWN.
UH HUH!
UH HUH!

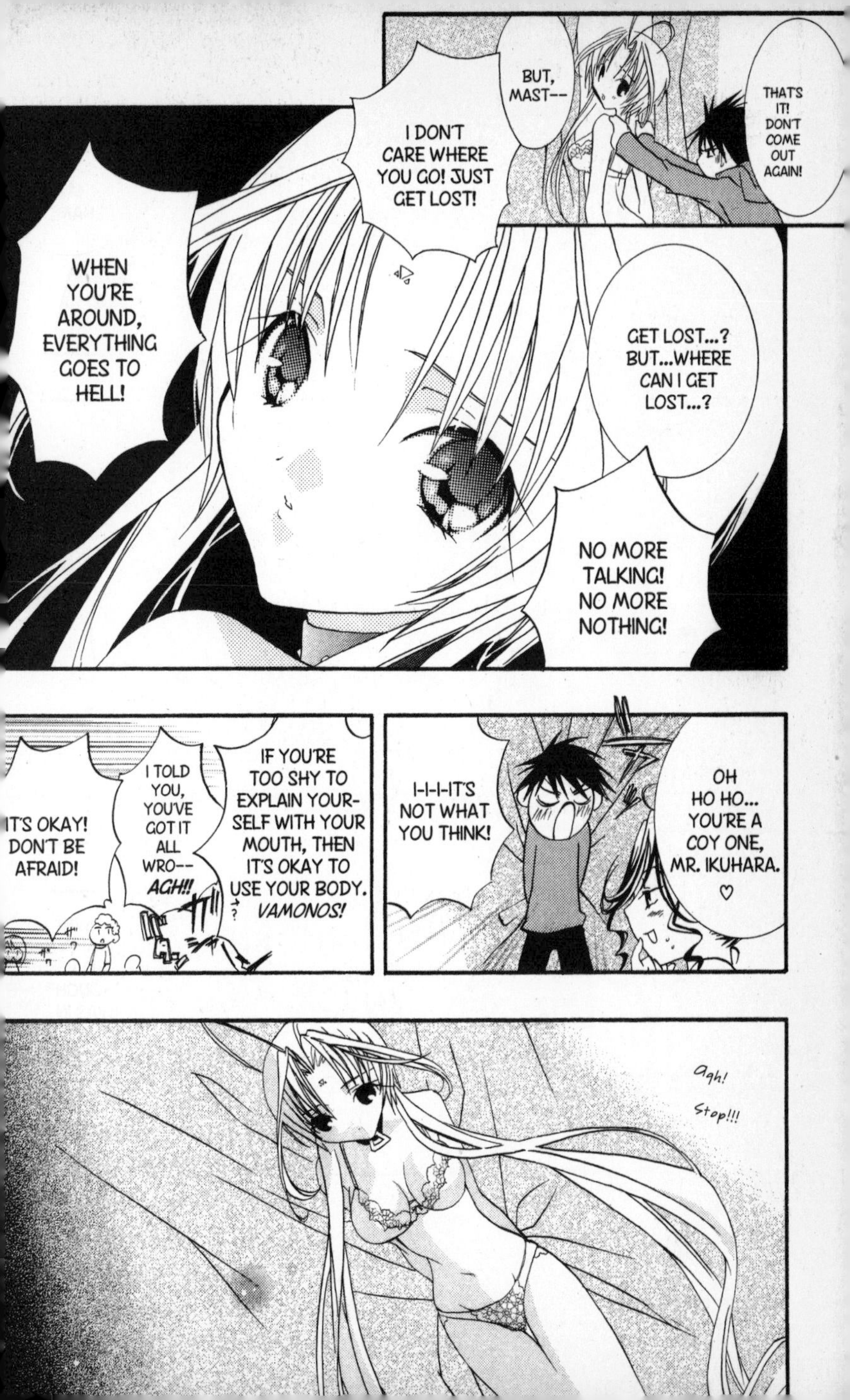
THAT'S IT! DON'T COME OUT AGAIN!
BUT, MAST--
I DON'T CARE WHERE YOU GO! JUST GET LOST!
WHEN YOU'RE AROUND, EVERYTHING GOES TO HELL!
GET LOST...? BUT...WHERE CAN I GET LOST...?
NO MORE TALKING! NO MORE NOTHING!
OH HO HO... YOU'RE A COY ONE, MR. IKUHARA. ♡
I-I-I-IT'S NOT WHAT YOU THINK!
IF YOU'RE TOO SHY TO EXPLAIN YOURSELF WITH YOUR MOUTH, THEN IT'S OKAY TO USE YOUR BODY. *VAMONOS!*
I TOLD YOU, YOU'VE GOT IT ALL WRO-- *AGH!!*
IT'S OKAY! DON'T BE AFRAID!
Agh!
Stop!!!

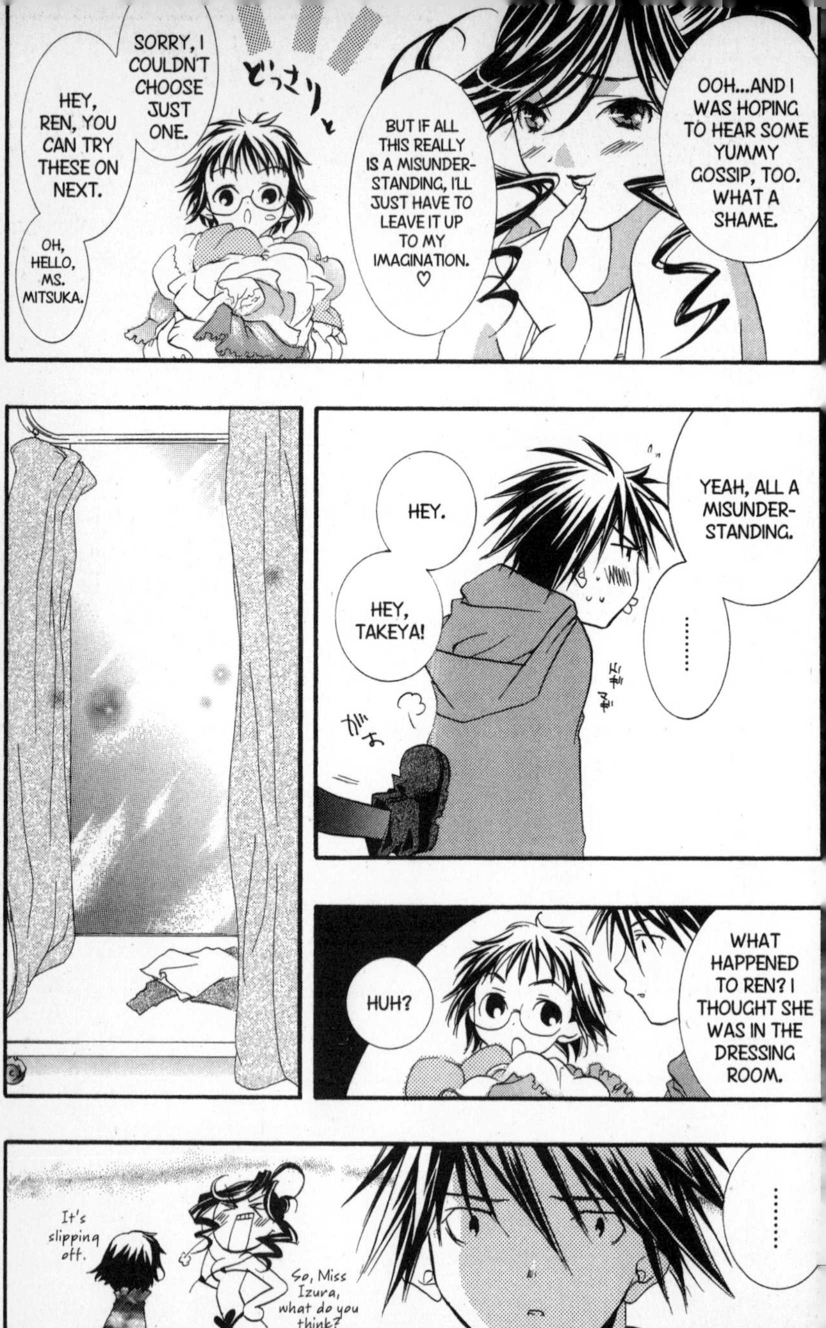

OOH...AND I WAS HOPING TO HEAR SOME YUMMY GOSSIP, TOO. WHAT A SHAME.
BUT IF ALL THIS REALLY IS A MISUNDERSTANDING, I'LL JUST HAVE TO LEAVE IT UP TO MY IMAGINATION. ♡
どっさりと
SORRY, I COULDN'T CHOOSE JUST ONE.
HEY, REN, YOU CAN TRY THESE ON NEXT.
OH, HELLO, MS. MITSUKA.
YEAH, ALL A MISUNDERSTANDING.
....
HEY.
HEY, TAKEYA!
がお
WHAT HAPPENED TO REN? I THOUGHT SHE WAS IN THE DRESSING ROOM.
HUH?
....
So, Miss Izura, what do you think?
It's slipping off.

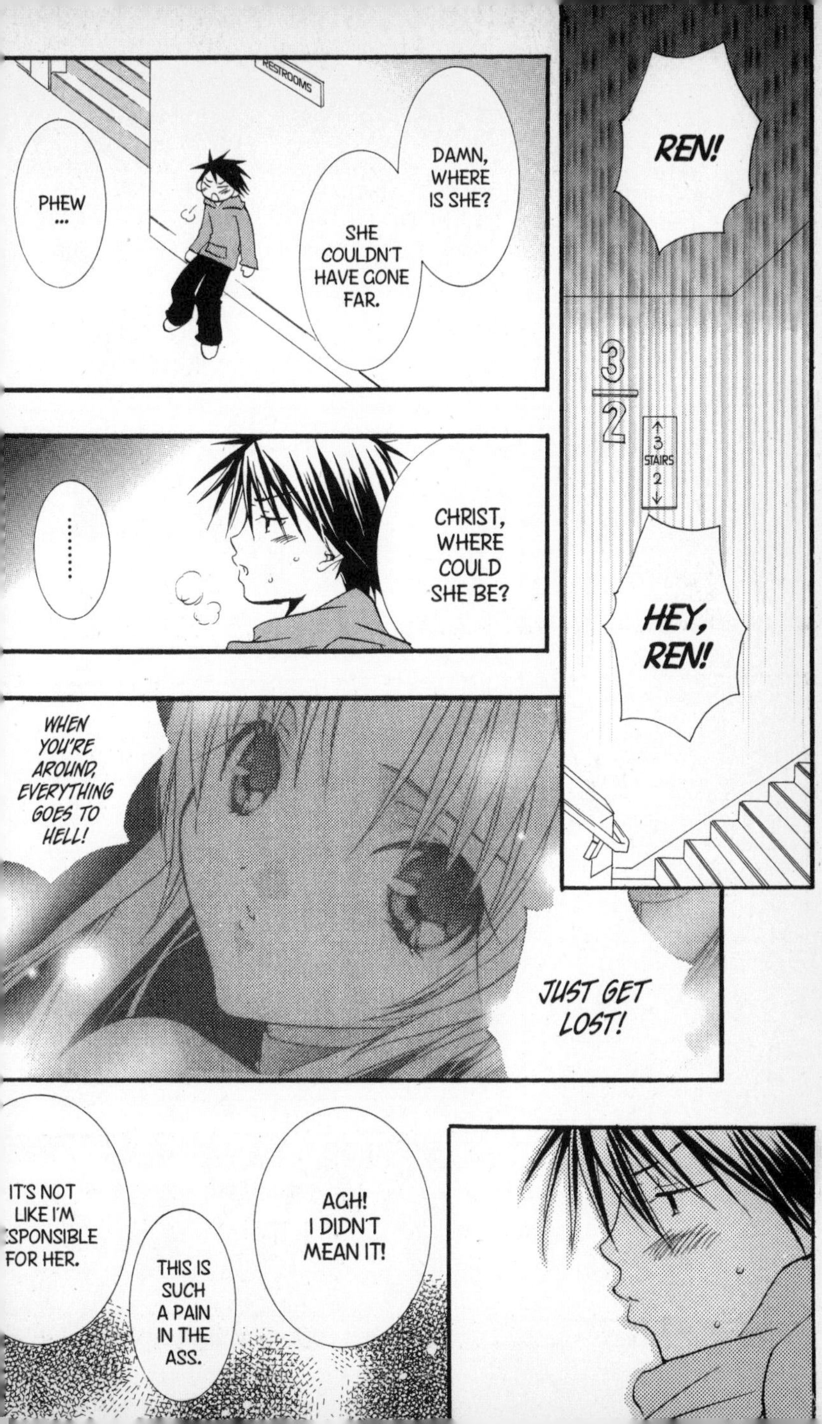
REN!
3
2
↑ 3 STAIRS 2 ↓
HEY, REN!
RESTROOMS
DAMN, WHERE IS SHE?
SHE COULDN'T HAVE GONE FAR.
PHEW...
CHRIST, WHERE COULD SHE BE?
....
WHEN YOU'RE AROUND, EVERYTHING GOES TO HELL!
JUST GET LOST!
AGH! I DIDN'T MEAN IT!
IT'S NOT LIKE I'M SPONSIBLE FOR HER.
THIS IS SUCH A PAIN IN THE ASS.

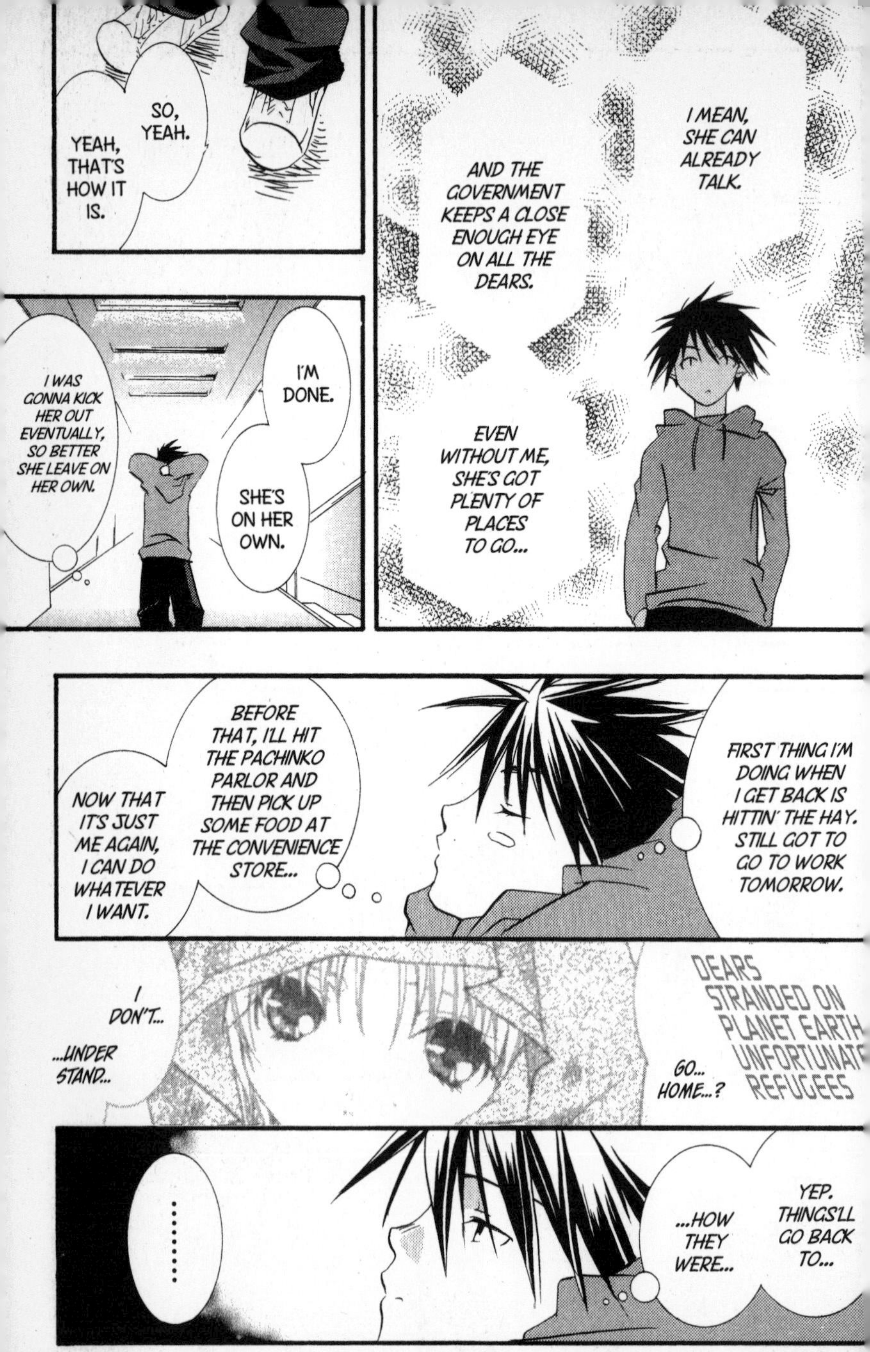
I MEAN, SHE CAN ALREADY TALK.
AND THE GOVERNMENT KEEPS A CLOSE ENOUGH EYE ON ALL THE DEARS.
EVEN WITHOUT ME, SHE'S GOT PLENTY OF PLACES TO GO...
SO, YEAH.
YEAH, THAT'S HOW IT IS.
I'M DONE.
SHE'S ON HER OWN.
I WAS GONNA KICK HER OUT EVENTUALLY, SO BETTER SHE LEAVE ON HER OWN.
FIRST THING I'M DOING WHEN I GET BACK IS HITTIN' THE HAY. STILL GOT TO GO TO WORK TOMORROW.
BEFORE THAT, I'LL HIT THE PACHINKO PARLOR AND THEN PICK UP SOME FOOD AT THE CONVENIENCE STORE...
NOW THAT IT'S JUST ME AGAIN, I CAN DO WHATEVER I WANT.
DEARS STRANDED ON PLANET EARTH UNFORTUNATE REFUGEES
GO... HOME...?
I DON'T...
...UNDER STAND...
YEP. THINGS'LL GO BACK TO...
...HOW THEY WERE...
......

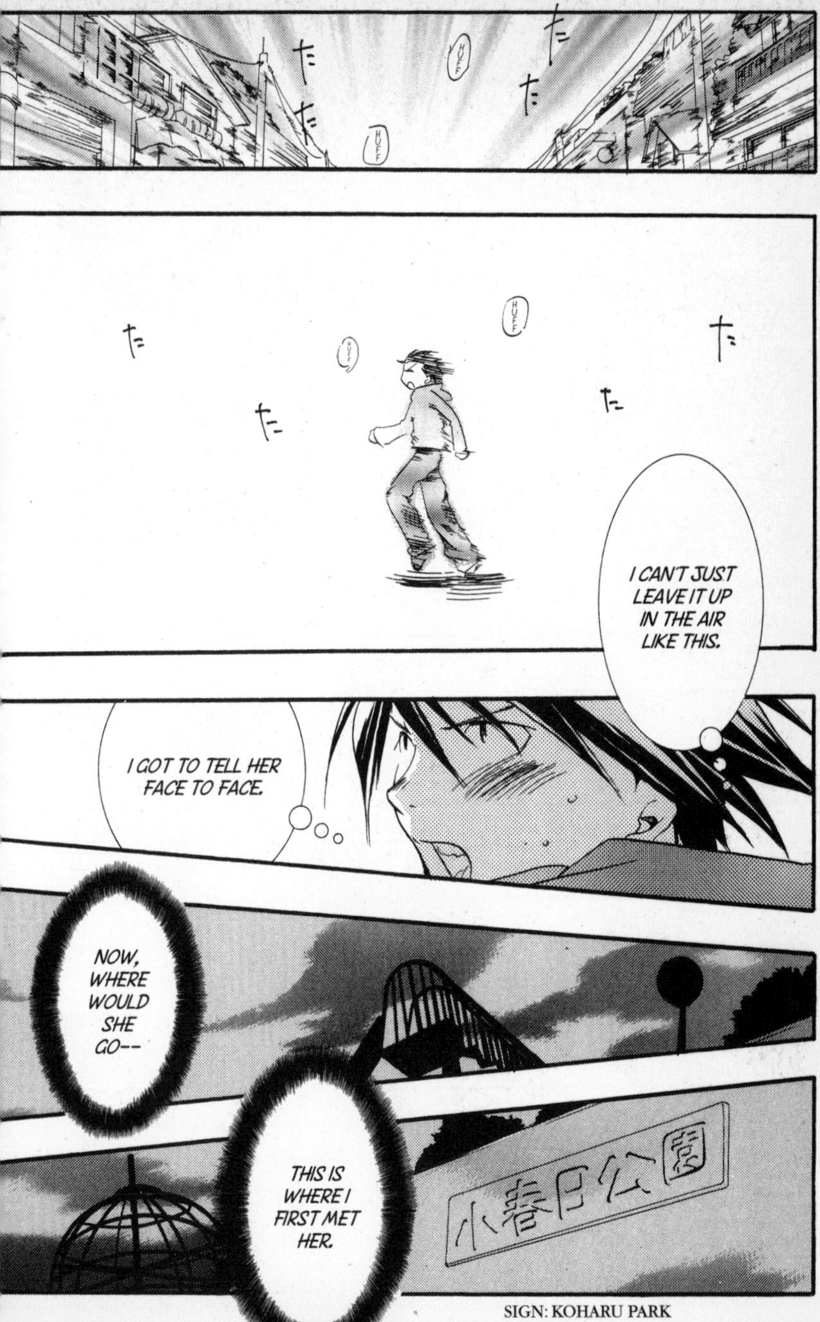

た
た
た
た
HUFF
HUFF
HUFF
HUFF
だ
た
た
た
I CAN'T JUST LEAVE IT UP IN THE AIR LIKE THIS.
I GOT TO TELL HER FACE TO FACE.
NOW, WHERE WOULD SHE GO--
小春日公園
THIS IS WHERE I FIRST MET HER.

SIGN: KOHARU PARK

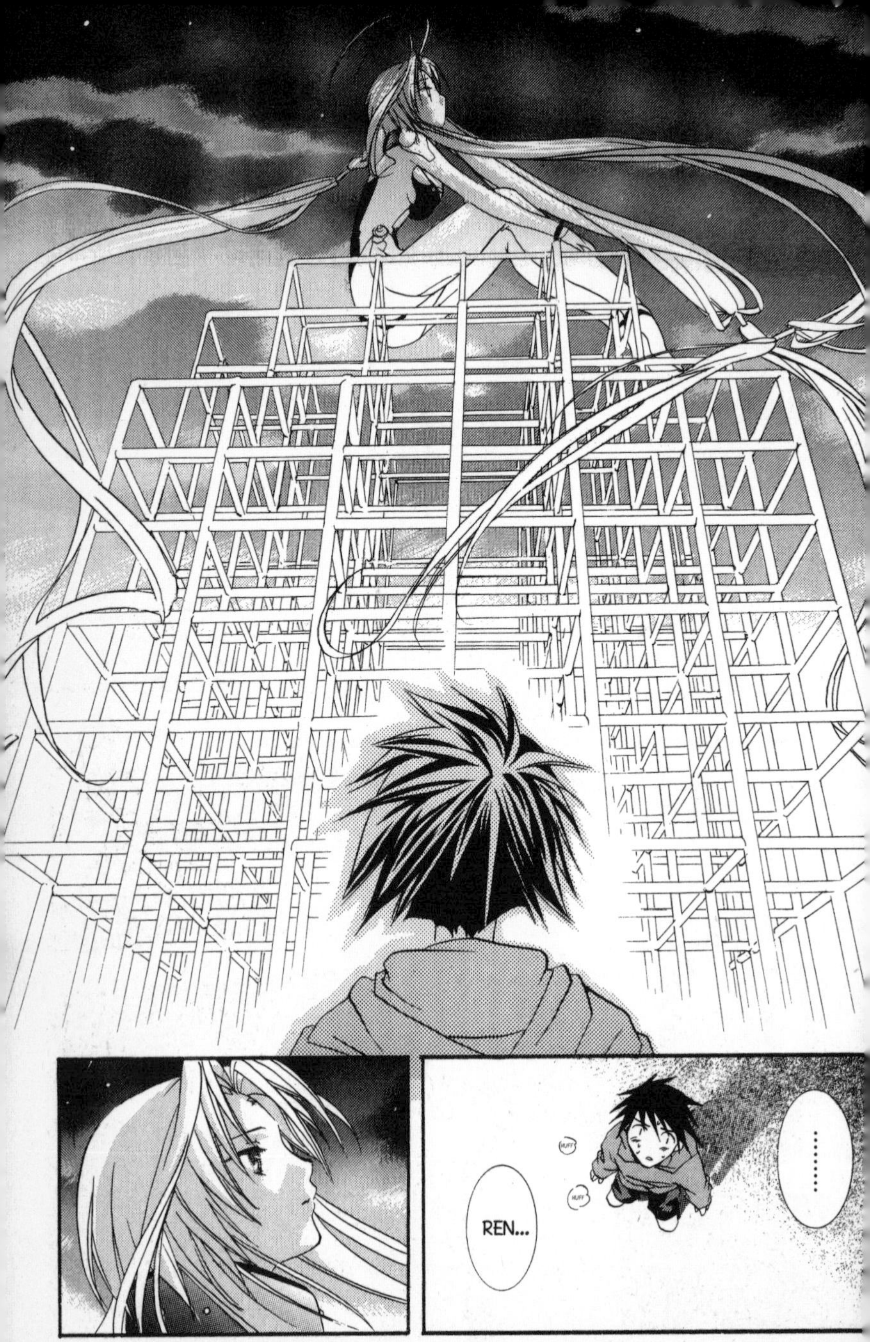
......
HUFF
HUFF
REN...

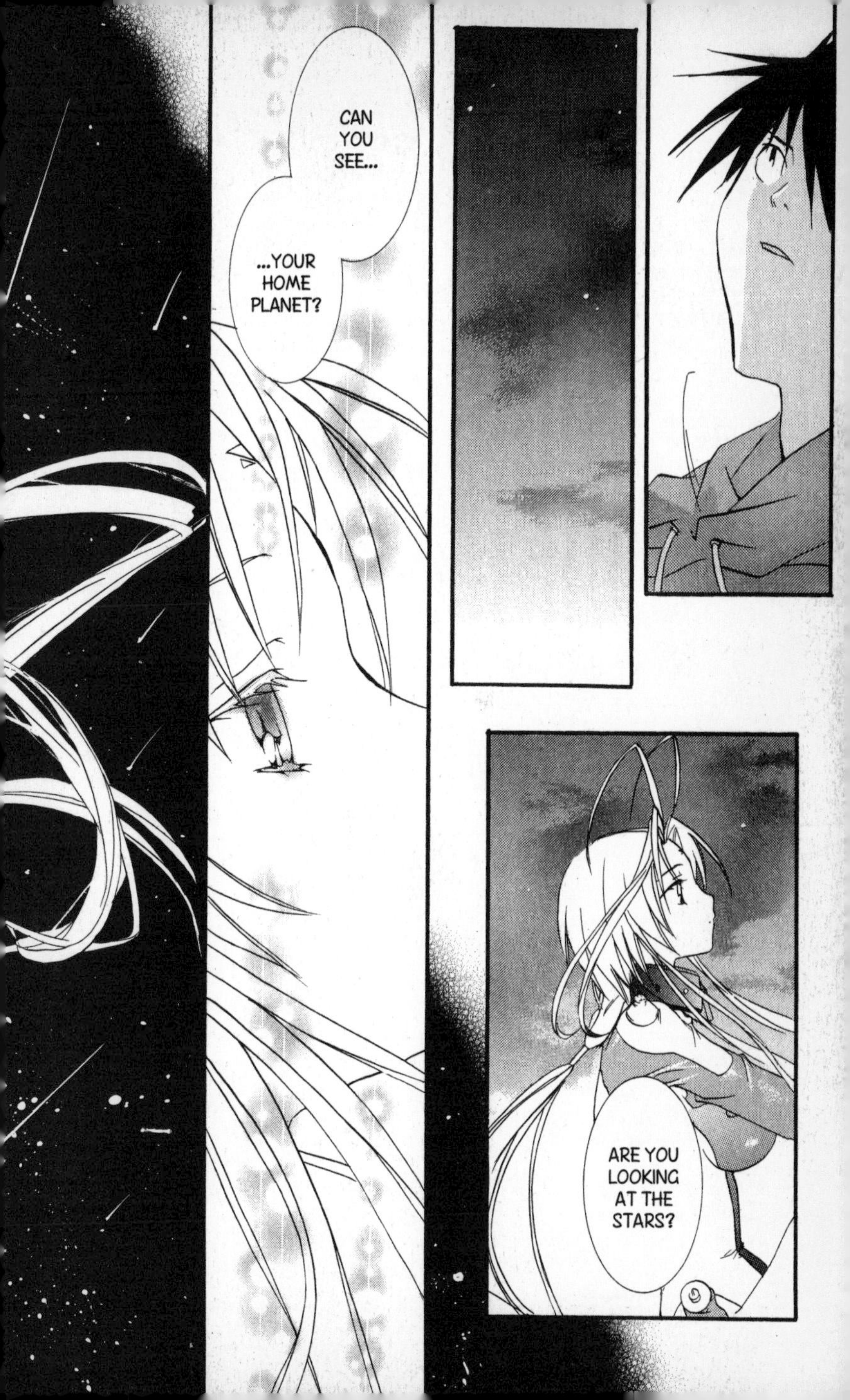
ARE YOU LOOKING AT THE STARS?
CAN YOU SEE...
...YOUR HOME PLANET?

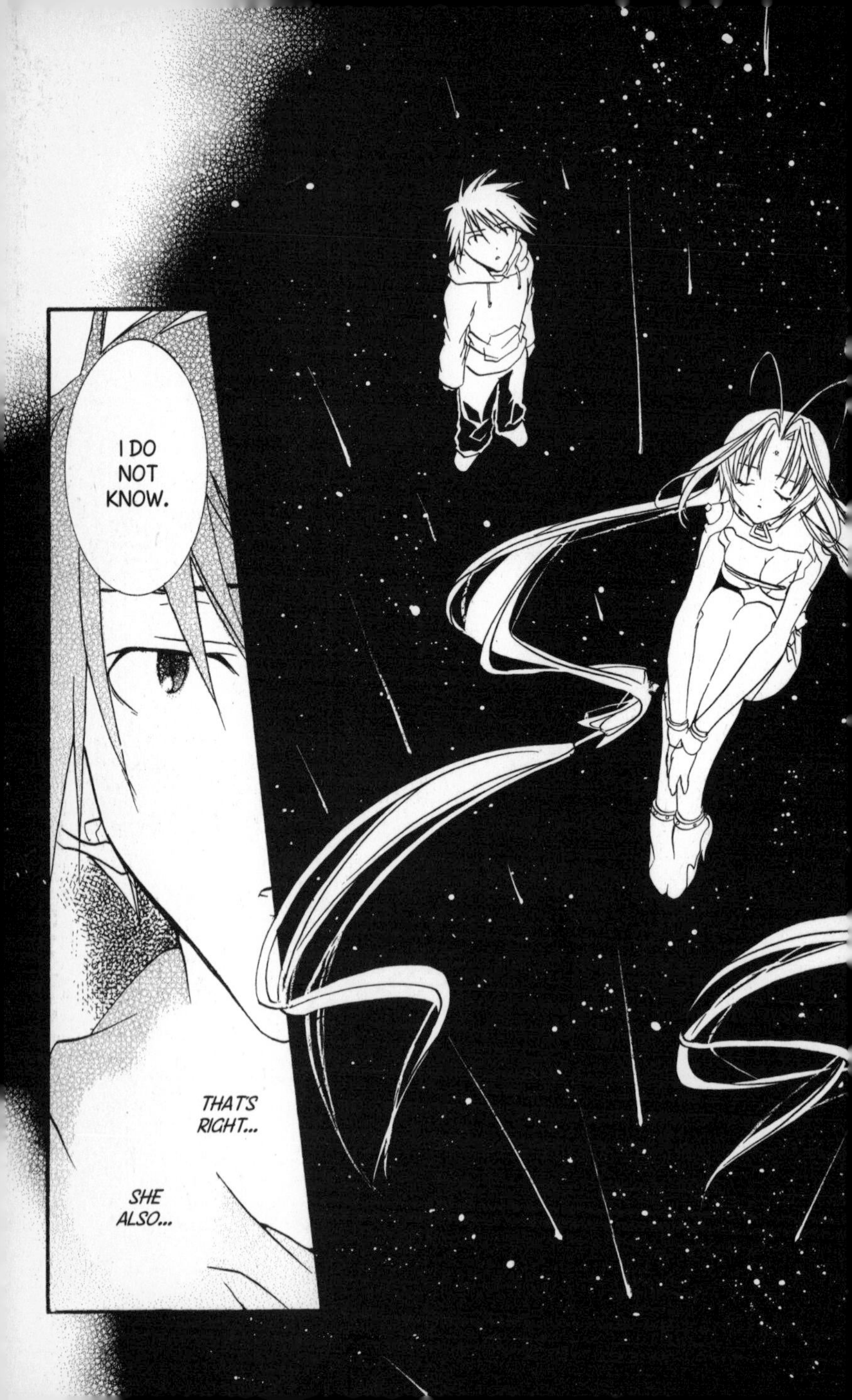
I DO NOT KNOW.
THAT'S RIGHT...
SHE ALSO...

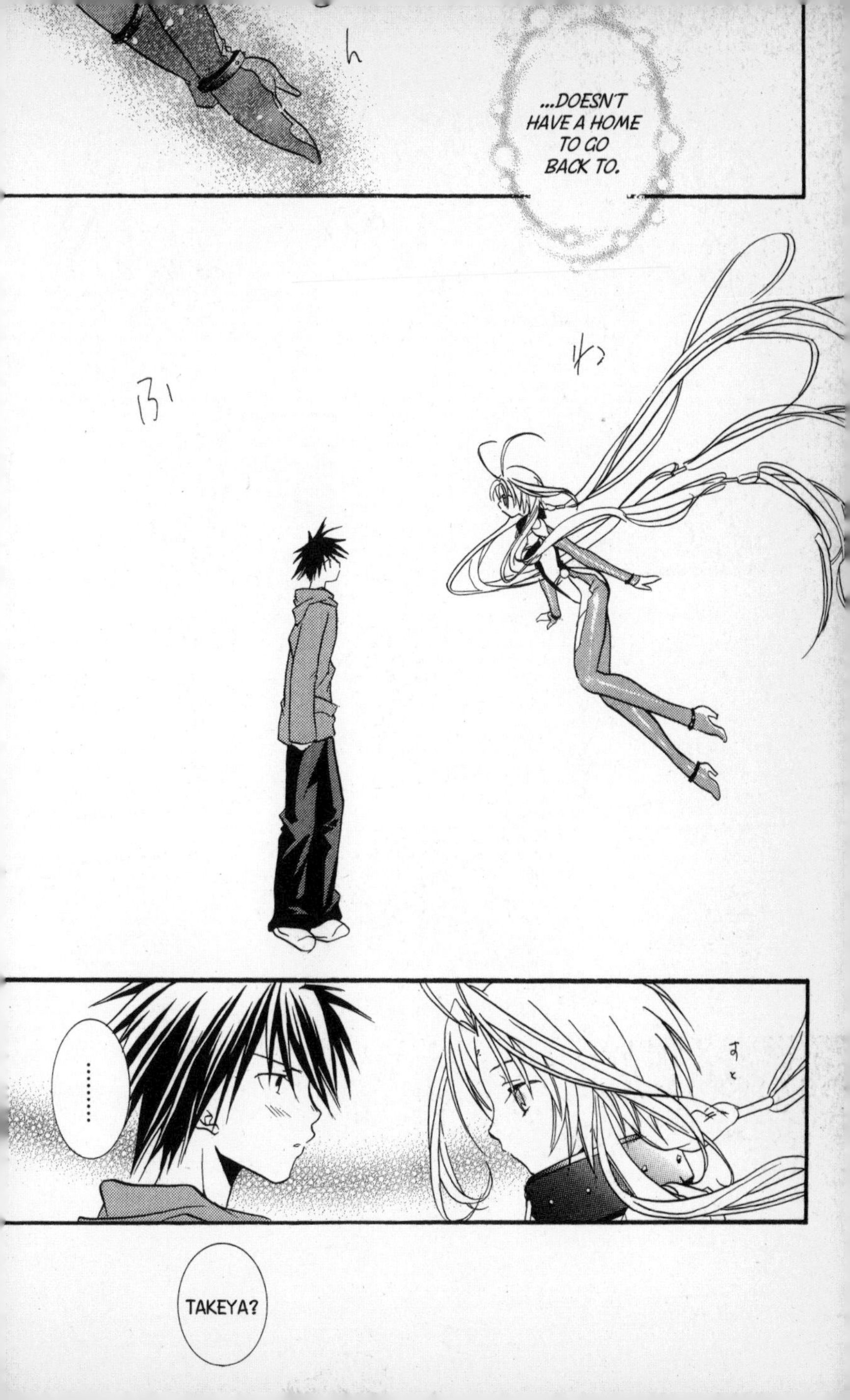
...DOESN'T HAVE A HOME TO GO BACK TO.
....
TAKEYA?

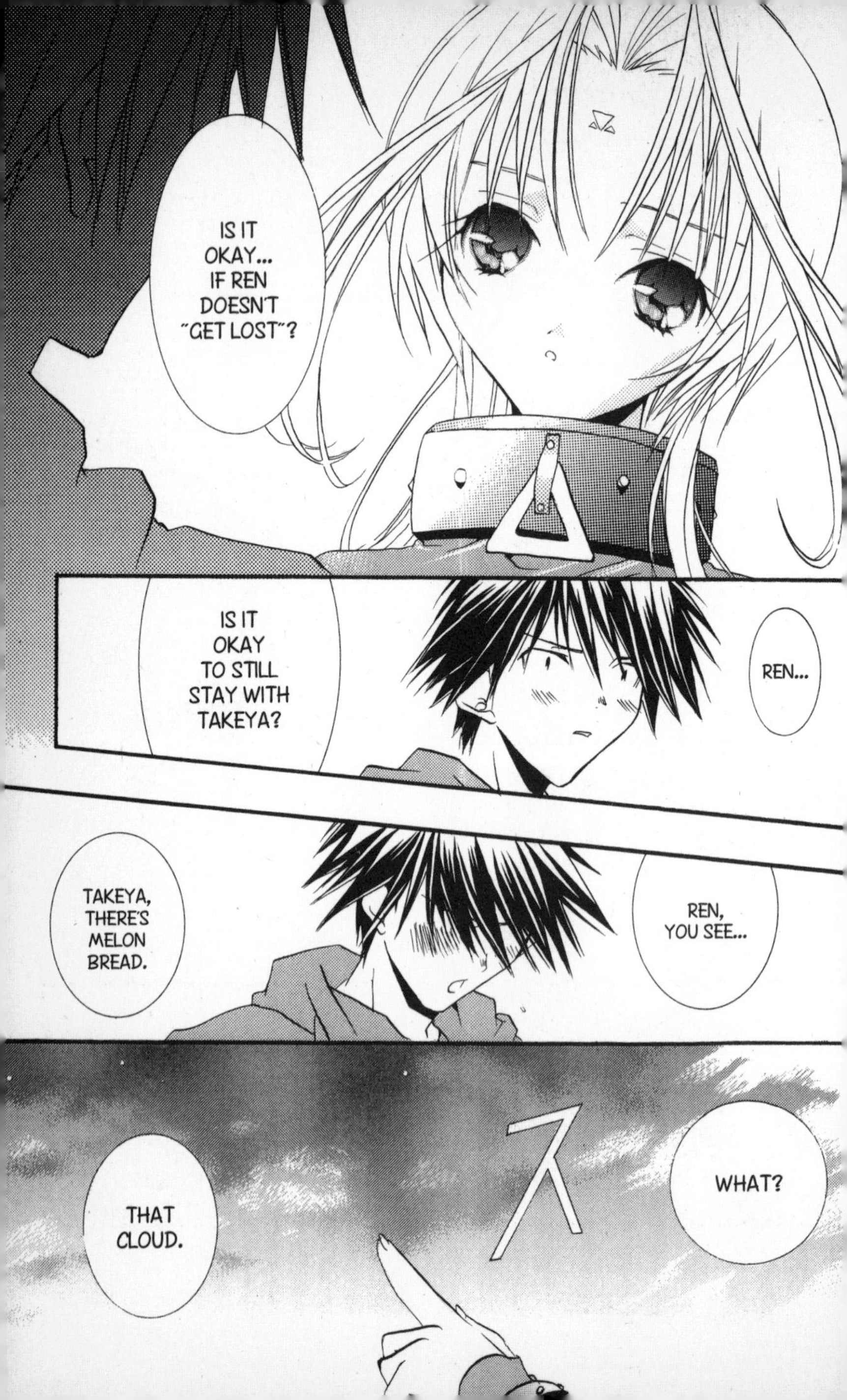
IS IT OKAY... IF REN DOESN'T "GET LOST"?
REN...
IS IT OKAY TO STILL STAY WITH TAKEYA?
REN, YOU SEE...
TAKEYA, THERE'S MELON BREAD.
WHAT?
ス
THAT CLOUD.

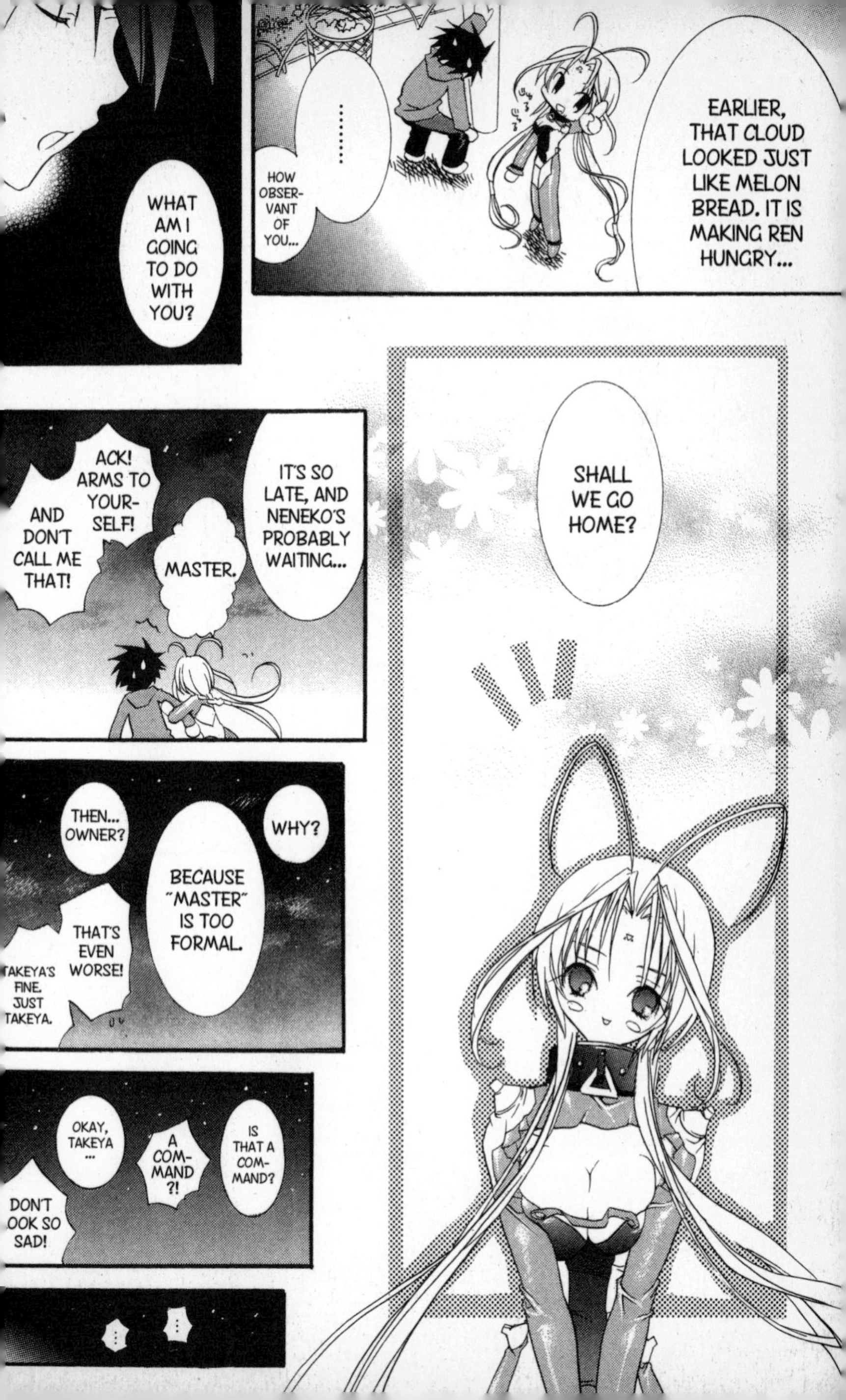

EARLIER, THAT CLOUD LOOKED JUST LIKE MELON BREAD. IT IS MAKING REN HUNGRY...
......
HOW OBSERVANT OF YOU...
WHAT AM I GOING TO DO WITH YOU?
SHALL WE GO HOME?
IT'S SO LATE, AND NENEKO'S PROBABLY WAITING...
MASTER.
ACK! ARMS TO YOURSELF!
AND DON'T CALL ME THAT!
WHY?
BECAUSE "MASTER" IS TOO FORMAL.
THEN... OWNER?
THAT'S EVEN WORSE!
TAKEYA'S FINE. JUST TAKEYA.
IS THAT A COMMAND?
A COMMAND?!
OKAY, TAKEYA...
DON'T OOK SO SAD!
...
...

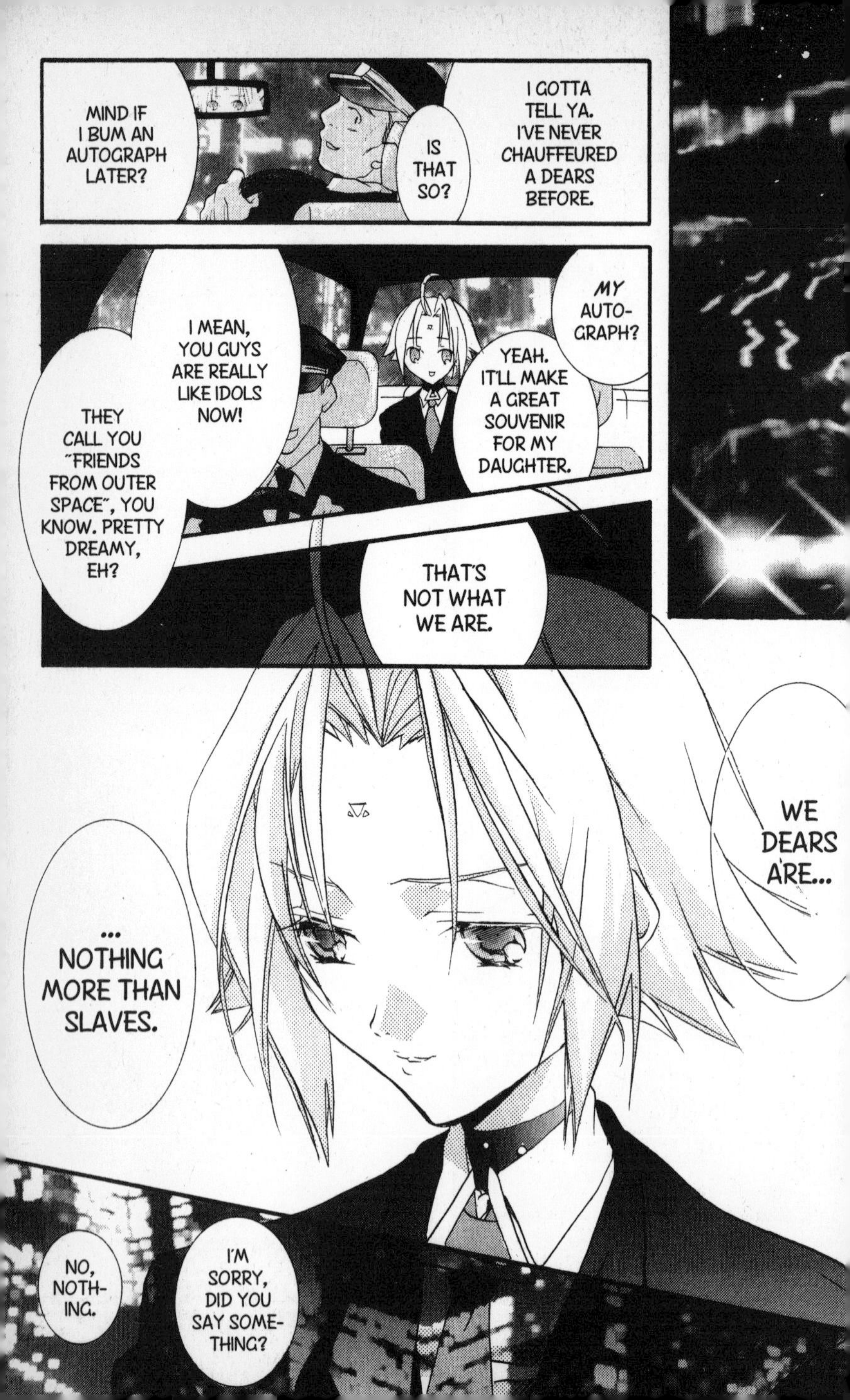
I GOTTA TELL YA. I'VE NEVER CHAUFFEURED A DEARS BEFORE.
IS THAT SO?
MIND IF I BUM AN AUTOGRAPH LATER?
MY AUTO-GRAPH?
YEAH. IT'LL MAKE A GREAT SOUVENIR FOR MY DAUGHTER.
I MEAN, YOU GUYS ARE REALLY LIKE IDOLS NOW!
THEY CALL YOU "FRIENDS FROM OUTER SPACE", YOU KNOW. PRETTY DREAMY, EH?
THAT'S NOT WHAT WE ARE.
WE DEARS ARE...
... NOTHING MORE THAN SLAVES.
I'M SORRY, DID YOU SAY SOME-THING?
NO, NOTH-ING.

AFTER SCHOOL SPECIAL
STAFF ROOM
Sigh
MS. MITSUKA, ARE YOU FEELING SICK?
NO, THAT'S NOT WHAT IT IS.
TODAY, AFTER SCHOOL, I'M GOING OUT TO BUY UNDERWEAR BECAUSE...
...RIGHT NOW, I'M NOT WEARING *ANY UNDER-WEAR!!*
ガタ
IMAGINE WHAT WOULD HAPPEN IF A STUDENT SAW ME! *AH! AH...!*
Nothing here →
Nor here →
OR IF PEOPLE FROM TOWN NOTICED ON MY WAY TO THE DEPART-MENT STORE...!
AAAHH!!
I COULD LEND YOU A SWEAT-SHIRT.

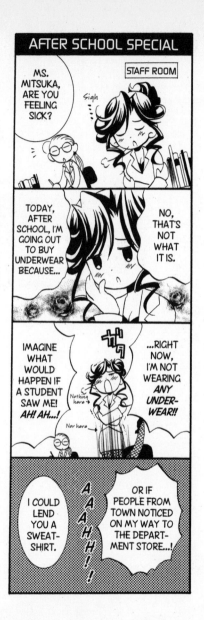

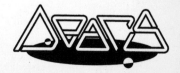

5th Contact

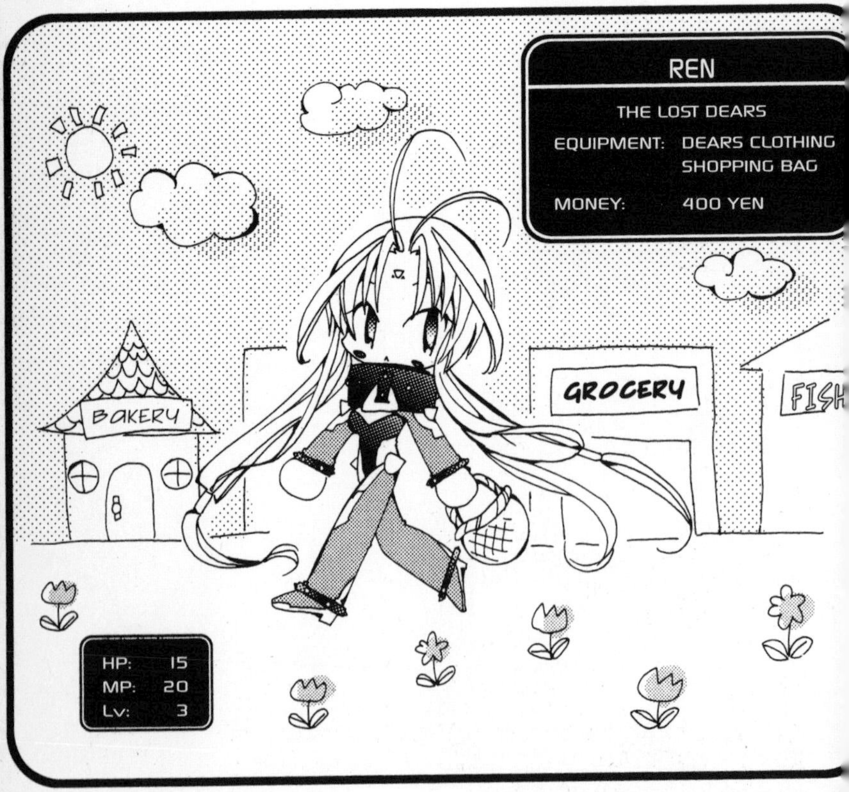
REN
THE LOST DEARS
EQUIPMENT: DEARS CLOTHING
SHOPPING BAG
MONEY: 400 YEN
BAKERY
GROCERY
FISH
HP: 15
MP: 20
Lv: 3

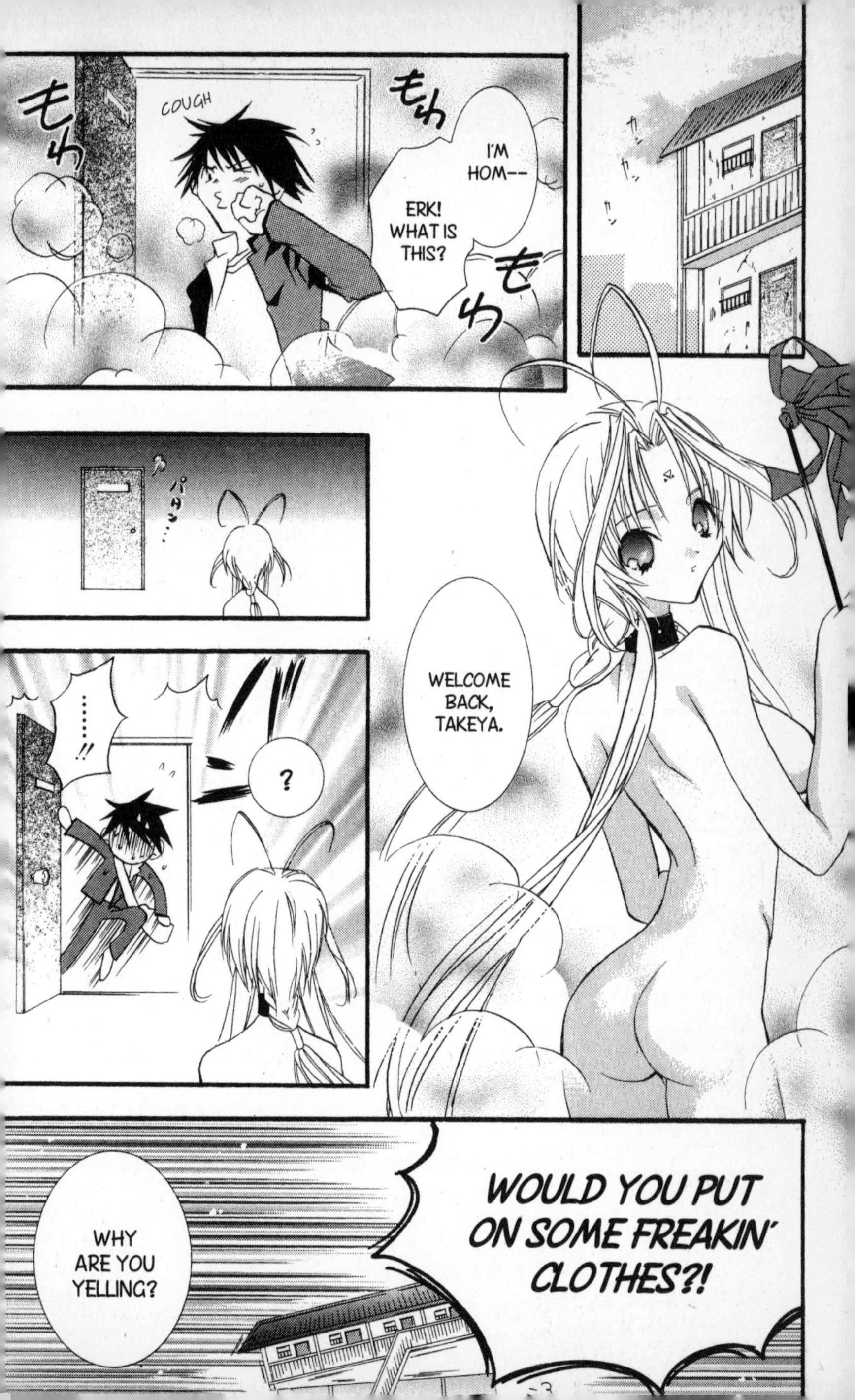
もわ
COUGH
I'M HOM--
ERK! WHAT IS THIS?
もわ
もわ
WELCOME BACK, TAKEYA.
パタン…
......!!
?
WOULD YOU PUT ON SOME FREAKIN' CLOTHES?!
WHY ARE YOU YELLING?

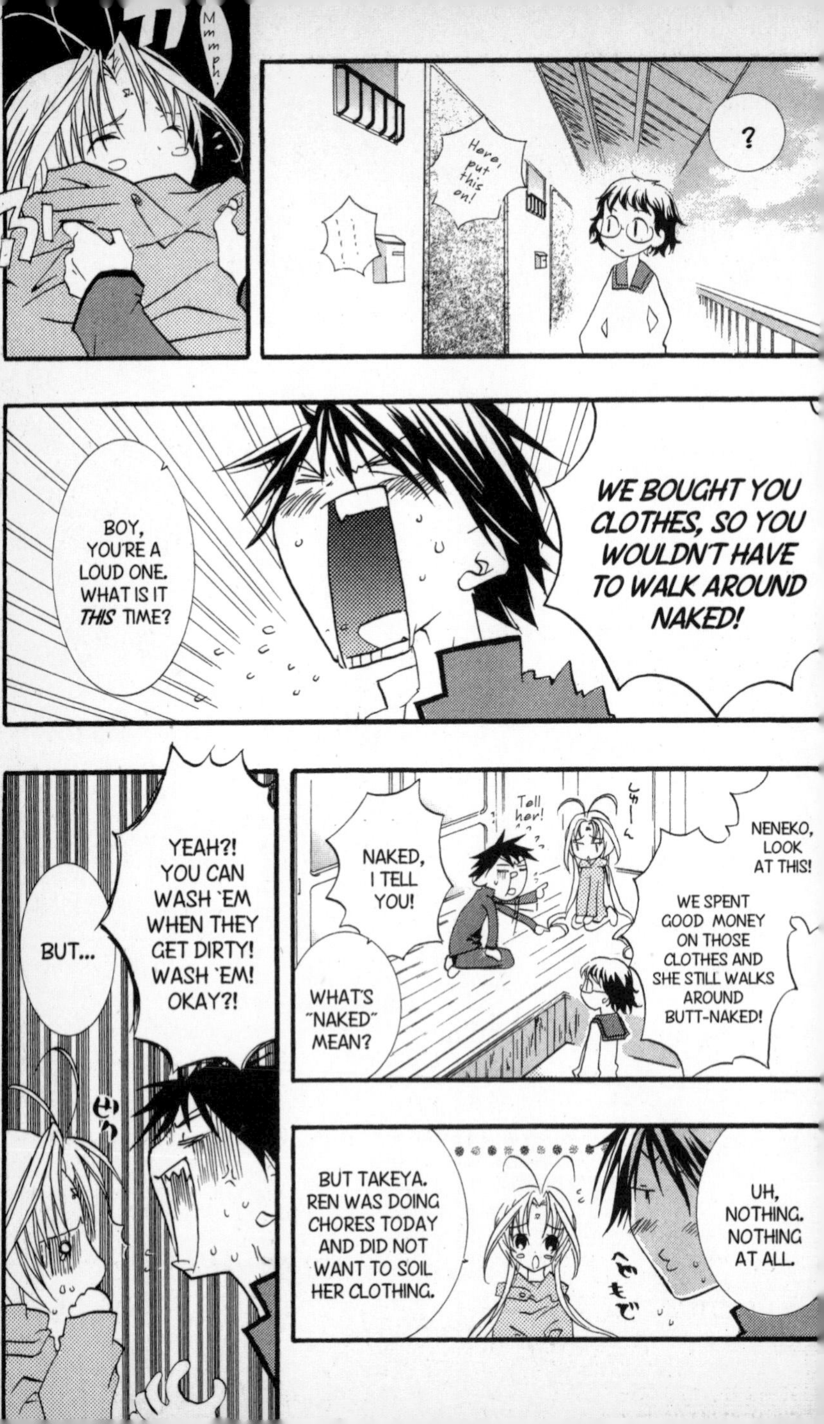
?
Here, put this on!
Mmmph.
WE BOUGHT YOU CLOTHES, SO YOU WOULDN'T HAVE TO WALK AROUND NAKED!
BOY, YOU'RE A LOUD ONE. WHAT IS IT *THIS* TIME?
NENEKO, LOOK AT THIS!
WE SPENT GOOD MONEY ON THOSE CLOTHES AND SHE STILL WALKS AROUND BUTT-NAKED!
Tell her!
NAKED, I TELL YOU!
WHAT'S "NAKED" MEAN?
UH, NOTHING. NOTHING AT ALL.
BUT TAKEYA. REN WAS DOING CHORES TODAY AND DID NOT WANT TO SOIL HER CLOTHING.
YEAH?! YOU CAN WASH 'EM WHEN THEY GET DIRTY! WASH 'EM! OKAY?!
BUT...

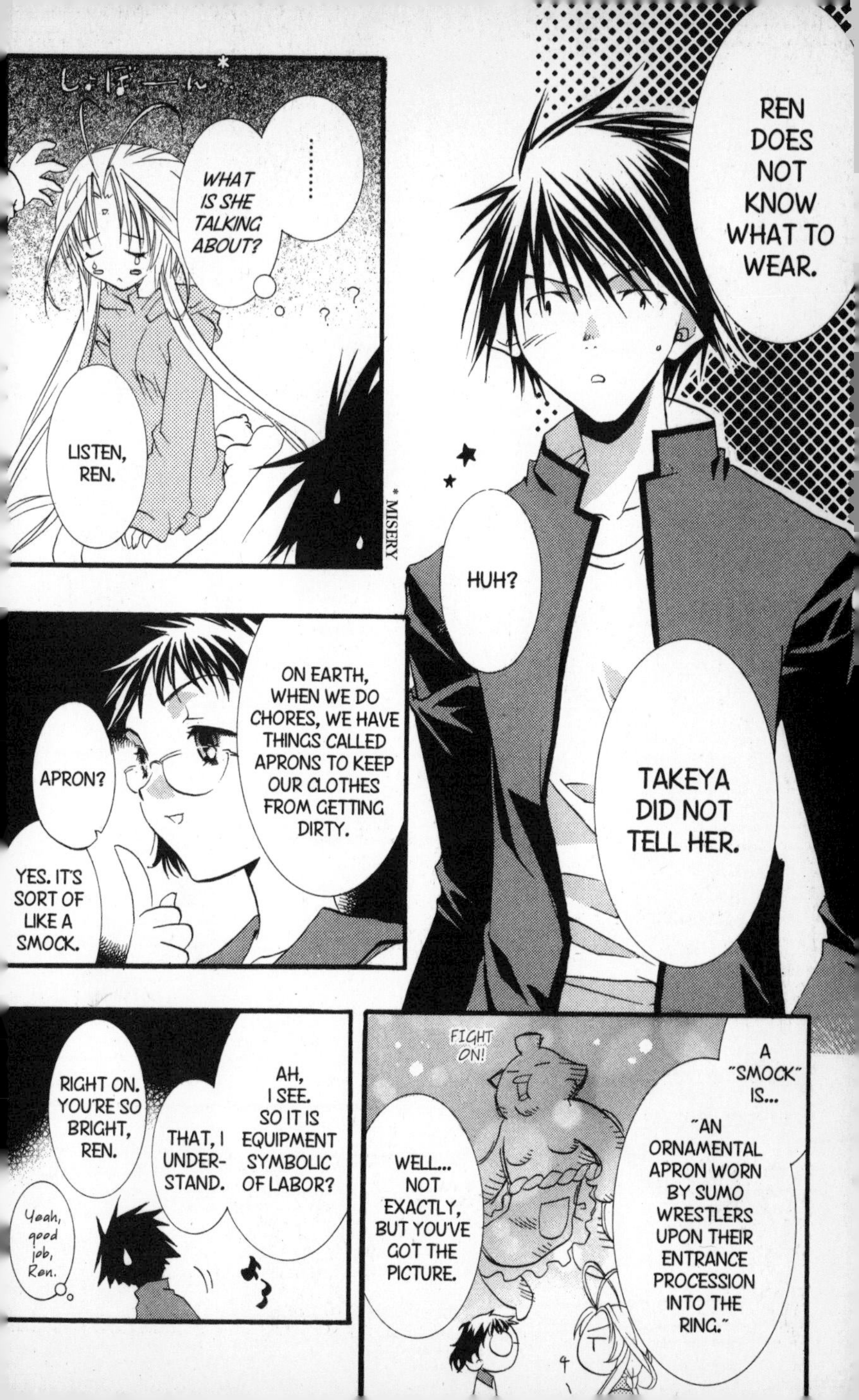
REN DOES NOT KNOW WHAT TO WEAR.
HUH?
TAKEYA DID NOT TELL HER.
しょぼーん...*
......
WHAT IS SHE TALKING ABOUT?
LISTEN, REN.
* MISERY
ON EARTH, WHEN WE DO CHORES, WE HAVE THINGS CALLED APRONS TO KEEP OUR CLOTHES FROM GETTING DIRTY.
APRON?
YES. IT'S SORT OF LIKE A SMOCK.
A "SMOCK" IS...
"AN ORNAMENTAL APRON WORN BY SUMO WRESTLERS UPON THEIR ENTRANCE PROCESSION INTO THE RING."
FIGHT ON!
WELL... NOT EXACTLY, BUT YOU'VE GOT THE PICTURE.
AH, I SEE. SO IT IS EQUIPMENT SYMBOLIC OF LABOR?
THAT, I UNDERSTAND.
RIGHT ON. YOU'RE SO BRIGHT, REN.
Yeah, good job, Ren.

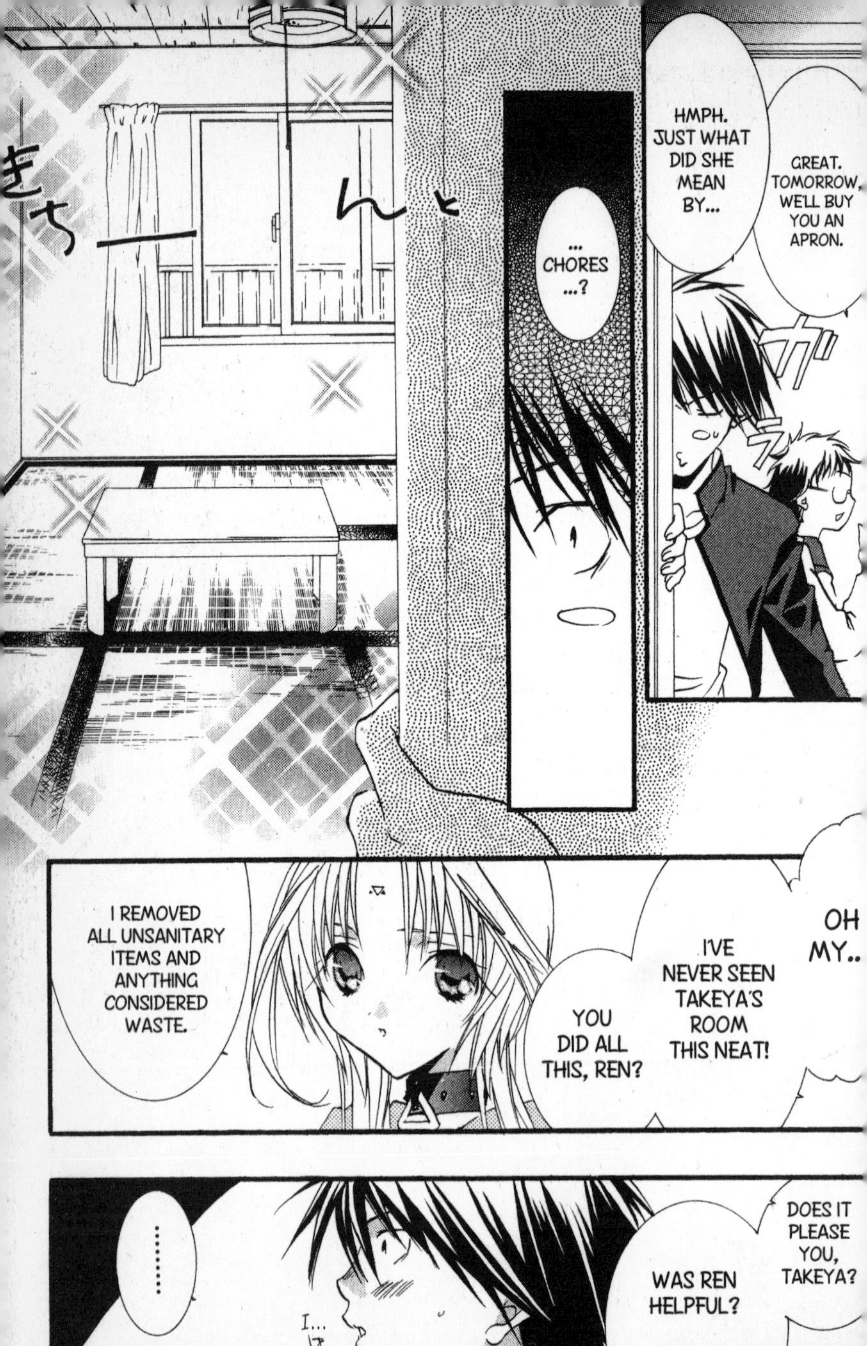
GREAT. TOMORROW, WE'LL BUY YOU AN APRON.
HMPH. JUST WHAT DID SHE MEAN BY...
...CHORES...?
きちーんと
OH MY..
I'VE NEVER SEEN TAKEYA'S ROOM THIS NEAT!
YOU DID ALL THIS, REN?
I REMOVED ALL UNSANITARY ITEMS AND ANYTHING CONSIDERED WASTE.
DOES IT PLEASE YOU, TAKEYA?
WAS REN HELPFUL?
I...
....

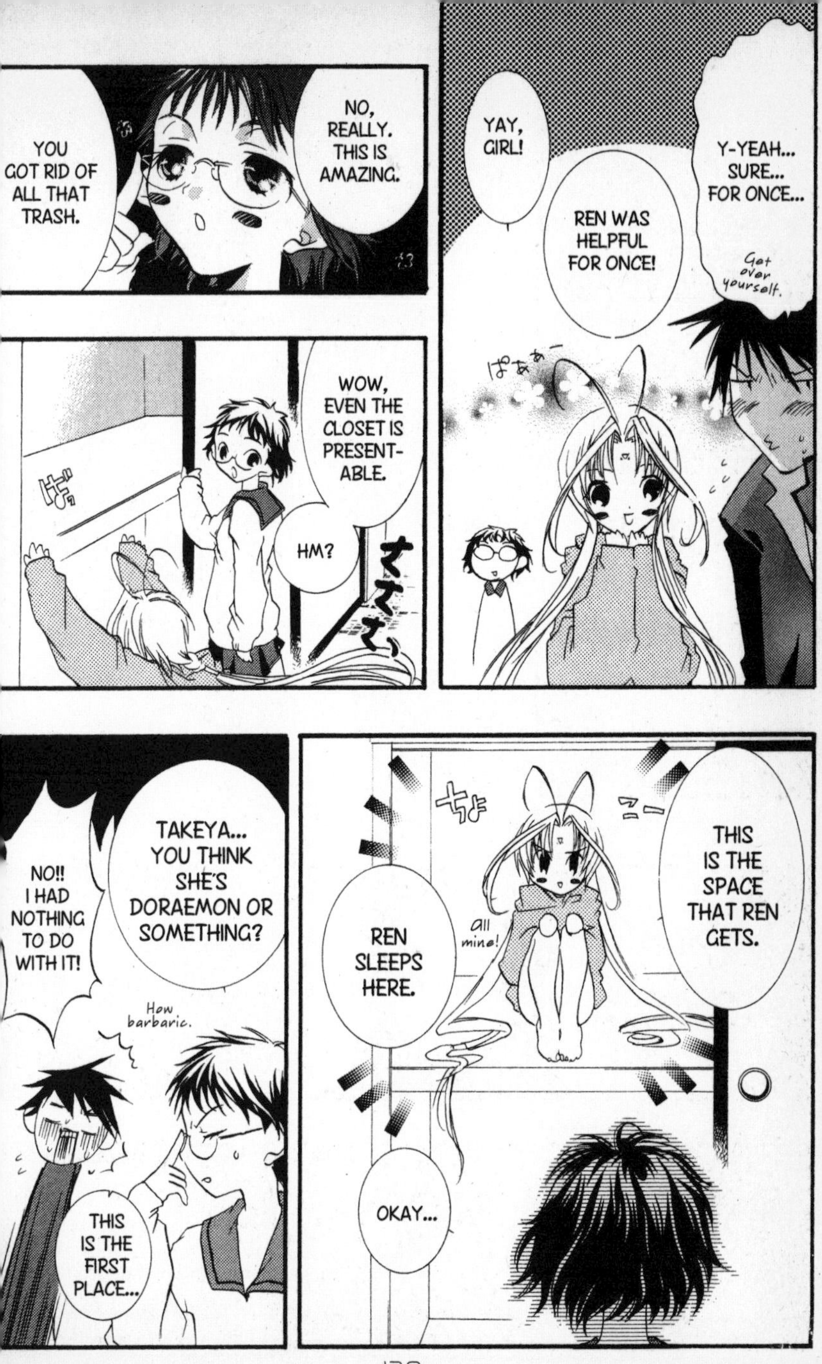
Y-YEAH... SURE... FOR ONCE...
Get over yourself.
YAY, GIRL!
REN WAS HELPFUL FOR ONCE!
NO, REALLY. THIS IS AMAZING.
YOU GOT RID OF ALL THAT TRASH.
WOW, EVEN THE CLOSET IS PRESENT-ABLE.
HM?
THIS IS THE SPACE THAT REN GETS.
ちょ
REN SLEEPS HERE.
all mine!
OKAY...
TAKEYA... YOU THINK SHE'S DORAEMON OR SOMETHING?
NO!! I HAD NOTHING TO DO WITH IT!
How barbaric.
THIS IS THE FIRST PLACE...

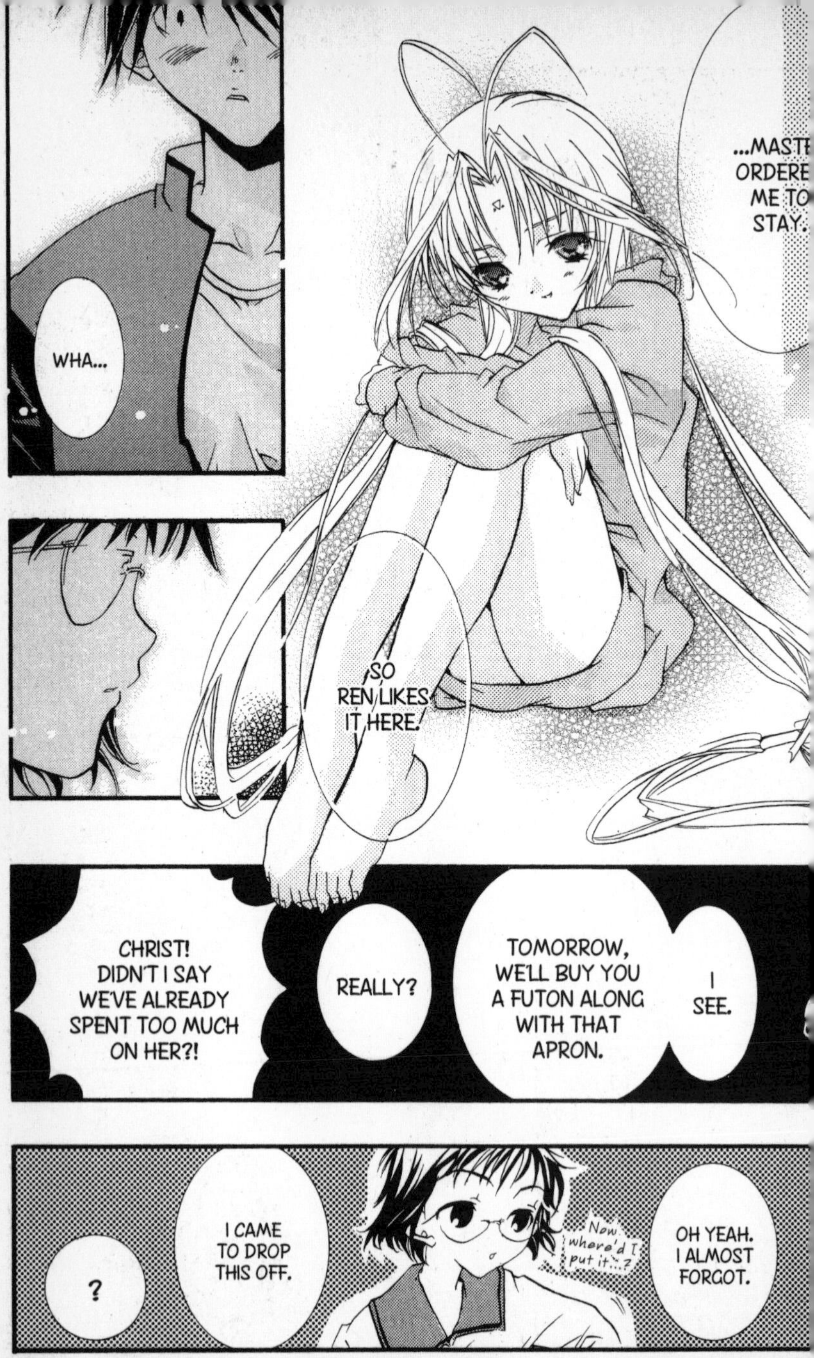
...MASTE ORDERE ME TO STAY.
SO REN LIKES IT HERE.
WHA...
I SEE.
TOMORROW, WE'LL BUY YOU A FUTON ALONG WITH THAT APRON.
REALLY?
CHRIST! DIDN'T I SAY WE'VE ALREADY SPENT TOO MUCH ON HER?!
OH YEAH. I ALMOST FORGOT.
Now where'd I put it...?
I CAME TO DROP THIS OFF.
?

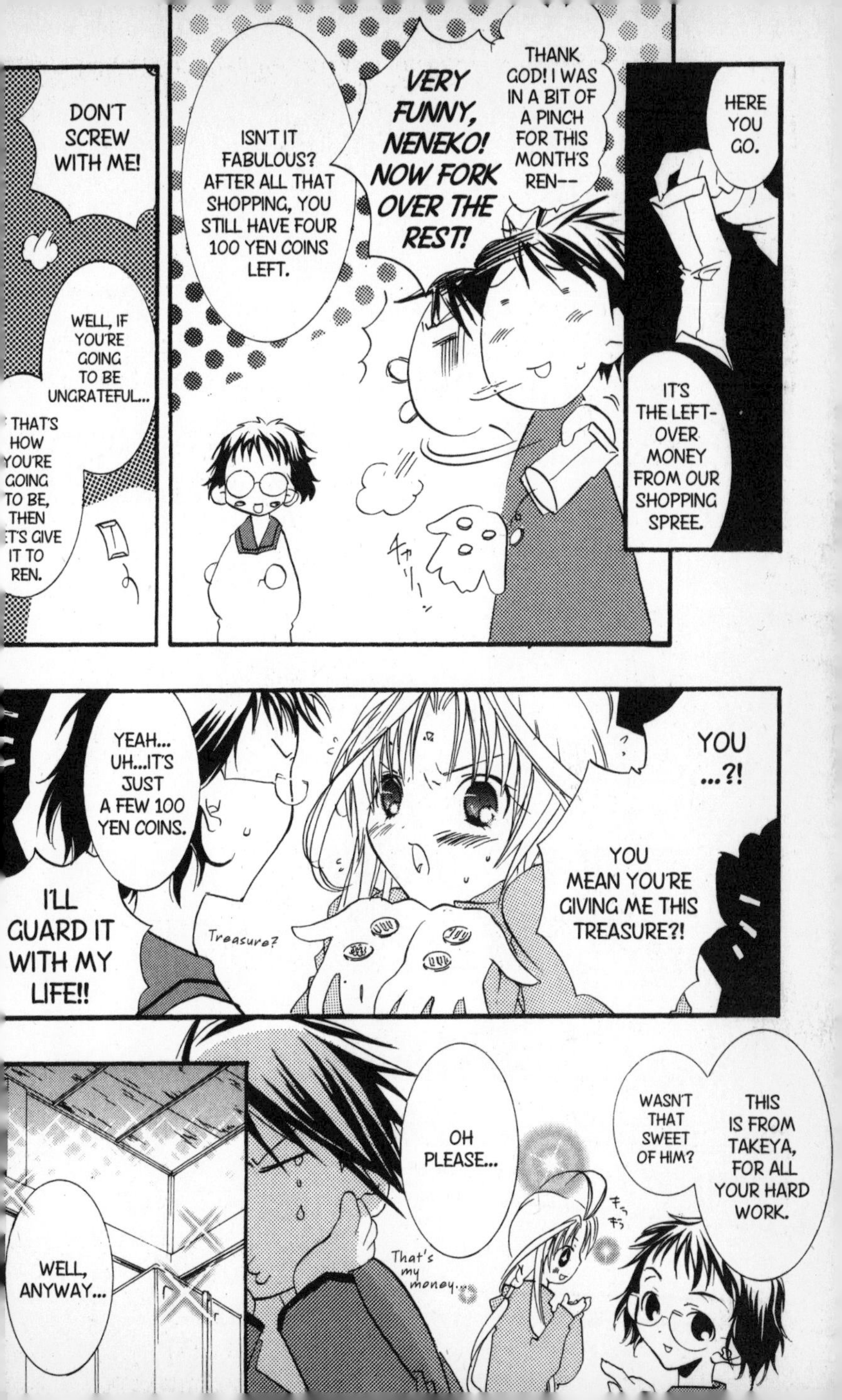
HERE YOU GO.
IT'S THE LEFT-OVER MONEY FROM OUR SHOPPING SPREE.
THANK GOD! I WAS IN A BIT OF A PINCH FOR THIS MONTH'S REN--
VERY FUNNY, NENEKO! NOW FORK OVER THE REST!
ISN'T IT FABULOUS? AFTER ALL THAT SHOPPING, YOU STILL HAVE FOUR 100 YEN COINS LEFT.
DON'T SCREW WITH ME!
WELL, IF YOU'RE GOING TO BE UNGRATEFUL...
THAT'S HOW YOU'RE GOING TO BE, THEN ET'S GIVE IT TO REN.
YOU ...?!
YOU MEAN YOU'RE GIVING ME THIS TREASURE?!
YEAH... UH...IT'S JUST A FEW 100 YEN COINS.
Treasure?
I'LL GUARD IT WITH MY LIFE!!
THIS IS FROM TAKEYA, FOR ALL YOUR HARD WORK.
WASN'T THAT SWEET OF HIM?
OH PLEASE...
That's my money...
WELL, ANYWAY...

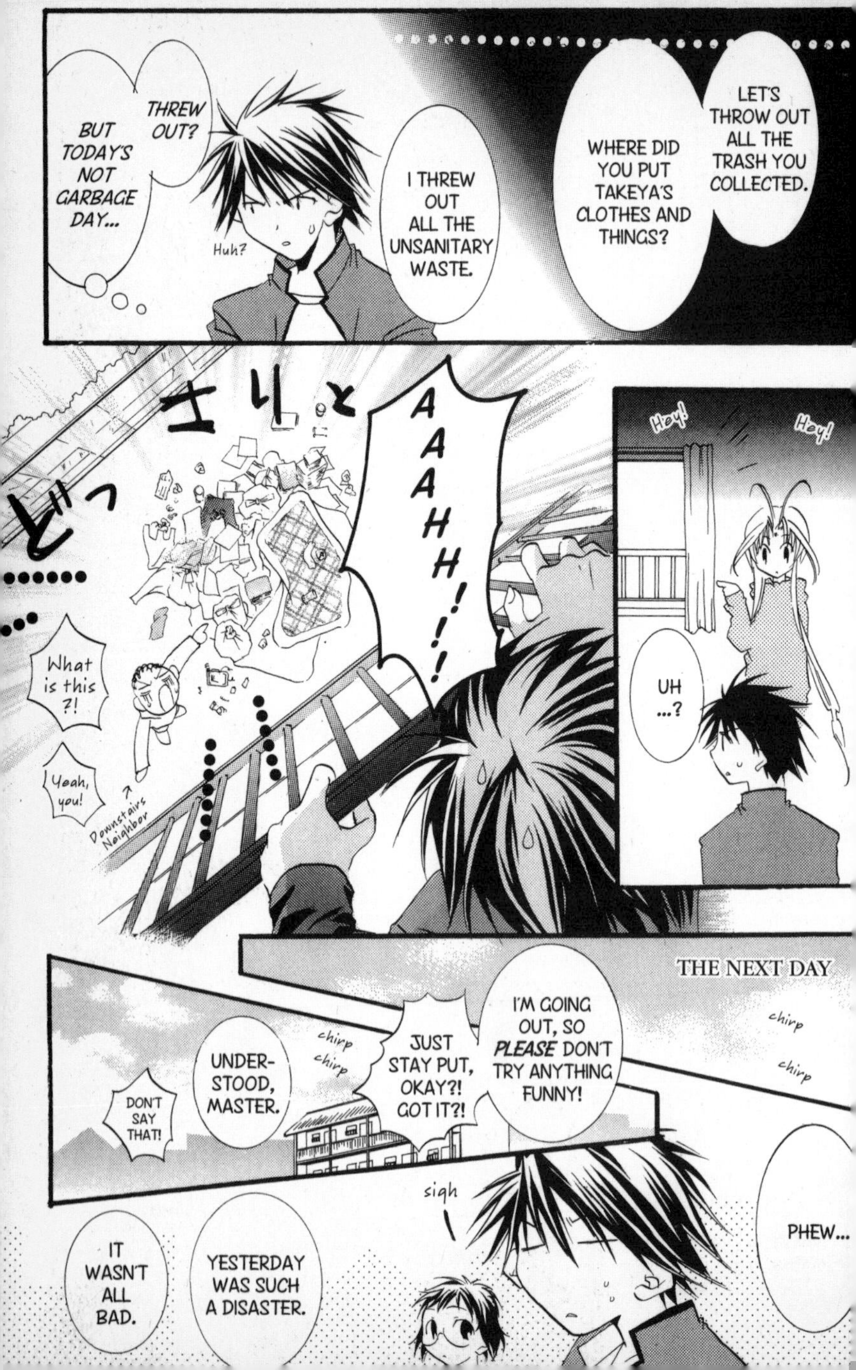
LET'S THROW OUT ALL THE TRASH YOU COLLECTED.
WHERE DID YOU PUT TAKEYA'S CLOTHES AND THINGS?
I THREW OUT ALL THE UNSANITARY WASTE.
Huh?
THREW OUT?
BUT TODAY'S NOT GARBAGE DAY...
Hey!
Hey!
UH ...?
AAAAHH!!!
どっ
....
What is this?!
Yeah, you!
Downstairs Neighbor
THE NEXT DAY
chirp
chirp
I'M GOING OUT, SO *PLEASE* DON'T TRY ANYTHING FUNNY!
JUST STAY PUT, OKAY?! GOT IT?!
chirp
chirp
UNDER-STOOD, MASTER.
DON'T SAY THAT!
PHEW...
sigh
YESTERDAY WAS SUCH A DISASTER.
IT WASN'T ALL BAD.

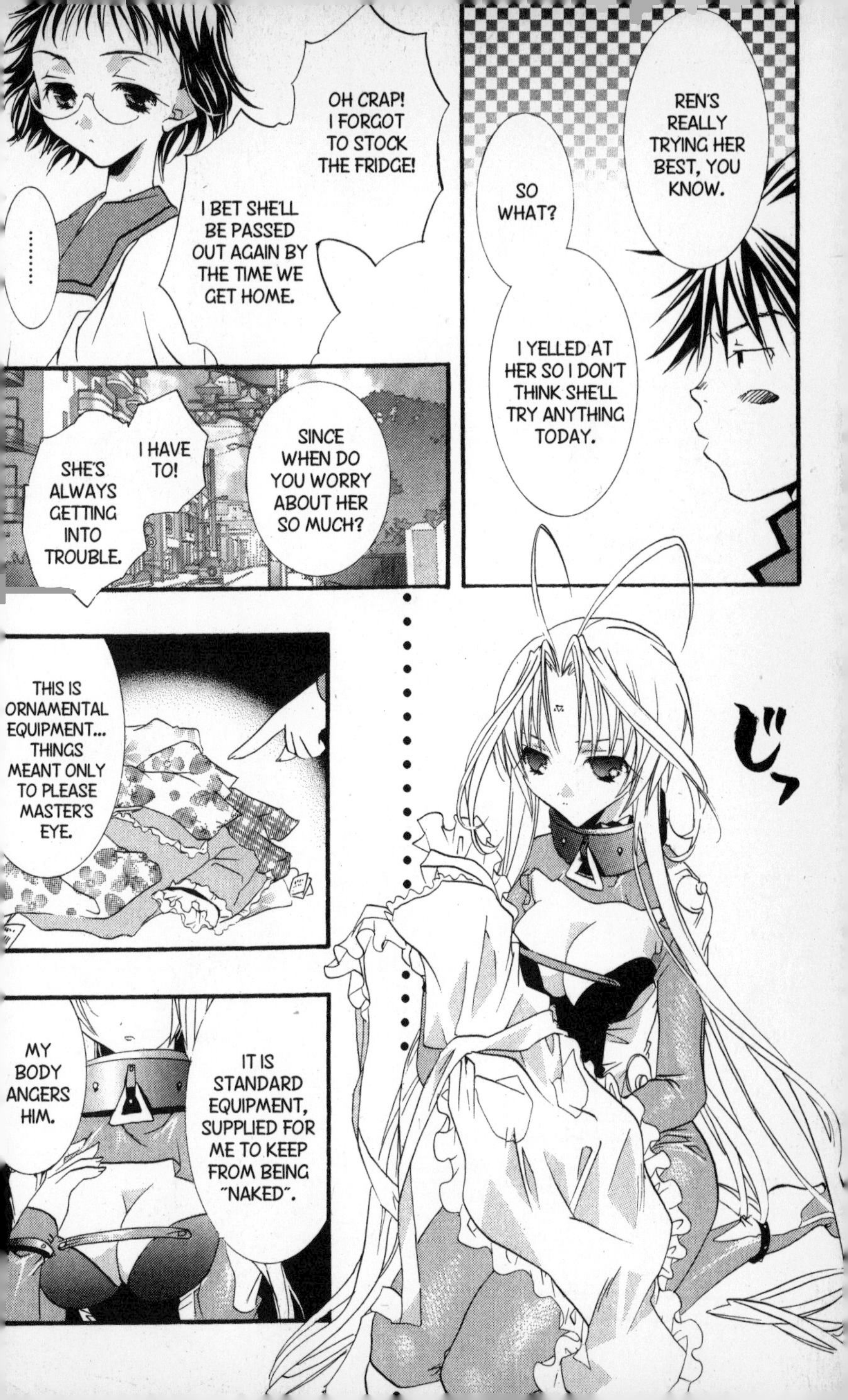
REN'S REALLY TRYING HER BEST, YOU KNOW.
SO WHAT?
I YELLED AT HER SO I DON'T THINK SHE'LL TRY ANYTHING TODAY.
OH CRAP! I FORGOT TO STOCK THE FRIDGE!
I BET SHE'LL BE PASSED OUT AGAIN BY THE TIME WE GET HOME.
......
SINCE WHEN DO YOU WORRY ABOUT HER SO MUCH?
I HAVE TO!
SHE'S ALWAYS GETTING INTO TROUBLE.
じっ
THIS IS ORNAMENTAL EQUIPMENT... THINGS MEANT ONLY TO PLEASE MASTER'S EYE.
IT IS STANDARD EQUIPMENT, SUPPLIED FOR ME TO KEEP FROM BEING "NAKED".
MY BODY ANGERS HIM.

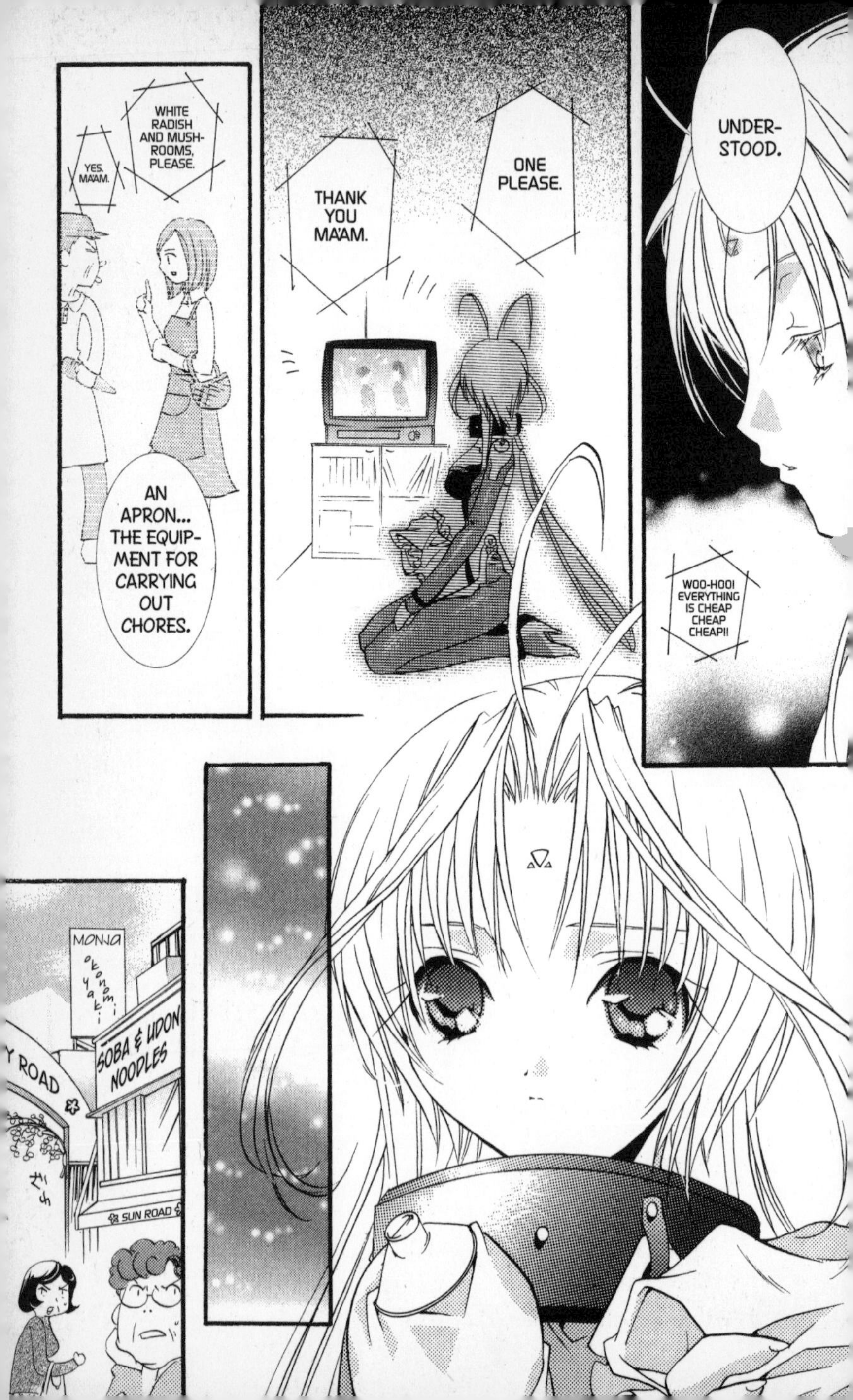
UNDER-STOOD.
WOO-HOO! EVERYTHING IS CHEAP CHEAP CHEAP!!
ONE PLEASE.
THANK YOU MA'AM.
WHITE RADISH AND MUSH-ROOMS, PLEASE.
YES, MA'AM.
AN APRON... THE EQUIP-MENT FOR CARRYING OUT CHORES.
MONJA
okonomiyaki
SOBA & UDON NOODLES
Y ROAD
SUN ROAD

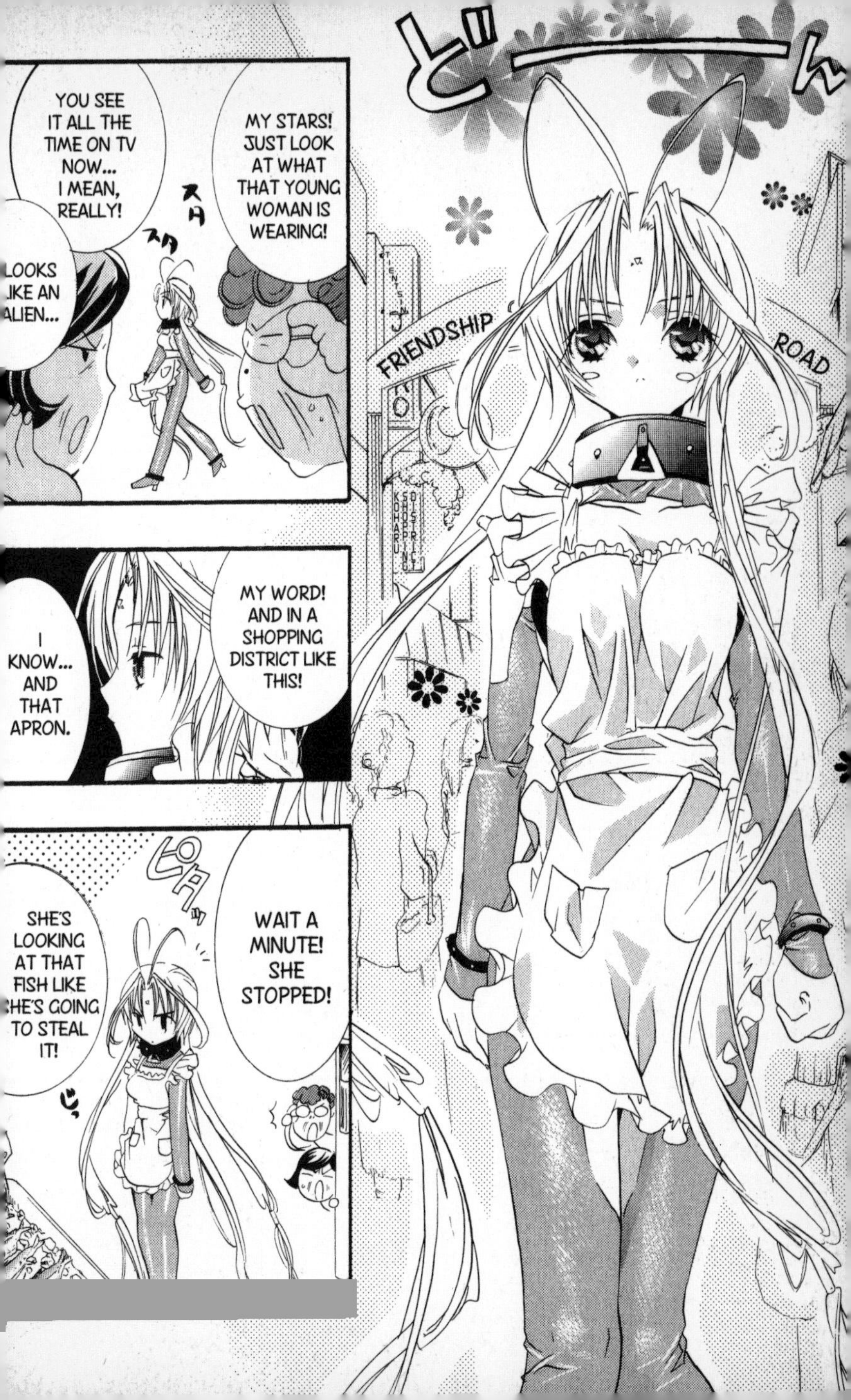
どーーん
FRIENDSHIP ROAD
KOHARU SHOPPING DISTRICT
MY STARS! JUST LOOK AT WHAT THAT YOUNG WOMAN IS WEARING!
YOU SEE IT ALL THE TIME ON TV NOW... I MEAN, REALLY!
スタ スタ
LOOKS LIKE AN ALIEN...
MY WORD! AND IN A SHOPPING DISTRICT LIKE THIS!
I KNOW... AND THAT APRON.
WAIT A MINUTE! SHE STOPPED!
ピタッ
SHE'S LOOKING AT THAT FISH LIKE SHE'S GOING TO STEAL IT!
じ

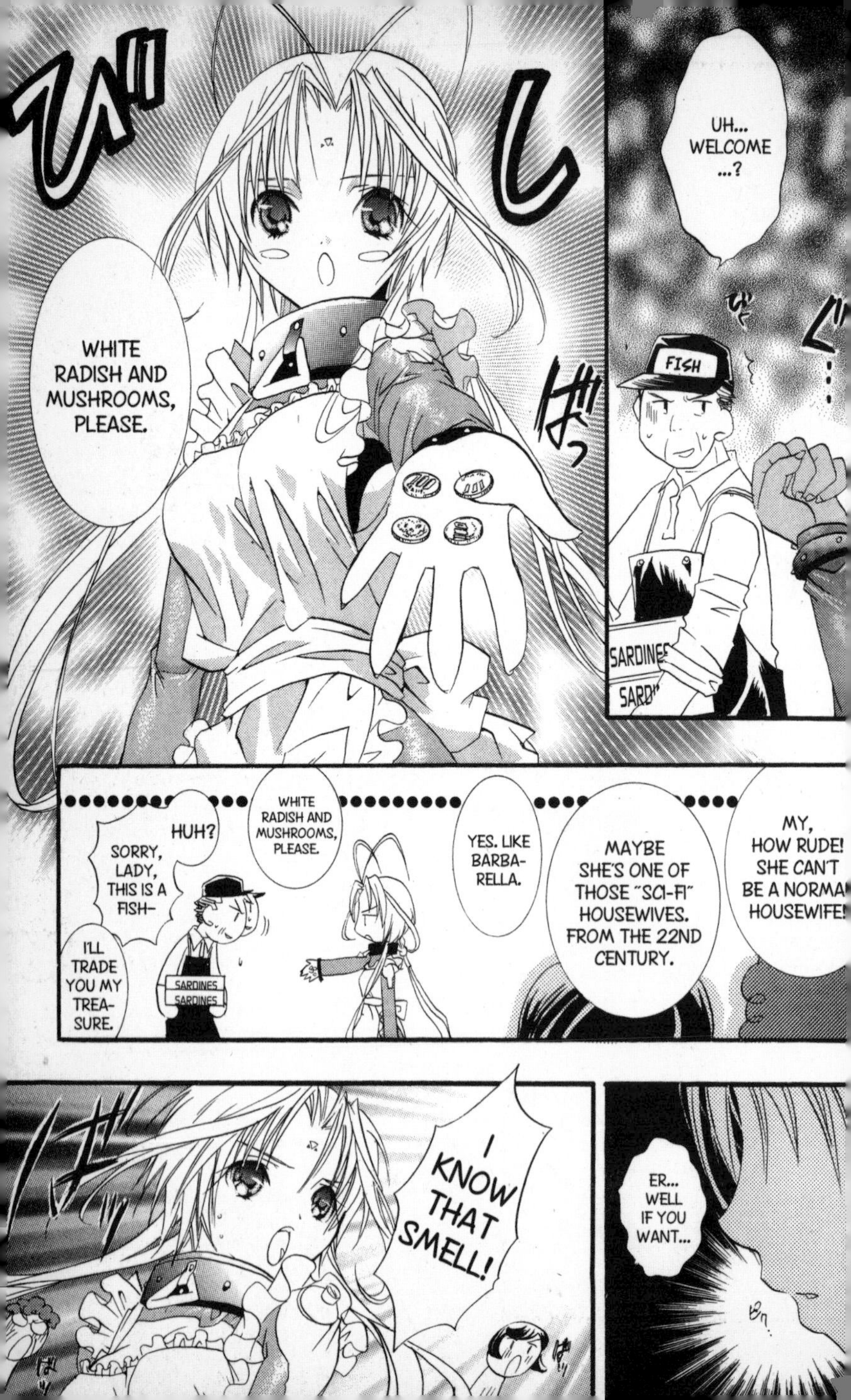
UH... WELCOME ...?
FISH
SARDINES
SARDI
WHITE RADISH AND MUSHROOMS, PLEASE.
MY, HOW RUDE! SHE CAN'T BE A NORMA HOUSEWIFE
MAYBE SHE'S ONE OF THOSE "SCI-FI" HOUSEWIVES. FROM THE 22ND CENTURY.
YES. LIKE BARBA-RELLA.
WHITE RADISH AND MUSHROOMS, PLEASE.
HUH?
SORRY, LADY, THIS IS A FISH-
I'LL TRADE YOU MY TREA-SURE.
SARDINES
SARDINES
ER... WELL IF YOU WANT...
I KNOW THAT SMELL!

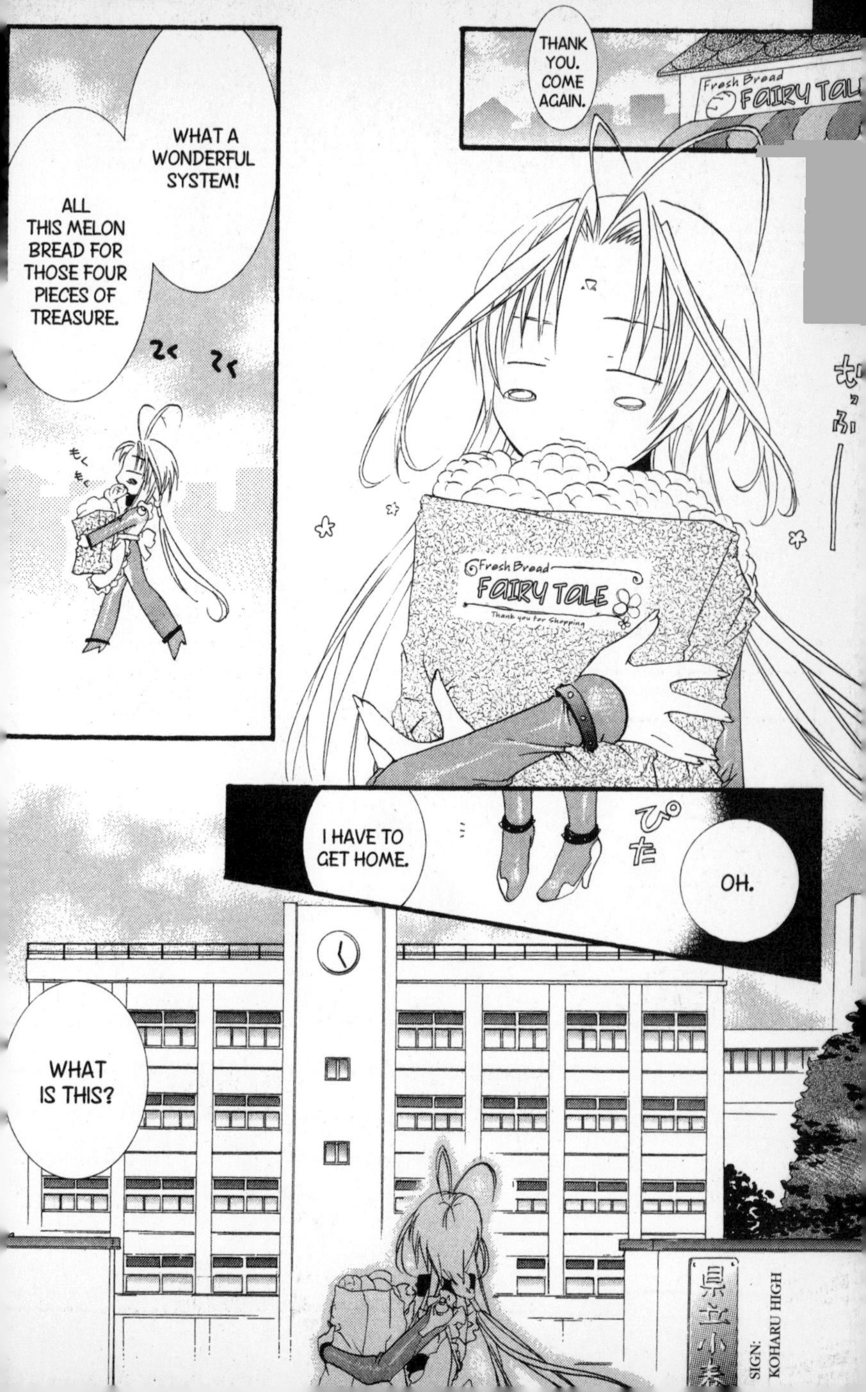
THANK YOU. COME AGAIN.
Fresh Bread FAIRY TALE
WHAT A WONDERFUL SYSTEM!
ALL THIS MELON BREAD FOR THOSE FOUR PIECES OF TREASURE.
もく もく
Fresh Bread FAIRY TALE
Thank you for Shopping
OH.
ぴた
I HAVE TO GET HOME.
WHAT IS THIS?
SIGN: KOHARU HIGH

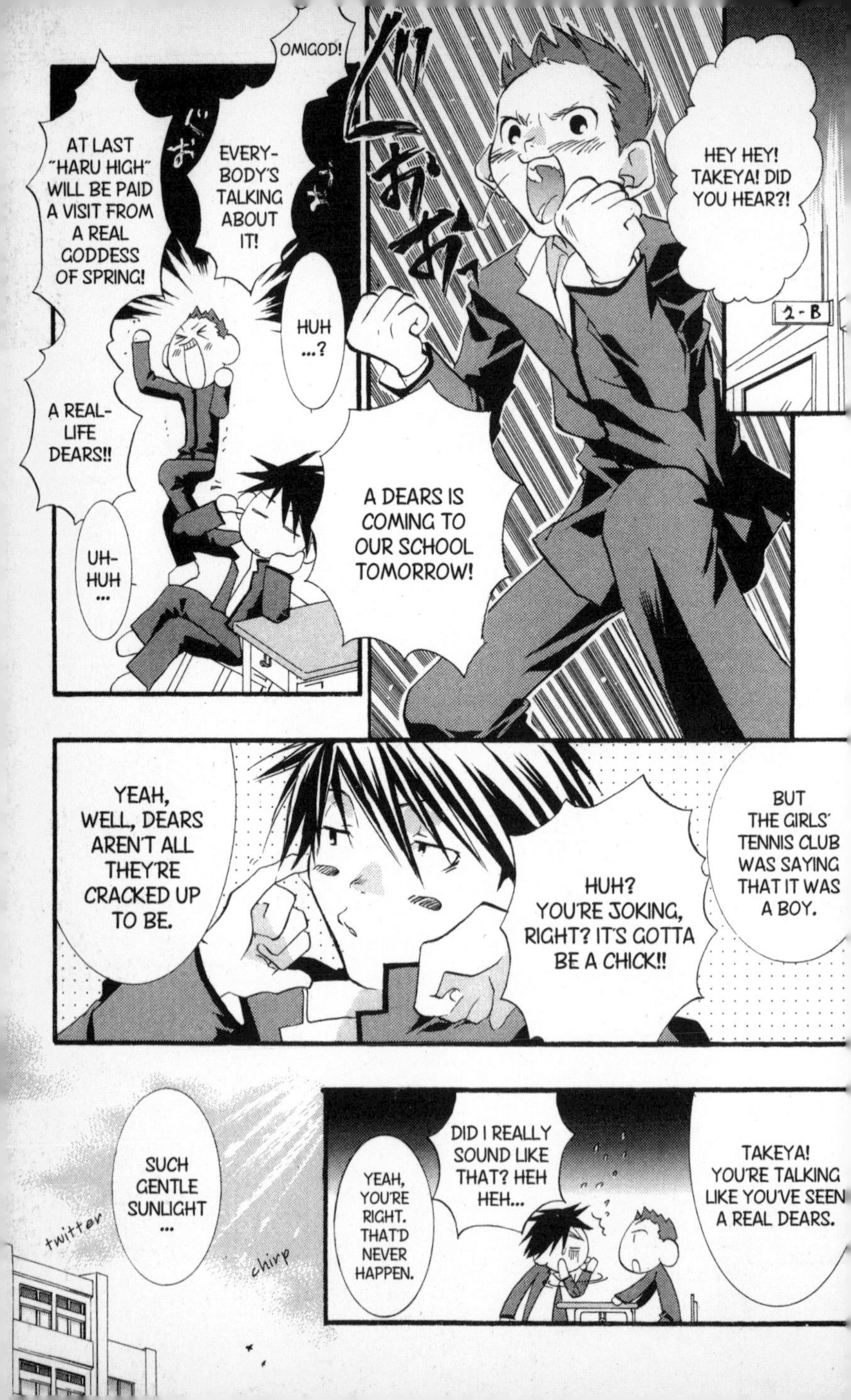
HEY HEY! TAKEYA! DID YOU HEAR?!
A DEARS IS COMING TO OUR SCHOOL TOMORROW!
OMIGOD!
EVERY-BODY'S TALKING ABOUT IT!
AT LAST "HARU HIGH" WILL BE PAID A VISIT FROM A REAL GODDESS OF SPRING!
HUH ...?
A REAL-LIFE DEARS!!
UH-HUH ...
2-B
BUT THE GIRLS' TENNIS CLUB WAS SAYING THAT IT WAS A BOY.
HUH? YOU'RE JOKING, RIGHT? IT'S GOTTA BE A CHICK!!
YEAH, WELL, DEARS AREN'T ALL THEY'RE CRACKED UP TO BE.
TAKEYA! YOU'RE TALKING LIKE YOU'VE SEEN A REAL DEARS.
DID I REALLY SOUND LIKE THAT? HEH HEH...
YEAH, YOU'RE RIGHT. THAT'D NEVER HAPPEN.
SUCH GENTLE SUNLIGHT ...
twitter
chirp

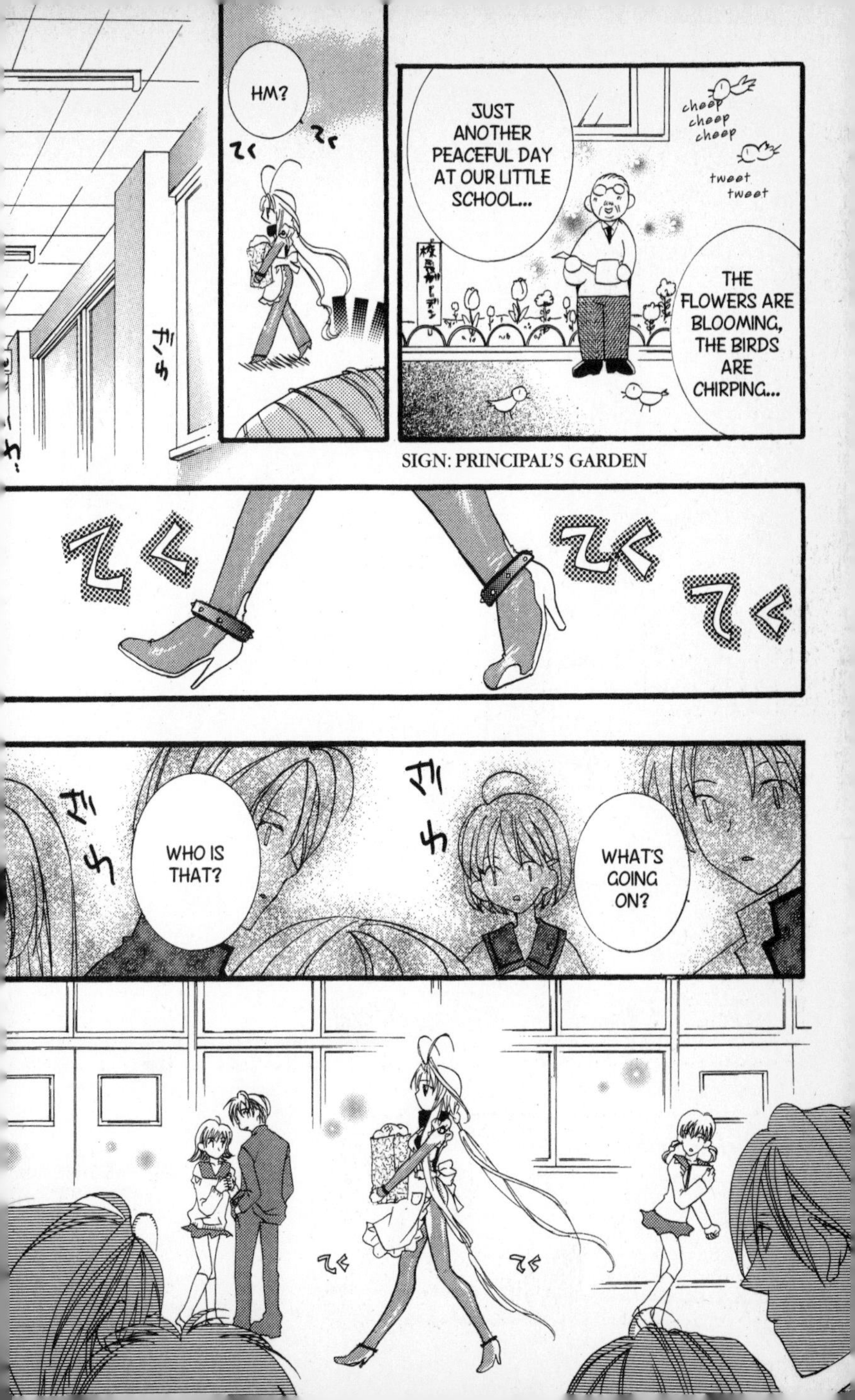
JUST ANOTHER PEACEFUL DAY AT OUR LITTLE SCHOOL...
cheep cheep cheep
tweet tweet
THE FLOWERS ARE BLOOMING, THE BIRDS ARE CHIRPING...
SIGN: PRINCIPAL'S GARDEN
HM?
WHAT'S GOING ON?
WHO IS THAT?

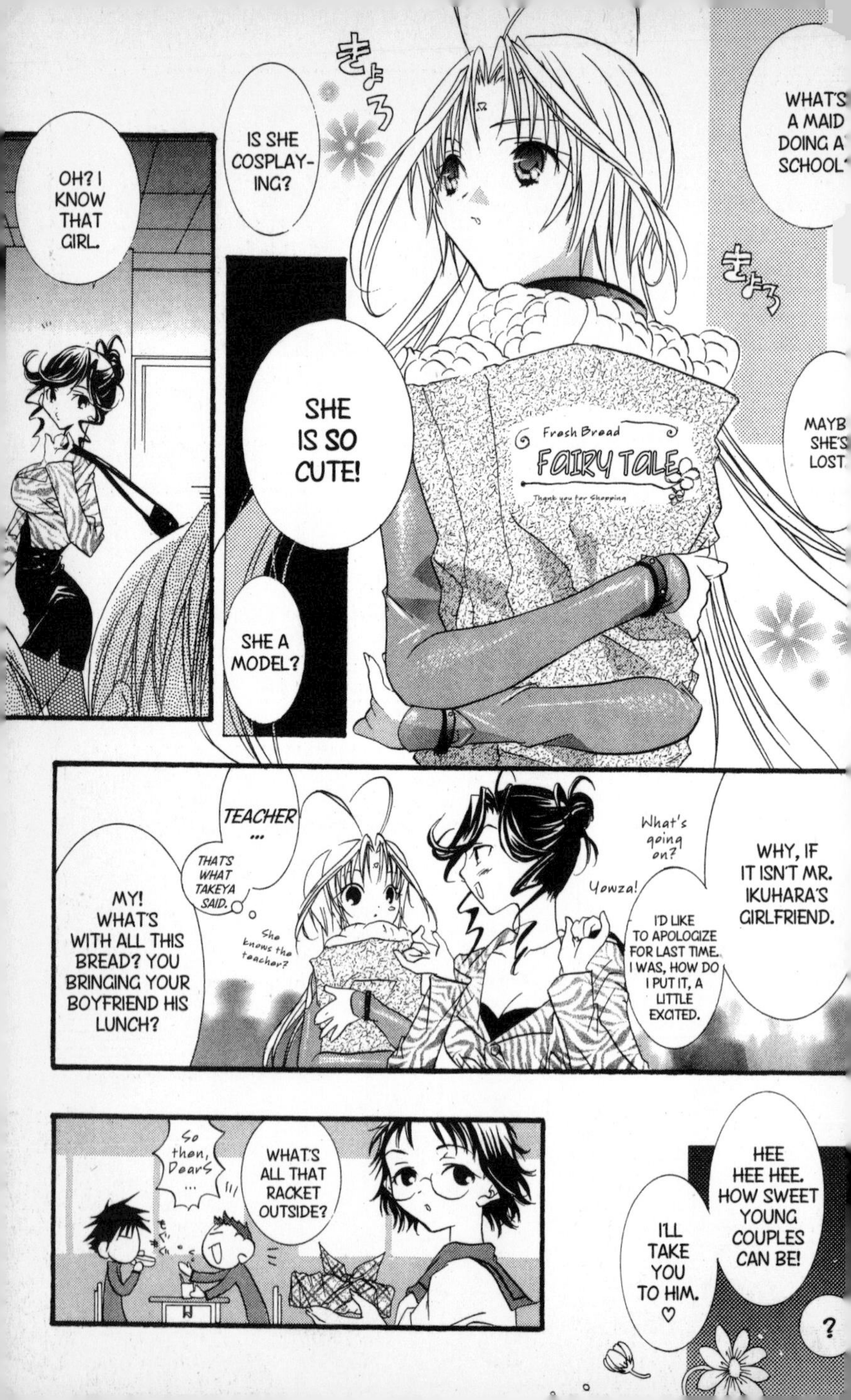
きょろ
WHAT'S A MAID DOING A SCHOOL
IS SHE COSPLAY-ING?
きょろ
Fresh Bread
FAIRY TALE
Thank you for Shopping
MAYB SHE'S LOST.
SHE IS SO CUTE!
SHE A MODEL?
OH? I KNOW THAT GIRL.
WHY, IF IT ISN'T MR. IKUHARA'S GIRLFRIEND.
What's going on?
Yowza!
I'D LIKE TO APOLOGIZE FOR LAST TIME. I WAS, HOW DO I PUT IT, A LITTLE EXCITED.
TEACHER...
THAT'S WHAT TAKEYA SAID.
She knows the teacher?
MY! WHAT'S WITH ALL THIS BREAD? YOU BRINGING YOUR BOYFRIEND HIS LUNCH?
HEE HEE HEE. HOW SWEET YOUNG COUPLES CAN BE!
I'LL TAKE YOU TO HIM. ♡
?
WHAT'S ALL THAT RACKET OUTSIDE?
So then, DearS...

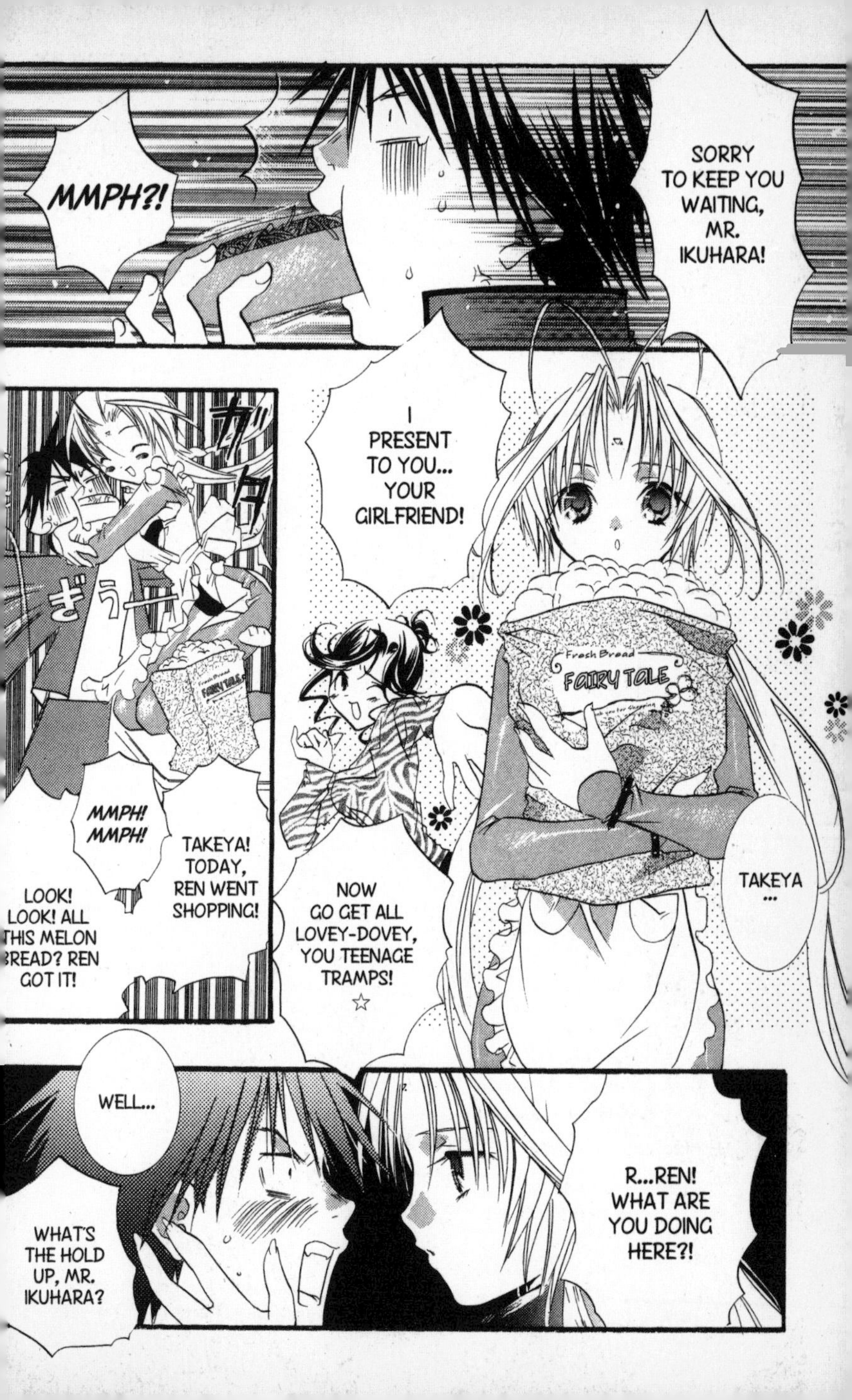
SORRY TO KEEP YOU WAITING, MR. IKUHARA!
MMPH?!
I PRESENT TO YOU... YOUR GIRLFRIEND!
TAKEYA ...
NOW GO GET ALL LOVEY-DOVEY, YOU TEENAGE TRAMPS! ☆
TAKEYA! TODAY, REN WENT SHOPPING!
MMPH! MMPH!
LOOK! LOOK! ALL THIS MELON BREAD? REN GOT IT!
R...REN! WHAT ARE YOU DOING HERE?!
WELL...
WHAT'S THE HOLD UP, MR. IKUHARA?

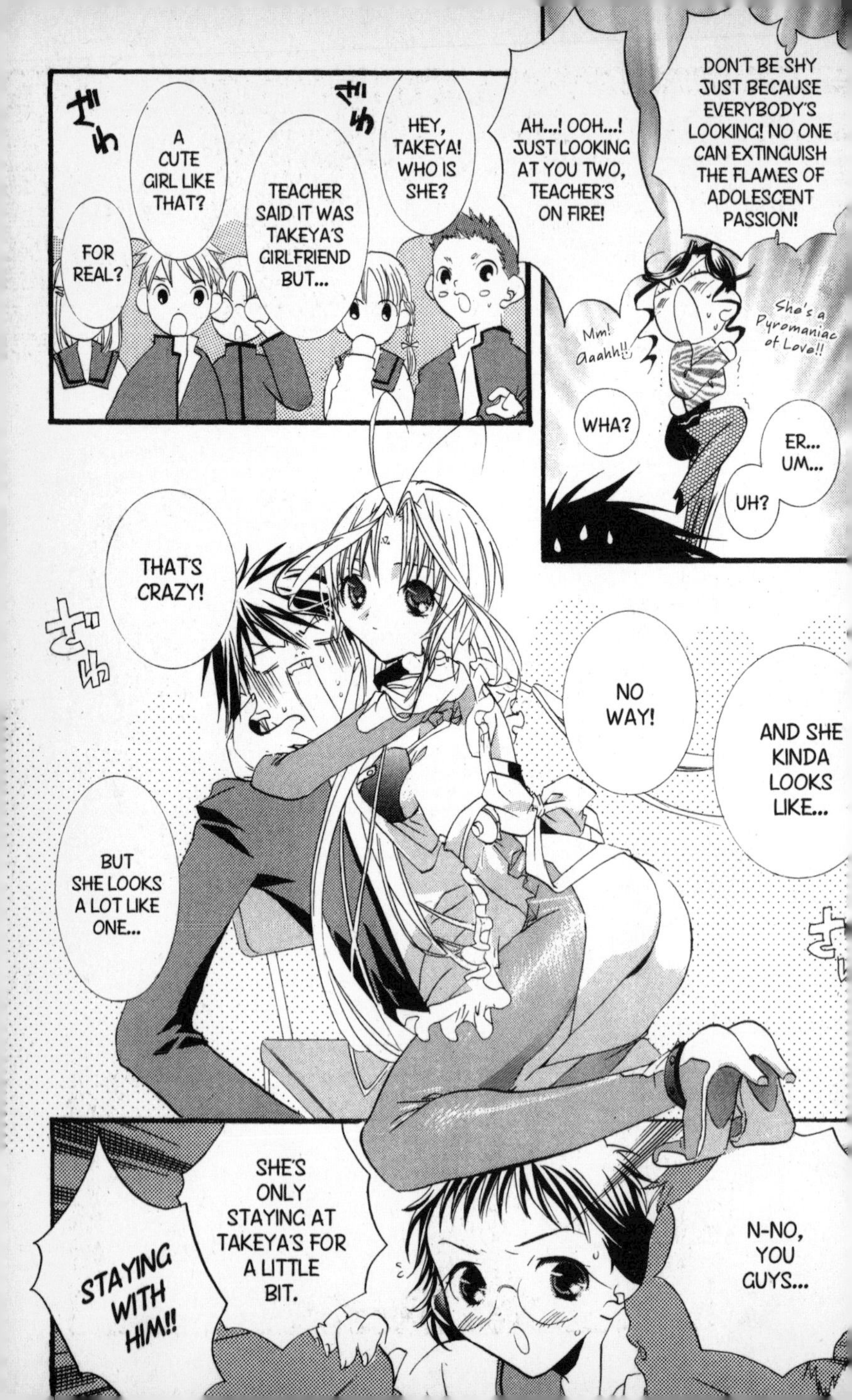
DON'T BE SHY JUST BECAUSE EVERYBODY'S LOOKING! NO ONE CAN EXTINGUISH THE FLAMES OF ADOLESCENT PASSION!
AH...! OOH...! JUST LOOKING AT YOU TWO, TEACHER'S ON FIRE!
She's a Pyromaniac of Love!!
Mm! Aaahh!!
ER... UM...
UH?
WHA?
HEY, TAKEYA! WHO IS SHE?
ざわ
TEACHER SAID IT WAS TAKEYA'S GIRLFRIEND BUT...
A CUTE GIRL LIKE THAT?
FOR REAL?
ざわ
AND SHE KINDA LOOKS LIKE...
NO WAY!
THAT'S CRAZY!
ざわ
BUT SHE LOOKS A LOT LIKE ONE...
N-NO, YOU GUYS...
SHE'S ONLY STAYING AT TAKEYA'S FOR A LITTLE BIT.
STAYING WITH HIM!!

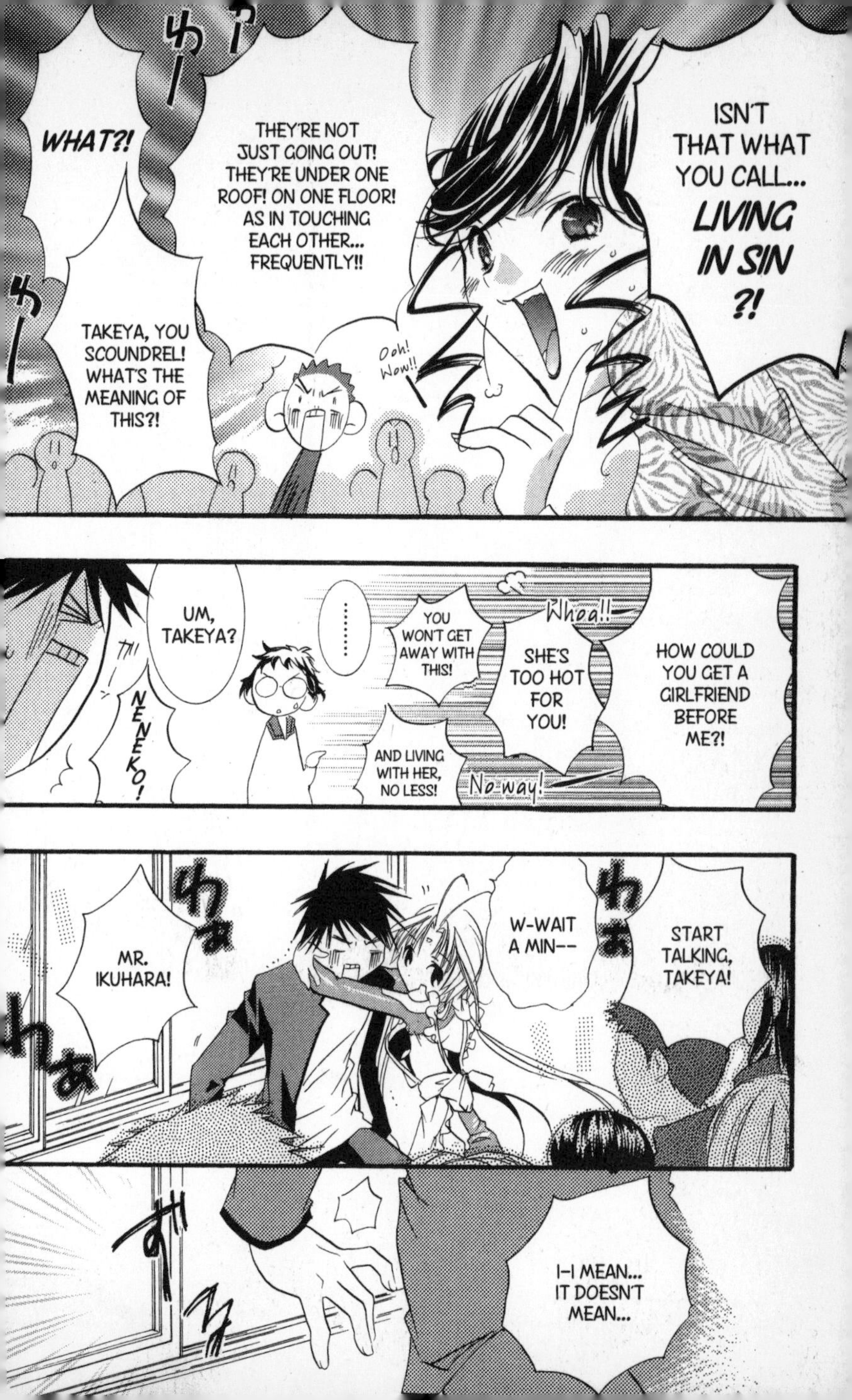
ISN'T THAT WHAT YOU CALL... LIVING IN SIN ?!
Ooh! Wow!!
THEY'RE NOT JUST GOING OUT! THEY'RE UNDER ONE ROOF! ON ONE FLOOR! AS IN TOUCHING EACH OTHER... FREQUENTLY!!
WHAT?!
TAKEYA, YOU SCOUNDREL! WHAT'S THE MEANING OF THIS?!
HOW COULD YOU GET A GIRLFRIEND BEFORE ME?!
Whoa!!
SHE'S TOO HOT FOR YOU!
No way!
YOU WON'T GET AWAY WITH THIS!
AND LIVING WITH HER, NO LESS!
....
UM, TAKEYA?
NENEKO!
START TALKING, TAKEYA!
W-WAIT A MIN--
MR. IKUHARA!
I-I MEAN... IT DOESN'T MEAN...

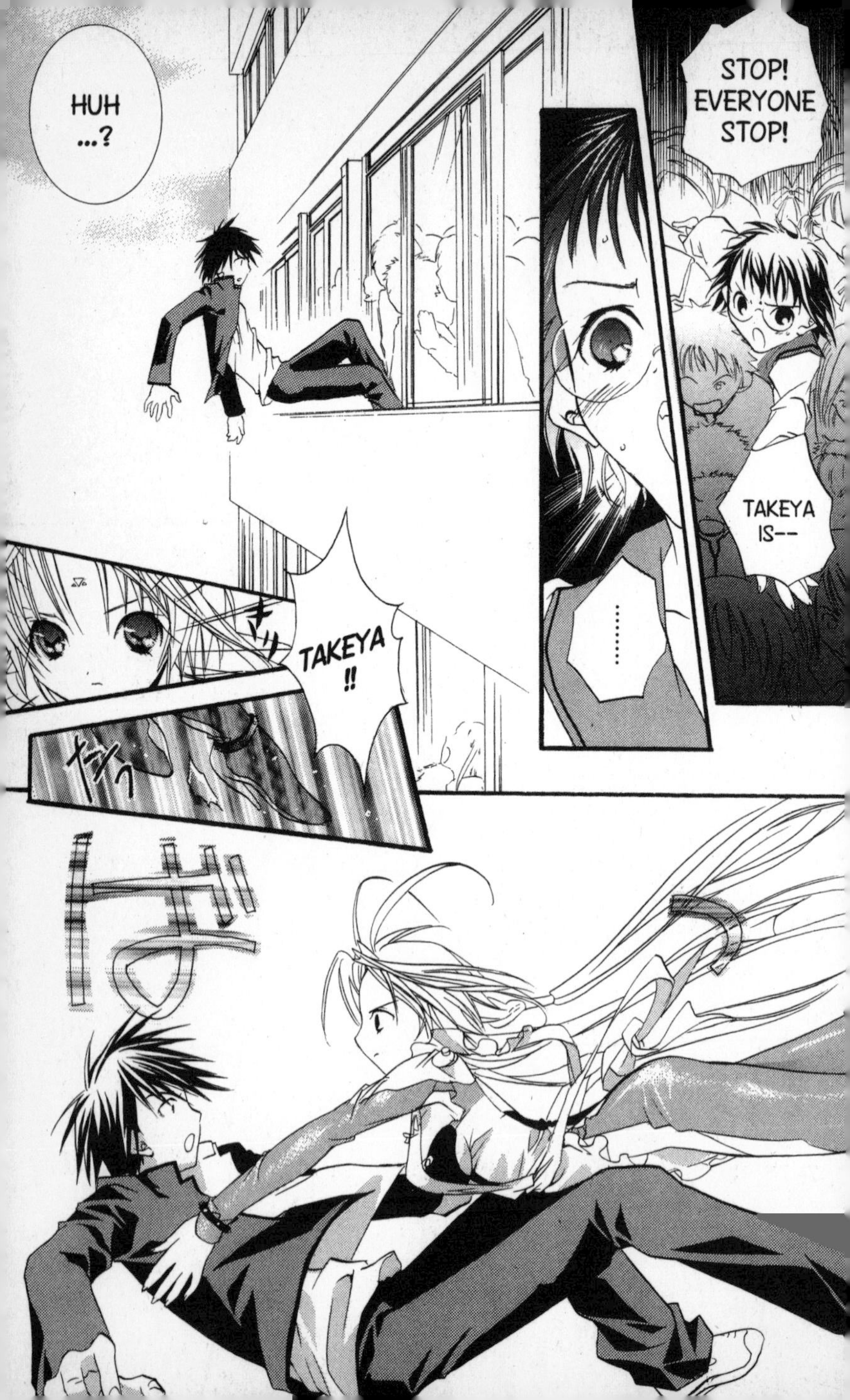
STOP! EVERYONE STOP!
TAKEYA IS--
......
HUH ...?
TAKEYA !!

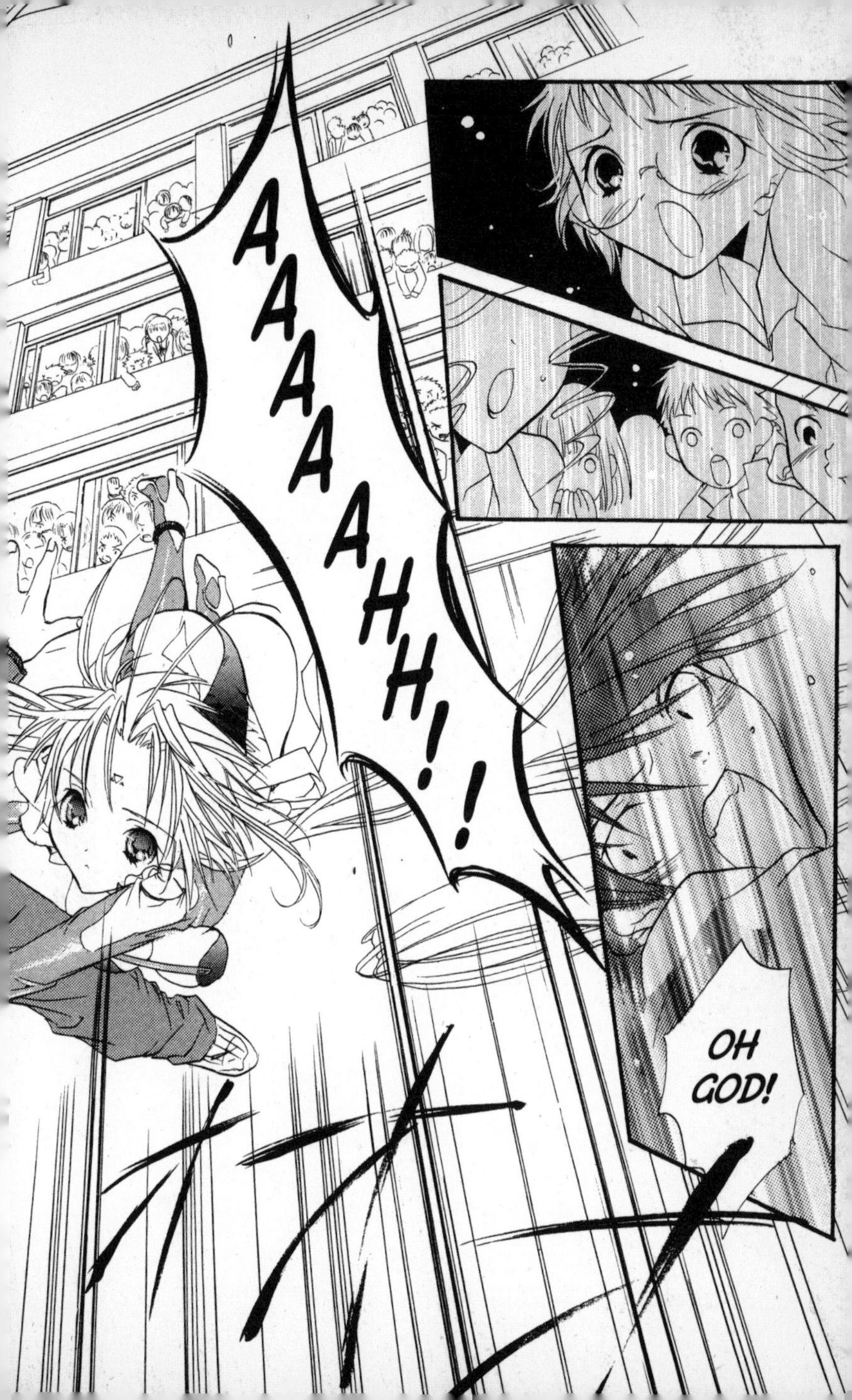
AAAAAAHH!!!
OH GOD!

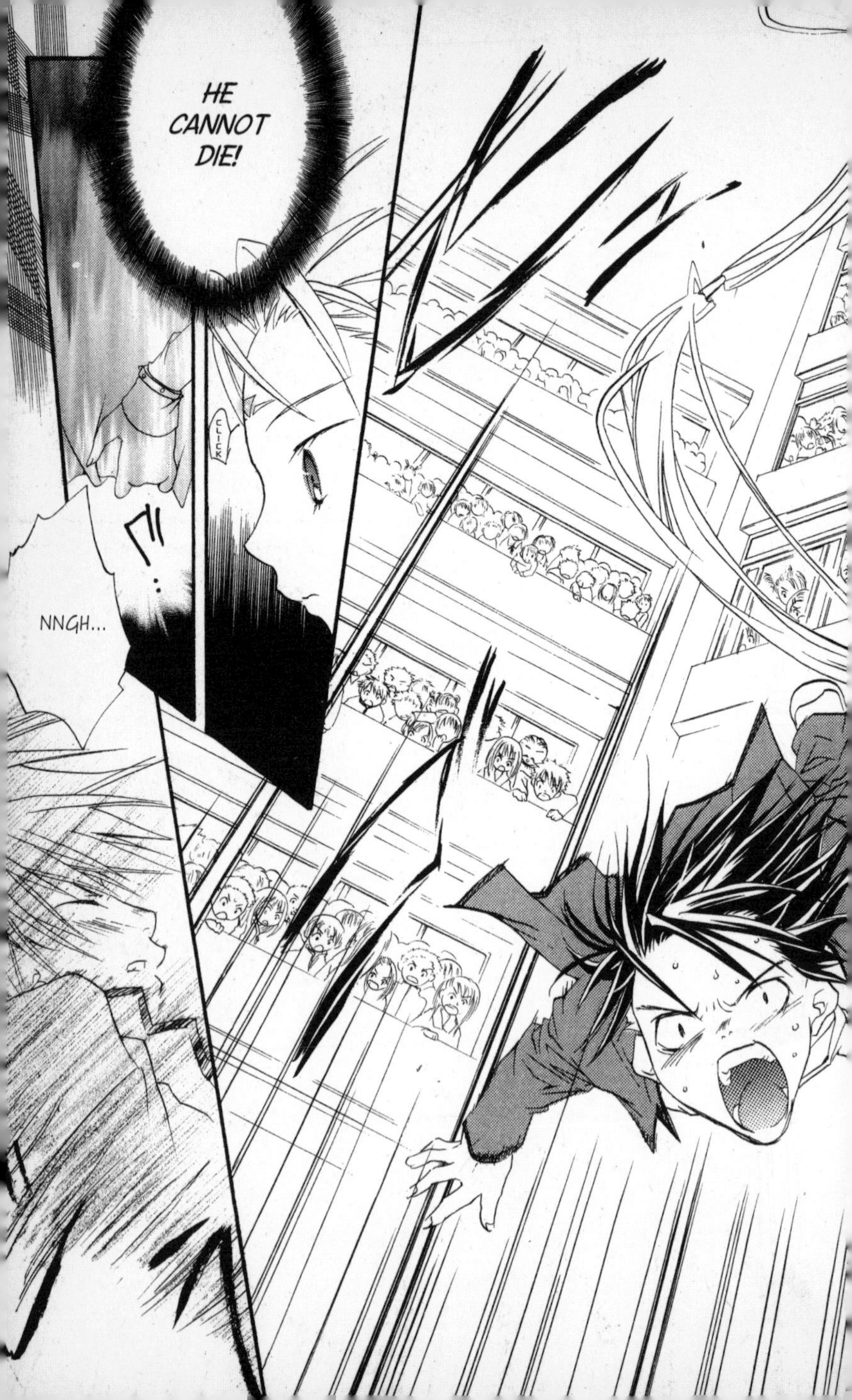
HE CANNOT DIE!
CLICK
NNGH...

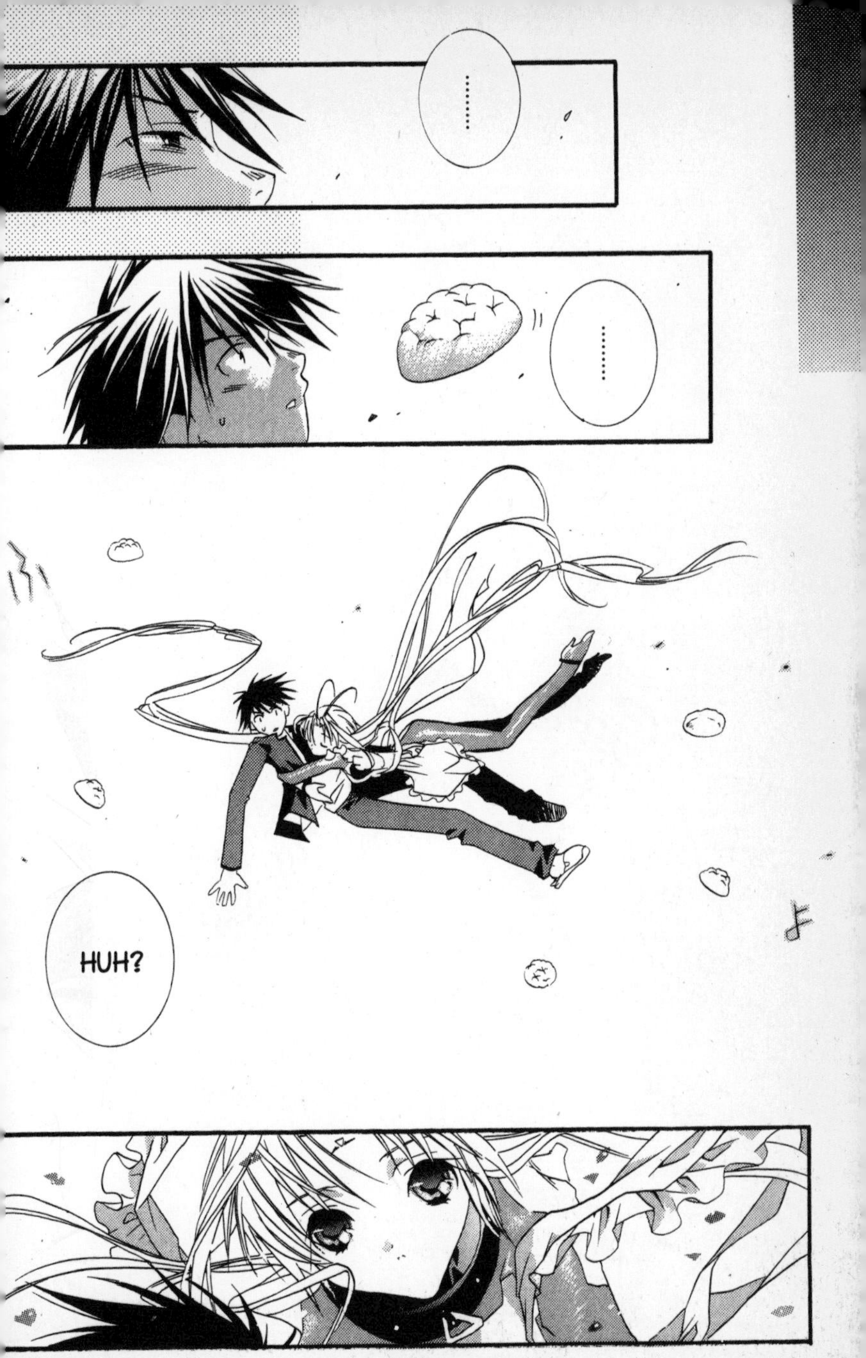
......
......
HUH?

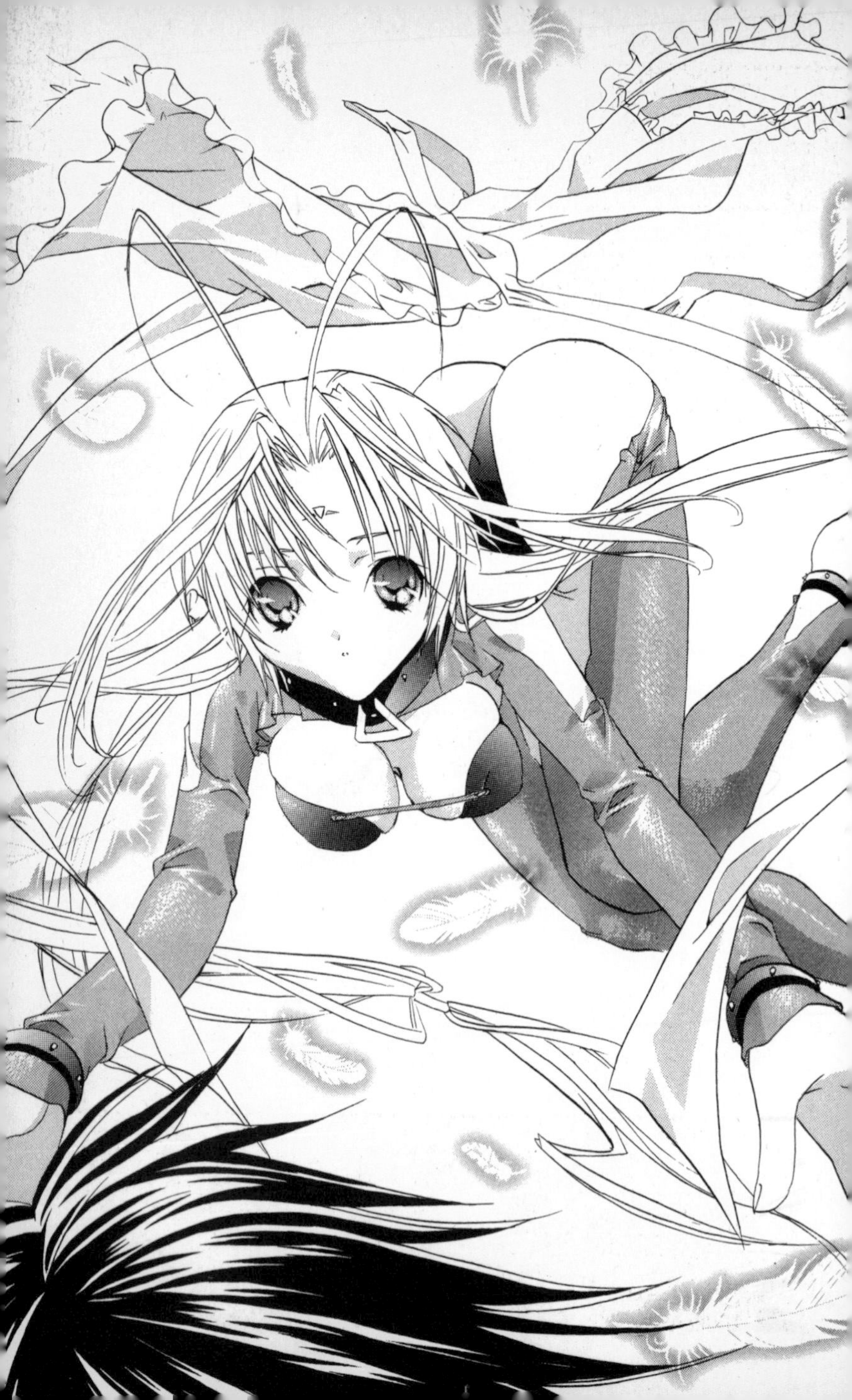

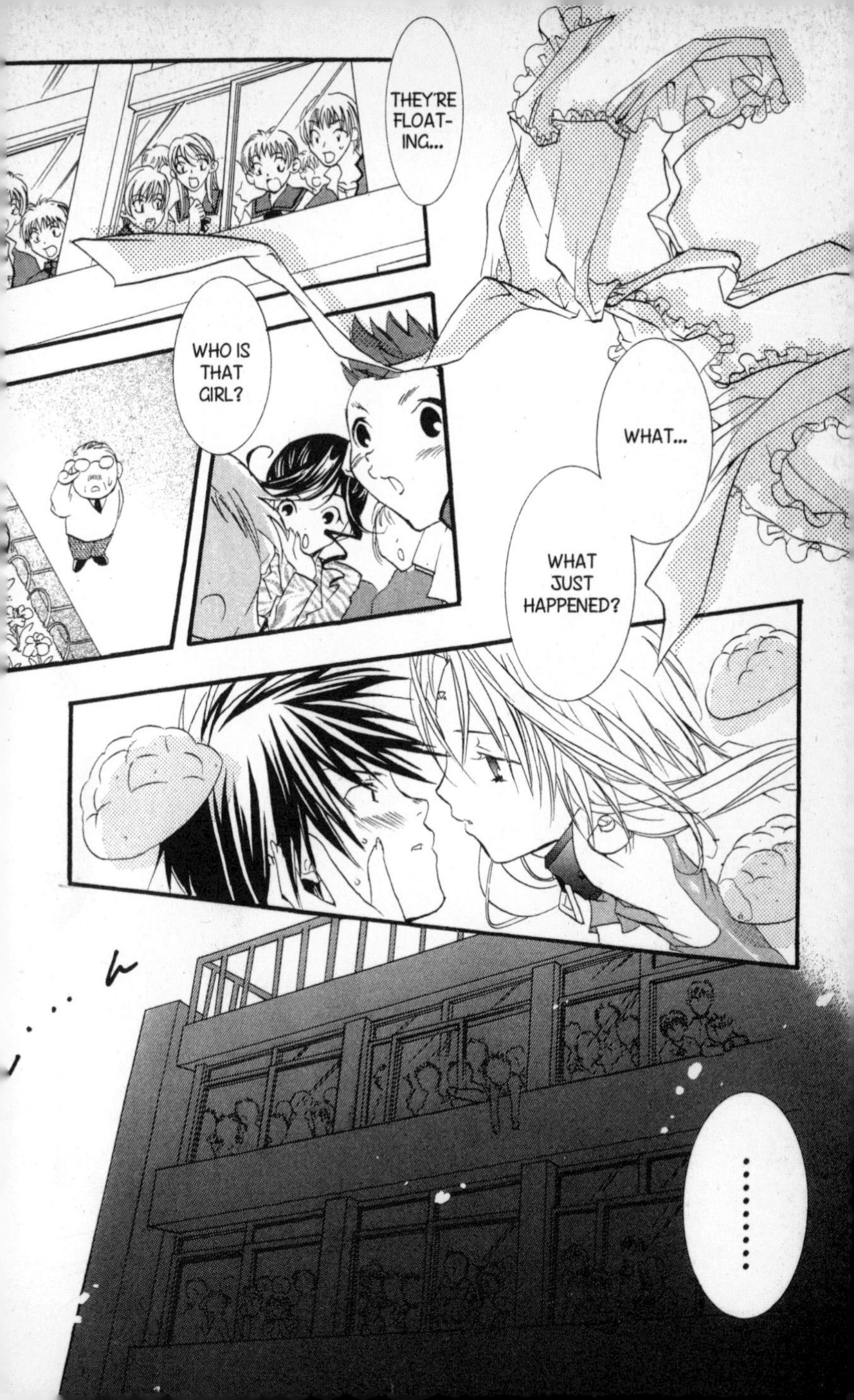
THEY'RE FLOAT-ING...
WHO IS THAT GIRL?
WHAT...
WHAT JUST HAPPENED?
......

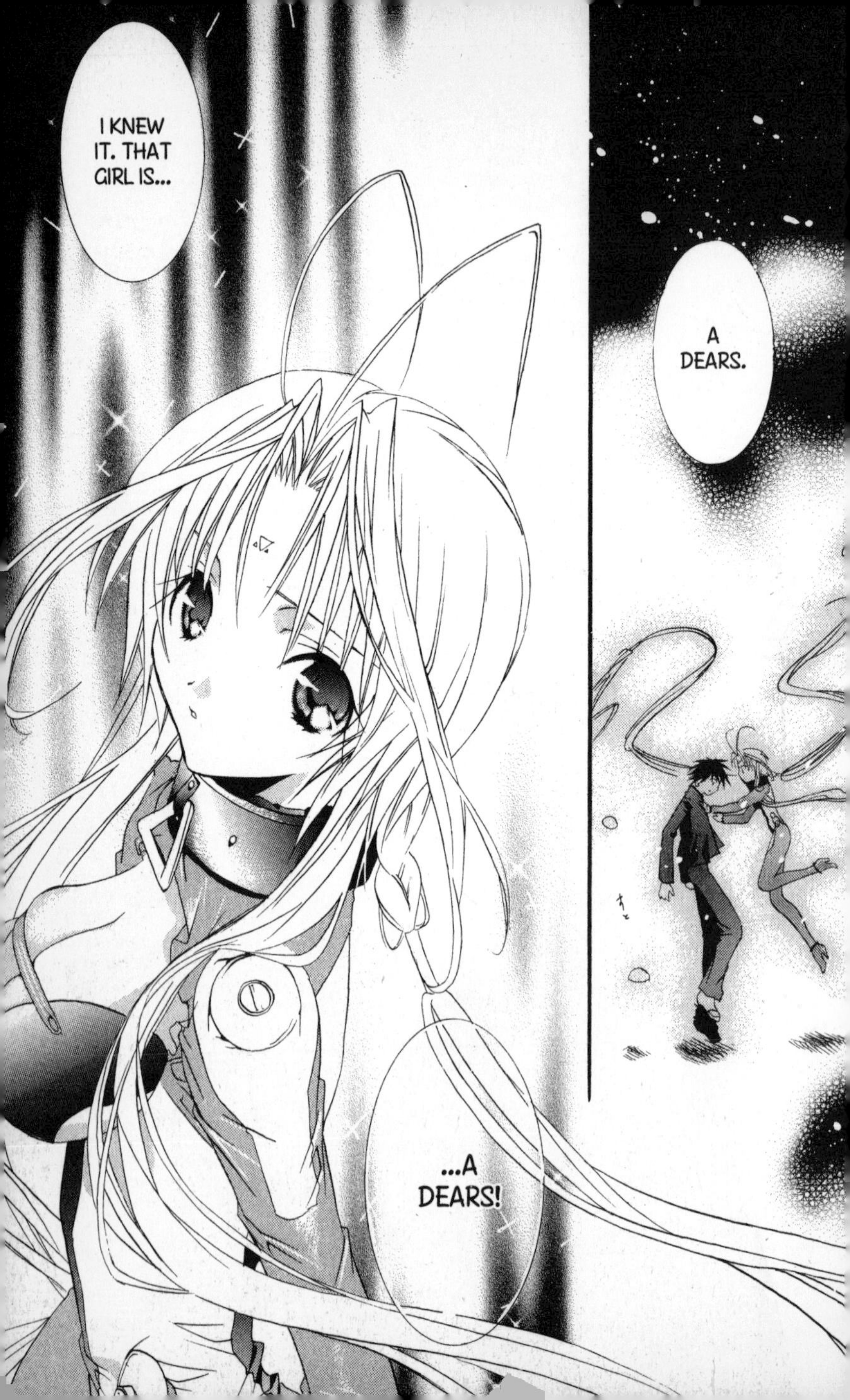
A DEARS.
I KNEW IT. THAT GIRL IS...
...A DEARS!

DearS

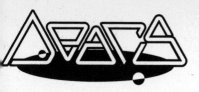

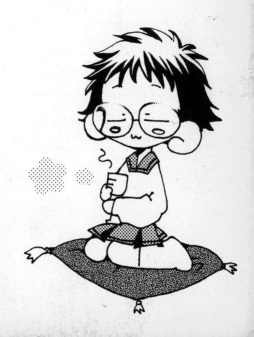

6th Contact

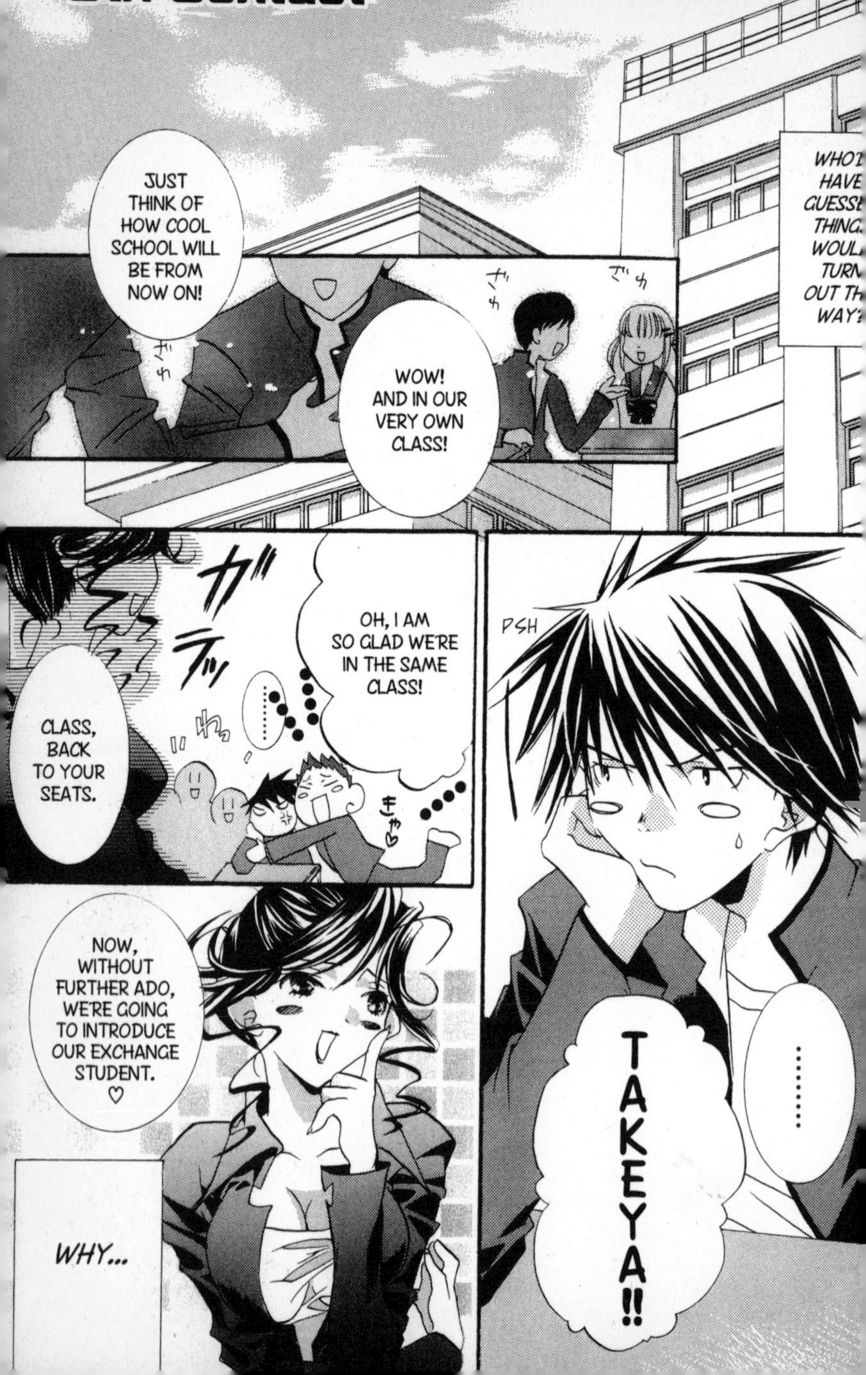
WHO'I HAVE GUESSE THING WOUL TURN OUT TH WAY?
WOW! AND IN OUR VERY OWN CLASS!
JUST THINK OF HOW COOL SCHOOL WILL BE FROM NOW ON!
PSH
......
TAKEYA!!
OH, I AM SO GLAD WE'RE IN THE SAME CLASS!
......
CLASS, BACK TO YOUR SEATS.
NOW, WITHOUT FURTHER ADO, WE'RE GOING TO INTRODUCE OUR EXCHANGE STUDENT. ♡
WHY...

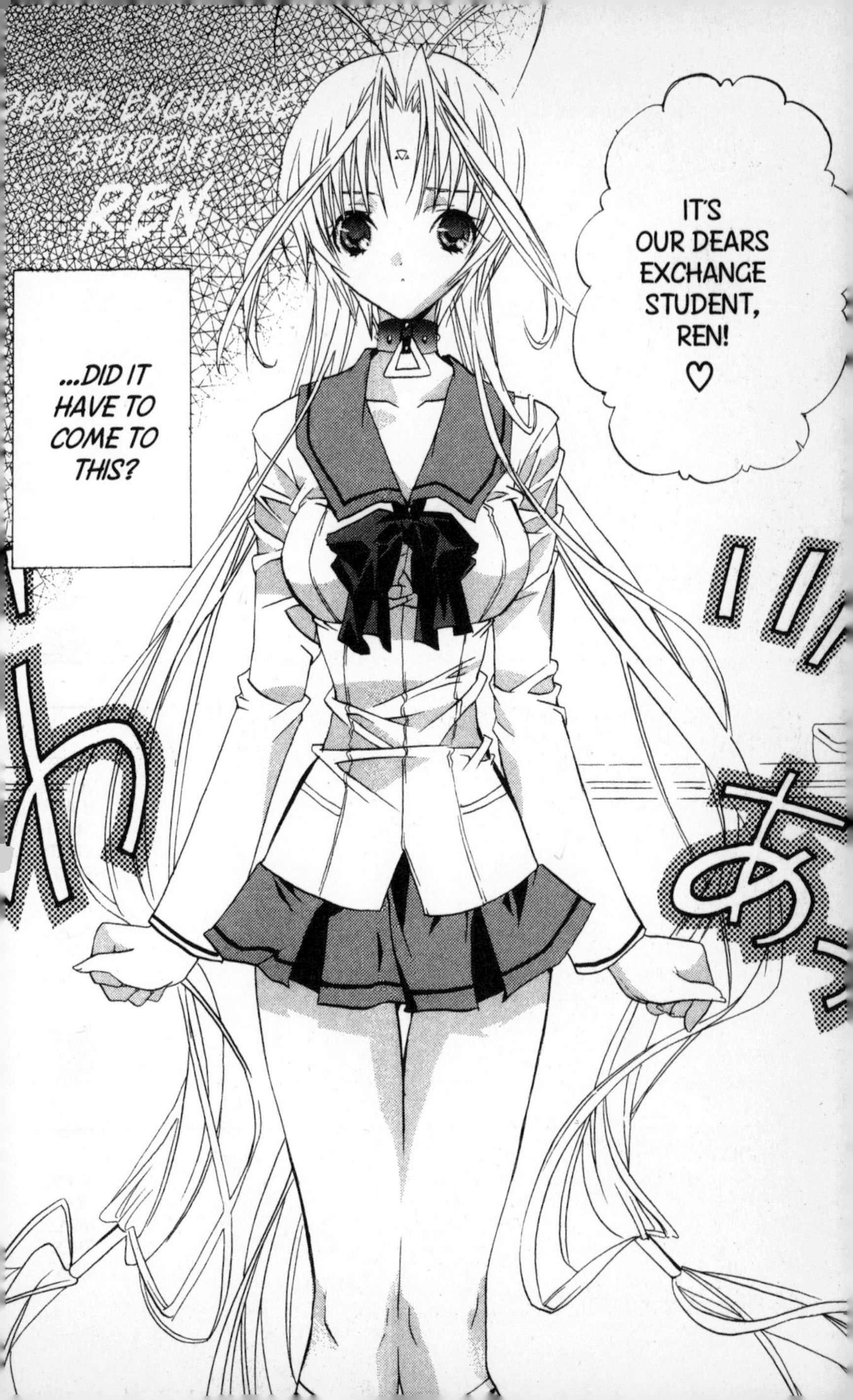
IT'S OUR DEARS EXCHANGE STUDENT, REN! ♡
DEARS EXCHANGE STUDENT REN
...DID IT HAVE TO COME TO THIS?

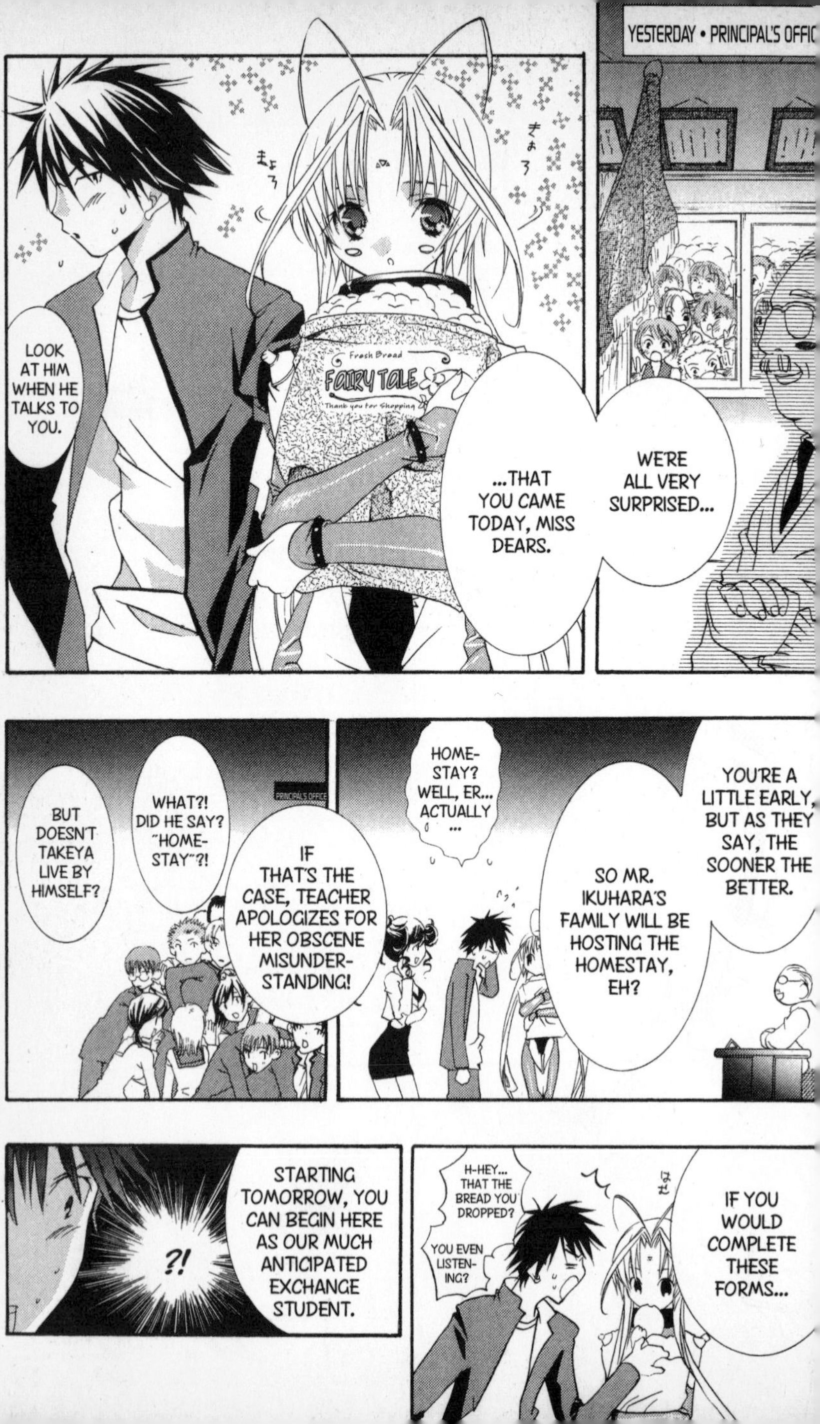
YESTERDAY • PRINCIPAL'S OFFIC
WE'RE ALL VERY SURPRISED...
...THAT YOU CAME TODAY, MISS DEARS.
Fresh Bread
FAIRY TALE
Thank you for Shopping
LOOK AT HIM WHEN HE TALKS TO YOU.
YOU'RE A LITTLE EARLY, BUT AS THEY SAY, THE SOONER THE BETTER.
SO MR. IKUHARA'S FAMILY WILL BE HOSTING THE HOMESTAY, EH?
HOME-STAY? WELL, ER... ACTUALLY ...
IF THAT'S THE CASE, TEACHER APOLOGIZES FOR HER OBSCENE MISUNDER-STANDING!
PRINCIPAL'S OFFICE
WHAT?! DID HE SAY? "HOME-STAY"?!
BUT DOESN'T TAKEYA LIVE BY HIMSELF?
IF YOU WOULD COMPLETE THESE FORMS...
H-HEY... THAT THE BREAD YOU DROPPED?
YOU EVEN LISTEN-ING?
STARTING TOMORROW, YOU CAN BEGIN HERE AS OUR MUCH ANTICIPATED EXCHANGE STUDENT.
?!

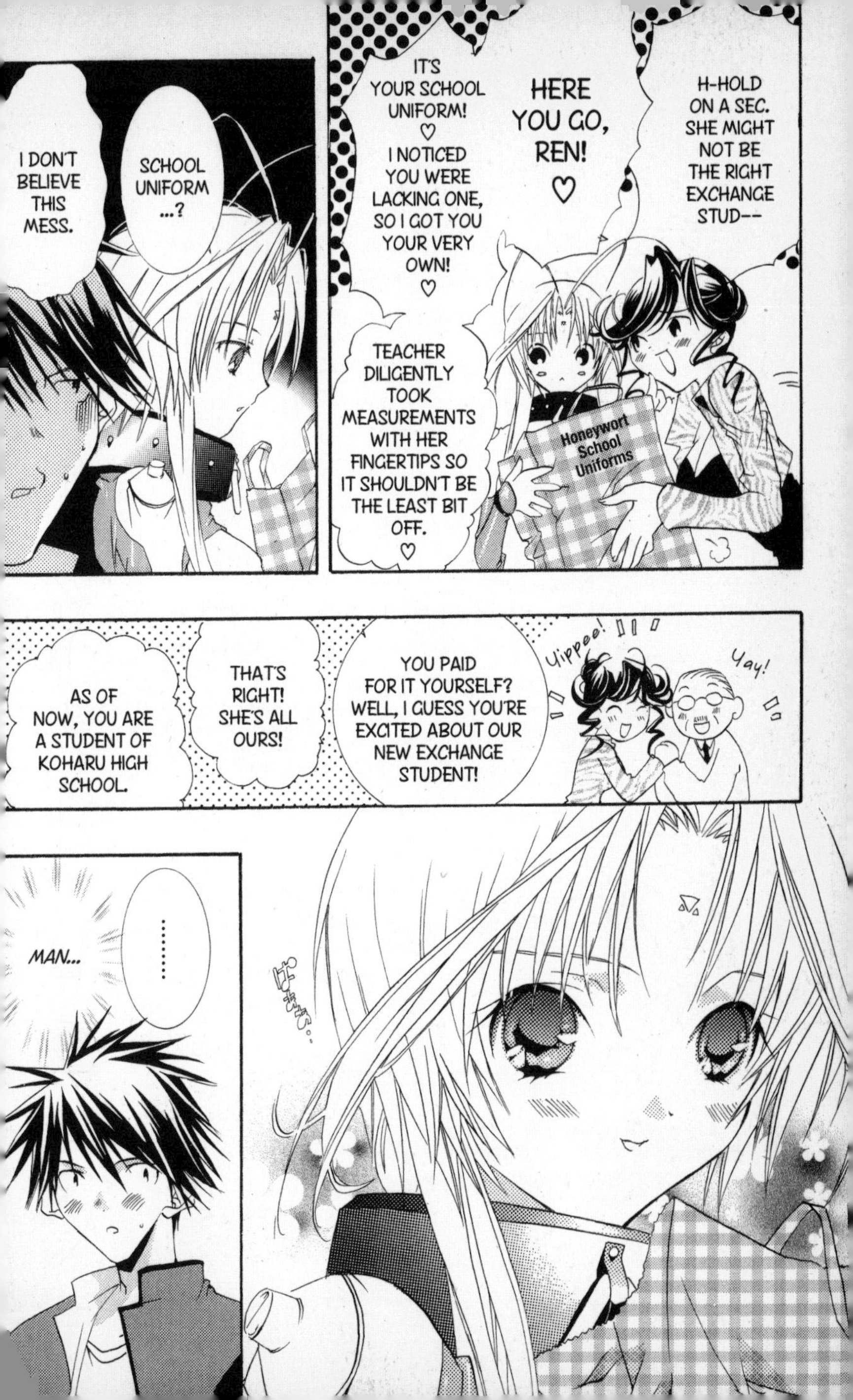
H-HOLD ON A SEC. SHE MIGHT NOT BE THE RIGHT EXCHANGE STUD--
HERE YOU GO, REN! ♡
IT'S YOUR SCHOOL UNIFORM! ♡ I NOTICED YOU WERE LACKING ONE, SO I GOT YOU YOUR VERY OWN! ♡
Honeywort School Uniforms
TEACHER DILIGENTLY TOOK MEASUREMENTS WITH HER FINGERTIPS SO IT SHOULDN'T BE THE LEAST BIT OFF. ♡
SCHOOL UNIFORM ...?
I DON'T BELIEVE THIS MESS.
Yay!
Yippee!
YOU PAID FOR IT YOURSELF? WELL, I GUESS YOU'RE EXCITED ABOUT OUR NEW EXCHANGE STUDENT!
THAT'S RIGHT! SHE'S ALL OURS!
AS OF NOW, YOU ARE A STUDENT OF KOHARU HIGH SCHOOL.
....
MAN...

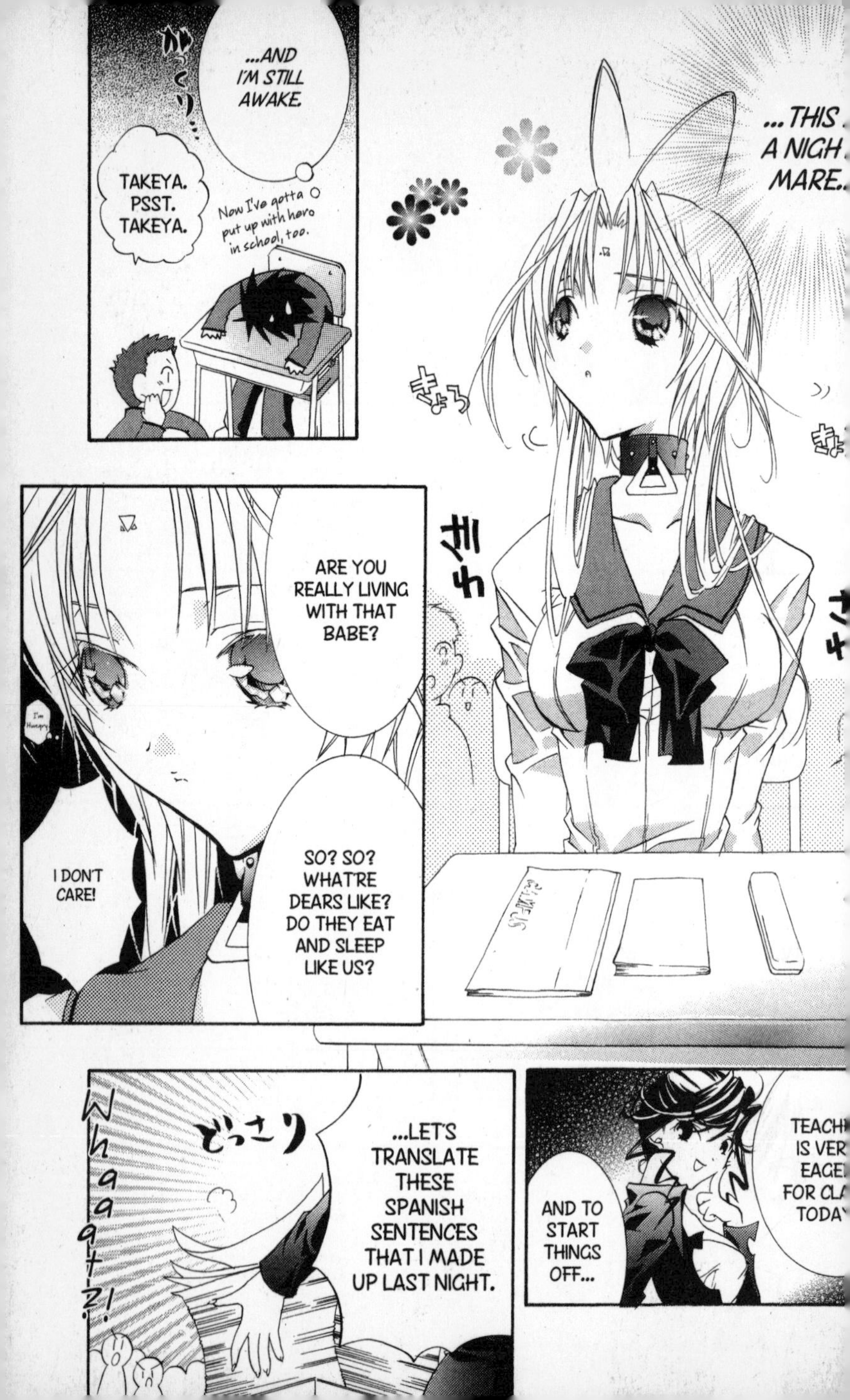
...THIS
A NIGH
MARE..
きょろ
きょ
ざわ
さ
がっくり…
...AND I'M STILL AWAKE.
TAKEYA. PSST. TAKEYA.
Now I've gotta put up with hero in school, too.
ARE YOU REALLY LIVING WITH THAT BABE?
I'm Hungry
SO? SO? WHAT'RE DEARS LIKE? DO THEY EAT AND SLEEP LIKE US?
I DON'T CARE!
TEACH
IS VER
EAGE
FOR CLA
TODAY
AND TO START THINGS OFF...
...LET'S TRANSLATE THESE SPANISH SENTENCES THAT I MADE UP LAST NIGHT.
どっさり
Whaaaat?!

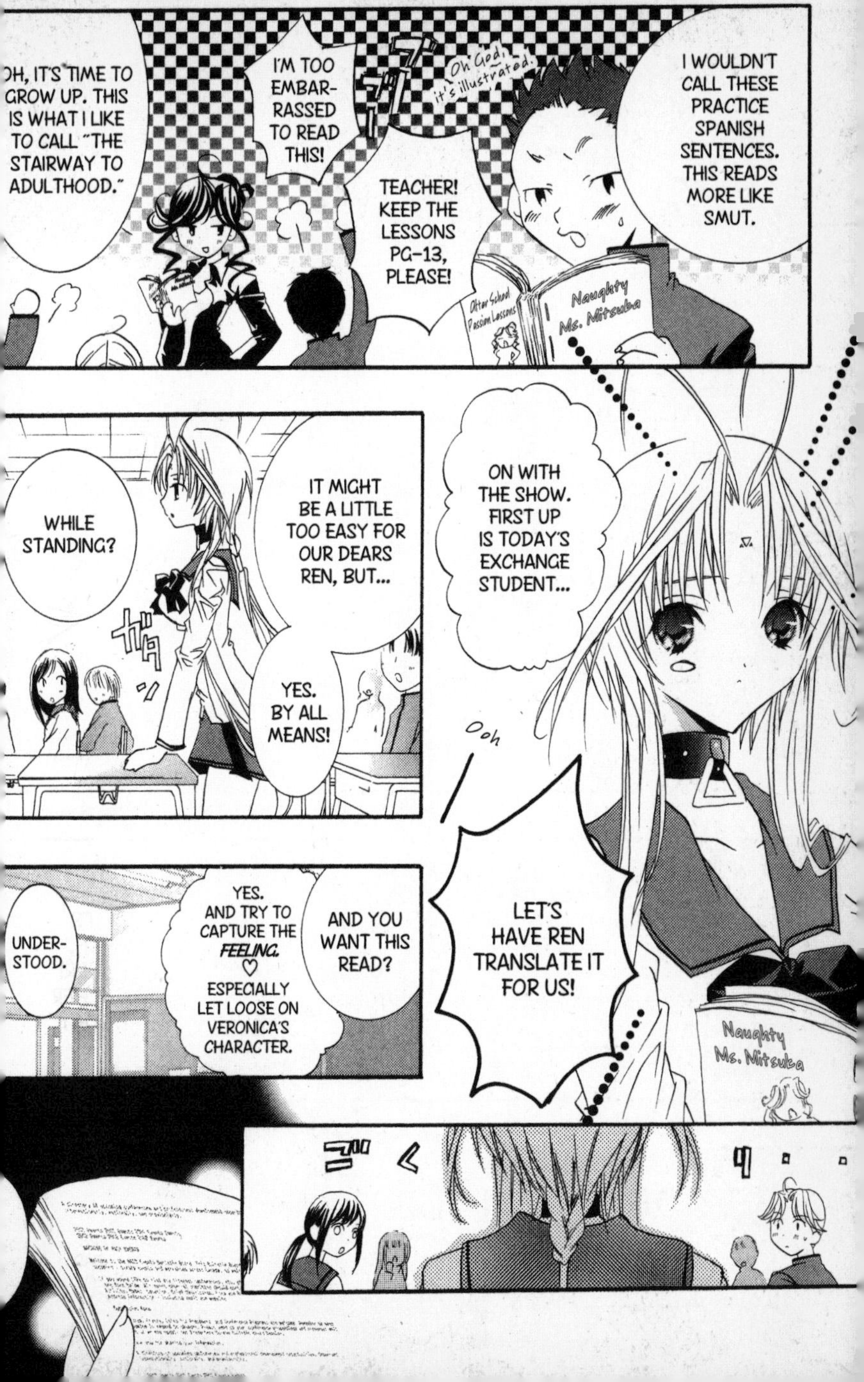
I WOULDN'T CALL THESE PRACTICE SPANISH SENTENCES. THIS READS MORE LIKE SMUT.
Oh God, it's illustrated.
Naughty Ms. Mitsuka
After School Passion Lessons
TEACHER! KEEP THE LESSONS PG-13, PLEASE!
I'M TOO EMBAR-RASSED TO READ THIS!
OH, IT'S TIME TO GROW UP. THIS IS WHAT I LIKE TO CALL "THE STAIRWAY TO ADULTHOOD."
ON WITH THE SHOW. FIRST UP IS TODAY'S EXCHANGE STUDENT...
Ooh
LET'S HAVE REN TRANSLATE IT FOR US!
Naughty Ms. Mitsuka
IT MIGHT BE A LITTLE TOO EASY FOR OUR DEARS REN, BUT...
YES. BY ALL MEANS!
WHILE STANDING?
AND YOU WANT THIS READ?
YES. AND TRY TO CAPTURE THE FEELING. ♡ ESPECIALLY LET LOOSE ON VERONICA'S CHARACTER.
UNDER-STOOD.

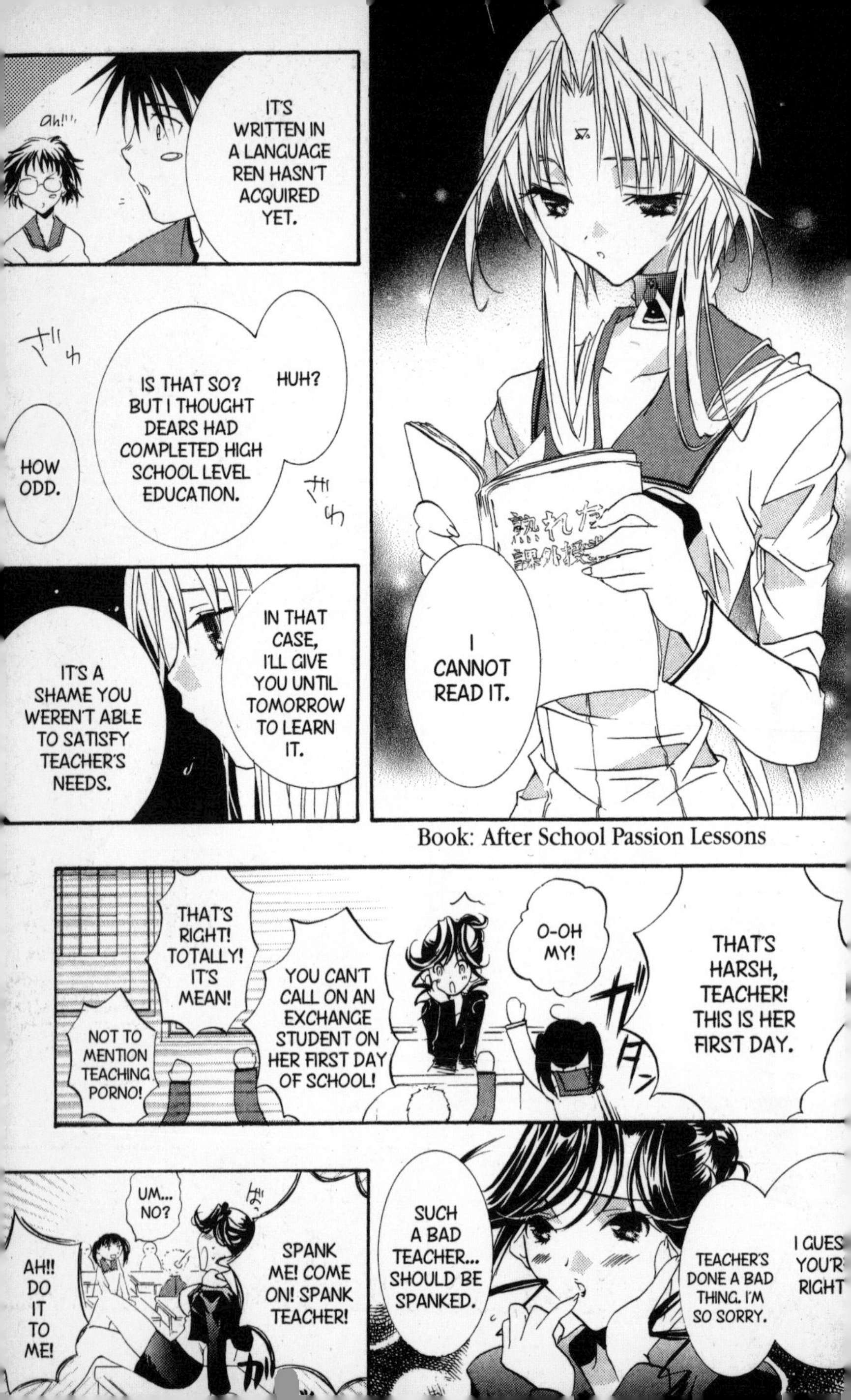
I CANNOT READ IT.
ah!!
IT'S WRITTEN IN A LANGUAGE REN HASN'T ACQUIRED YET.
HUH?
IS THAT SO? BUT I THOUGHT DEARS HAD COMPLETED HIGH SCHOOL LEVEL EDUCATION.
HOW ODD.
IN THAT CASE, I'LL GIVE YOU UNTIL TOMORROW TO LEARN IT.
IT'S A SHAME YOU WEREN'T ABLE TO SATISFY TEACHER'S NEEDS.
THAT'S HARSH, TEACHER! THIS IS HER FIRST DAY.
O-OH MY!
YOU CAN'T CALL ON AN EXCHANGE STUDENT ON HER FIRST DAY OF SCHOOL!
THAT'S RIGHT! TOTALLY! IT'S MEAN!
NOT TO MENTION TEACHING PORNO!
I GUES YOU'R RIGHT
TEACHER'S DONE A BAD THING. I'M SO SORRY.
SUCH A BAD TEACHER... SHOULD BE SPANKED.
UM... NO?
SPANK ME! COME ON! SPANK TEACHER!
AH!! DO IT TO ME!

Book: After School Passion Lessons

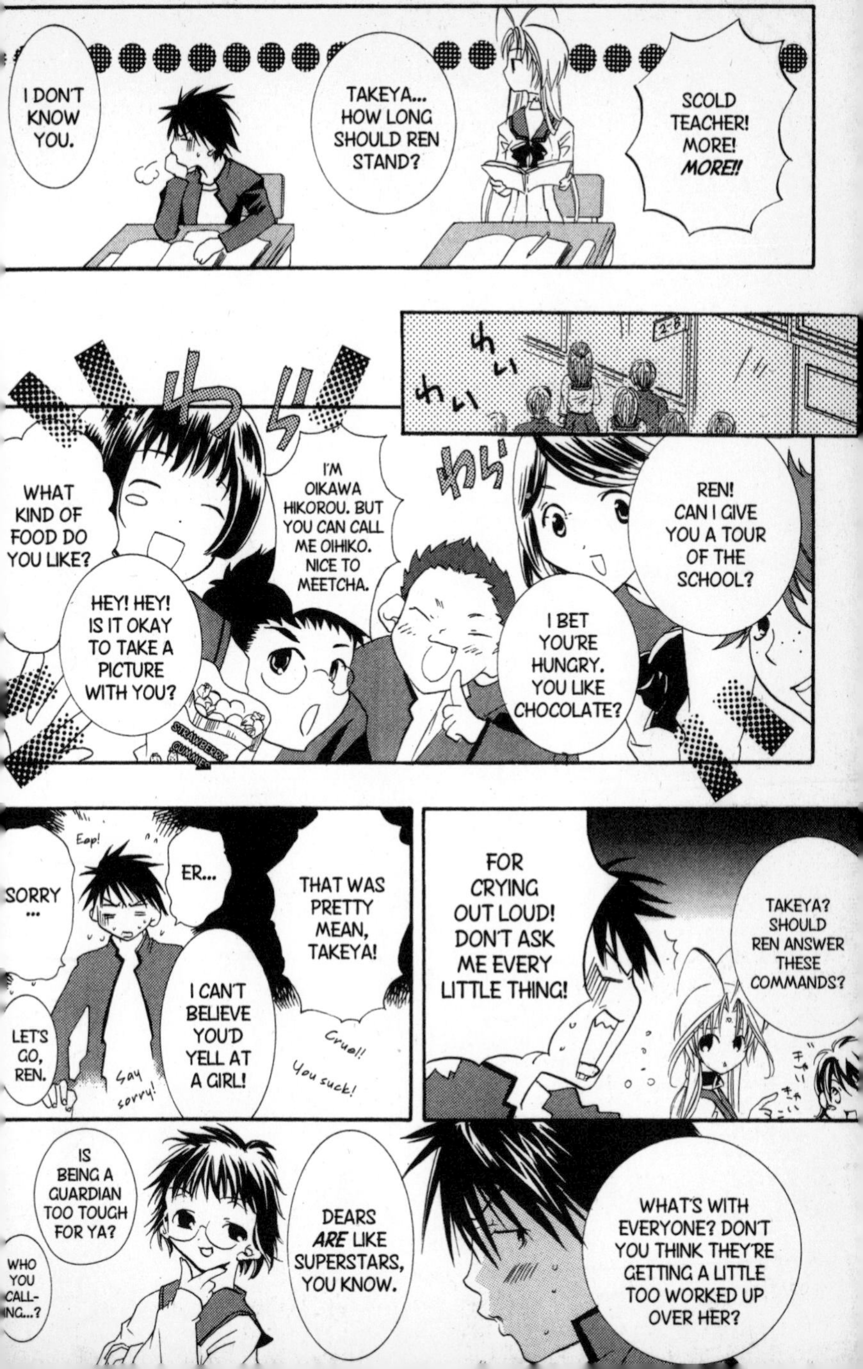
SCOLD TEACHER! MORE! *MORE!!*
TAKEYA... HOW LONG SHOULD REN STAND?
I DON'T KNOW YOU.
わい わい
わら
REN! CAN I GIVE YOU A TOUR OF THE SCHOOL?
I BET YOU'RE HUNGRY. YOU LIKE CHOCOLATE?
I'M OIKAWA HIKOROU. BUT YOU CAN CALL ME OIHIKO. NICE TO MEETCHA.
わら
WHAT KIND OF FOOD DO YOU LIKE?
HEY! HEY! IS IT OKAY TO TAKE A PICTURE WITH YOU?
STRAWBERRY GUMMIES
TAKEYA? SHOULD REN ANSWER THESE COMMANDS?
FOR CRYING OUT LOUD! DON'T ASK ME EVERY LITTLE THING!
THAT WAS PRETTY MEAN, TAKEYA!
ER...
Eep!
SORRY...
I CAN'T BELIEVE YOU'D YELL AT A GIRL!
Cruel!!
You suck!
Say sorry!
LET'S GO, REN.
WHAT'S WITH EVERYONE? DON'T YOU THINK THEY'RE GETTING A LITTLE TOO WORKED UP OVER HER?
DEARS *ARE* LIKE SUPERSTARS, YOU KNOW.
IS BEING A GUARDIAN TOO TOUGH FOR YA?
WHO YOU CALLING...?

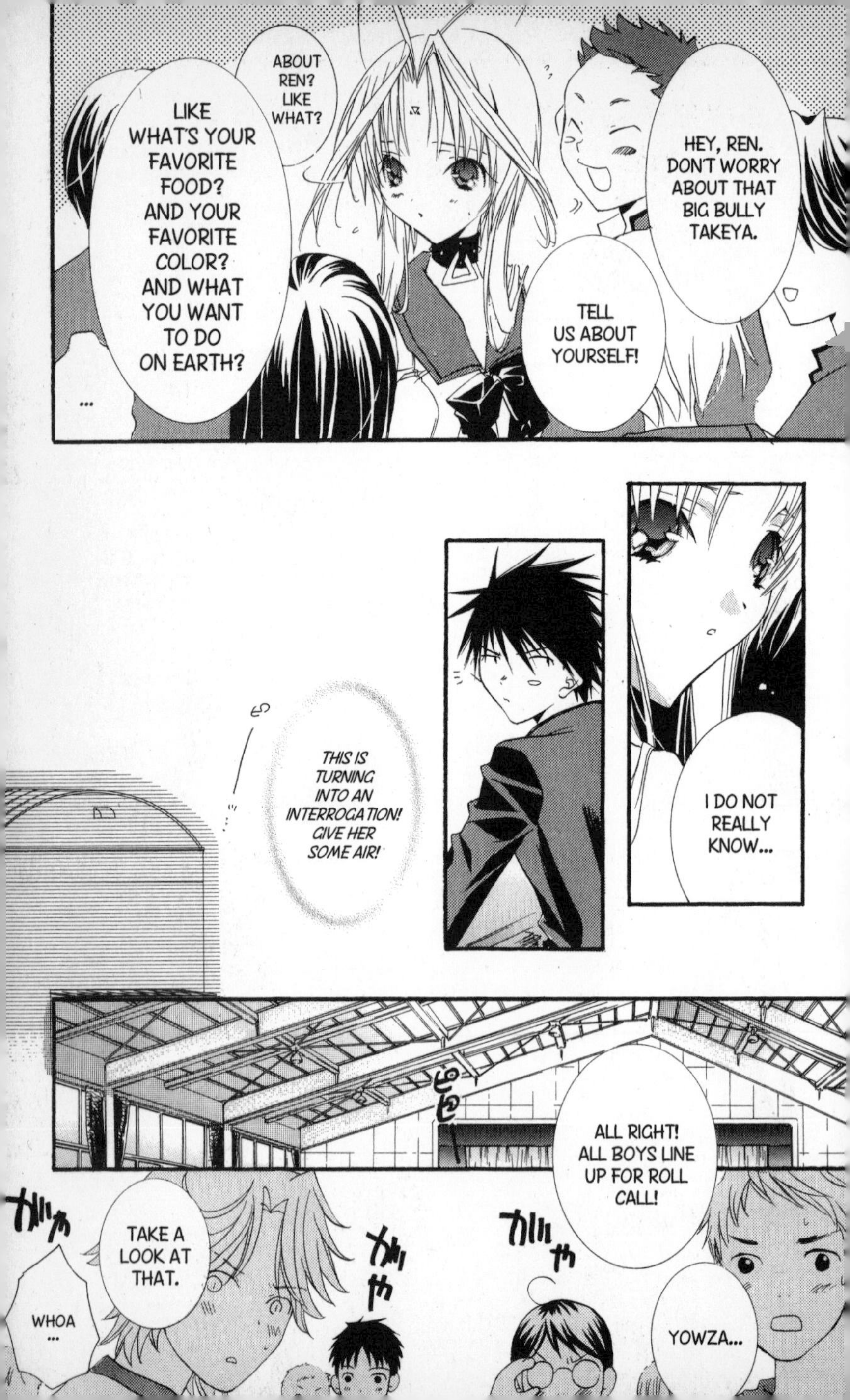
HEY, REN. DON'T WORRY ABOUT THAT BIG BULLY TAKEYA.
TELL US ABOUT YOURSELF!
ABOUT REN? LIKE WHAT?
LIKE WHAT'S YOUR FAVORITE FOOD? AND YOUR FAVORITE COLOR? AND WHAT YOU WANT TO DO ON EARTH?
...
I DO NOT REALLY KNOW...
THIS IS TURNING INTO AN INTERROGATION! GIVE HER SOME AIR!
ALL RIGHT! ALL BOYS LINE UP FOR ROLL CALL!
YOWZA...
TAKE A LOOK AT THAT.
WHOA ...

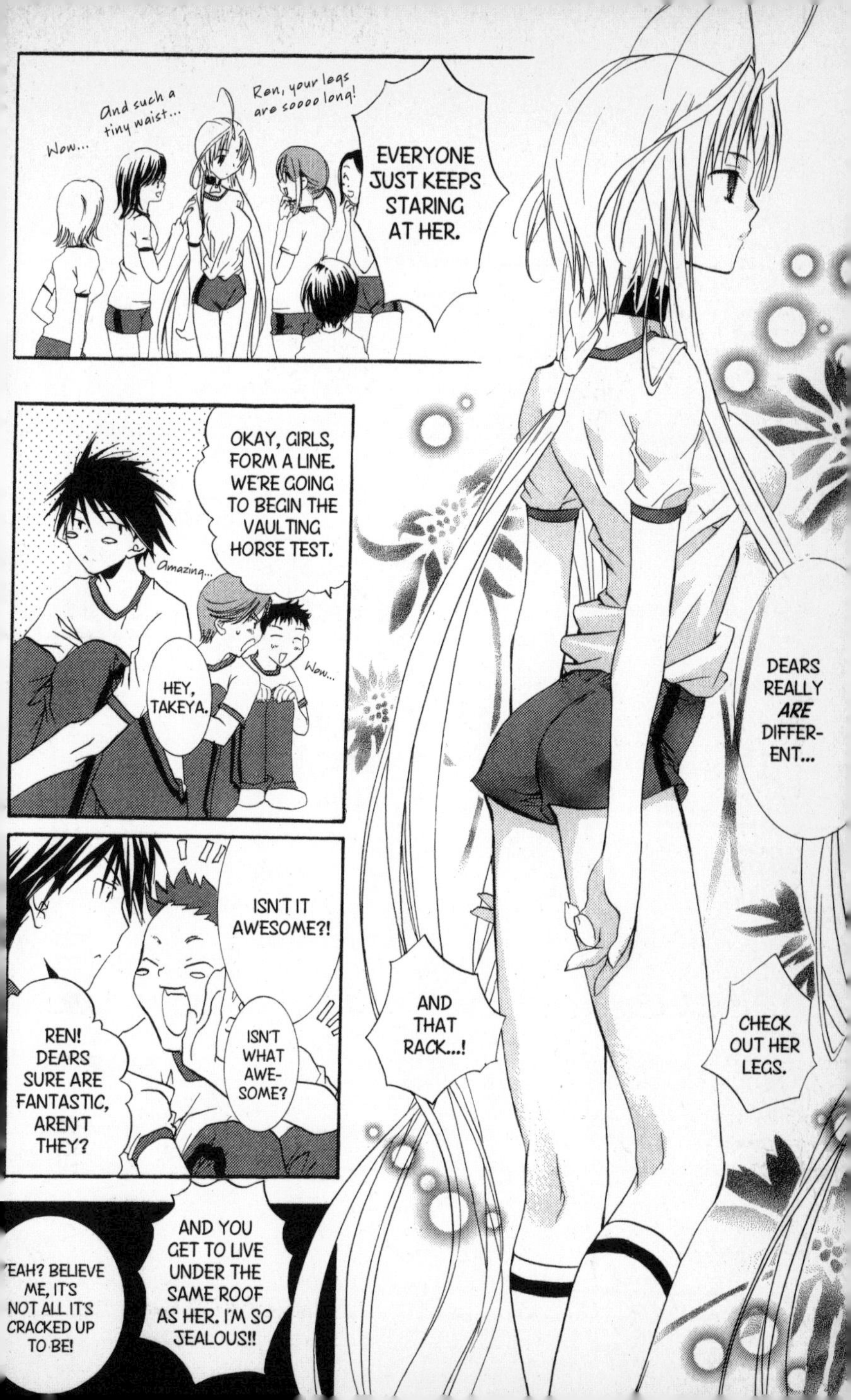
DEARS REALLY ARE DIFFERENT...
CHECK OUT HER LEGS.
AND THAT RACK...!
EVERYONE JUST KEEPS STARING AT HER.
Ren, your legs are soooo long!
And such a tiny waist...
Wow...
OKAY, GIRLS, FORM A LINE. WE'RE GOING TO BEGIN THE VAULTING HORSE TEST.
Amazing...
Wow...
HEY, TAKEYA.
ISN'T IT AWESOME?!
ISN'T WHAT AWESOME?
REN! DEARS SURE ARE FANTASTIC, AREN'T THEY?
AND YOU GET TO LIVE UNDER THE SAME ROOF AS HER. I'M SO JEALOUS!!
EAH? BELIEVE ME, IT'S NOT ALL IT'S CRACKED UP TO BE!

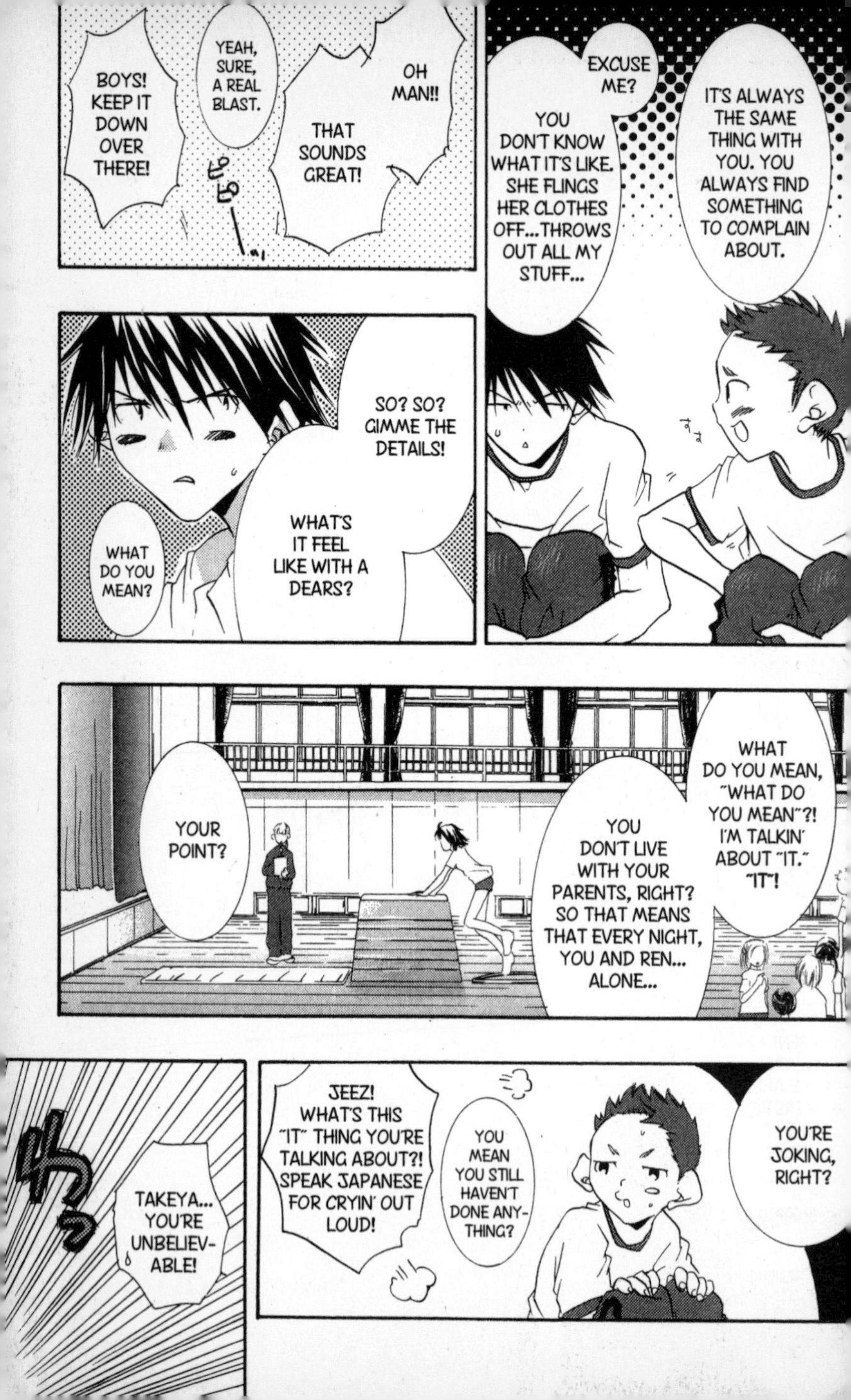
IT'S ALWAYS THE SAME THING WITH YOU. YOU ALWAYS FIND SOMETHING TO COMPLAIN ABOUT.
EXCUSE ME?
YOU DON'T KNOW WHAT IT'S LIKE. SHE FLINGS HER CLOTHES OFF...THROWS OUT ALL MY STUFF...
OH MAN!! THAT SOUNDS GREAT!
YEAH, SURE, A REAL BLAST.
BOYS! KEEP IT DOWN OVER THERE!
SO? SO? GIMME THE DETAILS!
WHAT'S IT FEEL LIKE WITH A DEARS?
WHAT DO YOU MEAN?
WHAT DO YOU MEAN, "WHAT DO YOU MEAN"?! I'M TALKIN' ABOUT "IT." "IT"!
YOU DON'T LIVE WITH YOUR PARENTS, RIGHT? SO THAT MEANS THAT EVERY NIGHT, YOU AND REN... ALONE...
YOUR POINT?
YOU'RE JOKING, RIGHT?
YOU MEAN YOU STILL HAVEN'T DONE ANY-THING?
JEEZ! WHAT'S THIS "IT" THING YOU'RE TALKING ABOUT?! SPEAK JAPANESE FOR CRYIN' OUT LOUD!
TAKEYA... YOU'RE UNBELIEV-ABLE!

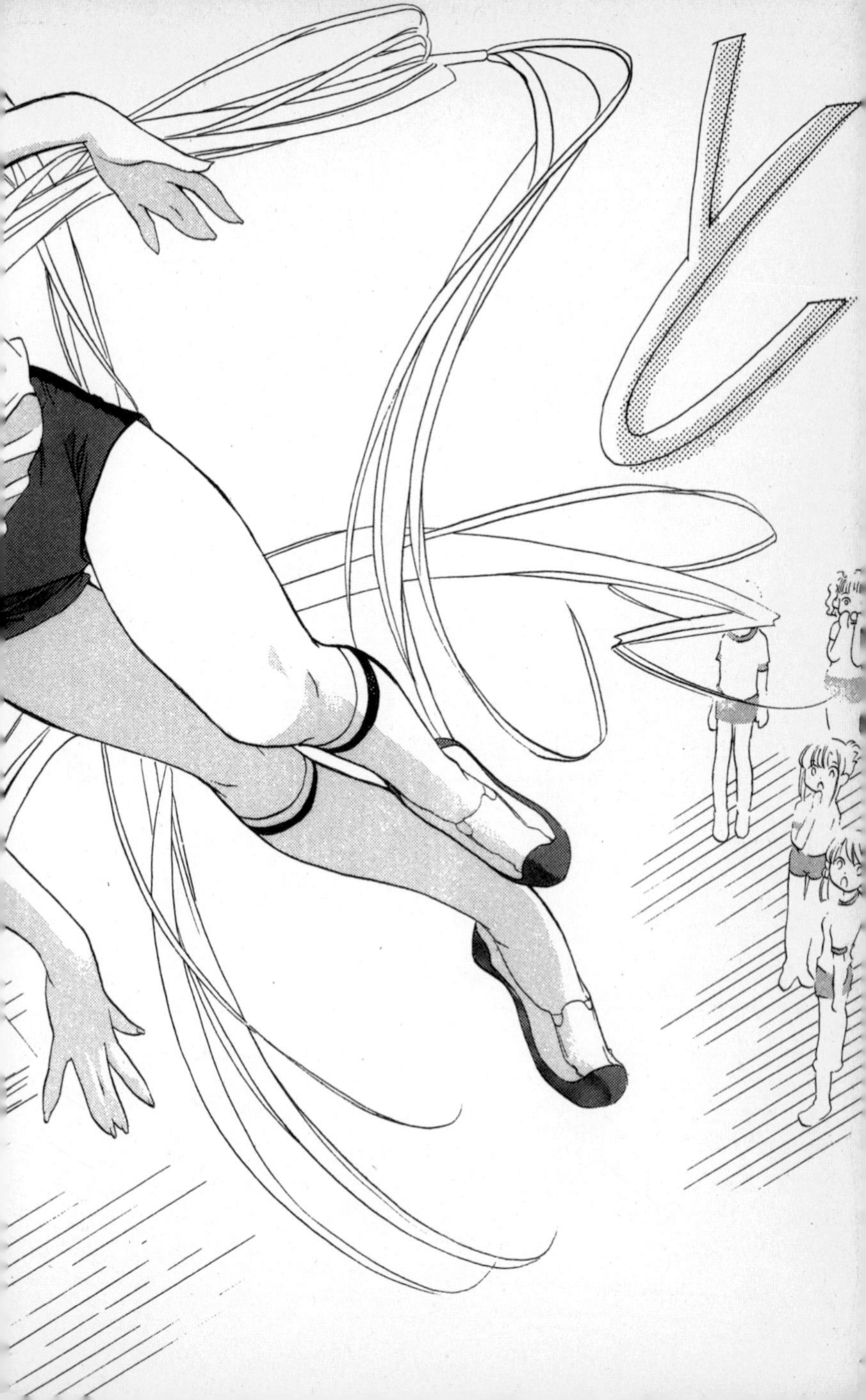

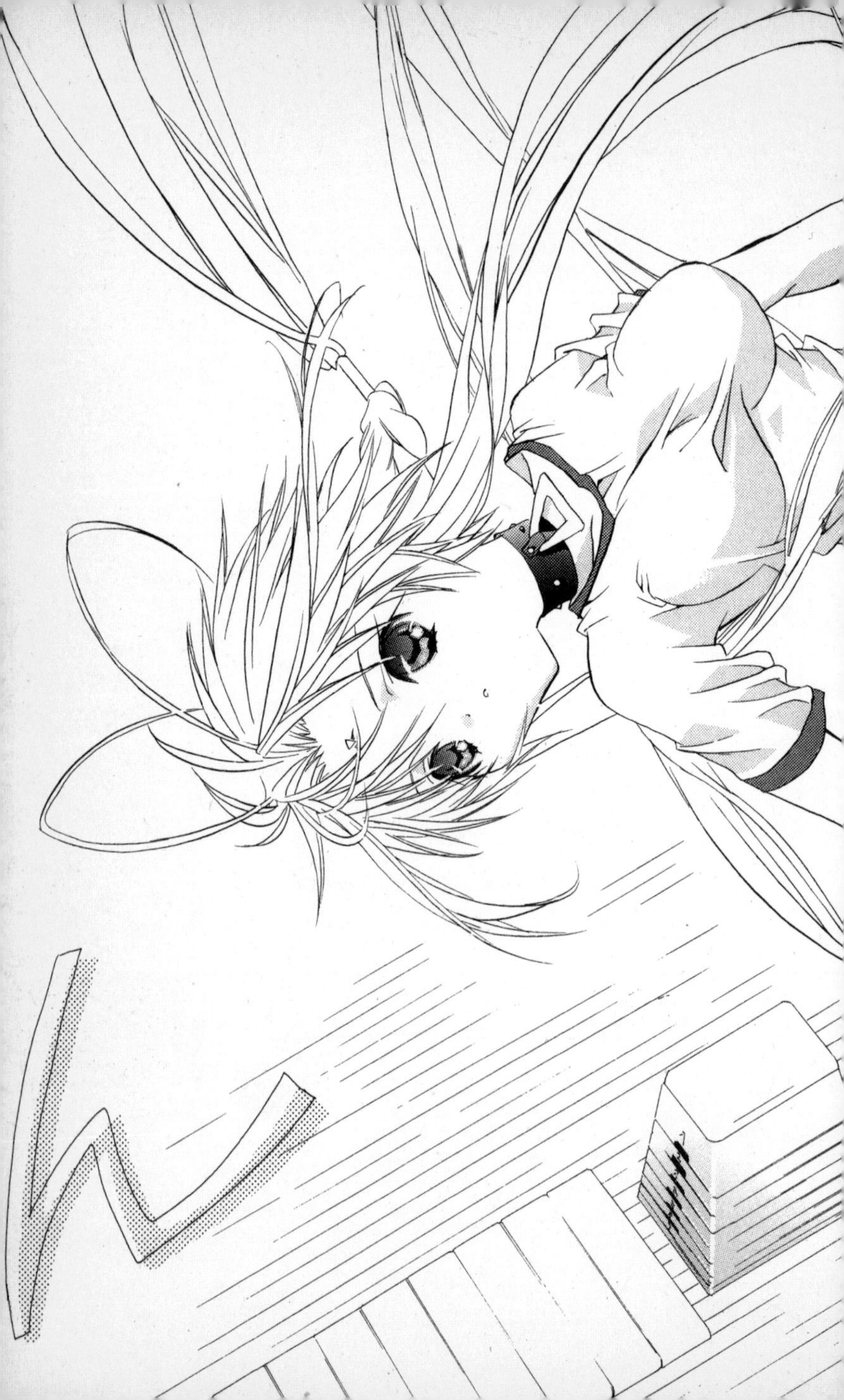

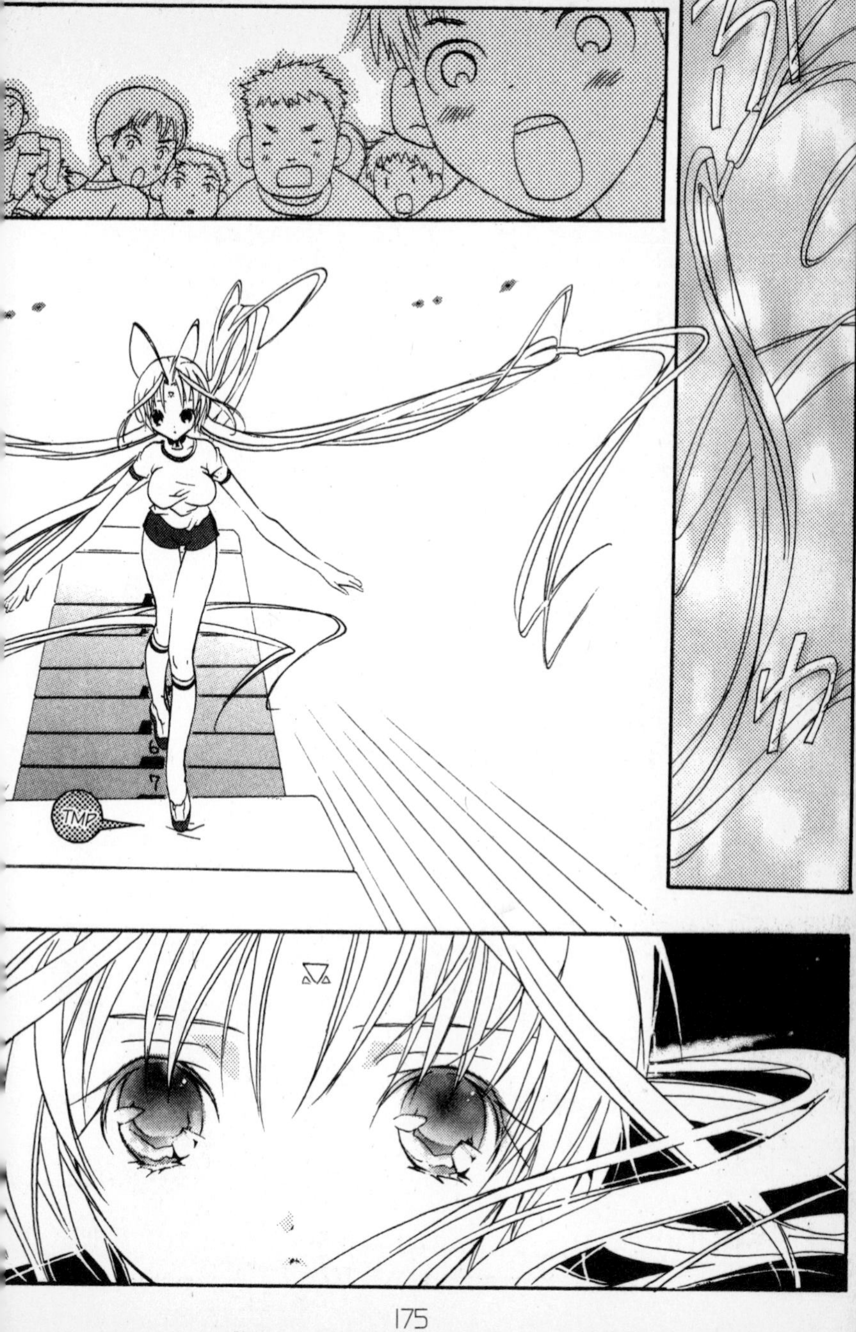
TMP

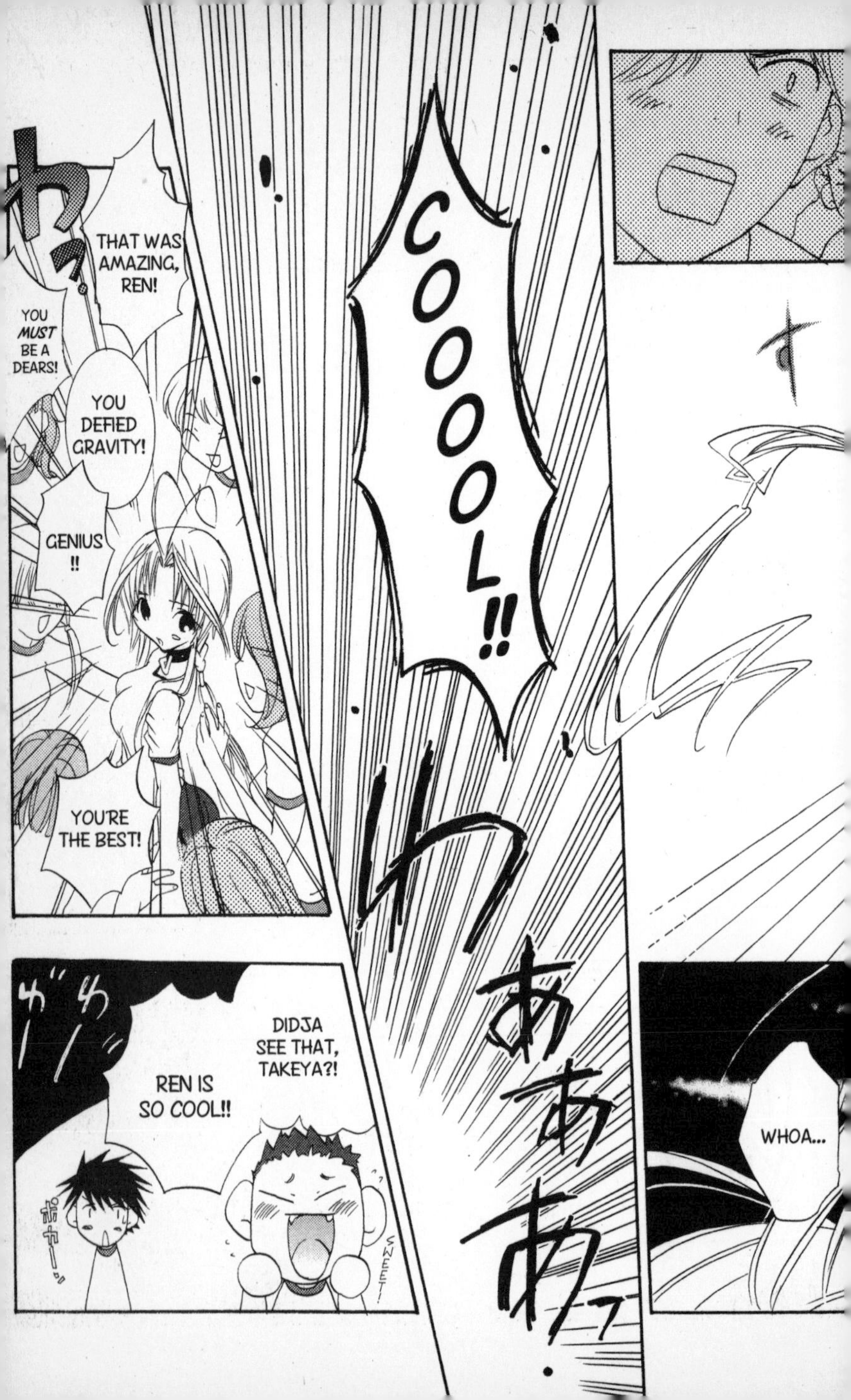
COOOOL!!
THAT WAS AMAZING, REN!
YOU *MUST* BE A DEARS!
YOU DEFIED GRAVITY!
GENIUS!!
YOU'RE THE BEST!
WHOA...
DIDJA SEE THAT, TAKEYA?!
REN IS SO COOL!!
SWEET!

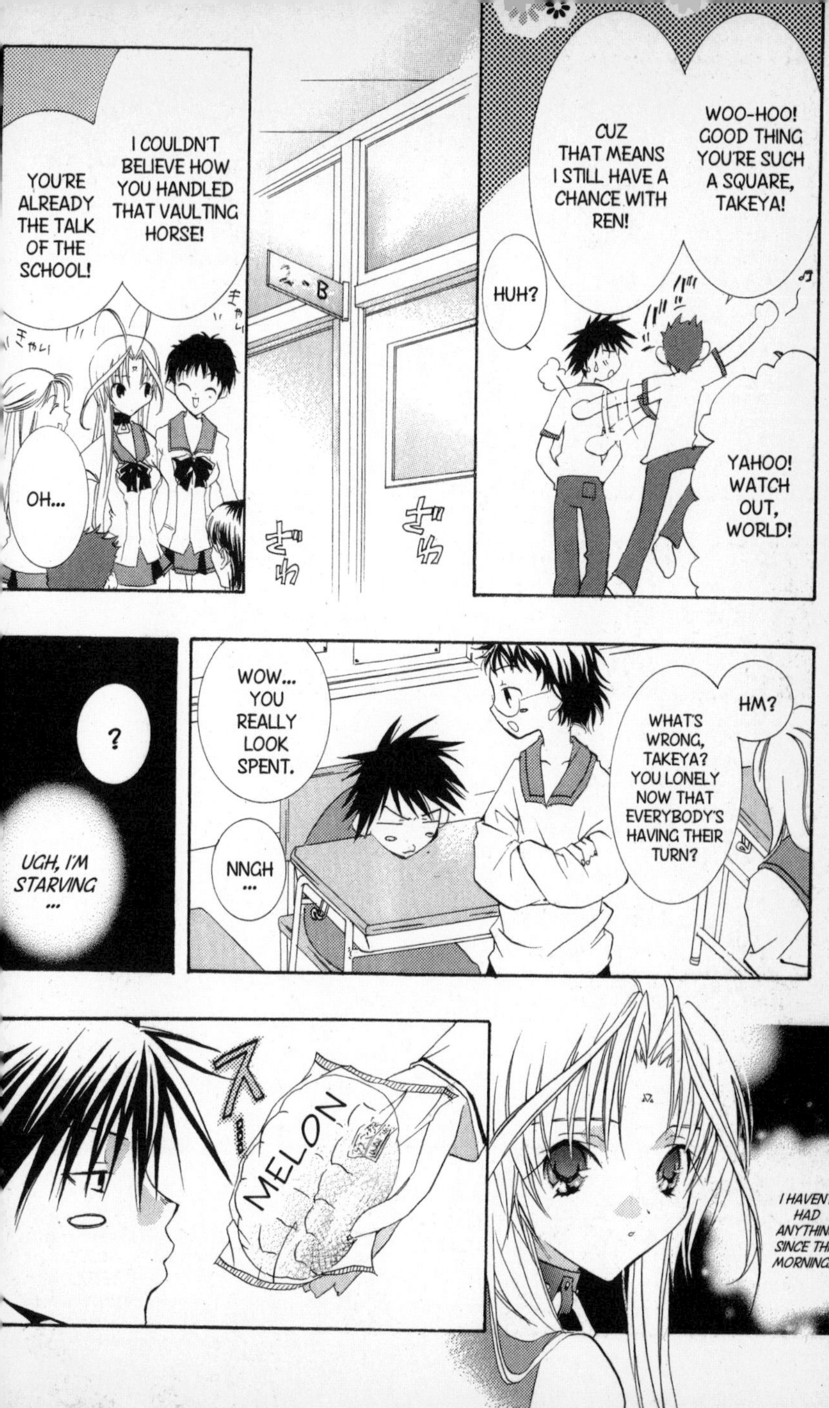

WOO-HOO! GOOD THING YOU'RE SUCH A SQUARE, TAKEYA!
CUZ THAT MEANS I STILL HAVE A CHANCE WITH REN!
HUH?
YAHOO! WATCH OUT, WORLD!
I COULDN'T BELIEVE HOW YOU HANDLED THAT VAULTING HORSE!
YOU'RE ALREADY THE TALK OF THE SCHOOL!
OH...
HM?
WHAT'S WRONG, TAKEYA? YOU LONELY NOW THAT EVERYBODY'S HAVING THEIR TURN?
WOW... YOU REALLY LOOK SPENT.
NNGH...
?
UGH, I'M STARVING...
I HAVENT HAD ANYTHING SINCE THIS MORNING...
MELON

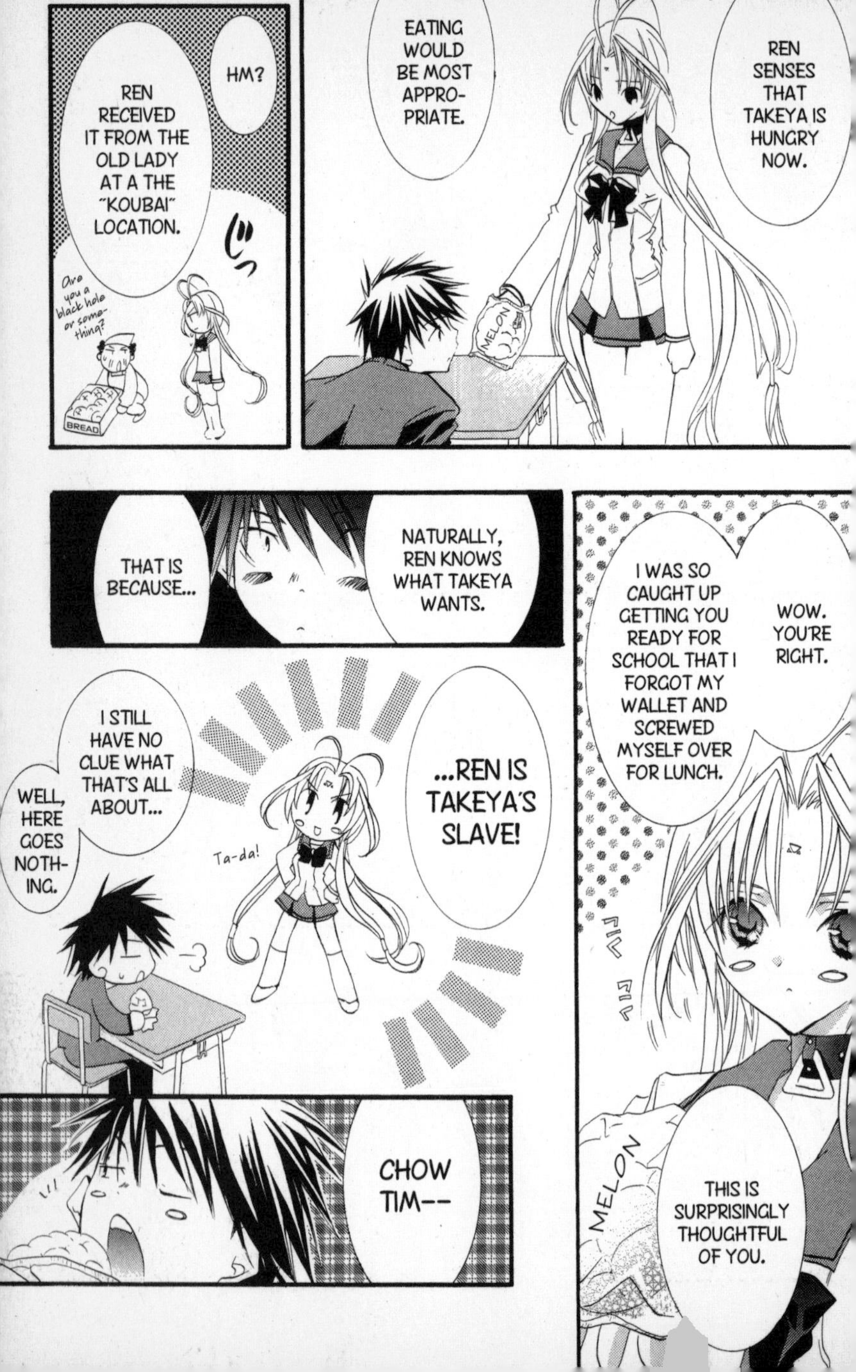
REN SENSES THAT TAKEYA IS HUNGRY NOW.
EATING WOULD BE MOST APPROPRIATE.
MELON
HM?
REN RECEIVED IT FROM THE OLD LADY AT A THE "KOUBAI" LOCATION.
じっ
Are you a black hole or some-thing?
BREAD
WOW. YOU'RE RIGHT.
I WAS SO CAUGHT UP GETTING YOU READY FOR SCHOOL THAT I FORGOT MY WALLET AND SCREWED MYSELF OVER FOR LUNCH.
THIS IS SURPRISINGLY THOUGHTFUL OF YOU.
MELON
NATURALLY, REN KNOWS WHAT TAKEYA WANTS.
THAT IS BECAUSE...
...REN IS TAKEYA'S SLAVE!
Ta-da!
I STILL HAVE NO CLUE WHAT THAT'S ALL ABOUT...
WELL, HERE GOES NOTH-ING.
CHOW TIM--

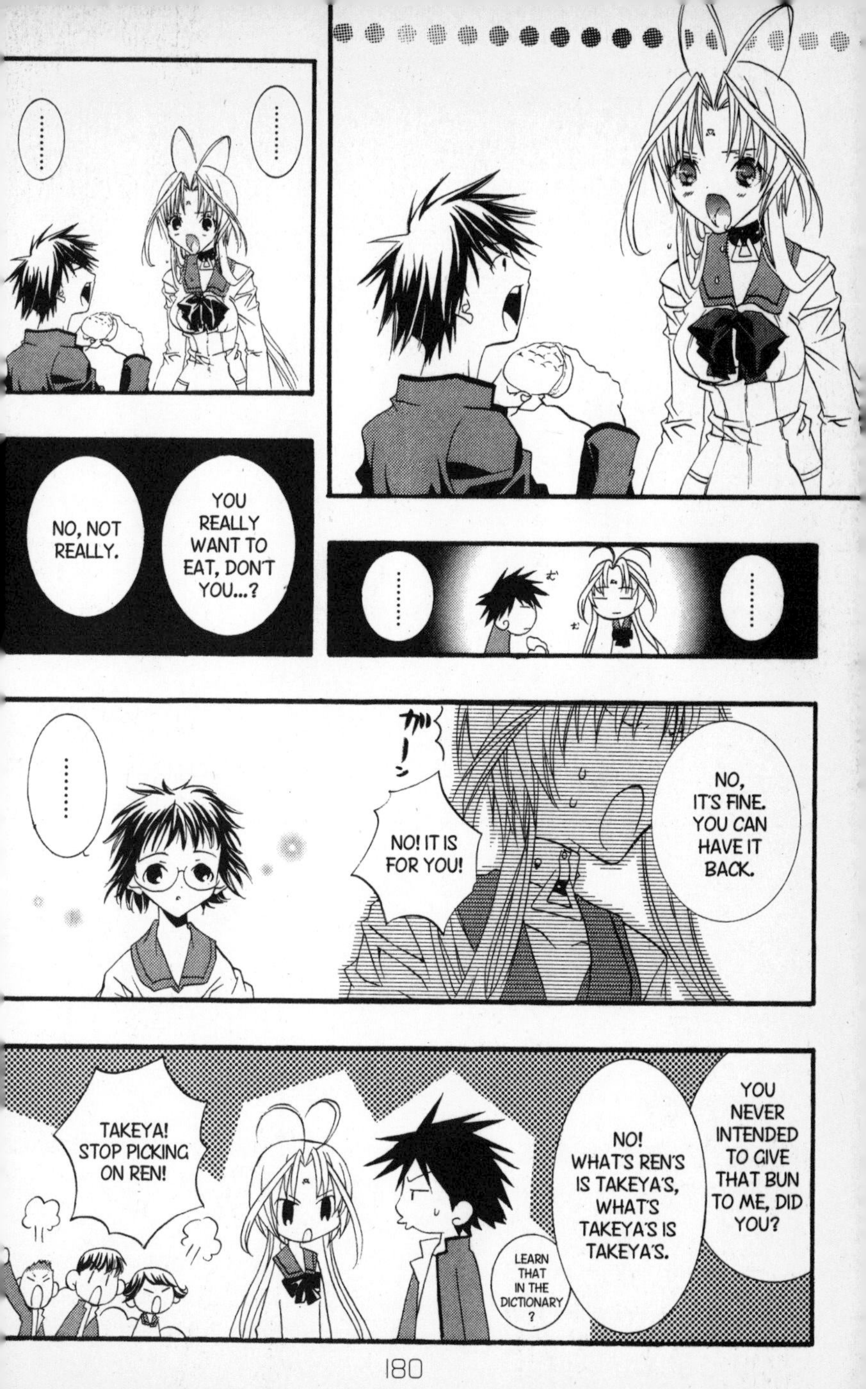
......
......
......
......
YOU REALLY WANT TO EAT, DON'T YOU...?
NO, NOT REALLY.
NO, IT'S FINE. YOU CAN HAVE IT BACK.
NO! IT IS FOR YOU!
......
YOU NEVER INTENDED TO GIVE THAT BUN TO ME, DID YOU?
NO! WHAT'S REN'S IS TAKEYA'S, WHAT'S TAKEYA'S IS TAKEYA'S.
LEARN THAT IN THE DICTIONARY?
TAKEYA! STOP PICKING ON REN!

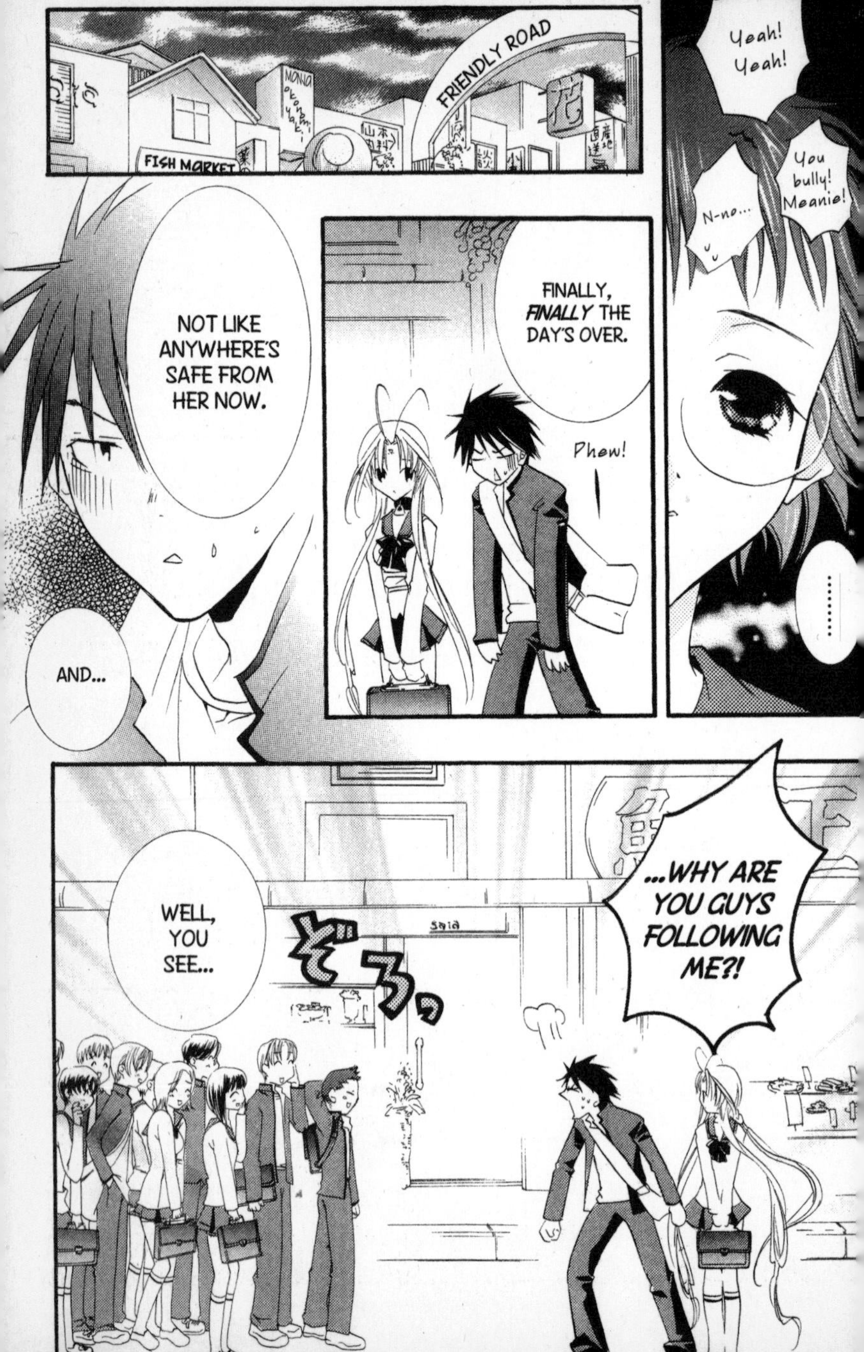
Yeah! Yeah!
You bully! Meanie!
N-no...
......
FRIENDLY ROAD
FISH MARKET
FINALLY, *FINALLY* THE DAY'S OVER.
Phew!
NOT LIKE ANYWHERE'S SAFE FROM HER NOW.
AND...
...WHY ARE YOU GUYS FOLLOWING ME?!
どろっ
WELL, YOU SEE...

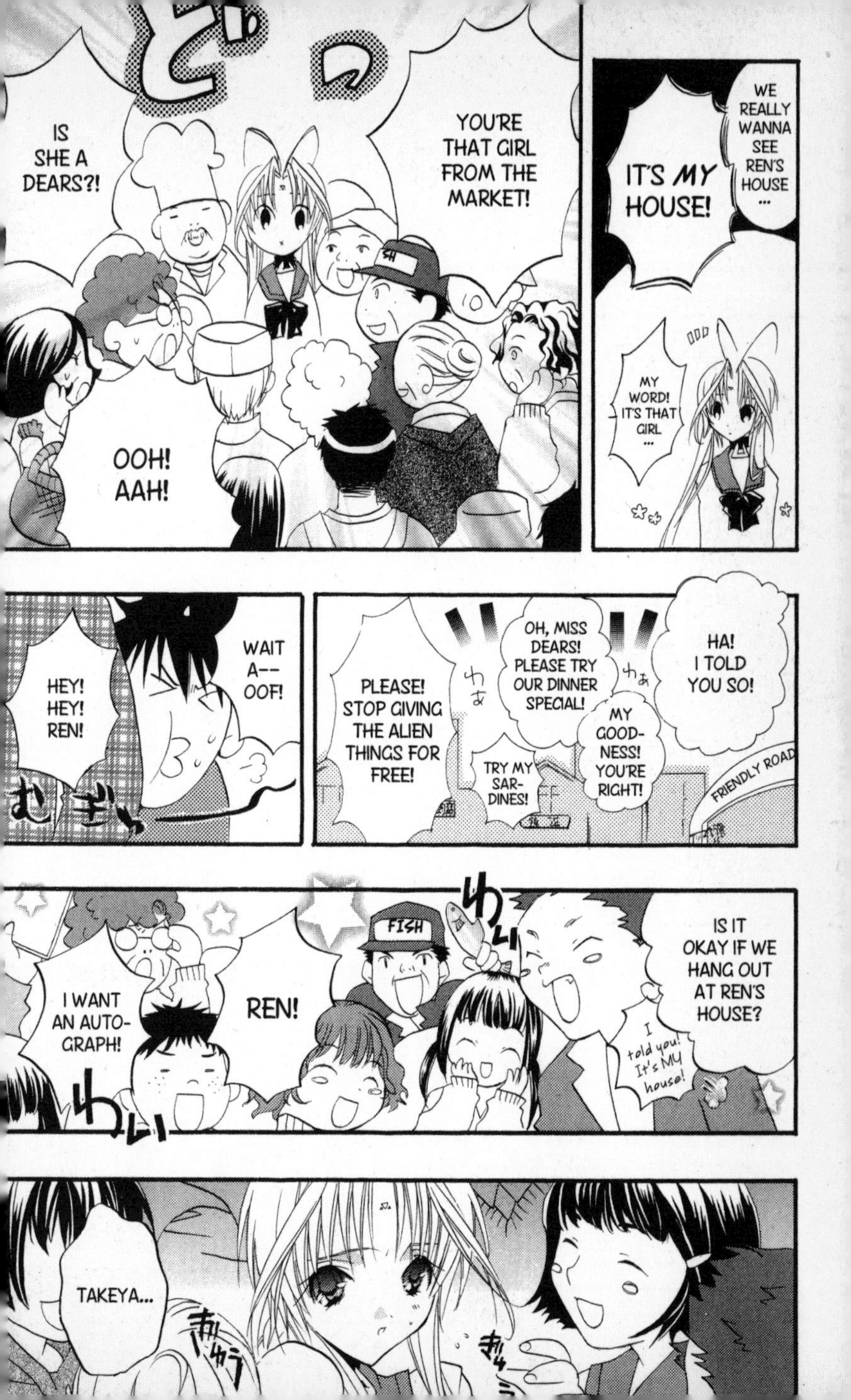
WE REALLY WANNA SEE REN'S HOUSE ...
IT'S MY HOUSE!
MY WORD! IT'S THAT GIRL ...
YOU'RE THAT GIRL FROM THE MARKET!
IS SHE A DEARS?!
OOH! AAH!
HA! I TOLD YOU SO!
OH, MISS DEARS! PLEASE TRY OUR DINNER SPECIAL!
MY GOOD-NESS! YOU'RE RIGHT!
FRIENDLY ROAD
TRY MY SAR-DINES!
PLEASE! STOP GIVING THE ALIEN THINGS FOR FREE!
WAIT A-- OOF!
HEY! HEY! REN!
IS IT OKAY IF WE HANG OUT AT REN'S HOUSE?
I told you! It's MY house!
FISH
REN!
I WANT AN AUTO-GRAPH!
TAKEYA...

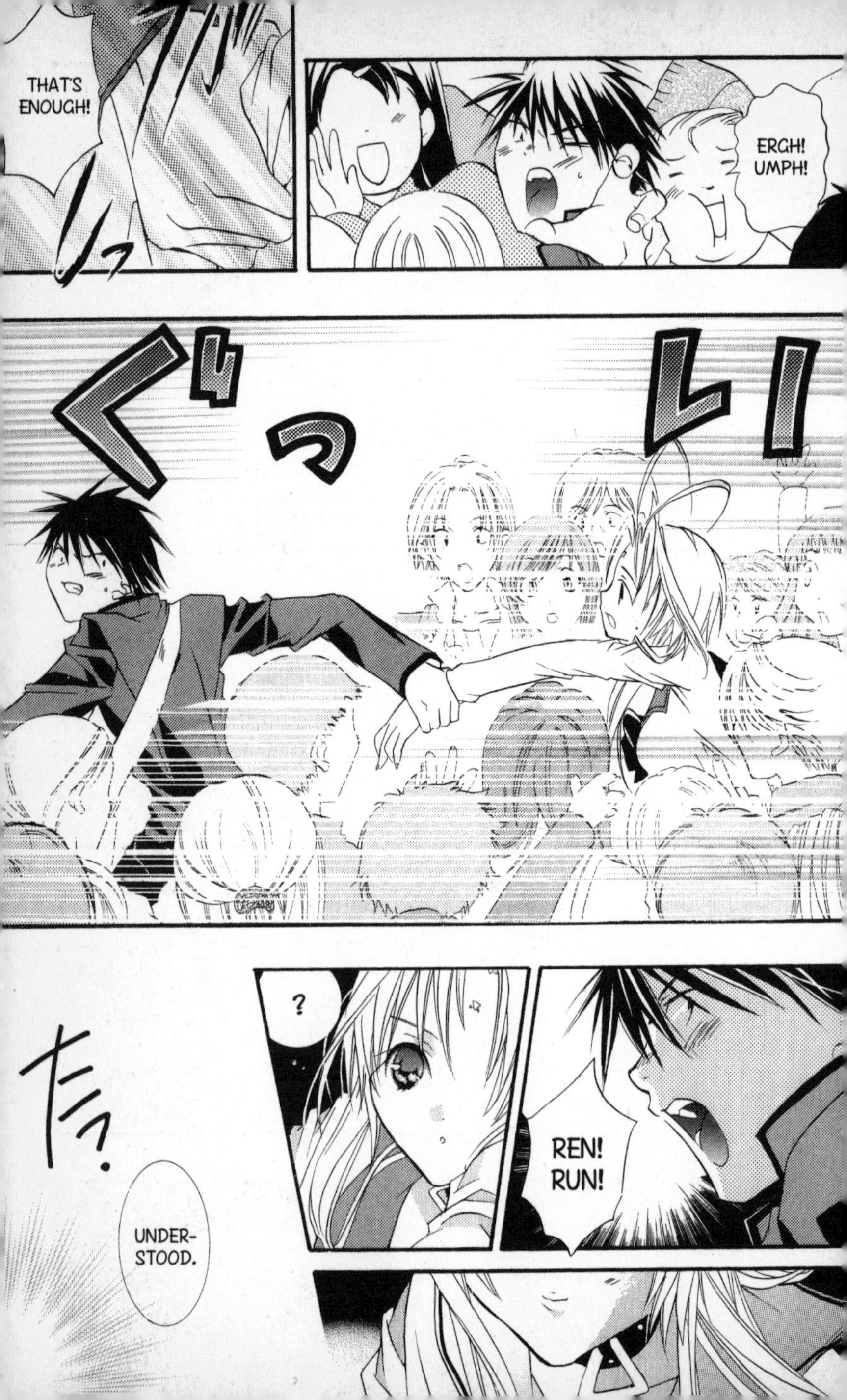

ERGH! UMPH!
THAT'S ENOUGH!
ぐっ
REN! RUN!
?
UNDER-STOOD.

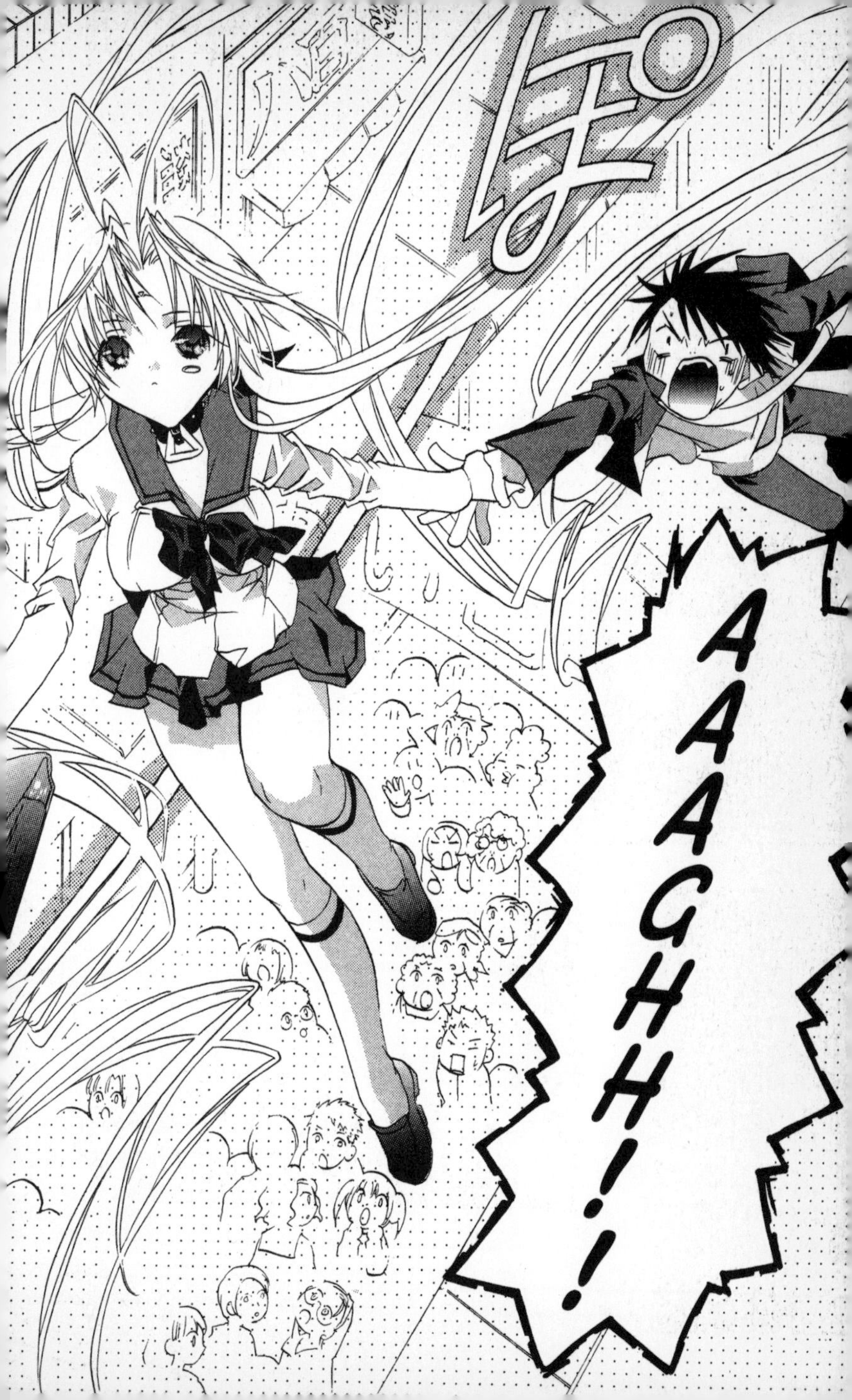
ぽ
AAAGHH!!!

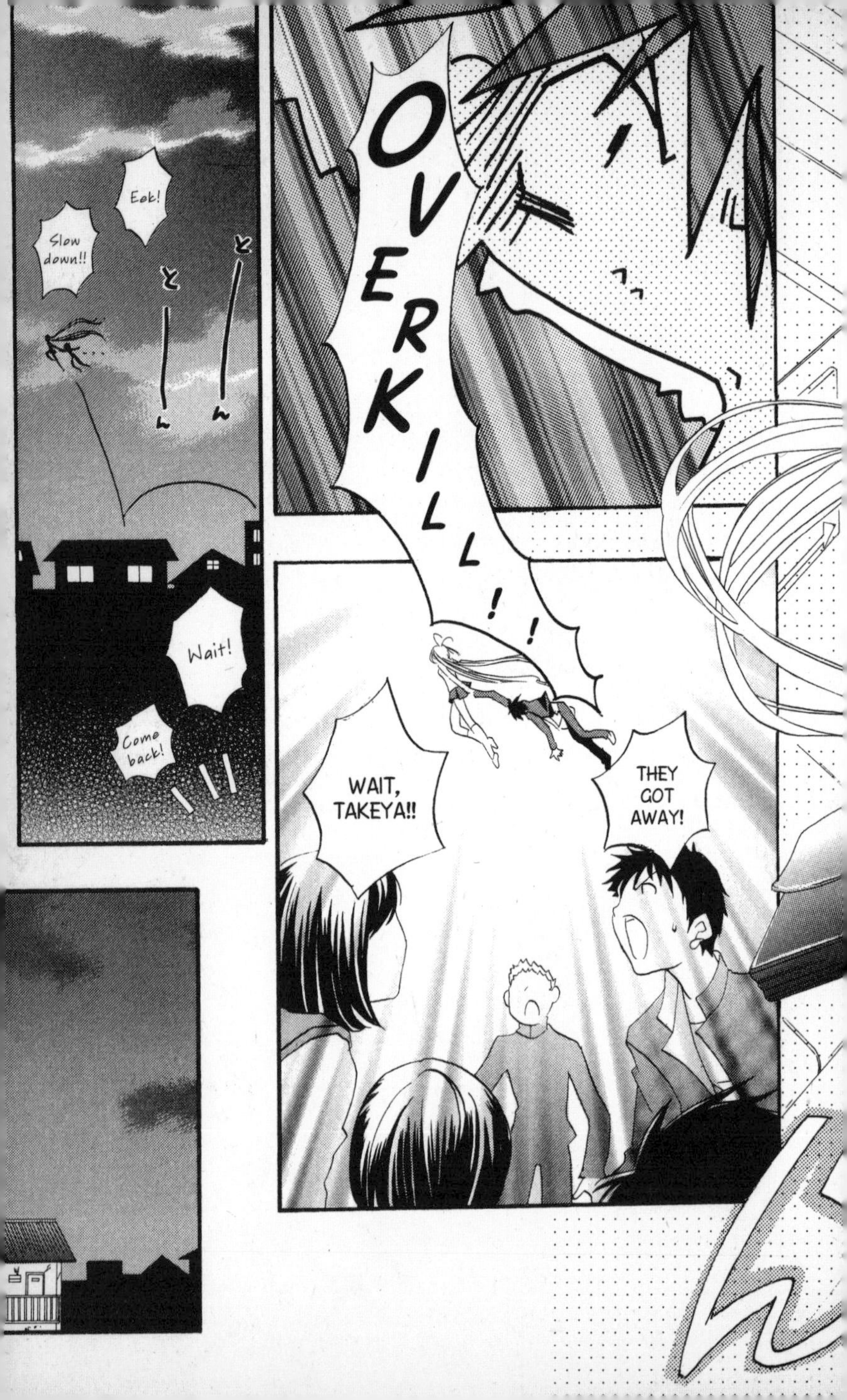
OVERKILLL!!
THEY GOT AWAY!
WAIT, TAKEYA!!
Eek!
Slow down!!
Wait!
Come back!

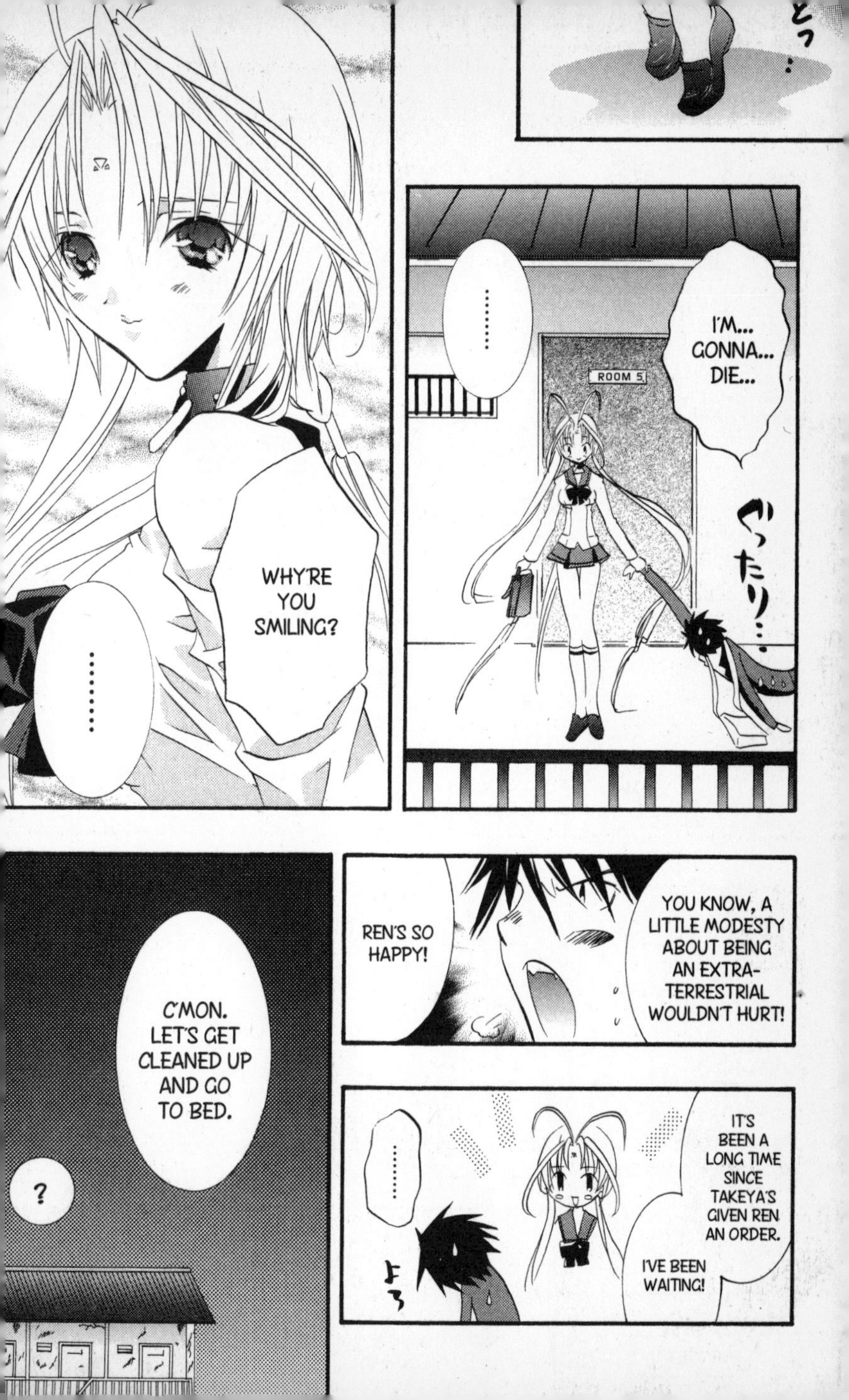
とっ…
I'M... GONNA... DIE...
....
ぐったり…
WHY'RE YOU SMILING?
....
YOU KNOW, A LITTLE MODESTY ABOUT BEING AN EXTRA-TERRESTRIAL WOULDN'T HURT!
REN'S SO HAPPY!
IT'S BEEN A LONG TIME SINCE TAKEYA'S GIVEN REN AN ORDER.
I'VE BEEN WAITING!
....
よろ
C'MON. LET'S GET CLEANED UP AND GO TO BED.
?

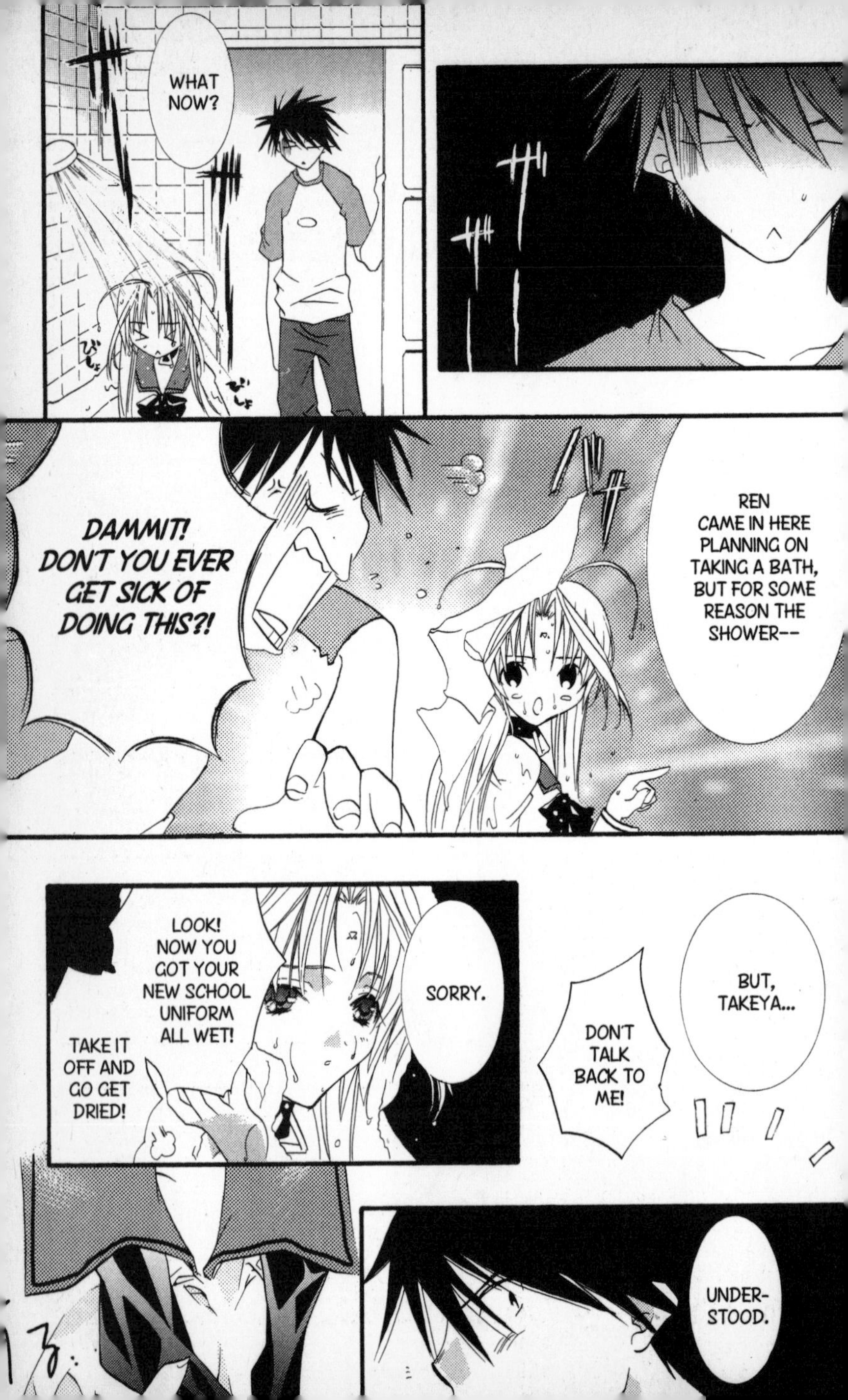
WHAT NOW?
REN CAME IN HERE PLANNING ON TAKING A BATH, BUT FOR SOME REASON THE SHOWER--
DAMMIT! DON'T YOU EVER GET SICK OF DOING THIS?!
BUT, TAKEYA...
DON'T TALK BACK TO ME!
SORRY.
LOOK! NOW YOU GOT YOUR NEW SCHOOL UNIFORM ALL WET!
TAKE IT OFF AND GO GET DRIED!
UNDER-STOOD.

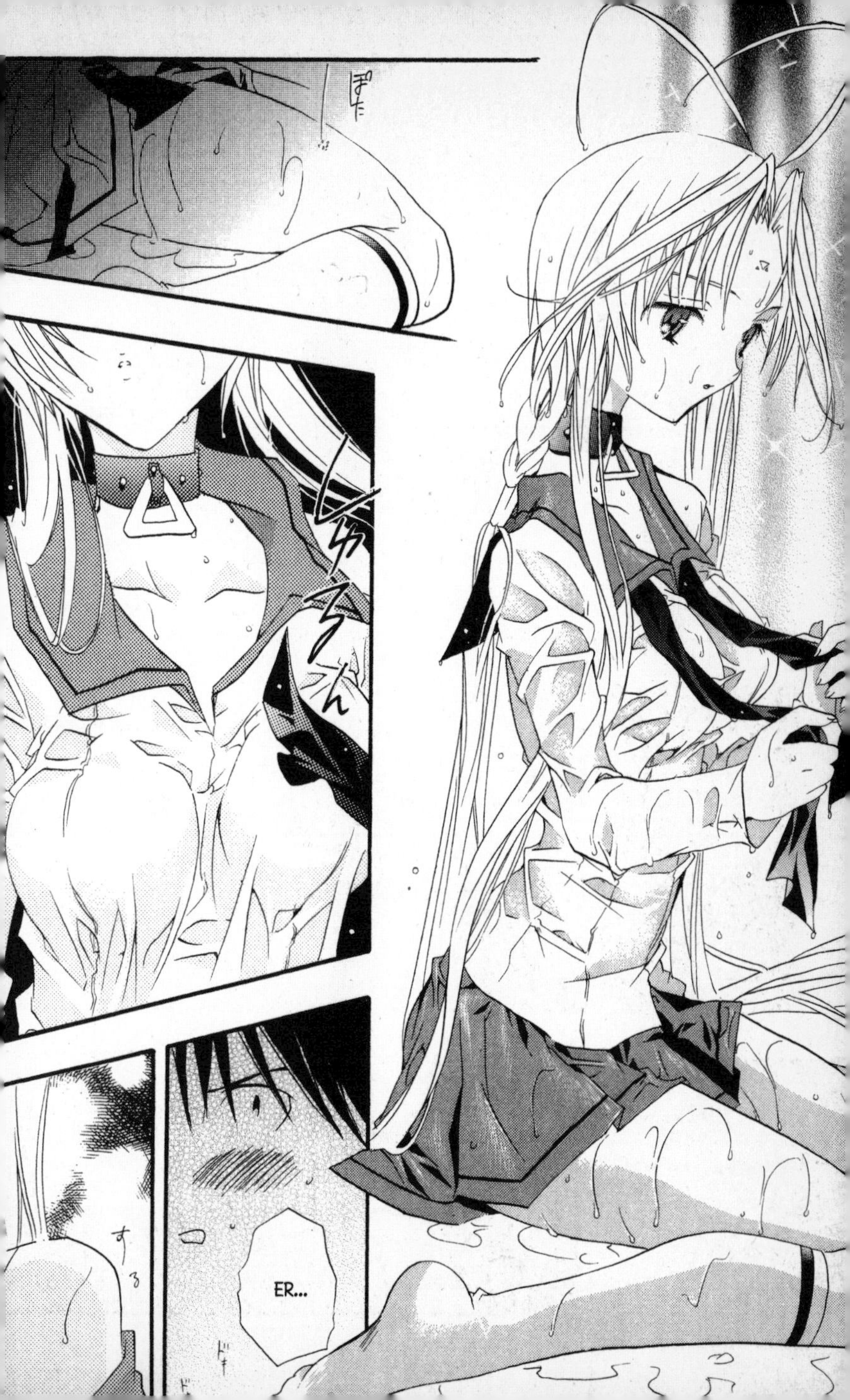
ぽた
しゅるん
ER...
ドキ
する

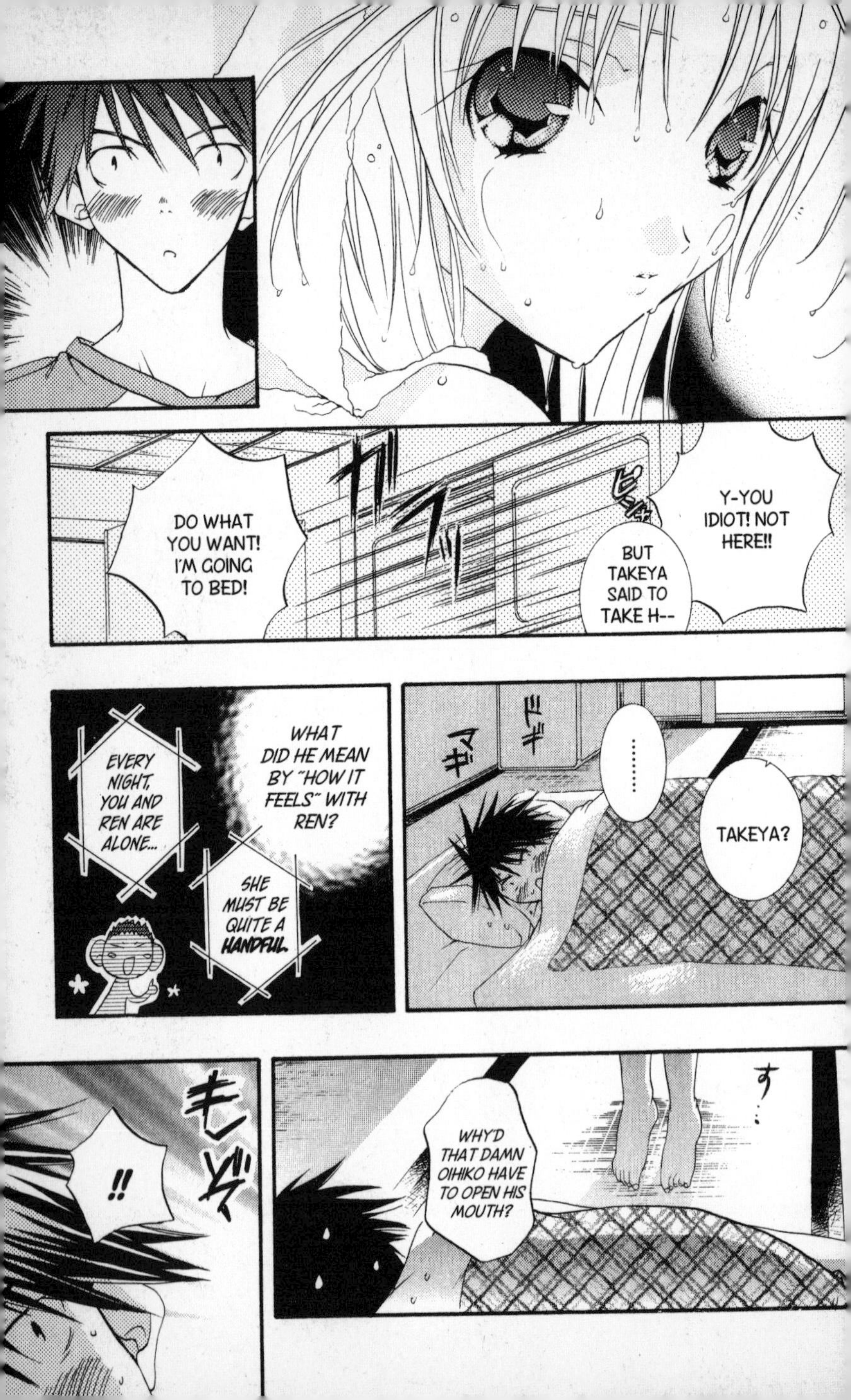
Y-YOU IDIOT! NOT HERE!!
BUT TAKEYA SAID TO TAKE H--
DO WHAT YOU WANT! I'M GOING TO BED!
ドギマギ
......
TAKEYA?
WHAT DID HE MEAN BY "HOW IT FEELS" WITH REN?
EVERY NIGHT, YOU AND REN ARE ALONE...
SHE MUST BE QUITE A HANDFUL.
す・・
WHY'D THAT DAMN OIHIKO HAVE TO OPEN HIS MOUTH?
!!

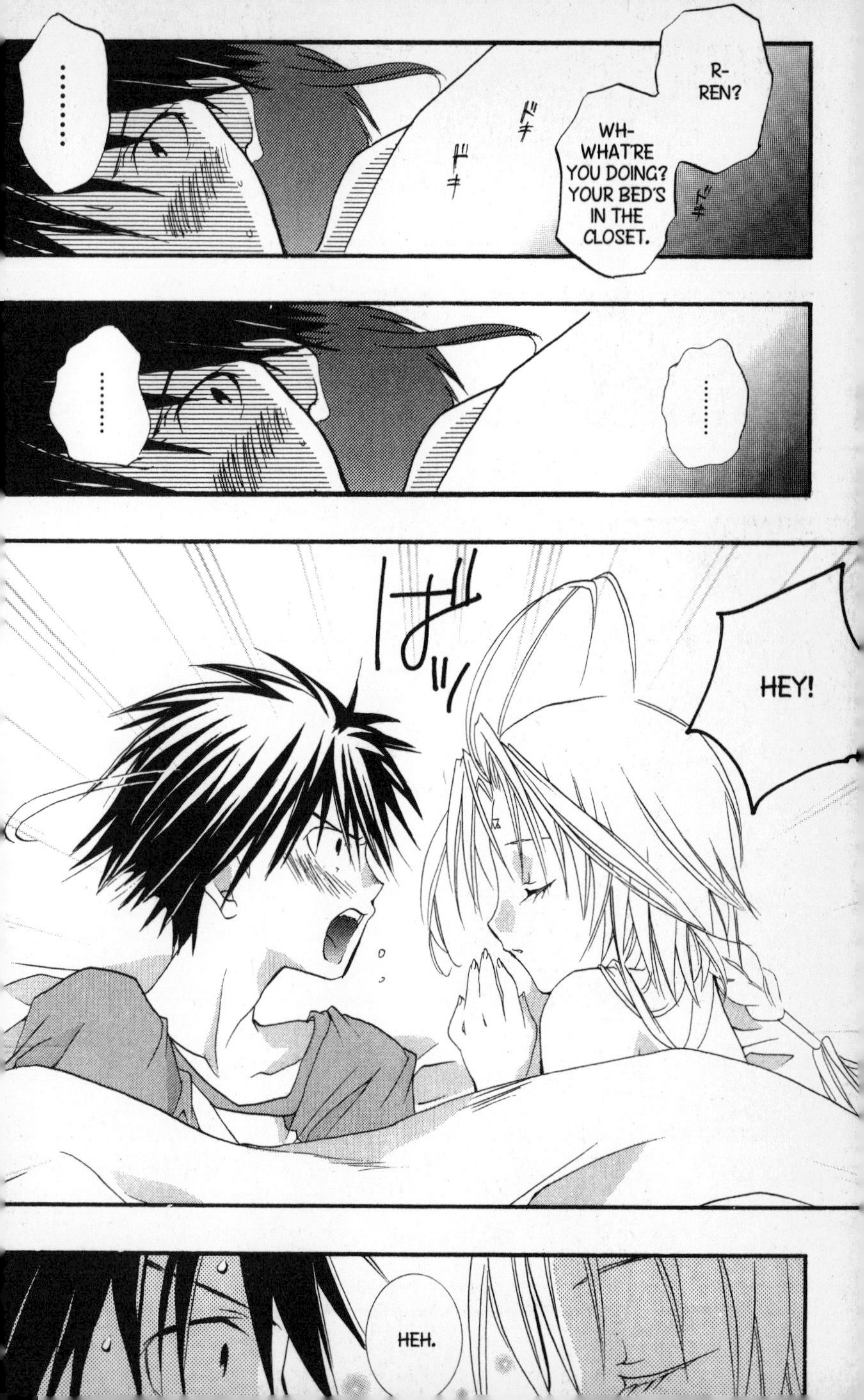
R- REN?
WH- WHAT'RE YOU DOING? YOUR BED'S IN THE CLOSET.
ドキ
ドキ
ドキ
......
......
......
ば
HEY!
HEH.

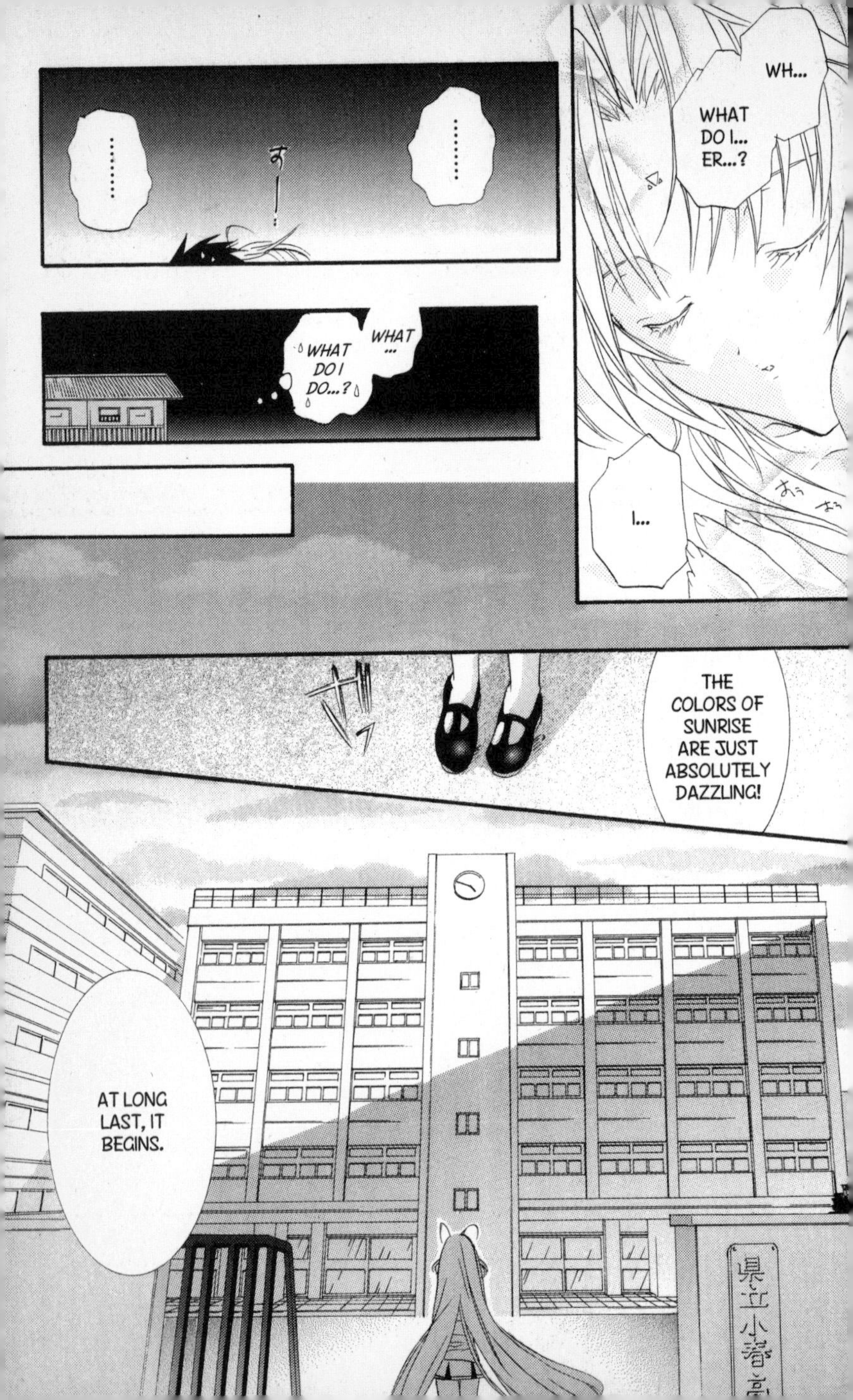
WH...
WHAT DO I... ER...?
I...
....
す—!
....
WHAT...
WHAT DO I DO...?
THE COLORS OF SUNRISE ARE JUST ABSOLUTELY DAZZLING!
AT LONG LAST, IT BEGINS.

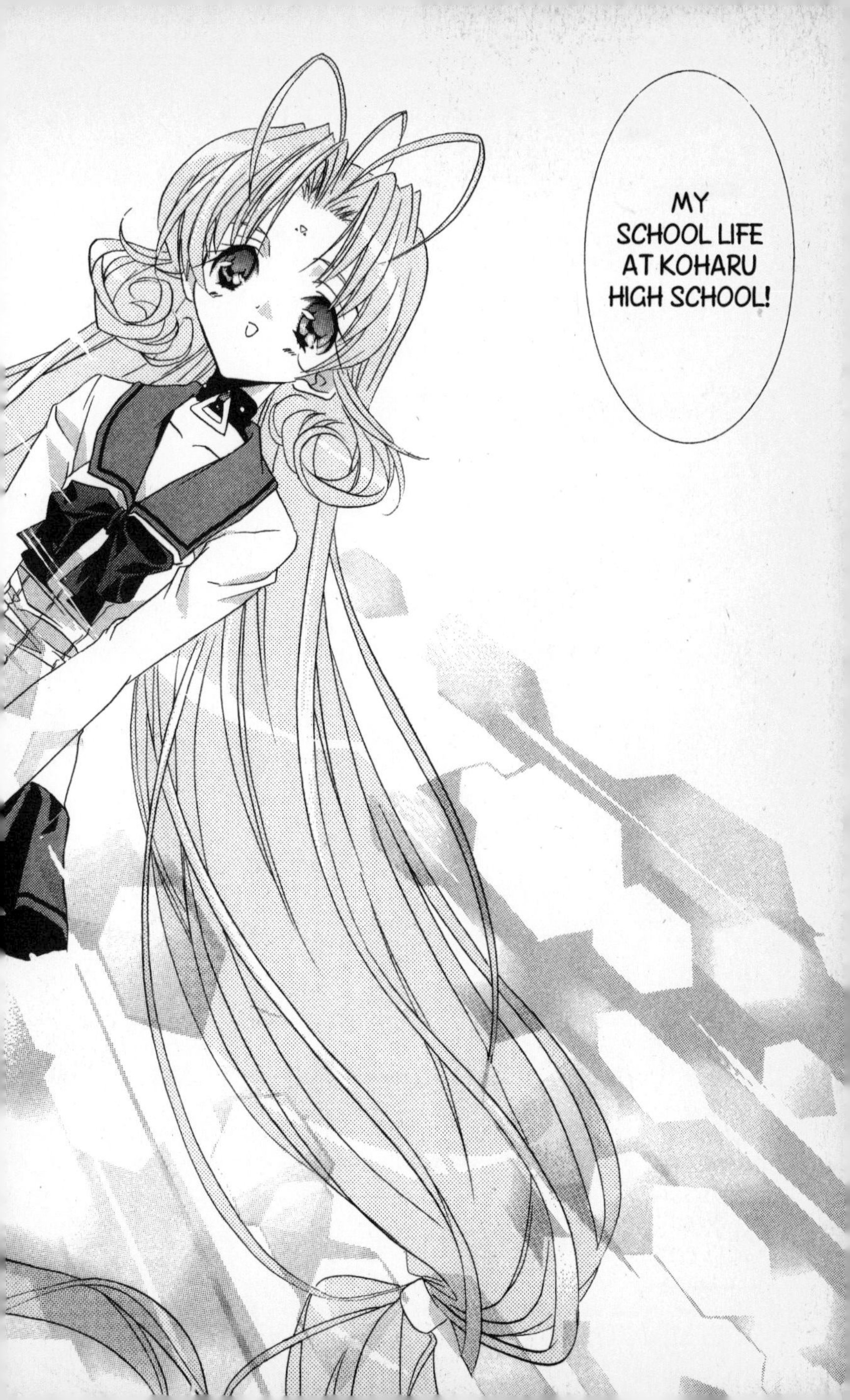
MY SCHOOL LIFE AT KOHARU HIGH SCHOOL!

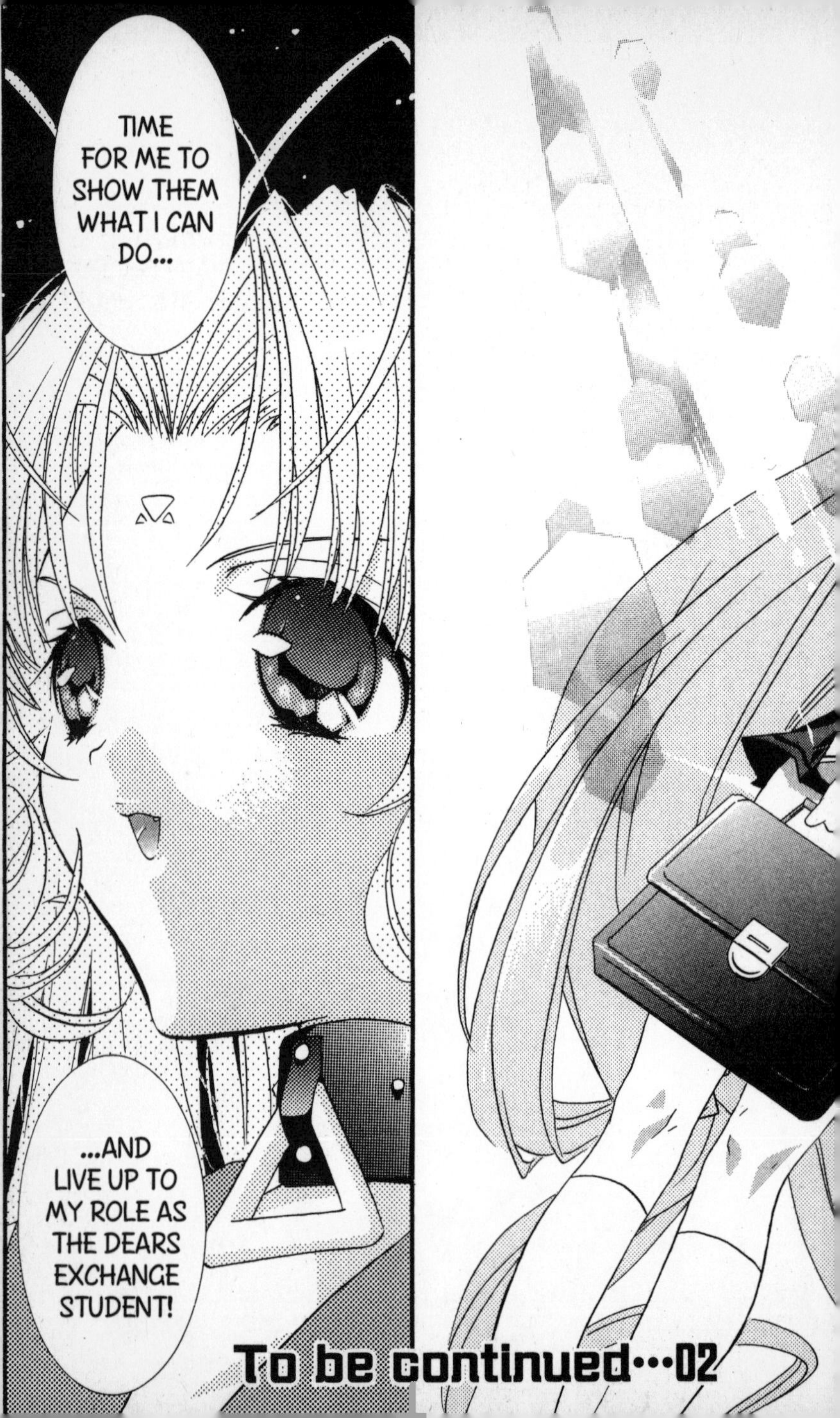
TIME FOR ME TO SHOW THEM WHAT I CAN DO...
...AND LIVE UP TO MY ROLE AS THE DEARS EXCHANGE STUDENT!
To be continued…02

>>>Thank you for reading>>>

>>>See you next "DearS" vol.2!>>>

all produced by
PEACH-PIT

Banri.Sendou ... Shibuko.Ebara

special thanks to
Nao
Mochi
Jiro
Momiji
Kao
Zaki
Kagawa
Y-fairy
joe

T.Hatano

DearS
ディアーズ

"DEARS" IS PEACH-PIT'S 2ND VOLUME PROJECT, AS WELL AS FIRST
ORIGINAL STORY. IT IS ALSO THE LONGEST STORY.
WITH ONE VOLUME OUT, OUR HEARTS ARE REALLY INTO IT.
WE'RE EXTREMELY HAPPY TO HAVE BEEN GIVEN SUCH A PROJECT.
THANK YOU VERY MUCH FOR READING.
THERE ARE STILL A LOT OF IMPERFECT POINTS, BUT
THOUGH THE READERSHIP WAS SMALL,
I DREW IT HOPING THAT PEOPLE WOULD ENJOY IT.
WE'RE STILL IN THE INTRODUCTION PART OF THE STORY, BUT
BECAUSE I'M STILL ITCHING TO DRAW SO MUCH MORE,
I'LL BE EVEN HAPPIER WHEN WE GET TO MEET AGAIN.
SO, UNTIL VOLUME TWO!

TO BE C

http://p-pit.ktplan.ne.jp/

DearS
VOLUME 2

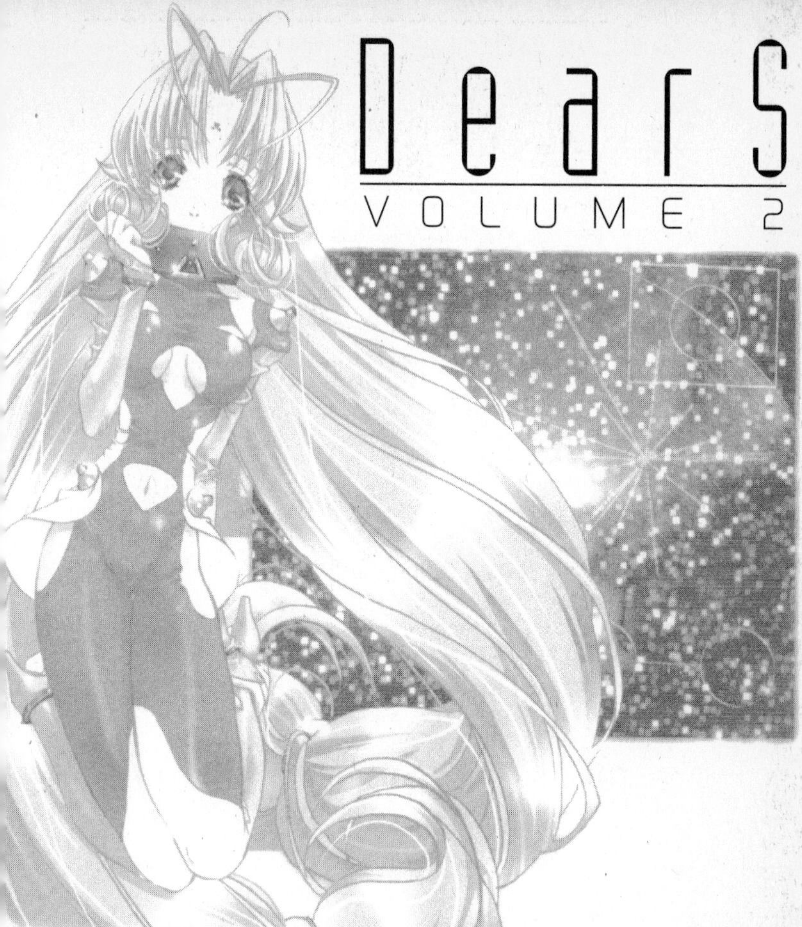

What's going to happen when the real DearS shows up? Wide-scale panic, mass hysteria, and maybe, just maybe, a few yards of clothing removed. But things really get stirred up when a DearS boy comes into the picture. And terror strikes in the form of a mysterious man who refers to Ren as one of the Zero Numbers and threatens to take her back to the DearS community. Ren will have to learn free will if she is going to be Takeya's slave forever!

Check back in April when DearS Volume 2 hits manga shelves everywhere!

TOKYOPOP®

BOYS:BE™

A GUY'S GUIDE TO GIRLS

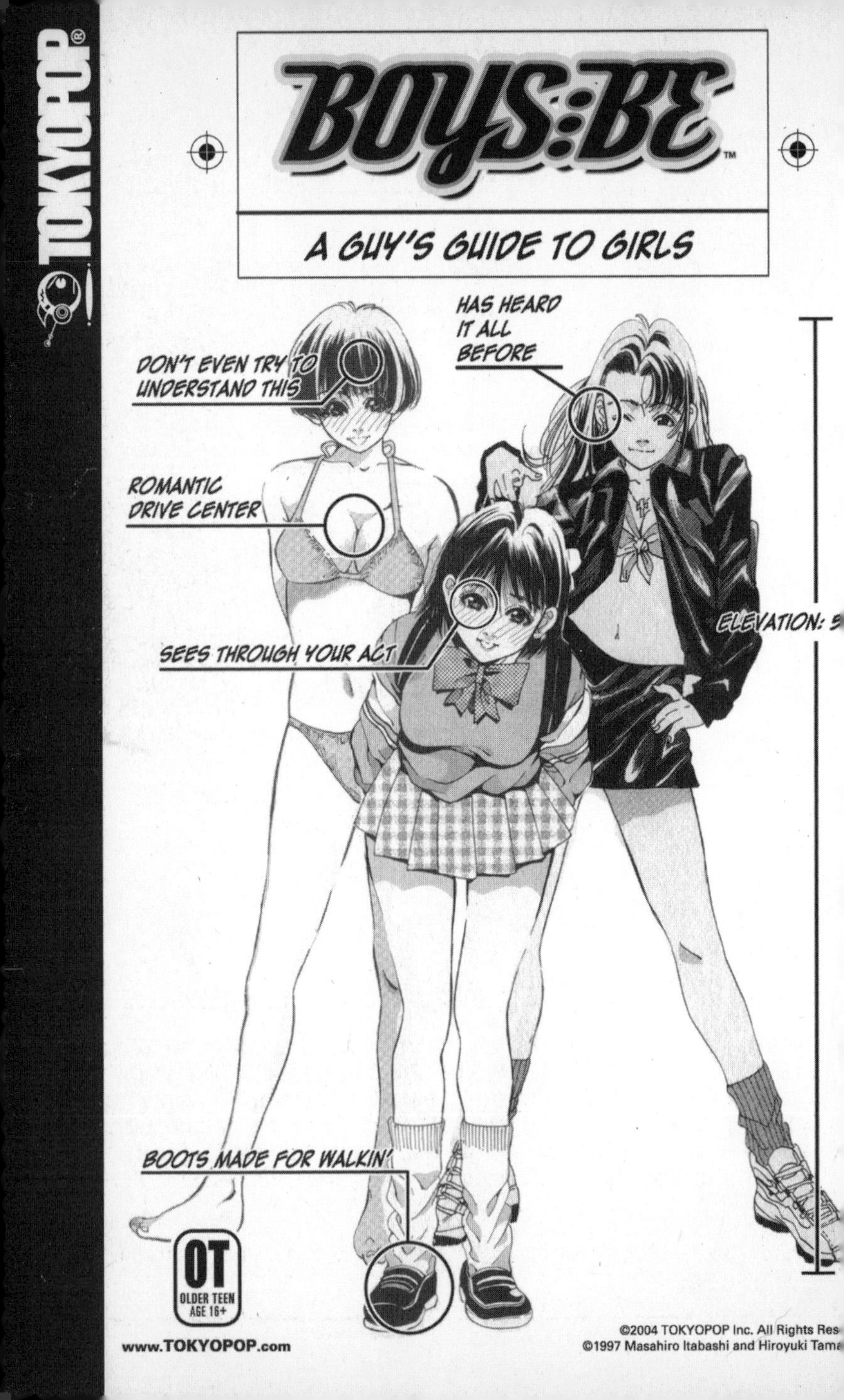
HAS HEARD IT ALL BEFORE
DON'T EVEN TRY TO UNDERSTAND THIS
ROMANTIC DRIVE CENTER
SEES THROUGH YOUR ACT
ELEVATION: 5
BOOTS MADE FOR WALKIN'
OT
OLDER TEEN AGE 16+

www.TOKYOPOP.com

COMIC PARTY ™

Behind-the-scenes with artistic dreams and unconventional love at a comic convention

TEEN
AGE 13+

ALSO AVAILABLE FROM TOKYOPOP®

MANGA

.HACK//LEGEND OF THE TWILIGHT
@LARGE
ABENOBASHI: MAGICAL SHOPPING ARCADE
A.I. LOVE YOU
AI YORI AOSHI
ALICHINO
ANGELIC LAYER
ARM OF KANNON
BABY BIRTH
BATTLE ROYALE
BATTLE VIXENS
BOYS BE...
BRAIN POWERED
BRIGADOON
B'TX
CANDIDATE FOR GODDESS, THE
CARDCAPTOR SAKURA
CARDCAPTOR SAKURA - MASTER OF THE CLOW
CHOBITS
CHRONICLES OF THE CURSED SWORD
CLAMP SCHOOL DETECTIVES
CLOVER
COMIC PARTY
CONFIDENTIAL CONFESSIONS
CORRECTOR YUI
COWBOY BEBOP
COWBOY BEBOP: SHOOTING STAR
CRAZY LOVE STORY
CRESCENT MOON
CROSS
CULDCEPT
CYBORG 009
D•N•ANGEL
DEARS
DEMON DIARY
DEMON ORORON, THE
DEUS VITAE
DIABOLO
DIGIMON
DIGIMON TAMERS
DIGIMON ZERO TWO
DOLL
DRAGON HUNTER
DRAGON KNIGHTS
DRAGON VOICE
DREAM SAGA
DUKLYON: CLAMP SCHOOL DEFENDERS
EERIE QUEERIE!
ERICA SAKURAZAWA: COLLECTED WORKS
ET CETERA
ETERNITY
EVIL'S RETURN
FAERIES' LANDING
FAKE
FLCL
FLOWER OF THE DEEP SLEEP
FORBIDDEN DANCE
FRUITS BASKET
G GUNDAM
GATEKEEPERS
GETBACKERS
GIRL GOT GAME
GRAVITATION
GUNDAM SEED ASTRAY
GUNDAM SEED ASTRAY R
GUNDAM WING
GUNDAM WING: BATTLEFIELD OF PACIFISTS
GUNDAM WING: ENDLESS WALTZ
GUNDAM WING: THE LAST OUTPOST (G-UNIT)
HAPPY MANIA
HARLEM BEAT
HYPER POLICE
HYPER RUNE
I.N.V.U.
IMMORTAL RAIN
INITIAL D
INSTANT TEEN: JUST ADD NUTS
ISLAND
JING: KING OF BANDITS
JING: KING OF BANDITS - TWILIGHT TALES
JULINE
KARE KANO
KILL ME, KISS ME
KINDAICHI CASE FILES, THE
KING OF HELL
KODOCHA: SANA'S STAGE
LAGOON ENGINE
LAMENT OF THE LAMB
LEGAL DRUG
LEGEND OF CHUN HYANG, THE
LES BIJOUX
LILING-PO
LOVE HINA
LOVE OR MONEY
LUPIN III
LUPIN III: WORLD'S MOST WANTED
MAGIC KNIGHT RAYEARTH I
MAGIC KNIGHT RAYEARTH II
MAHOROMATIC: AUTOMATIC MAIDEN
MAN OF MANY FACES
MARMALADE BOY
MARS
MARS: HORSE WITH NO NAME
MINK
MIRACLE GIRLS
MIYUKI-CHAN IN WONDERLAND
MODEL
MOURYOU KIDEN: LEGEND OF THE NYMPH
NECK AND NECK
ONE
ONE I LOVE, THE
PARADISE KISS
PARASYTE
PASSION FRUIT
PEACH FUZZ
PEACH GIRL
PEACH GIRL: CHANGE OF HEART
PET SHOP OF HORRORS
PHD: PHANTASY DEGREE
PITA-TEN
PLANET BLOOD
PLANET LADDER

10.19

STOP!

This is the back of the book.
You wouldn't want to spoil a great ending!

This book is printed "manga-style," in the authentic Japanese right-to-left format. Since none of the artwork has been flipped or altered, readers get to experience the story just as the creator intended. You've been asking for it, so TOKYOPOP® delivered: authentic, hot-off-the-press, and far more fun!

DIRECTIONS

If this is your first time reading manga-style, here's a quick guide to help you understand how it works.

It's easy... just start in the top right panel and follow the numbers. Have fun, and look for more 100% authentic manga from TOKYOPOP®!